Religions of the Book

of the

Book

EDITED BY

Gerard S. Sloyan

THE ANNUAL PUBLICATION OF THE
COLLEGE THEOLOGY SOCIETY
1992
VOLUME 38

UNIVERSITY
PRESS OF
AMERICA

Lanham • New York • London

Annual Publication • 38

The paper used in this publication meets the minimum requirements of
American National Standard for information Sciences—Permanence
of Paper for Printed Library Materials,
ANSI Z39.48—1984

CONTENTS

INTRODUCTION

Gerard S. Sloyan

Jews and Christians have lived for long in close proximity in this country, although there are places where Jews are not found in numbers. Recent decades have come to see the remarkable growth of an Islamic population in our midst. Some are refugees from an oppressive Iranian regime, but there are also immigrants from Egypt, Palestine and West Africa who have come to American cities—and universities—for the same reasons that brought Europeans to these shores. These newcomers are usually amazed at the vigor of Muslim membership among African-Americans. Sometimes adherents to the three groups have lived in comparative peace in their homelands with those of one or the other religious persuasions, sometimes not. Immigrants from the former Soviet Union and the state of Israel are prepared for the highly secularized culture they find here. Muslim new Americans seldom are. It is not long before new arrivals discover the widespread black-white or Anglo-Hispanic antipathies in the United States and some, tragically, decide to make them their own. The prevailing anti-Judaism of gentile culture in all of North America is not lost on them either, although they find that it takes more subtle forms than in their lands of origin.

This last cancerous growth has long cried out for extirpation, along with the allied phenomenon of Jewish anti-Christian sentiment. Mutual ignorance of the two religious traditions is a heavily contributing factor to the tension. To it is now added an anti-Islamic hatred in the U.S. and Canada more virulent than any previous anti-Jewish or anti-Catholic antipathy, because rooted in profounder ignorance and stereotype. The news and entertainment media pour daily fuel on these flames, both for political reasons that are thought to be religious and because it is so easy to pillory a distant, unknown people. Arab Christians, whose existence is scarcely known, suffer the same slanderous accusations.

The country's public schools and civic organizations work hard at fostering intergroup understanding. Unfortunately, our conspiracy of silence over religion keeps both from being as effective as they might be.

Colleges and universities, especially those not yet corroded by the secular spirit, suffer no such handicap. Those who instruct in all such institutions, however, even teachers of theology or religion, know that they do not know enough in depth to make an adequate exposition of the convictions and practices of the others in the triad. Christians who know biblical Israel are generally ignorant of rabbinic religion, which is to say Judaism. Jews tend to know Christianity by hearsay and exposure to its worst representatives, and understandably get it wrong. The two together, and Jews for special reasons, are likely to suppose "Islamic fundamentalism" (read: violent action) and Islam to be the same thing.

The college classroom is an optimum place to get it right, once professors of religion, history, politics and sociology have troubled to get it right themselves. Some not quite 200 members of the College Theology Society (founded 1954) met over four days at Allentown College of St. Francis de Sales in May, 1992 to reduce their common ignorance. These papers convey something of their intellectual and human exchange, but necessarily little of the many fruitful conversations that followed from them.

THE EXILE OF REDEMPTION IN JUDAISM

Susannah Heschel

I feel very honored to have been asked to contribute this paper, in the context of an interfaith dialogue. I have been asking myself during the past months what it means to me to represent Judaism in this way. What is my connection to Judaism and what shall I say as a spokesperson on its behalf? I was raised in a religious Jewish home. My parents were two people committed to spiritual as well as intellectual lives, my father as a theologian and my mother as a pianist. At the same time, whenever I left my home to encounter Judaism outside—in the synagogue, in the homes of other Jews—I discovered that my position, and my identity, were suddenly very different. At home, everything Jewish was open to me: I was expected to pray myself, to lead the family prayers at the table, to study Jewish texts and demonstrate my knowledge, and so on. When I went to our synagogue, however, I was expected to be a passive observer. Within the flock of children at Sabbath morning services, only the little boys were asked to come forward and open the ark. When I grew to adolescence, I had to leave my special seat next to my father and move to the women's section; for me, it represented an emotional circumcision, a tearing away of a part of myself.

These two experiences—of feeling completely at home in Judaism, identifying Judaism with home, and feeling utterly alienated and trivialized and unnecessary within the larger community—became intensified after my father's death. Then, I wanted with all my heart to go to the synagogue twice each day and say *kaddish* for him but was not allowed to in most of the synagogues that held daily services. It was Mary Daly's book, *Beyond God the Father*, that gave me the language to express my frustration and also to begin to analyze the situation from a feminist perspective.

I mention this personal story not only to introduce myself to you, but also because I believe that feminism reveals something very basic to Judaism. It is this: that women's experience, precisely because it is so marginal, helps us to see something that is otherwise not readily visible.

I wish to argue that the experience of alienation is central to Judaism. I further wish to discuss in my paper a few of its manifestations in the history of Jewish thought, and some of the ways modern Judaism uses alienation as a positive strategy. In this strategy exile itself becomes the value that is affirmed instead of an awaited redemption. Exile and redemption are central theological categories in Judaism. They have an added significance because they are not only doctrinal concepts but reveal the emotional and spiritual sensibilities of the Jewish people through the centuries.

Exile enters the first Jewish text from the earliest moment. We think immediately of the exile from the Garden of Eden, which is followed by the exile of the patriarchs and matriarchs from the land promised by God to Abraham, then the exile to Egypt which meant slavery to Israel. In historical terms, we have the exile from the Northern Kingdom as a result of the Assyrian conquest and from the South Kingdom following the Babylonian conquest.

The question of exile is intriguing to explore in Jewish thought because it is refracted in so many different ways. There is, for example, a question of who is in exile, and who redeems whom. With the expulsion from Eden, it is not only Adam and Eve who go into exile, but God who, in the later midrashic readings, by their rejection of his commandment is also exiled. Clearly, in the biblical Exodus story, it is the Children of Israel who are in exile, but Pharaoh's heart must be hardened in order that the redemption be properly a divine act. The Egyptian ruler is exiled by God as a result of his initial willingness to allow the Jews to depart.

Following the Roman destruction of Jerusalem, it was not only the Jewish people who went into Diaspora but perhaps more significantly, as rabbinic Judaism states, it was God, too, who went into exile with the Jewish people and now is in need of redemption. How is God to be redeemed, and by whom? By the Jewish people, observing the divine commandments. This is a fascinating theological assertion that reaches its pinnacle in kabbalistic thought. In classical *kabbalah* (Heb., tradition) God's exile is mythicized as a detachment of female from male; each *mitzvah* or good deed in response to commandment that a Jew performs has the potential of reuniting female with male and bringing about a redemption of God by ending the inner-divine exile.

Throughout Jewish descriptions of the state of exile, God is not absent from the Jewish community. On the contrary, God was always fully present, as in the period of the wilderness following the Exodus when God hovered in a cloud and pillar. The (Babylonian) exile was God's punishment of the Jews for their sins; but the meaning of the exile is not an exile from God or a punishment in which God abandons the Jewish people. Rather, it is that God so loves and so identifies with the Jews that God has gone into exile with them.

What follows from this belief is that, not only the Jewish people, but God, too, requires redemption—by the Jewish people. Theirs is a common fate. In the present state of exile, the ultimate redemption will be not only of the Jewish people but of God as well. In this theology, God is not an omnipotent deity who will redeem us poor humans; the question of who redeems whom is far more complex, and definitely two-sided.

> A teaching found frequently in midrashic literature is the following: Whenever Israel went into exile, the Divine Presence was exiled with them. When they were exiled to Egypt, the Divine presence was with them; when they were exiled to Babylon, the Divine present was with them . . . and when they are destined to return, the Divine Presence will return with them . . . All the time that Israel is in bondage, the Divine Presence, so to speak, is in bondage with them. And when they are destined to return, the Divine Presence will return with them.

This belief that God accompanies the Jewish people in exile is a strong current in rabbinic literature. One statement in the Talmud asserts that God cried as the Temple in Jerusalem went up in flames. In another striking passage in a midrash God says, "I am God and you are my witnesses; and if you are not my witnesses as it were, then I am not God." This trend in Jewish theology which sees God, not as remote and transcendent, but as immanent and involved in people's lives is dominant in rabbinic thought. It becomes a central contention of Jewish mysticism.

In the mystical literature, a major attribute of God is compassion and empathy. In fact, beginning at least in the Zohar, the classic, most influential text of Kabbalah composed in thirteenth-century Spain by Moshe de Leon, a sacramental theology can be traced which has some close parallels with Catholic sacramental theology. According to the Zohar, every commandment performed by a Jew has ramifications in the divine realm. Every commandment becomes holy through the deed; the person performing the act acquires sanctity; the action itself participates in the sacred history of Israel; and the performance of the act has an impact that alters the inner life of God. While the first three aspects seem to parallel Christian understandings of the sacraments, the fourth aspect strikes me as uniquely Jewish: that God responds to human deeds and, conversely, that human actions have a profound effect on the divine reality. Here is a brief illustration from the Zohar:

> Every time the righteous do the will of God they add strength to the might of the heavens, as it is written, "And now the strength of the Lord is increased." And if not, then as it were, "You were unmindful of the rock that begot you, and you forgot the God who gave you birth."

This aspect of Jewish theology has implications, not only for the nature of God, but also for the nature of human actions, for the covenant of commandments. Deeds become highly significant, allowing Jews to participate in bringing about the redemption of God from exile and, simultaneously, their own redemption.

Why was the exile of God appealing, theologically and spiritually? It allowed a sacramental interpretation that brought meaning and vitality to the commandments, and it encouraged a transformation of the relationship between God and the Jewish people from one of estrangement to connection. The despair over the destructive events of 70 C.E. might have been viewed as leading to a divorce from God, or God's rejection of the Jews. Instead, speaking of the neediness of God created a relationship that seems best described by the metaphor of the *aqunah*, a woman whose husband has disappeared either by accident or deliberately. His death cannot be confirmed, so she is not a widow, and since he has not sent her a bill of divorce, she is not free to remarry. She may or may not long for him but, in any case, she is permanently bound to him.

The nightmare this situation causes women has long been discussed in Jewish legal texts. Various solutions have been proposed to alleviate the situation of the *aqunah* and allow her release but none has been accepted. To this day, there are tens of thousands of Jewish women who live their lives as *aqunot*, bound to husbands whose exact whereabouts may be unknown to them or who deliberately deny them a divorce in order to extort money, custody of the children, or simply to be cruel.

It seems to me that the problem of the *aqunah* has not been resolved by Jewish legal experts primarily because women are powerless in the Jewish legal system and in the Jewish community. But on the theological level, the *aqunah* also plays a role. The situation of being bound to a man who has disappeared but whose death cannot be proven evokes so well the relationship between the Jews and God in the postexilic literature: not a divorce, nor a death—certainly no utter rejection—but a continued relationship in the face of disappearance.

Within Hasidim exile describes the spiritual state of being a Jew, with Egypt as its metaphor. In this view, living the life of a Jew, observing the commandments, does not necessarily bring us closer to God but may actually estrange us further. Levi Yitzhak of Berdichev describes two ways of serving God: one by means of attachment of oneself to God, the other by serving God through the commandments and good deeds. He writes, "Now, one who serves God through dedication alone sees God with one's own eye, while one who serves God through commandments and actions sees God through a glass, since his means of service is an existing thing." It is, of course, surprising to find even the suggestions of a negative attitude toward the commandments within a pietistic, Hasidic text, but ambivalence toward the *mitzvot* is characteristic of some Hasidic literature. For our purposes, what is interesting about the text is its description of the religious life: following the commandments results in an estrangement, seeing God through a glass, rather than achieving closeness and attachment.

Valorizing exile as the central metaphor for Jewish religious experience is, therefore, not new to the modern period. It did, however, take on particular connotations during modernity, precisely, I would argue, in those movements of thought that attempted to overcome exile. Here are a few examples. The effort to write Jewish history began in the early nineteenth century as an attempt to recover Jewish identity. It hoped to discover what had been constant in the course of Jewish history over the centuries and what it really meant to be a Jew, particularly if the system of *mitzvot* and beliefs was no longer convincing. Yet the history that was initially written was a history of persecutions and sufferings, the history of Jews at the hands of non-Jews. What emerged was not an answer to the question of Jewish identity but a further sense that Jews have no history, that what happened to Jews through the course of the centuries was not of their own making, but the result of antisemitism. The Hebrew writer Haim Hazaz, in his short story, *The Sermon*, which is set in a kibbutz in the early years of Israeli statehood, has one of his characters complain:

. . . we have no history at all. That's a fact. . . . Because we didn't make our own history, the gentiles made it for us. Just as they used to put out our candles on the Sabbath, milk our cows and light our ovens on the Sabbath, so they made our history for us to suit themselves, and we took it from them as it came. But it's not ours, it's not ours at all! Because we didn't make it, we would have made it differently, we didn't want it to be like that, it was only others who wanted it that way and they forced it on us, whether we liked it or not, which is a different thing altogether. In that sense, and in every other sense, I tell you, in every other sense, we have no history at all.

Feminism, too, writes a history in which women are not the protagonists but the victims of patriarchy. While feminists increasingly propose visions of future reconciliations that will overcome sexism, the vibrant energy of feminist though lies in the critique. Indeed, there is a tendency within feminist theory to portray patriarchy as so intrinsic, so deep, that it can never be overcome. Not only our religious teachings and laws but our symbols; not only our symbols but our language; not only our language but our very imaginations are so imprinted with false patriarchal constructions of "woman" that recovery of our true selves seems impossible. In reading feminist theorists, I come away feeling we are doomed as females to live the artificial lives of patriarchal women.

Or, let us take Zionism. Using metaphors drawn from the traditional religious language of exile and redemption, Zionism claimed that by creating a state of Israel the exile of the Jewish people would be brought to an end. The question is, redemption from what? Certainly, redemption from political dependency and physical vulnerability. Yet, although each of the Zionists for the last one hundred years has called for Israel to be a state like all other states, creating a "normalization" of Jewish political life and, hence, personal identity, Zionism in fact created a new form of exile. Rather than a state among the states, Israel has become, for most of its history, an alien among the nations, even a pariah to many. For Israeli Jews, there is a sense of alienation from Judaism, a loss of Jewish identity even while Israeli identity has yet to be defined. Zionism opposes itself to Judaism even more than it draws from it; Zionism wants to create a new kind of Jews, one who is strong and unafraid, independent and invulnerable. Zionism, too, wants to overcome the past of Jewish history, the piety, the bookishness of religious life. It is no accident that masculine metaphors abound in Zionist rhetoric: as Miriyam Glazer has pointed out, to overcome the diaspora means literally, in Hebrew, to become a man. The Diaspora Jew is the feminized Jew, the Israeli is the masculine, macho Jew. To be in exile is to be a woman, or an effeminate man.

There has been, through Zionism, no real overcoming of exile. Instead, we see a transfer of the state of exile from a collection of individual Jews to a political state that suffers an alienation from both its Jewish roots and the surrounding world. Needless to say, the political ramifications are grave when both Israelis and Palestinians view themselves as being in exile. It is hard to make concessions for peace or feel secure and strong when locked in a mentality of exile.

What I am arguing is that exile has become so ingrained into Jewish self-understanding on so many levels—politically, historically, spiritually—that we can ask whether the major thrust of Judaism really wants to overcome exile, really wants redemption. It may even be that the deliberate intention of the myth of redemption is to inculcate the unconscious wish not to be saved. Hazaz's character tells his fellow kibbutz members his view of Israelis:

> They really believe redemption will come, I repeat it, again, they believe in all truth and sincerity, they hope for it, aspire to it, and yet they intend that it should not come. this is not deceit, it's not duplicity at all. I'm sure of it. Here something is at work beneath the surface, something rooted in the depths of their heart, something unconscious. . . . It's not for nothing that the myth became so beloved among the people, and holds such sway that they became like some kind of poets, not concerned at all with the world as it is, but altogether given up to dream and legend. Two thousand years it has consoled them, and for two thousand more they will live by its warmth, in dream, in mourning, in expectation, and in secret fear of it, and never will they tire.

It is not that redemption in one of its various modern forms, whether feminism, historical scholarship, or the State of Israel, has brought us out of exile or can even do so; rather, exile has so overtaken the religious imagination that redemption may no longer be a realistic possibility or even a desired possibility. Movements that claim they can redeem us may serve at best to expose the depth of the exile and in that way to deepen and intensity it.

Perhaps herein lies an aspect of the great distance between Judaism, Christianity, and Islam. For Christians, the great exile of Jesus from his people and his disciples in the crucifixion is overcome through his resurrection. Whatever the despair of Good Friday, it is followed immediately by Easter. For Jews, the redemption has not yet come, and the state of exile remains. On the other hand, the triumph of resurrection over death might also be a source of the triumphalism that permeates Christianity, based on a self-confidence that the ultimate miracle has happened and therefore can happen, simply as a gift to Christians from God.

For Muslims, this entire conversation might seem rather bizarre. There is certainly ambivalence toward Jesus' divine sonship. On the one hand, Jesus' divinity is denied, but on the other hand, the Qur'an rejects the claim of his crucifixion, relating that a substitute for him was found at the last moment. This may be because it cannot accept the notion that a prophet of God so close to the divine was put to death. For Muslims, Judaism's anthropomorphic notion of a divine exile is similarly unacceptable theologically. Divine omnipotence is too important to be sacrificed at the altar of divine pathos.

It is doubtful that theological differences can ever be breached on the level of doctrine; exile is just one of the many differences of belief among us that are rooted as much in our religious imagination and self-understanding as they are in our exegesis of our respective Scriptures. At another level, however, that of religious experience, perhaps we can in speaking of our unique concerns find a common language of mutual understanding.

THE BRIDGE OF PARTNERSHIP:
CHRISTIANS, JEWS, AND MUSLIMS AS
PARTICIPANTS IN THE STRUGGLE FOR
WORLD TRANSFORMATION

Joseph W. Devlin

Jerusalem provides us with a dramatic symbol of the present situation besetting the three faiths which trace their origin to the call of Abraham. A recent article about that city, site of the ancient Jerusalem Temple, Mount Calvary, and the place of Muhammad's ascension, described it as a place where people live side by side but not together. Professor Michael Cook, of Hebrew Union College, some time ago told the story of a lion who escaped from an urban zoo and was found a few blocks away pacing up and down behind a fence only thirty feet long. He could not turn the corner. Professor Cook saw this as an image of the present status of Jewish-Christian relations—going over old ground but never turning the corner. In the case of the relations of both with Islam, it could be said that the lion has not yet escaped. Yet there are signs of hope.

The contemporary world is undergoing tremendous changes as we head toward the year 2000. Vaclav Havel has described what is happening as the "end of the modern era." Havel says: "The modern era has been dominated by the culminating belief, expressed in different forms, that the world, and being as such--is a wholly knowable system governed by a finite number of universal laws that man can grasp and direct for his own benefit. . . . This, in turn, gave rise to the proud belief that man, as the pinnacle of everything that exists, was capable of objectively describing, explaining and controlling everything that exists, and of possessing the one and only truth about the world." Communism as an expression of this world has collapsed. Capitalism, to the extent that it participates in the same outlook favoring control, as evidenced in the

Pentagon document of a few years ago outlining future policy, is also in poor health.

These upheavals have resulted in a retribalization of the world. The loss of a universal center in modernity has given rise to what many are describing as postmodernism. This term is defined by Fredric Jameson as characterizing a "time which is out of joint"---a time that has lost its continuity with the past. One of the features of this postmodern period is the rise of consumerism and the radical individualism of people who have no connection with a tradition of any kind. Such a society can be called "loose-bounded" (R. Merelman). It is so differentiated internally that there is no focus of unity other than the private self. The outcome of all this, not surprisingly, has been the rise of fundamentalisms and sectarian movements of all kinds, each endeavoring to restore to the pertinent culture some sense of partnership and community. Fundamentalisms are thus modern movements against the postmodern pluralization of life worlds. A global system of consumption in which an elite would leave the masses behind is on the agenda of the powerful in many lands. It is at this point that the relevance of religion and, in particular, of the three Abrahamitic faiths is seen.

It is no secret that religion has been used and is now being used as an ideology to support power structures. One of the functions of religion is to integrate a society, providing it with a plausibility structure. Muhammad Arkoun has noted, in a study of Islam, the importance of the distinction between the spiritual experience itself and its formulation into the official ideologies used by centralizing states competing for power. Judaism, Christianity, and Islam are all movements of the spirit which have been concretized in institutions. The logic of maintaining these institutions has always tended historically to override the logic of mission that these faiths have. The story is not a pleasant one. Today, as never before, there is a need to discover what it is we are about as descendants of Abraham, Moses, Jesus and Muhammad. We need to search for a vision of what it is in common that we are engaged in. Rabbi Abraham Heschel has said that the key issue in interfaith relationships was whether there is a divine Reality which mysteriously impinges upon everything and is concerned not least with the destiny of humanity.

Abraham was called to give up his fixed faith in a changeless world and to go out seeking a new city. It is this vision of a new heaven and a new earth which has inspired Jew, Christian and Muslim to see their reponses as ones of pilgrimage, of journeys to the future. For several reasons, not excluding political intrigue, members of these faiths have not generally seen their journeys as part of a larger enterprise fostered by the God of history. With the advent of globalism, made possible by rapid transport and instant communication, the question of each faith's theological imperialism has come under scrutiny by believers and non-believers alike.

All religious traditions have historical birthplaces. It might be said that they have outgrown them and should outgrow them. Our God is a God of the living. Hence it would seem incumbent upon those who see themselves in a relationship with God to dialogue as equals in attempting to understand the heart of the message we have in common. What each of us holds distinctively is all too well known. One writer has noted that all three traditions see God's image in every human being and that we are called not to rule over others—even theologically—but to empower others. Empowerment, not domination, is the law in a world where only God rules. This insight provides a basic tool to critique not only our theologies but the world as well.

THE SAME RELIGIOUS TRADITION--A NEW PARADIGM

Authors such as Hans Küng call this development of a common vision, or common theology a "paradigm shift," using the term canonized by Thomas Kuhn in discussing change in the field of science. Models have been employed in approaching the task of interfaith relationships in the past. The most common has been "exclusivism." Exclusivism sees other faiths as basically false and considers how persons of another faith can nevertheless "be saved, i.e., enjoy the world to come, enter paradise." The other side of this approach has come to be called "inclusivism." Inclusivism sees other faiths as having many good elements. They are preparations for the acceptance of the true faith. Bernard Lewis, a Jewish scholar of Islam at the Institute for Advanced Studies of Princeton University, notes that Christianity and Islam have this problem more directly since they have expressed more universal claims and aspirations. Raimundo Panikkar, retired from the University of California at Santa Barbara, rejects both exclusivism and inclusivism as inadequate. These two approaches are anxious to preserve the tradition each is committed to and avoid the dangers of relativism they suspect in a pluralistic approach, e.g., that of a John Hick, who sees a universal religious experience prior to its concretization in various cultural forms called religious traditions. The new problem focuses upon how all religious traditions relate to each other, beginning by assuming that they do. The old one concerned itself with "the salvation of the non-believer," assuming that there could be such.

RELIGION AS LANGUAGE AND AS STORY

Panikkar's view, well described in a volume by Michael Barnes, entitled "Christian Identity and World Pluralism-Religions in Conversation," is called parallelism and interpenetration. Panikkar stresses the importance of encounter between members of different faiths--in our case between pairs among Muslims, Jews and Christians. The first task is the careful study of the faith of the dialogue partner so as to ascertain what is really being said. Religion, says Barnes, is a *language*, using the model proposed by George Lindbeck and very like that of Wilfred Cantwell Smith. Religion introduces people into the shared language or *story* of the group. It accounts for the total worldview and practice of a particular people. Dialogue, therefore, is not done by abstracting certain themes or ideas in order to compare them with other ones. This approach deals more adequately, not only with the elements of continuity within a tradition, what keeps it the same, but with elements of change. Smith expresses this well: "Religion is original every morning."

There is a dialectic in every religious story between tradition and challenges to it. Abraham, Moses, Jesus and Muhammad each challenged the tradition they received, broadening and deepening it. Religion is thus less a set of answers than a set of questions requiring response—a conversation. This conversation is seen in the Hebrew Bible, in the parabolic language of Jesus, and in the very structure of the Qur'an. Since stories can be shared and language learned, those who dialogue will be changed. This has always happened, as the historical work of scholars like Smith has ably demonstrated. But it is our task to dialogue so as to struggle with the limitations of language in coping with our common future in the global city--a new Jerusalem where we can live not just side by side but together. The struggle to live side by side in the old Jerusalem is both paradigm and test. What may be impossible in the short run in the old world may be possible in the land we inhabit.

FAITH IS NOT BELIEF

Many engaging in such a dialogue are helped by the reminder that faith is not the same as belief. When faith is identified with belief it becomes exclusivist and may even become fanatic. A key question is identity. If my indentity is tied to beliefs, I am going to be threatened by any questioning of them. The ability to dialogue, then, requires conversion. In Hebrew this word is *teshuvah* which means a turning around and a walking on the straight path in a new direction. All three Abrahamitic faiths share this image. As Barnes has put it, "The change of understanding which comes with conversion is often a profound revelation of what one has always believed. Perhaps it may be compared to learning a new language. The old does not disappear; it becomes more highly prized. The new appears as an alternative way of articulating that which one has always held most dear."

PROPHETIC COMMUNITIES: JEWISH, CHRISTIAN, MUSLIM

The new language that we all need to learn includes, importantly, that of caring for the earth. I am aware that all three faiths have beautiful expressions of the responsibility of the believer for creation. I am here suggesting the development of a language of *common* responsibility—the responsibility of prophetic communities: Muslims, Jews, and Christians as transnational actors for peace and justice. I believe that dialogue and ecumenical convergence should begin here. Technology, communications and transport have already brought us together, despite their unfortunate side-effect of diluting, even debasing cultures. We must begin to reflect deeply about the religious significance of these "signs of the times."

It is noteworthy that while all three faiths have theologies which call for world transformation, these calls have taken a decidedly political turn in recent years. Modern structures of power are not overly happy with this situation, preferring faiths which teach submission and other-worldliness. A deeper examination of the way in which these structures have encouraged Jewish, Christian and Muslim hatreds needs to be made. As Jurgen Habermas has noted, fostering this strife has been and still is a way of stifling the potential that truly universal religions have for criticizing unjust political/economic power. Jewish return to the ancestral homeland, Christian liberation theologies, and modern Muslim religion-political movements, despite the legitimate criticisms that can be made of their execution, are nevertheless expressions of a call to change political, economic and cultural structures which establish and reinforce dehumanizing tendencies. Our prophets understood the meaning of collective evil. The privatizing tendencies and excessive individualism found in modern religion needs to be directly confronted.

With an increasing awareness of ourselves as Jews, Christians and Muslims, dedicated as coworkers in a global movement to establish justice and harmony, there would come the recognition that this task is not a moral option for a holy elite but a condition for survival on this planet. The task is none other than what it takes for people to live together on earth. To paraphrase Rosemary Haughton, the prophetic communities of our time are not only calling for a return to tradition but are struggling to see that the world may live at all. The list suggested by Paul Knitter--human suffering, socio-economic oppression, the evils of the arms race, nuclear holocaust, and ecological disaster, provide a daunting agenda. Many of these issues are tied together, as can be seen by surveying the damage done by conspicuous consumption and mindless pollution. The advice of philosopher Richard Rorty is pertinent here. We should eschew grand schemes and proceed in a reformist manner, sketching "a concrete alternative institution, an alternative that does not presuppose the existence of a new kind of human being."

THE TASK OF MUTUAL UNDERSTANDING

With the new paradigm suggested above as the heart of a dialogue, the importance of spirituality is underlined. *Jihad* as struggle with the self to overcome obstacles to God's will is the beginning of external reform. One might also describe the task as one of "de-privatizing" the messages that these three faiths are giving. A fruitful discussion could develop concerning how much de-privatization is needed in each faith community and why. The importance of understanding faith as conviction and action (Heb., *emunah*) would emerge. Another relevant issue, as Darrell Fasching has noted, is the development of models of faith that encourage questioning as contrasted with those which call for unquestioning obedience.

With this in mind, I thought it would be well to conclude with the mention of several issues that have caused misunderstanding between Jews and Christians and likewise between Muslims and Christians. Also included below are matters that would seem to be points of convergence.

Issues Concerning Jews and Christians

1. The importance of overcoming "blaming myths," e.g., is a religion of legalism (or worse, of fear). These stereotypes are still promoted by some Christian teachers and clerics (much of it out of ignorance, but not always). Of great importance here, as noted by Rabbi Michael Cook, is the work of Norman Beck, *Mature Christianity*, a study of anti-Jewish polemic in the New Testament. Polemic is found in these sacred texts. A beginning of the solution to the problem is understanding the historically conditioned nature of these first-century, emotional diatribes. The Christian is not bound to see eternal verities in battles occasioned by, among other things, the emergence of two rival groups claiming to interpret the religion of Israel and destruction of the Second Temple. These are time-bound situations and fail to shed light on the circumstances of the present age. If taken uncritically, they prevent us from exercising much needed self-criticism. An attack on first-century religious leaders of any group is part of the past. What is to be said about religious leadership at the present time? Dealing with this question would be, in Beck's term, *mature* Christianity.

2. The problem of theologies of supersessionism. Jewish authors can even detect these views in such irenic work as that of Paul Van Buren. Talk of Christianity "fulfilling" Judaism needs to be replaced with dialogue about different religious experiences based upon the same sources.

3. The value of Jewish emphasis upon the historical dimension of faith. Hellenized Christianity has always tended to move toward eternal, timeless truths untouched by the particularities of history. The teaching of religion in such an abstract manner is the cause of much loss of faith. The example of the Holocaust provides a lesson in the danger of reducing faith to a calculating rationality, that provides a neat set of answers to every problem. The love affair with "timeless truths" has resulted in a desiccated Christianity. This has been a special temptation to Catholics. The opposite temptation of fundamentalist Protestants is also to be feared: the reduction of Scripture to a set of selectively chosen propositions, unaffected by the circumstances in which these texts arose.

4. The importance of dealing with the contemporary Jewish community and its experience. For example, showing support for its struggle to deepen its understanding of the covenant in modern times, an issue addressed by Arthur Hertzberg, Eugene Borowitz and Emil Fackenheim

among others. As Catholic scholar Johannes Metz has said: Avoid any theology that could have been the same before as after the Holocaust. The development of a self-critical theology concerned with human liberation is an imperative. We have seen the results of the other kind. Rabbi Jacob Agus said long ago that Christians and Jews need to compete only in the doing of good works. And, as Borowitz has indicated, there is no need to find any universal common denominator. Pluralism and particularity are not evils *per se.*

5. The importance (for Christians) of a much deeper understanding of the Jewishness of Jesus and the entire early movement associated with him. Jesus did not reject the Jewish people despite the attempts of some of his Jewish followers to make it seem so by their ardent verbal attacks on other Jews. He was critical of his own community of disciples for failing to get his message. A deeper penetration of this dimension would be a helpful beginning on the road to partnership. It helps to understand the polemics. Separating Jesus off from the early evangelizers creates new problems for Christians and Jews.

Issues concerning Muslims and Christians

1. A deeper understanding of Islam as a liberation movement. Seeing the importance of *Jihad Akbar*—the greater struggle spoken of above--and the call to be trustees for humanity, *Khilafah*, against the injustices to the poor at the hands of economic and political powers, local and Western. A dialogue should bring to light that so-called "Islamic fundamentalism" has much to do with the rejection of a consumerist mentality and threats to family and social life found in what is called "late capitalism." A convergence with Christian liberation theologies is obvious and could be developed.

2. The work of Mahmoud Taha concerning the two messages of the Qur'an—the eternal and the time-conditioned—would seem to provide a bridge for understanding. His discussion of "the dictates of the time," i.e., the historically conditioned development of legislation in Medina, seems very similar to what some consider the enduring achievement of Vatican II: the historically conscious approach to world problems. Khalid Duran has spoken of the call of Muhammad back to the faith of Abraham and Islam as a separate institution as two aspects of the problem. Solving this dilemma will be of utmost importance for establishing "the best community."

3. The Muslim example of prayer as expressed in the lifestyle of Muhammad combined with this-worldly concern is of great help to the Christian who sees both characteristics in Jesus. Muslim scholars have often remarked about the "other-worldliness" of Christianity. This may very well be a legitimate criticism of a Western rejection of Semitic awareness of the sacred in the secular, and a product of the Gnostic escapism that Christianity never completely exorcized.

4. The question of religious pluralism in the context of *dahr al Islam* (the household is Islam). The importance of Qur'anic *surah* 2:256, "There is no compulsion in religion," in determining the situation of religious minorities. Added to this is the question of "mission" as partnership rather than competition, which is undoubtedly the hardest thing for both traditions to accept. Religious partnership may be eons off, but working together to solve the problems of a suffering humanity is at the doorstep in places where believers of the two religions live close.

CONCLUSION

A dialogical approach to relationships among the adherents to Judaism, Christianity and Islam is said to be very unlikely by sociologist Byran Turner. More precisely, he says that "at present there seems to be little possibility of global ecumenism on a fundamentalist basis." He goes on to say:

> The problem on a global level, when dealing with exclusive fundamentalist religious movements, is clearly more difficult, and the future relations between the Abrahamic faiths in particular is uncertain. The poignancy of the relationship between the Abrahamic faiths is nowhere better illustrated than in their separate, exclusive, and largely incompatible claims to Jerusalem. The first problem then is how to contain, within a single global environment, absolutist religious positions presented by mutually conflictual religious systems.

His statement is a challenge to us all. Do the religious positions have to be "absolutist"?

We conclude where we began: In a global society we need to live, not just side by side, but together. This is the wisdom of all the children of Abraham.

SELECTED BIBLIOGRAPHY

Akhtar, Shabbir, *A Faith for All Seasons: Islam and the Challenge of the Mod ern World.* Chicago: Ivan R. Dee, 1990.

Barnes, Michael, *Christian Identity and Religious Pluralism, Religions in Con versation,* Nashville: Abingdon, 1989.

Beck, Norman A., *Mature Christianity. The Recognition and Repudiation of the Anti-Jewish Polemic of the New Testament.* Susquehanna, Pa.: Susquehanna University, 1985.

Borowitz, Eugene B., *Renewing the Covenant: A Theology for the Postmodern Jew.* Philadelphia: Jewish Publication Society of America, 1991.

Boulares, Habib: *Islam, the Fear and the Hope.* Zed Books, 1990.

Charlesworth, James (ed.), *Jews and Christians: Exploring the Past, Present and Future.* New York: Crossroad, 1990.

Cragg, Kenneth, *Jesus and the Muslim.* London: Allen & Unwin, 1985.

Fischer, M. J. and Mehdi Abedi, *Debating Muslims: Cultural Dialogues in Postmodernity and Tradition.* Madison: University of Wisconsin, 1990.

Griffiths, Paul, *Christianity through Non-Christian Eyes.* Maryknoll, N. Y.: Orbis, 1990.

Haas, Peter J. and Rosemary Ruether, "Recent Theologies of Jewish Christian Relationships," *Religious Studies Review,* 16/4, (October 1990) 316ff.

Harrelson, Walter, and Randall Falk, *Jews and Christians. A Troubled Family.* Nashville: Abingdon, 1990.

Hick, John and Edmund S. Meltzer, *Three Faiths One God: A Jewish, Chris tian, Muslim Encounter.* Albany: State University of N. Y., 1989.

_____. *Truth and Dialogue in World Religions. Conflicting Truth Claims.* Philadelphia: Westminster, 1974.

Knitter, Paul, *No Other Name. A Critical Survey of Christian Attitudes Toward the World Religions.* Maryknoll, N. Y.: Orbis, 1985.

Koening, John, *Jews and Christians in Dialogue.* Philadelphia: Westminster, 1979.

Küng, Hans, *Theology for the Third Millennium,* Garden City, N. Y.: Double day, 1988.

_____ et al,. *Christianity and the World Religions. Paths to Dialogue with Islam, Hinduism and Buddhism.* Idem, 1986.

Lawrence, Bruce B., "Current Problematics in the Study of Islam," *Religious Studies Review,* 16/4, (October 1990) 293ff.

Lee, Bernard, *The Galilean Jewishness of Jesus.* Mahwah, N. J.: Paulist, 1988.

Lindbeck, George, *The Nature of Doctrine. Religion and Theology in a Post Liberal Age.* Philadelphia, Westminster, 1984.

Panikkar, Raimundo, "The Silence of the World," *Cross Currents.* XXIV/ 2 and

3, (Summer/Fall 1974) 154ff.; also "Symposium in Honor of Raimundo Panikkar," *Cross Currents*, XXIX/ 2 (Summer 1979).

----. *On Catholic Identity*. Warren Lecture Series in Catholic Studies 17. University of Tulsa, 1991.

----, *The Intrareligious Dialogue*, New York, Paulist, 1978.

Peck, Abraham, *Jews and Christians After the Holocaust*. Philadelphia, Fortress, 1982.

Pontifical Council for Interreligious Dialogue, *Guidelines for Dialogue between Christians and Muslims*. Prepared by Maurice Borrmans, translated by R. Marston Speight. Mahwah, N. J.: Paulist, 1990.

Robinson, Neal, *Christ in Islam and Christianity*. Albany: State University of N. Y., 1991.

Robertson, Roland and William R. Garrett, *Religion and Global Order*, New York: Paragon, 1991. See especially article by Bryan S. Turner, "Politics and Culture in Islamic Globalism" pp 161ff.

Shermis, Michael, and Arthur Zannoni, *Introduction to Jewish-Christian Rela tions*. Mahwah, N. J.: Paulist, 1991.

Sloyan, Gerard S., *Jesus in Focus. A Life in its Setting*. 2d, rev. ed.; Mystic Ct.: Twenty-Third, 1993.

Smith, Wilfred Cantwell, *Towards a World Theology*, Philadelphia: Westmin ster, 1980.

Swidler, Leonard et al, *Death or Dialogue? From the Age of Monologue to the Age of Dialogue*; Trinity Press International, 1990.

_____. (ed): *Toward a Universal Theology of Religions*. Maryknoll, N. Y.: Orbis, 1987.

_____, Gerard S. Sloyan, Lewis John Eron, Lester Dean, *Bursting the Bonds? A Jewish-Christian Dialogue on Jesus and Paul*. Idem, 1990.

_____. (ed): *Muslims in Dialogue*. Lewiston, N. Y.: Edwin Mellen, 1992.

van Buren, Paul, *A Theology of the Jewish Christian Reality*. 1. *Discerning the Way* (1980); 2. *A Christian Theology of the People Israel*. (1983); 3. *Christ in Context* (1988). New York: Seabury Crossroad.

Watt, William Montgomery, *Islamic Revelation in the Modern World*. Edin burgh: University of Edinburgh, 1969.

ISLAM AND CHRISTIANITY BETWEEN TOLERANCE AND ACCEPTANCE

Mahmoud Ayoub

The dictum *cuius regio eius religio*, so well recognized in medieval Christendom as a general but unalterable rule of socio-political and state relations, exists also in Arabic. Some have even claimed for it Prophetic authority in the famous saying, *al-nāsu ʿalā dini mulūkihim* (people adhere to the religion of their monarchs).[1] The significance of this principle in Islam can be clearly discerned in the title and methodological structure of the most important classical world history by the great historian Tabari who called his ambitious work "The History of Apostles and Kings."[2]

The two great powers here meant, which provide the context for both the Christian and Islamic view of the world and of human history, are the divine and temporal powers. These two powers are represented in Islam by the prophetic history, which is the framework within which human history moves, and the temporal power, represented by the ruler. In Christianity they are the "city of God," represented here on earth by the Church, and human secular power. The first is eternal and immutable, the second ephemeral and transient.[3] Both concepts, moreover, are based in the scriptures of the two communities: "the Kingdom of God" of the Gospel and God's absolute dominion (*mulk*) of the Qur'ān.[4]

In classical Muslim piety these two powers were seen as reflecting one another. When the ruler is just and good, nature is good as well. But nature becomes less giving and harsher when the ruler is harsh and unjust.[5] Therefore it may be argued that in Islam the temporal and religious powers are closely intertwined. They are two dimensions of one absolute divine power without which no power, be it good or evil, can exist. This is to say, power in human society ultimately belongs to God alone.

This principle and its implementation have, since the death of the Prophet, been the issue which split the Muslim community into warring factions. They are the challenge to the legitimacy of any authority in Muslim society. This challenge was proclaimed early in Muslim history in the uncompromising dictum, "No authority or judgment except God's judgment or authority."[6] This principle, moreover, which is common to all three monotheistic traditions, has been a source of strength and moral cohesion for the pious, but also a justification for exclusiveness, conflict and bloodshed.

From the preceding it may be concluded that religion in the Middle East has always been, and remains to this day, not merely a set of beliefs, or even a theological system. It is rather the framework of a socio-political identity: a culture and way of life, a communion of worship and liturgy. Therefore, the ultimate aim of religion is not orthodoxy or "right belief" but holiness and healing. This phenomenon has been well investigated, and need not occupy us further in this discussion.[7]

The Qur'ān did introduce a new element, or at least a new emphasis, to this religious identity. This is the challenge of active and responsible faith which the Qur'ān presents, not only to the Muslims at the time of the Prophet Muhammad, but to all those who believe in God throughout human history. Here again, faith is not simply right belief, but true *islām*, or the total surrender of the human will and destiny to God. Faith, moreover, is a source of blessing, healing and salvation not only for those who live by it, but through them, for the whole society.

For instance, in narrating the story of Lot and God's judgment over his wicked people, the Qur'ān concludes, "We brought out of it [that is Lot's city] those in it who had faith, but We found in it only one house of the *muslims*" (Q. 51:36). As in the Genesis account of the same story (Gen. 9:1-29), the implication is that there was not a sufficient number of people of faith living in the wicked city for God to spare it. Faith can become, not only a source of blessing and salvation, but also a cause of judgement and chastisement.

Thus, in discussing the fate of the martyrs of Najrān,[8] the Qur'ān asserts that they were martyred for their faith and thus lays God's curse on those who subjected them to martyrdom by fire, only because "they had faith in God." In the same context, the Qur'ān further threatens those who seek to tempt people away from their faith by means of coercion, torture or death with the punishment of hell-fire in the hereafter (Q. 85:4-10).

It may be further concluded from the above discussion that the Qur'ān posits a two-level faith identity. The first is an identity which is legal, cultural, and social, expressed in the individual's membership in the Muslim community. The framework of this identity is Islam as an institutionalized religion and legal system. The second is a deeper identity which is based on faith, or *īmān*. It belongs to God alone to decide as to the truth or falsity of this identity. The Qur'ān speaks of the nomadic Arabs (*al-aʿrāb*) who said, "We have faith." The Qur'ān counters, "Rather say, 'We have become Muslims,' for true faith has not yet entered your hearts" (Q. 49:148).

This point is again brought home with graphic irony in the following exchange between the Prophet and a young and enthusiastic fighter for the new faith, Usāma b. Zayd:

> In battle with the polytheistic tribe of the Bani Murrah, Usāma killed a man after he pronounced the *shahāda*, "There is no god but God," adding, "Do not kill me, I am a Muslim." The Prophet reproached Usāma for killing another Muslim. But Usāma protested, "He declared the shahāda under my sword." The Prophet ironically retorted, "Then you did not of course neglect to split open his head," to determine whether the man had indeed accepted faith or not.[9]

These two levels of identity stood side by side in the formative years of the Muslim community, and their legal and theological legitimacy is clearly affirmed in the Qur'ān and early *hadith* tradition. Faith as a universal and primordial basis of true religious identity was not limited to the Muslims. Rather, it was extended to the Jews and Christians as people of the Book, and to all those who have true faith in God.

In a rare case where a qur ānic verse is repeated, almost verbatim, once near the beginning of the Prophet's mission in Medina and again towards its end (Q. 2:62; 5:69), we read, "Surely those who have faith, the Jews, the Christians, and the Sabaeans, whoever accepts faith in God and the last Day, and performs good deeds; they shall have their reward with their Lord, no fear shall come upon them nor will they grieve" (Q. 2:62).[10] This verse presents again two criteria whereby a genuine religious identity can be ascertained: possession of a Divine revelation, or scripture (*kitāb*), and faith in God. Faith, to be more precise, is the primary, universal, and overarching principle within which scriptures are a concomitant but not absolutely necessary criterion.

The Jews and Christians here represent the first criterion as people of the Book (*ahl al-kitāb*). This criterion, however, could be extended to include all other faiths based on scriptures. This in fact the Muslims soon did as they treated first the Zoroastrians (*mājūs*) and later the Hindus as "people of the Book." The Sabaeans may be taken to represent all those who had faith in God other than the Jews and Christians. This is because classical Qur'ān commentators and traditionists generally differed as to whether the Sabaeans actually possessed a sacred book.[11]

As for the legal religious identity which determined the status of an individual or group in Muslim society, it was more often than not subject to cultural and political considerations. For example, the Christian Arab tribes in early Islam were torn between their own faith-identity as Christians and an ethnic and cultural affinity with the Muslims. They therefore decided to fight alongside the Muslims rather than pay the poll-tax, which they regarded as a humiliation for true Arabs. They were not only exempted from the poll-tax, but allowed to share in the booty.[12] Eventually, more on cultural than religious grounds, I believe, these people were largely assimilated into Muslim society.

In yet another example of Christian-Muslim relations we see reflected the principles of religious tolerance and even mutual acceptance, on the one hand, and of polemical debate, repudiation, and subjugation on the other. In Mecca, the Qur'ān presents the Christians of Najrān to the oppressed Muslims as an example of faith-martyrs to be emulated. In Medina, the Christians of Najrān become the model community of *dhimmis* living under Islamic protection with all the positive and negative elements that this status entailed.[13]

When, under the leadership of the Prophet, the Muslim commonwealth of Medina became increasingly recognized as the principal religio-political power in Arabia, a number of delegations from neighboring tribes and communities were sent to the Prophet to pledge allegiance or make peace with Medina. The delegation of Najrān came to the Prophet, according to tradition,[14] with two aims in view, to share their faith in hope of winning Muhammad to Christianity and, failing this, to establish a peace-covenant with the Muslim state that would insure for them religious freedom and social independence. The men, who included religious and political leaders, were allowed to offer their prayers in the Prophet's mosque in spite of the protestations of some of the Companions.

The Qur'ān clearly indicates that a sharp debate concerning the divinity and humanity of Christ took place between the Prophet and the men of Najrān, but does not report the actual disputation. Accounts of this debate are late, and appear to reflect an already developed legal system governing the social, religious, and political status of non-Muslims in a vast Islamic state (Q. 3:59-63).[15] The two elements that are of interest to us in this encounter are, first the fact that the men of Najrān were allowed to worship in the Prophet's mosque, and second that, while the Prophet and the Christians of Najrān did not agree theologically, they worked out a mutually acceptable relationship.

The first of these two elements indicates, in my view, an acceptance of both faith-communities of the essential truth of each other's faith, and hence the legitimacy of both Christian and Islamic worship. The second demonstrates an attitude of mutual tolerance in spite of profound and irreconcilable theological differences. This tolerance unfortunately had within it the seeds of intolerance and hostility, nurtured by a long history of conflict, rivalry, and domination. This is because it was a tolerance dictated by military rather than moral strength and by political exigencies rather than the imperatives of a common faith in God.

This encounter, moreover, along with the on-going interaction of the first generation of Muslims with their Jewish and Christian neighbors raises another important question. What is the qur'ānic demand of non-Muslims, particularly the people of the Book, as far as their relationship with Islam goes? This question is important because it bears directly on Muslim-Christian relations today. I am convinced that the Qur'ān and early prophetic tradition generally demanded from Jews and Christians no more than what we are struggling to come to terms with today. It is the recognition that Muhammad is one of the prophets of God, the Qur'ān is the Book of God, and that Islam must exist alongside the two previous religions as an authentic religion based on an authentic revelation from Heaven. In support of this view may be cited the Qur'ān's repeated claim to be "a Book confirming the scriptures that were before it" (Q. 2:97; 3:3; 3:50; 4:47; 5:46).

To be sure, there are verses in the Qur'ān which appear to evince not harmony and concord but discord and conflict between Muslims and the other people of the Book. Most notable among these is the famous *jizya* verse which reads, "Fight those among the people of the Book who do not have faith in God and the Last Day, and do not prohibit what God and His Messenger had prohibited, and do not abide by the true faith, until they give the *jizya* with their own hand, humbled" (Q. 9:29). The verse, however, lays down three important conditions for fighting, two of which are unverifiable: "not having faith in God and the Last Day" and "not abiding by the true faith." It may be argued that these and the third condition, namely not abiding by the sanctions of the Qur'ān and the Prophet, apply to Muslims as well. Conversely, all three conditions may, at least from the Islamic point of view, equally apply to all faith communities.

Like all legislative verses of the Qur'ān, the ultimate purpose of this verse is not legislation but moral and religious guidance. This may be inferred from the many conditions and qualifiers which the Qur'ān attaches to its legal sanctions and prohibitions. Often this purpose is obscured by the juristic purely legal or political rules formulated on the basis of moral and religious precepts. Who is therefore to decide that such and such Jews and Christians do not have faith in God, or do not abide by the true religion? Obviously, if the judgement concerning the true *islām* of Muslims ultimately belongs to God, then should not the sincerity and truth of faith of Jews and Christians also be left to God to decide?

This question raises yet another problem. If we cannot decide who of the people of the Book have true faith in God and who do or do not follow the true religion, how are we to apply the Islamic law of the *jizya* to these people? Yet, jurists legislated not for the exception but for the rule. Furthermore, jurists often broadened the applications of qur'ānic sanctions far beyond their apparent sense to include Jews and Christians within their purview.

I believe that only after the Qur'ān was codified, and there were no longer any "associators" (*mushrikūn*) of other gods with God in Arabia, that terms like Associators, previously restricted to non-Muslim Arab tribes came to designate Christians and even Jews.[16] The Qur'ān consistently refers to Jews and Christians as people of the Book. In the *hadith* tradition, which is the second source of Islamic sacred law after the Qur'ān, the word *dhimma* was used to designate the people of the Book as people with a special covenant of protection with the Muslims, but the term did not imply a second-class status. Rather, the word *dhimma* was used as an expression of the responsibility of the Muslims for their non-Muslim subjects.

The people of *dhimma* were sometimes referred to as the "people of the *dhimma* of the Messenger of God." At other times they were called the "people of the *dhimma* of God." This is to say, the charge for the wellbeing of these people primarily rested with God. The entire community is to represent God and His Messenger in safeguarding their covenant of protection with the people of *dhimma*. Thus did the protection and wellbeing of Christians and Jews in Muslim lands become the sacred charge of all Muslims.

With the development of the schools of jurisprudence (*fiqh*) and the deepening conflict between Christendom and the World of Islam, the people of *dhimma* came to be regarded as a special category, not only different from, but inferior to the Muslims. This development may be contrasted with the original Muslim attitude illustrated by the following anecdote:

> Hizām b. Hakim, one of the Prophet's Companions, saw one day in Syria a group of Christians standing out in the hot sun. He was told that they were being punished because they had not paid their land taxes in full. Hizam went to the governor of Syria-Palestine ᶜUmayr b. Saᶜd and reproached him saying, "I heard the Messenger of God, peace and blessings be upon him, say, 'He who torments men in this world, God will torment him on the Day of Resurrection.'" Hearing this, the governor ordered that the men be set free.[17]

The development of a legal system and the institutions to implement it, however necessary for the survival of Islam as a faith and civilization, resulted in the reification of *Islām* into a closed religion. It rendered Islam the final religion and Muhammad the final Prophet. Theologically and juristically, this finality meant that Islam superseded all previous religions, and the Qur'ān abrogated all previous scriptures. These exclusivist ideas and the exclusivist attitudes which they engendered belonged to the development of the Islamic religious disciplines such as theology, jurisprudence and the qur'ānic sciences.

It must again, however, be stressed that religious exclusivism does not accord with the spirit and worldview of the Qur'ān. The Qur'ān states, "To everyone have we appointed a way and a course to follow" (Q. 5:48), and "For each there is a direction toward which he turns; vie therefore with one another in the performance of good works. Wherever you may be, God shall bring you all together [on the day of judgment]. Surely God has power over all things" (Q. 2:148).

By the end of the eleventh century, both the Christians and Muslim communities had different concerns: the Muslims had established an

Arabo-Islamic culture in Spain, hence the Catholic *reconquista* and the Christians embarked on two centuries of crusades in the name of Christ. Thus the voice of God in the Qur'ān and the Gospel was completely drowned by the clamor of human folly and the cries of victims of war and oppression.

In such circumstances, the ideals of love, universalism and openness which are basic to both faiths gave way to ideas of exclusivism and hostility on both sides. Motivated by the affirmation that salvation is by Christ alone, Christians sent both missionaries and armies to colonize and convert the Muslims. For Muslims, the people of the Book became the rejecters of faith (*kuffār*) who obstinately refused to accept God's final revelation; that is, they refused to become Muslims. Thus they took the place of the Meccan "associators" as legally legitimate objects of religious warfare and domination.

Muslim and Christian men and women have lived together in the Middle East for the most part as good neighbors. Given the mosaic character of Middle Eastern societies throughout their long history, Muslims, Christians and Jews lived with a good measure of concord and harmony. This was due, at least in part, to social courtesy, which is a common characteristic of Eastern peoples regardless of their religious affiliations. There were, of course, outbreaks of conflict, but often these were incited either by a particular group of people for particular political ends or by outside influences.

Within the framework of this common courtesy, dialogue between Muslims and Christians in the Middle East has not been a dialogue about religious beliefs and theological doctrines. It is rather a neighborly relationship of sharing, sharing in each other's festivals and other joyous celebrations and in sad occasions of death and calamity. In short, they shared a daily life as one community of different but mutually respected faiths.

Among the many things Middle Eastern Christians and Muslims have learned from the West is to do dialogue, western style. This kind of dialogue is, however, too foreign to the whole culture and mentality of the people. It is therefore not going very far and many people are suspicious of both the form and purpose of this dialogue. Communities which have long taken for granted that everyone must have a socio-religious identity naturally live the ideal of religious pluralism.

The cultural courtesy, of which I have made so much in this discussion, is based on an old Arab adage which is in turn inspired by the

Qur'ān. The Qur'ān says, "To you your religion, and to me my religion" (Q. 109:6). The adage goes, "To each his religion, and may God help him," that is to live by it.

The Qur'ān speaks to us today as directly as it did to the people of its time of revelation more than fourteen centuries ago. It enjoins all the people of the Book, Jews, Christians and Muslims, mutually to accept one another on one basis alone, "that we worship no one except God, and that we do not take one another as lords besides God" (Q. 3:64). This invitation to the people of the Book to come to one word of common purpose remains a challenge for all of us today as it was for the Prophet and his people.

It may be further argued that the Qur'ān legislates for a pluralistic society in which diverse religious communities can live side by side in mutual and creative acceptance that would far transcend mere tolerance. No doubt, in both Christianity and Islam this ideal exists. Both the Catholic and Orthodox Churches have long had a historical and philosophical tradition of interfaith relations, and many Protestant churches and other religious and civic organizations are playing a major role in the effort to realize this ideal.

The challenge of the Qur'ān, I believe, and more to Muslims than to Christians, is to regard the people of the Book as a large family of faith, speaking different languages but worshipping the One God. The Qur'ān employs two terms to denote peoples bound by a common faith or destiny: *ashāb* and *ahl*. It calls '*ashāb*' the inhabitants of Paradise (*ashāb al-janna*) and people with a shared destiny, such as the "people of the Cave" (*ashāb al-kahf*) (Q. 2:39; 2:257; 7:42; 10:26; 18:9), while the immediate family of such prophets as Noah, Abraham, Moses and Muhammad, it calls *ahl* (Q. 3:33; 11:45; 3:121).

Consistently, the people of the Book are referred to in the Qur'ān as *ahl al-kitāb*. The word *ahl* always signifies a family relationship. The *ahl* of a person are his or her family, wife, husband and children. Therefore, the phrase, *ahl al-kitāb* should be translated as "the family of the Book." The Qur'ān, furthermore, enjoins Muslims and all the people of faith to show kindness to their near relations.

Muslims, certainly more than Christians if not Jews, are in the strict literal sense, people of the Book. For Muslims, therefore, "a true religion" is faith in a revealer-God and His revelations. Islam to a large extent shares a deep reverence for the sacred word with Eastern Christianity and all the ancient Semitic cultures of the Middle East. The

Christian concept of the incarnate, divine Word notwithstanding, it still cannot be argued that Islam has imposed on Christianity a concept or idea which it did not already have. The Church had, until Martin Luther, argued for the equality, if not primacy, of tradition over Scriptures. This is because the New Testament is a product of the Church and a record of its early history and witness. But with Luther's proclamation, "*sola scriptura*," Islam and Christianity again came closer together in the recognition of the centrality of the Scriptures as a source of moral, legal and spiritual authority. The centrality of the "revealed Divine Word" in the life and worship of the Church has been especially emphasized by Vatican II in its eucharistic theology, where the faithful are urged to turn for spiritual nourishment to "the divine Scriptures," "since from the table of both the word of God and of the body of Christ she unceasingly receives and offers to the faithful the bread of life, especially in the sacred liturgy."[18]

Thus the "revealed Word of God" (*al-kitāb*) may once more become the common bond that binds all the people of faith together. The qur'ānic emphasis on the centrality of the Book could help Jews, Christians and Muslims become for the first time the reconciled children of Abraham, to become one happy family.

Notes

[1]This saying has no basis in the *hadīth* tradition. It is, however, reported in the Prophetic tradition as a moral indictment of the community's laxity: "*Kamā takūnū yuwallā ʿalaykum*" (just as you are, so will be those in authority over you). *Mishkāt al-Masābih*. Trans. James Robson (Lahore: Sh. Muhammad Ashraf, 1975), 789.

[2]*Taʾrikh al-Rusul wal-Mulūk* by Muhammad b. Jarir al-Tabari [d. 310/923] is a publication project [in English translation] of State University of New York Press. For the life of the author and his methodology, see *The History of Tabari*, vol. 1, "General Introduction and From Creation to the Flood," trans. and annot. by Franz Rosenthal (Albany: State University of New York Press, 1989), 5-140.

[3]The classical expression of this idea is St. Augustine's *The City of God* which is the first major attempt at presenting a Christian philosophy of history.

[4]See the Lord's Prayer in Mt. 6:9-13 where the addition to v.13 in later manuscripts, "For yours is the kingdom and the power and the glory for ever. Amen," stresses this idea further. In the Qurʾān this idea provides the framework of God's role in human history, see Q. 3:26 as well as 2:107; 3:189.

[5]See Geo. Widengren, *Muhammad, the Apostle of God, and His Ascension* (Uppsala, 1950); also Nizām al-Mulk, *Siyar al-Mulūk* or *siyāsat-nāmah*, trans. Hubert Drake as *The Book of Government or Rules for Kings* (London: Henley and Boston: Routledge and Kegan Paul, 1978), pt. 1, ch. 5 (pp. 32-42).

[6]"*Lā hukma illā li-llāh*" (cf. Q. 6:57; 12:40) was the slogan raised by the Khārijites against ʿAli b. Abi Tālib, the fourth of "the rightly guided caliphs," first Shiʿi Imam and one of the most venerated personalities in Muslim history.

[7]See J. Spencer Trimingham, *Christianity Among the Arabs in Pre-Islamic Times* (London and New York: Longmans/Librairie du Liban, 1979), 100-16 passim.

[8]See the illuminating study of this pre-Islamic South Arabian Christian community by Irfan Shahid, *The Martyrs of Najrān: New Documents* (Brussels, 1971).

[9]Ibn Qayyim al-Jawziyyah, *Zād al-Maʿād*, ed. Shuʿayb ʿAbd al-Qādir al-Armaʾūt, 6th ed., vol. 3 (Beirut: Muʾassasat al-Risālah, 1304/1984), 361. See also note for a comprehensive discussion of this tradition.

[10]For a comprehensive discussion of the major interpretations of this verse, see M. Ayoub, *The Qurʾān and its Interpreters*, vol. 1 (Albany: State University of New York, 1984), 108ff.

[11]See the previous note.

[12]Marshall G.S. Hodgson, *The Venture of Islam*, Vol. 1 (Chicago and London: University of Chicago Press, 1974), 199; 229.

[13]For a discussion of the term *dhimma* in the Qurʾān and its legal significance for Jews and Christians under Muslim rule, see M. Ayoub, "Dhimma in Qurʾān and hadith," *Arab Studies Quarterly*, 5 (1983), 172-82. For a very useful presentation of numerous primary text translations into English on the status of *dhimmīs*, see Bat Yeʾor, *The Dhimmi: Jews and Christians under Islam* (Rutherford, Madison, Teaneck: Fairleigh Dickinson University Press/London and Toronto: Associated University Presses, 1985),

passim.

[14]For a discussion of this event and the traditions concerning it, see M. Ayoub, *The Qur'ān and its Interpreters*, vol. 2 (Albany: State University of New York), Introduction: Occasion of revelation of Sura 3 (*Āl ʿImrān*) and commentaries on the *mubāhala* verse (Q. 3:61).

[15]See the previous note.

[16]See Q. 9:30 and my articles "Dhimma in the Qur'ān and Hadīth," *Arab Studies Quarterly*, 5 (1983), 172-82 and "ʿUzayr in the Qur'ān and Muslim Tradition." In *Studies in Islamic and Judaic Studies: Papers Presented in the Institute for Islamic and Judaic Studies*. Brown Judaic Studies, 110. Center for Judaic Studies, University of Denver (Atlanta: Scholars Press, 1986), 3-18.

[17]Ahmad b. Hanbal, *Musnad Ibn Hanbal*, vol. 3 (Beirut: Dar Sadir, n.d.), 403.

[18]Cf. Ch. 6 ("Sacred Scripture in the Life of the Church") of the Dogmatic Constitution on Divine Revelation of Vatican Council II, in Walter M. Abbott, ed., *The Documents of Vatican II* (New York: Guild Press, 1966), 125ff.

THE TWO-HANDED GOD: COMMUNION, COMMUNITY AND CONTOURS FOR DIALOGUE

Ralph Del Colle

INTRODUCTION

"Children of Abraham," a phrase that accurately captures the religious kinship among Jews, Christians and Muslims, not only recalls the patrimony of the three semitic, monotheistic faiths but reminds adherents of these traditions that their ultimate loyalty, faith or submission is to the God who, in the biblical account, calls one forth to a far country and in the Qur'anic one ensures the disowning of all idols along the way. The common heritage of these three faiths is so obvious as not have to be stated. Still the most basic fruits of interreligious dialogue—tolerance, mutual respect, conversation—are still sadly lacking in many parts of our conflict-ridden world. Not the least of these conflicts is centered in the region that is their birthplace. This obvious commonality is the linkage between the speaking God, the prophetic messenger and the birth of a community. Shared attestation, however, is the most obvious aspect of the common heritage; differences of message and situation divide the traditions sharply. Despite the differences, the canonical reception of the Hebrew Bible by Judaism and Christianity, and the Qur'anic witness to those who in Christian hearing are familiar messengers—Abraham, Moses and Jesus—invites dialogue. All of this is to say that, at least for Christians, if not for Jews and Muslims, dialogue among these three traditions cannot be just instances of generic interreligious dialogue or the working out of a model of dialogue that is not already informed by their unique kinship of commonality and difference.

Where does one begin? Do we not have to negotiate and perhaps even take a stand among the prevailing theoretical models that have emerged in theologies of interreligious dialogue? Are we Christians, for example, to be inclusivist or pluralist in approach, christocentric or theocentric in our theological bearings? Or, must we start with the basic fact that is common to these traditions: a prophetic rather than mystical religiosity, according to the typologies of Hans Küng and David Tracy?[1] The latter author would inform Christian dialogue with the religious traditions of South and East Asia while the former best expresses our Abrahamic traditions. Although I have already hinted at the usefulness of the commonality of prophetic mediation in this dialogue I propose to begin even more specifically within the ambit of Christian particularity, then relate my Christian specific to Judaism and Islam respectively.

The particularity to which I am referring is the Christian apprehension of God. It is, in the event, both christological and pneumatological. Borrowing a figure from Irenaeus, we may image Christ and the Spirit as "the two hands of God." Apart from these "hands" the divine economy is neither experienced nor known. A Christian accounting of ultimate reality since the apostolic age is matter of God revealed through the Son and the Holy Spirit. The situation of global religious pluralism and the intent toward dialogue, however, seem together to call that claim into question. Are not there other ways to the divine in the Christian reading? In the inclusivist reading cannot the grace of Christ be spoken of as present within the religious experience, ritual acts and communal structures of other traditions? In the debate over theoretical models, do not the the other traditions compel the Christian to some decision over the claimed absolute normativity of Jesus Christ in the quest for religious truth? Inevitably, the answer to these questions will inform the perception and understanding of Christian identity, since no one emerges from the encounter with the other quite the same as before.

It is my contention that Christians cannot really answer these questions without initially recovering the full pneumatological dimension of Christian faith. This means a trinitarian knowing of the divine. In its christological focus I refer to this as Spirit Christology. This is intended not merely to provide a new modifier for the doctrine of Jesus Christ but to suggest a full trinitarian perspective for the understanding of God's work in the world. To be specific, the filiological and pneumatological dimensions of christology—God as Son and Spirit—are neither identical nor separated but convergent and mutual. This christological perspective is, I believe, the most fruitful model for exploring issues of Christian identity. How this awareness could enrich the prospects for Christian-Jewish and Christian-Islamic dialogue will, I hope, become evident.

SPIRIT CHRISTOLOGY AND THE CHALLENGE OF CHRISTIAN IDENTITY

By observing both a unity and a distinction between the "two hands of God," between what we can identify as the *Christus praesens* and the *Spiritus praesens*, we are enabled to witness to the divine activity, as we seek conversation between the pluralism of human culture and religious expression, and the ecclesial confession of Christian identity. In such conversations the alternatives of christocentrism or theocentrism are surely inadequate. The Christian awareness of God always includes a christological focus and a pneumatic knowing. Only by the Holy Spirit can one say "Jesus is Lord" (1 Cor. 12:3).[2]

The problem, especially in Western Christianity, has been the subordination of the mission of the Holy Spirit to that of the Son, thereby rendering it merely instrumental to the latter. One such example is that the Spirit can become the subjective dimension of the objective work of the Son. Nor is it helpful to rectify this by so separating the mission of the Spirit from that of the Son that one could identify the pneumatological without the christological. I prefer, rather, the axiom suggested by Yves Congar: "No Christology without pneumatology and no pneumatology without Christology."[3] In other words, the Christian knows God "through Christ and in the Spirit," according to the patristic formula. All issues affecting the existential embodiment of Christian identity will have these two coextensive but distinct theologies of godhead as markers for the journey of Christians along the way. Whether it be questions arising from culturally specific readings of the human experience or emancipatory imperatives arising out of human suffering and oppression, Christian discernment is both a christological and pneumatological affair. Neither one displaces the other or is more important than the other. And neither does anything to threaten the divine unity or unicity.

Coming to interreligious dialogue and specifically, Christian-Jewish and Christian-Islamic dialogue, our concern is with the God whom Jews, Christians and Muslims bear witness to as One who is both hidden and revealed. Whether it be the burning bush of Sinai, the hill of Golgotha, or the cave of Mount Hira, it is the hidden God who speaks. The eventual effectual result of this speech is the formation of religious community: a People, an Ekklesia, an Abode. For the Christian this revealing God is known in Christ Jesus by the power of the Holy Spirit. Jesus of Nazareth, crucified and risen, is the material content, the sacramental presence, and the eschatological hope of Christian faith. Coextensive with this, the Holy Spirit is the incarnating co-agent, the contemporaneous evocation and the promissory downpayment of the divine economy. As Kilian McDonnell has remarked, pneumatology is the epistemology of our theological recognition of "the presence of God in history and the face of the Son in His Church."[4]

Spirit Christology, as I am suggesting it, distinguishes between the filial and pneumatic dimensions of the person and work of Jesus Christ. Spirit Christology does not displace Logos/Son christologies but complements them in the direction of a fully trinitarian context for all christological reflection. It also avoids the philanthropic or merely human tendencies of some contemporary Spirit Christologies, e.g., those of Hick and Lampe.[5] Jesus Christ is the enfleshed image of God's communicative and relational being in a human life, which was witnessed most profoundly in his "Abba" prayer. Jesus Christ is also present in the *ekklesia* through the presence of the Spirit, the risen *Kyrios* as sender of the Spirit. His origins, ministry and paschal passage lie under the agency of the Spirit, so that we can say with Piet Schoonenberg that "in Jesus himself both Logos and Spirit are present" although in his glorification the Spirit and not the Logos is given to the Christian community.[6]

On the one hand, to the Jewish and Muslim dialogue partners it can be said that when Christians confess Jesus Christ, they witness to the outpouring of God, protologically as Wisdom and Word, eschatologically as Spirit.[7] This counters a premature categorization of the doctrine of the trinity as tritheism. On the other hand, the classical trinitarian distinction between the temporal missions of the Son and the Spirit is also preserved. It is the Word who becomes incarnate and the Spirit who is efficacious in the world as the graced presence of the divine economy. But we also seek an integration, not an undue separation, between the divine sendings of Son and Spirit. The mission and ministry of Jesus Christ, the Word incarnate, is suffused by the Spirit. Full of the Spirit and as Spirit-bearer, Jesus in his paschal passage to resurrection/exaltation becomes the sender of the Pentecostal Spirit. And it is the efficacious presence of the Spirit (the *Spiritus praesens*) who enables the self-presentation of the risen Christ (the *Christus praesens*) that thus constitutes the reality of the church and its apostolic mission. In sum, God's self-communicating Word incarnate as a human being in Jesus Christ and now transfigured in total presence to God is the source of the life-giving Spirit who is consummating all of creation in God, a work only to be fully realized in a new advent of divine agency at the parousia.

In interreligious dialogue, especially the dialogue with Jews and Muslims, Christians need to stress how God's protological speech—"In the beginning . . . God said" (Gen. 1:1-3) or "In the beginning was the Word" (Jn.1:1)—becomes covenantal or prophetic speech formative of both scripture and community. The christological moment or gestalt of revelation contains within it a pneumatological impulse in which the event and reception of divine speech entails both divine agency and human praxis. These constitute the most primordial dimensions of a tradition's religious experience. In the words of the apostles and elders at the council held at Jerusalem (Acts 15:28), "It is the decision of the Holy Spirit and Us." This is perhaps a hint that divine agency is present in human agency but always transcends it beyond the limitations of human reflection and decision. Indeed, attention to these two hands of the divine economy, never separate but never confused, enables us to interpret analogically the full possibilities that dialogue with another tradition affords. It is one that offers, in my opinion, an authentic communion as an eschatological foretaste of divine presence across the boundaries of the confessional and historical particularities of our respective communities.[8] To this I now turn.

CHRISTIAN-JEWISH DIALOGUE:
COVENANTAL COMMUNION AND MESSIANIC OPENNESS

A descriptive account of the Judaic encounter with God would refer to election, covenant, Torah, the land and latterly halakha. Each relates to the other and expresses an aspect of the essentials of Judaism. For the Christian, it is helpful to focus on covenant as the premier paradigm since it locates one's attempt at listening and conversing within the framework of a familiarity that is already a difference. Christians cannot presume an intimate knowledge of Judaism when they only know the Hebrew scriptures and go ignorant of rabbinic interpretation and halakhic observance. In other words, what is familiar--the agency of the God of the covenant--immediately recedes into the otherness of sage and rabbi. A familiarity with evangelist and apostle does little to right this balance when attempting religious dialogue with Jews.

The first task for the Christian in this dialogue always entails coming to terms with the living reality of Judaism. Engaging in a biblical anamnesis of the faith of ancient Israel is palpably insufficient. For

Christians as well as for Jews covenant is the enactment of the divine-human encounter. The identity of the hidden God is revealed in conjunction with the covenantal partnership with the people Israel beginning with Abraham. Yet it is precisely in this covenantal relation that the *novum* of Christian faith appears, the new covenant (as *kaine* is usually translated) enacted in the paschal supper. Whether it be the contrast between old and new in the Epistle to the Hebrews, the schema of promise and fulfillment in the Gospel of Matthew, or the motif of type and antitype in the Fourth Gospel, the Christian is schooled in the obsolescence or irrelevance of contemporary Judaic practice. The understanding of the covenant as "new" rather than "renewal" has much to do with this, but there are other factors.

One way beyond this impasse from the Christian side is a close query of the Christian *novum* in both its christological and pneumatological dimensions. Rejecting the notion of Christianity as an additional covenant to God's covenant with Israel (the "double covenant" theory), we are better led in the direction of seeing a new dimension of the one covenant of God with Israel. If Christians claim an authentic rabbinic *novum* regarding the pattern of divine speech and redemption (the christological moment) and human praxis and hope (the pneumatological dimension), they have not disturbed the oneness of God but only claim to have heard God speak in two not entirely new ways. God is enfleshed in Torah given to a people, hence to a people, and guides this people through the divine Spirit poured out in its midst.

The question for the Christian is a simple one in the theological assessment of Judaism. Is God's covenant with Israel still valid? This seems patronizing, not to say insulting, to the Jew but it has to be put in this form because Christianity has so long denied it. The answer to the question is a resounding yes, whether we derive it from Paul in Romans 11:28-29 or the bishops' restoration of it at the Second Vatican Council (*Nostra Aetate* #4).[9] The issue, for Christianity of course, is how God's covenant with Israel, never revoked, is fully operative in light of the Christian claim that it has been renewed in Christ. Here the Gospel of Matthew is quite helpful. For Matthew the covenantal drama which culminates in Jesus identifies the claimed fulfillment as prophetically representative of the whole people: "Out of Egypt I called my Son" (Matt. 2:15). Jesus as an utterly faithful Jew is the instantiation in a human life of God's self-outpouring and kenosis that is an invitation to all nations. Jesus' baptism by John is viewed as the fulfillment of all righteousness

(Matt.3:15). His is to be the perfect righteousness. The polemic of the Matthean community portrays as exceeding that of the "scribes and Pharisees" (Matt. 5:20), an especially unfortunate claim in the event because it convinced Christians that their Law observance in the spirit of Jesus' teachings rendered nugatory all other Law observance.

Beyond the emergent conflict between church and synagogue lies the modality of the *novum* in the covenantal encounter between God and the people. The church traditionally assumed that the christological *novum* and its coextensive pneumatological witness ("We are witnesses of these things as is the Holy Spirit that God has given" Acts 5:32) negates or transforms the existing Judaic reality. This disregards the fact that that reality was not really static; it too was experiencing a *novum* in the form of the emergent rabbinic interpretations of the Torah to be enshrined in Mishnah and Talmud. As Norbert Lohfink has recently argued, a Christian affirmation of the fulfillment of Jeremiah's promise of a new covenant (31: 33-34), followed by Ezekiel's prophecy of a new heart and a new spirit (36:25-27) need not deny that there is a fulfillment in the House of Israel during the Second Temple period well before the time of Jesus. Eschatological-christological fulfillment in Jesus Christ--which is still on its way until the parousia--can be mutually related to the new heart loyal to the Torah which the sages and scribes of Israel had in their fidelity to God after the return.[10] This notion of an authentic *novum* in Judaism continues to the formative period following the destruction of the Second Temple, through to the completion of the Talmuds, along with *Tanak* the "classical Judaism of the dual Torah" to borrow the language of Jacob Neusner.

Neusner suggests that the challenge of Christianity had a part in leading to the validation of the authority of the Mishnah beyond the shared scriptures of Jews and Christians. Sages, not prophets, elevated the status of the oral Torah. History as the subject of messianic salvation gave way to the sanctification of Israel through Torah loyalty in the circumstances of Israel's this-worldly disempowerment.[11] Eventually with the completion of the Talmuds the entire Torah, written and oral, becomes the symbol of salvation. The promised Messiah would appear in the image of a Rabbi/Sage. In a similar vein, David Hartman speaks of the "Rabbinic renewal of the covenant," one that is an internalization of the covenantal ideal. Religious immediacy and anticipation is focused on the observance of God's precepts (*mizvot*). God reigns through the Torah, thus molding all expressions of Jewish life even when Israel's enemies are not defeated.[12] This internalization of the Torah, God's gift to Israel, has to be called a *novum* of both divine and human proportions.

By identifying this *novum* within Rabbinic Judaism we are able analogically to perceive the divine mystery in Judaic life and praxis from a Christian perspective. Here we can utilize the model of Spirit Christology already explicated. This is not to impose a Christian framework on what is distinctly Judaic but rather to enable the Christian to interact theologically with Israel's continuing witness to the God of the covenant. I propose that the christological analogue is Torah and messianic openness and the pneumatological analogue is halakhic observance and Talmudic engagement. The former bespeaks the presence of God in human speech and history while the latter highlights the covenantal response as human fidelity and the divine sanctification of creation.

For the Christian the christological moment centers on a human life, a crucified and risen human being. This simultaneously transforms previous messianic models and keeps the future open. Triumphalist interpretations of Jesus' exaltation tend to betray the staurological locus of fulfillment, the profound insight of the Fourth Gospel that Jesus' exaltation is in his cross. The cross joined to resurrection also delivers a paradigm of discipleship as cross-bearing "between the ages," until the arrival of the parousia. The apocalyptic sufferings of Christ are definitive for Christian messianic expectation, a mark which was never entirely lost on the Great Church even after the Constantinian settlement. Martyrs, confessors, saints in actuality bear the marks of the crucified Christ even as the liturgy of the church sacramentally represents it.

In Judaism both the Torah and messianic expectation similarly exclude triumphalistic notions. The Rabbis fashioned a Judaism for a time of waiting in an unredeemed world, as Michael Wyschogrod puts it, "A sober Judaism in which the word of God through prophecy was no longer being heard."[13] Torah as revelation of God is placed in human hands where God's interpretation can even be outvoted by the majority, as in the well-known aggadic story in which God replies to this defeat at the hands of the Rabbis by laughing and saying: 'My sons have defeated me, My sons have defeated Me' (*Bava Metzia* 59b).[14] With messianic hopes still unfulfilled, the speech of God finds its home or embodiment within the people through their study, interpretation and observance. Torah without Talmud, messianic hope without halakhic life, is inconceivable to the Rabbinic mind (even within the Reform tradition with its turn from *halakha* to ethics). To return to our analogical model: "No

Christology without pneumatology and no pneumatology without Christology."

Pneumatological christology suggests, as I have already stated, a mutual and reciprocal relationship between the Son and the Spirit. Although only the Son becomes incarnate and only the Spirit is pentecostally given, to know Jesus Christ is to attest that the "sender" of the Spirit, i.e., the risen Kyrios, was the "bearer" of the Spirit and in his origins was "out of" or "from" the Spirit. Each of these entails the cooperation of human and divine agency, respectively that of the glorified Christ, Jesus of Nazareth, and Mary. Likewise, in the Judaic tradition coextensive with the gift of Torah and messianic hope is the entrustment of the gifts and promises of God into the hands of human agency that Talmud and *halakha* represent. *Kavvanah*, the attentiveness to God that the *mitzvot* elicit, is where the divine indwelling is realized in the sanctification of creation, daily life and the covenant community. As its analogue in Christian faith suggests, it is the flowing together of human praxis and divine purpose. It is with this covenantal communion of Israel with God that the Christian may fruitfully dialogue.

CHRISTIAN-ISLAMIC DIALOGUE:
PROPHETIC COMMUNION AND DIVINE ZEAL

If the Christian-Jewish dialogue is primarily a conversation between an elect people and a portion of that people in continuity who witness to the singularity of Jesus Christ, Christian-Islamic dialogue pairs off two singularities which may in fact be irreconcilable. Some Christian theologians, among them the writer, do not have too much difficulty arguing that the Judaic "no" to Jesus as Messiah is really a "yes" to the God of the covenant, and that it behooves Christians to recognize the positive aspects of that assent even for Christian faith. But how does a final prophet and apostle/envoy follow upon the "once for all" revelation that is Jesus Christ? Not only is there a conflict of finalities but also there is the younger tradition enlisting the messengers and prophets of the biblical account, including Jesus, seeing in them a preparation for *the* Prophet. Francis E. Peters observes in his book, *Children of Abraham*, that if the Christian scriptures (especially the Pauline corpus) present Jesus as a "Jewish revolutionary" who abrogates the Law, the Qur'an presents Muhammad as an "Israelite fundamentalist" who does not reread the older scriptures of Jews and Christians but returns "to the source, the 'natural' pre-Torah religion of Abraham, the father of all believers."[15] Muslims would, of course, remind Peters of what he very well knows, namely, that Jews and Christians both altered their own writings and Islam restored their original meanings.

Despite these difficulties framing the question from the Christian perspective is relatively simple. Upon hearing the witness or recitation of Muhammad one inquires: is he a prophet of God? Is the Qur'anic message from God? While prophets leave little room for maneuver, the Christian is exhorted not to despise prophetic utterances, while simultaneously being required to test everything and retain what is good (1 Thess. 5:19). Hans Küng, for example, is able to give an affirmative answer to this question with all the nuances of historical criticism and comparative interpretation that he applies in other contexts to Jesus and Buddha. At the very least, quoting from Surah 46.9--"I only follow what has been revealed to me;/I am only a clear warner"--Küng proffers Muhammad as a "prophetic corrective for Christians in the name of the one and only God."[16] Indeed, the points he cites, that the one God is absolute and incomparable, without association, and one whose guidance disallows a separation between faith and life (including politics) are surely points that all Christians can agree to. As much was said by *Nostra Aetate* (#3).[17] But Küng and others, especially Kenneth Cragg (to whom I owe much in these reflections), are seeking a deeper dialogue with the Islamic tradition.

I begin by again employing Spirit Christology in analogical fashion, in this instance, to Islam. As I have already attended to the explication of this model I will immediately attempt a theological reading of Islam from the perspective of Spirit christology. First, the Qur'anic messengers and prophets familiar to the biblical account confront the Christian with the kinship of commonality and the otherness of difference. It is a common sacred history read in a key that is almost at the point of non-recognition. The issue is not so much historical faithfulness--the Qur'an claiming to correct the errors within the sacred books of Jews and Christians--as a particular theological rendering of the witnesses and their message.

Muslims will not assent, constrained by a literalist theory of inspiration, but the Christian seeks the pattern of divine speech in correlation with the convergence of human and divine agency. Prophetic communion and zeal for God are the two foci of the Islamic experience. The words of the Prophet, which are, the words of God, announce the creative power of the divine presence, the guidance necessary to establish the human being "in submission" as the vicegerent of God, and the coming judgment which ultimately establishes the creation as wholly God's. By "submission" the Muslim enacts in human life the totalizing consciousness of the divine imperative.

The condemnation of *shirk*--the association of anything at the level of God—along with its corresponding *takbir* and *tawhid*—respectively the magnification of God (*Allahu akbar*—"Greater is God") and the affirmation of divine unity—characterize Islamic faith and piety. Nevertheless, in the disassociation there is an association and in magnification of God there is an elevation of the human. God's absoluteness and incomparability are known because there is an enactment in human speech, while the attestation of God always includes the evocation of the divine messenger in the *Shahadah* (witness)[18]. So much is it the case that there is an association of God with the human that the legal/societal and affective/mystical dimensions of Islam are based on their recognition in Muhammad as the supreme embodiment of Islamic life. The pious Muslim celebrates the prophet (*tasliyah*=celebrating)[19] because God and the angels bless him (Surah 33.56). Islamic law (*shari'ah*) is grounded in *hadith*, traditional sayings of the Prophet, from which (along with the Qur'an) are derived the obligatory *sunnah* (customs, practice).

Analogically we are enabled to read christological and pneumatological moments in this religious complex. The pattern of revelation is one of uncompromising warning and guidance. To hear the divine speech is to listen to its recitation from the mouth of the Prophet (Surah 96.1) and respond to it with all the dignity inherent in God's original creative intent for the human being. This pattern requires the prophetic communion of the messenger, beginning with Adam and extending beyond Abraham to Jesus and Muhammad, each of whom bears witness in speech and action to the absolute claims of God.[20]

The pneumatological dimension is reflected in the formation of the Islamic community, an Abode (as in *Ummah* and *Dar al-Islam*) where *shari'ah* and *tasliyah* mark the legal and devotional boundaries of Islam, the latter extending into mysticism in the Sufi traditions. The divine zeal evoking human response and leading ultimately to *jihad* is certainly meritorious in the internal forum of heart and soul and even in community, short of coercion and Holy War. Despite this difficulty, the Christian cannot immediately dismiss *jihad* and the possible convergence of human and divine agency.

With respect to this particular theological reading of Islam through the lenses of Spirit Christology, Islam stands between Christianity and Judaism. Like Judaism its pneumatological moment is pervaded by instruction, guidance and law. Like Christianity, it evokes the human witness of singular individuals in the modality of prophetic communion. Here as well is where the Christian interlocutor suggests that the nature of this human witness and its coextensive pneumatological agency may be regarded in a modality that is more than prophetic (Matt. 11:9).

The Qur'an testifies to Jesus (*Isa*) and his gospel (*Injil*)—as it does to Moses and the Torah (*Taurat*)—but in a manner which clearly Islamizes him. The issue of whether God raptured Jesus before (or from) the cross or raised Jesus after the cross penetrates to the heart of how prophetic communion is enfleshed in human praxis: either success through struggle or surrender through suffering. Subsequent praxis may in fact render the truth of each confession. Prophetic communion and incarnational communion lend themselves to a deeply spiritual dialogue each aspiring to the eschatological fulfillment wherein God is all in all (1 Cor. 15:28).

CONCLUSION

This essay has been largely suggestive of how interreligious dialogues with Judaism and Islam are best illumined from the perspective of a pneumatological christology. By emphasizing the convergent integration of the distinct agencies of Christ and the Spirit in the divine economy Christians are enabled to identify analogous workings of God's presence in their kindred Abrahamic faiths. I have not approached questions of absolute or relative religious claims. What I have attempted to demonstrate is that all interreligious dialogue is conducted "on the way" to the promised kingdom within the economy of the "two hands of God." While on the journey the Christian may enter into dialogue, even communion, with faithful Jews and Muslims in whom we see the encounter with the divine word and the transformative response of human praxis.

NOTES

[1]Hans Küng, *et al. Christianity and the World Religions: Paths to Dialogue with Islam, Hinduism, and Buddhism* (New York: Doubleday, 1986), pp. 174ff. David Tracy, *Dialogue with the Other: The Inter-Religious Dialogue* (Grand Rapids: Eerdmans, 1991).

[2]All biblical quotations are taken from the *New American Bible* with Revised New Testament (New York: Oxford, 1990).

[3]Yves Congar. *The Word and the Spirit*, (San Francisco: Harper & Row, 1986), p. 1.

[4]Kilian McDonnell, "A Trinitarian Theology of the Holy Spirit?" *Theological Studies*, 46 (1985), 223.

[5]Geoffrey Lampe. *God as Spirit*, (London: SCM, 1977); John Hick. "An Inspiration Christology for a Religiously Plural World," in *Encountering Jesus: A Debate on Christology*, Ed. Stephen Davis (Atlanta: John Knox, 1988), pp. 5-38.

[6]Piet J. A. M. Schoonenberg. "Spirit Christology and Logos Christology," *Bijdragen*, 38 (1977), 374.

[7]Ibid., pp. 371-74.

[8]This approach to interreligious dialogue I borrow from Aloysius Pieris, S.J. *Love Meets Wisdom: A Christian Experience of Buddhism*, (Maryknoll: Orbis, 1988).

[9]" . . . the Apostle Paul maintains that the Jews remain very dear to God, for the sake of the patriarchs, since God does not take back the gifts he bestowed or the choice he made." *Vatican Council II: The Conciliar and Post Conciliar Documents*, ed. Austin Flannery, O.P. (Grand Rapids: Wm. Eerdmans, 1988), p. 741.

[10]Norbert Lohfink, *The Covenant Never Revoked* (Mahwah: Paulist, 1991), pp. 52-57.

[11]Jacob Neusner, *Death and Birth of Judaism* (New York: Basic Books, 1987), pp. 42-72.

[12]David Hartman, *A Living Covenant* (New York: The Free Press, 1985), pp. 220-25.

[13]Michael Wyschogrod, *The Body of Faith* (San Francisco: Harper & Row, 1983), p. 255.

[14]As quoted in Hartmann, *The Living Covenant*, p. 33.

[15]Francis E. Peters, *Children of Abraham* (Princeton, NJ: Princeton University, 1982), p. 197.

[16]See his *Christianity and the World Religions*, p. 129.

[17]"The Sacred Council urges that a sincere effort be made to achieve mutual understanding [between Christians and Muslims]; for the benefit of all men, let them together preserve and promote peace, liberty, social justice and moral values." *Vatican Council II: The Conciliar and Post Conciliar Documents*, p. 740.

[18]Especially in the witness of the Islamic profession of faith: "There is no god but God and Muhammad is the Envoy of God."

[19]As in: "May God send down blessing upon him and give him the greeting of peace."

[20]This christological moment is similar to those readings and reconstructions of the historical Jesus as the eschatological prophet. Thus it is not unusual that Küng resurrects Adolf Schlatter and Adolf von Harnack to suggest that Islam's early contact with Christianity was with Jewish-Christianity and its servant christology. *Ibid.*, pp. 122-26.

Tanakh, Bible and Qur'an:

Assumptions and Methods

of Interpretation

Alice L. Laffey

Introduction

Over ten years ago the members of the religious studies department at Holy Cross received a grant from the National Endowment for the Humanities to construct a course for first-year students, which would introduce them to Judaism, Christianity and Islam in a comparative manner. The course we designed proceeds phenomenologically, with classes devoted to an understanding of *God* in each tradition, the major *prophet* in each tradition, the sacred *writings* of each tradition, the notion and expression of *tradition* in each, the notion of *community* in each, the function of *law/theology* in each tradition, and the presence and role of *mysticism* in each. The final section of the course is directed to the consequences which the Enlightenment/Modernization has had on each tradition.

In the years which have followed since the introduction of that course, I have tried to teach the *Old Testament* in a way which acknowledges the Christian perspective from which I view it and which, therefore, I inevitably bring to the texts. This perspective implicitly understands the Old Testament as the first part of the Christian Bible. I also try, however, to assure the students that this is *one* perspective only, that the Jews have their own trajectory from which they read and interpret the *Hebrew Bible*, a trajectory which began shortly after the exile and which continued through the formation of the Talmud and on to this day.

Rarely, however, in my "Introduction to the Old Testament" course do I make any explicit references or connections to Islam, although I am keenly interested in how to teach the Old Testament, and Christianity in general, in a way that leaves students truly open to, and respectful of, other religious traditions. It is for this reason that the College Theology Society's theme this year so interested me that I was prompted to volunteer a presentation which would discipline my thinking more deeply about the assumptions and methods of each of the three religious traditions which they have brought to their respective scriptures at diverse points in history.

What I have discovered is, I think, the basis for a comparative course. In addition to the course which compares, in a general way, the three religious traditions, I believe there is potential for a course which studies specifically the Scriptures of the three traditions—the Hebrew Bible, the Christian Bible and the Qur'an—comparing and contrasting their assumptions and methods of interpretation. Each of the three traditions began with similar assumptions about the inspired nature of the sacred text. The assumptions led to interpretations which were both literal and symbolic. Such assumptions and interpretations proceeded in each tradition almost unchallenged until the Enlightenment and its aftermath in the West. Since that time they have been challenged by those who demand that the Hebrew and the Christian Bibles be examined critically: that their contents be subjected to the constraints of reason and history. This challenge has led to the development of methods of interpretation which assume human involvement in the production of the texts, and reasonable explanations for the contents contained therein. Nor did the Islamic community escape the consequences of the Enlightenment, though its ramifications for interpreting the Qur'an were delayed. Finally, Judaism and Christianity have now called into question both the assumptions and the methods of the Enlightenment, and these have begun to give way to post-modern interpretation. The same holds true for Islam, although with *seemingly* very different religiopolitical motivations and consequences. What I wish to explore in this paper, and what I wish eventually to develop into a comparative course, are the changes which have taken place in the ways in which the foundational writings of the three traditions have been understood and explained. Because a course has at least twenty-seven 75-minute sessions, or comparable, this presentation is merely an overview. In order to avoid being *too* general, however, I will provide greater detail for at least one aspect of each religious tradition.

THE PRE-MODERN PERIOD: FROM ORIGIN TO ENLIGHTENMENT

Tanakh: Assumptions as to its Nature and Its Appropriate Interpretation

In the pre-modern period before the Enlightenment, most Jews assumed that the Tanakh was divinely authored and divinely inspired. The Torah (that is, the five books of Moses) was understood as *the* teaching, *par excellence*; all else was commentary on it. The text was considered to be so sacred that "when Rabbi Meir came to Rabbi Ishmael and gave his profession as a scribe of the Torah Rabbi Ismael required of him the utmost care, saying, 'If you leave out a single letter or write a single letter too much, you will be found as one who destroys the whole world'."[1] And according to Avot 5:21, "Ben Bag-Bag said: 'Learn it and learn it (that is, the Torah), for everything is in it'."[2]

However, the Rabbis in the formative period of Judaism held sacred not only the Scriptures, which they considered Written Torah, but also the Oral Torah. They believed that the Written Torah was "intentionally incomplete, and meant to be supplemented by the Oral Torah," which had been "simultaneously given to Moses." The function of the Oral Torah was to explain, elaborate, and interpret "the obscurities and ambiguities of the written text." The Rabbis held that "the text and its interpretation are not two separate entities," but "twin aspects of the same revelation."[3] They consequently believed that even the "principles of tradition were given at Sinai," and that whatever was "drawn from the text by application of the principles" was "not an addition but a latent aspect of the text which was revealed in its relevant time and place. Morevoer, what was deduced by common human reasoning was given the same authority and status as that which was derived from the divinely given hermeneutic principles."[4] Because the Torah is divine word, it is inexhaustible. In fact, it was even said that "In the days of King David innocent children could interpret the Torah in forty-nine ways positively and forty-nine ways negatively."[5]

Tanakh: Methods of Interpretation[6]

The core of the rabbinic interpretive system is the Thirteen Middot or principles of Rabbi Ishmael which were developed in the first and second centuries of the Comon Era. They include the following:[7]

1. *Kal ve-Chomer*, which translated literally means, "from the light in weight to the heavy."

This principle argues from something of minor importance to something greater. For example, in Exod. 6:12 God tells Moses to go to Pharaoh to tell him to relieve the Israelites. To this Moses replies, "The Israelites have not harkened to me; how then shall Pharaoh hear me...?" (Pharaoh in this instance is understood to hold greater power than the Israelites.) In Deut. 31:27 Moses says to the Israelites, "While I am still alive you have been rebellious; how much more after my death?" (In this case the time of Moses' absence after death is a greater threat to the Israelites' faithfulness to God than the time of his presence among them.)

Using the same principle, the Rabbis argued that the "eye for an eye" passage in Exod. 21:24 allows for *monetary compensation* on the basis of Exod. 21:29-30. In the latter passage, a beast known to be dangerous has killed someone; although the owner could be liable to capital punishment, the punishment may be redeemed through monetary compensation. The Rabbis concluded that if law allows monetary compensation instead of capital punishment in one case, "how much more so" is monetary compensation reasonable in the other case which does not involve capital punishment.

2. *Gezerah Shava* translated literally means, "a comparison with the equal."

This principle is concerned with linguistic similarities between texts, that is, analogous expressions in two different passages of Scripture. It concludes, on the sole basis of *the identity of the expression*, that the provisions of one law may also apply to the other. By way of example, this principle was used to determine whether or not it was permitted to sacrifice the Paschal lamb on the Sabbath. Normally all labor is forbidden on the Sabbath. However, Num. 28:10 expressly provides for the *daily* offering to be brought *on the Sabbath* and Num. 23:2 allows for the *daily* offering "in its appointed season." Since in the law concerning the Paschal lamb the same expression, "in its appointed season" occurs, Rabbi Hillel concluded—and Rabbi Ishmael concurred—that the Paschal sacrifice was permitted on the Sabbath (Peshitta 66a).

3. *Binyan Av*, "from the particular to the general."

This principle asserts that a general rule derived from one biblical text, or from two related texts, is applicable to all similar cases, though they are not specified in detail. That is, from a single, special provision in one passage, a general principle may be constructed which is applicable to other related passages. By way of example, Deut. 24:6 directs that "no man shall take the mill or the upper millstone as a pledge; for he takes a man's life to pledge." In that case, the law is particular, referring to the hand mill and the millstone. However, a general reason for the prohibition is given: pledging those specific utensils would deprive the pledger's family of the means of preparing food. The Rabbis generalized this law and concluded that "nothing which is used for preparing food should be taken as a pledge" (Mishnah Baba Metzia 9.13). This principle provides that any law in Scripture may be applicable to similar or analogous cases. Only where Scripture itself indicates that a particular law is specifically limited to the case mentioned may one *not* generalize therefrom. The principle is based on the assumption that the particular case is an illustrative example for its general application. (The *binyan av* principle may also be deduced from two biblical passages instead of from only one special provision.)

4. The *clal u-frat* principle provides that when a general rule is followed by a specific particular, the rule is limited to the specific particular.[8]

Accordingly, particulars are not to be taken as merely illustrative examples of the general, but the contents of the general rule are to be restricted solely to those particulars. When this principle is applied to Deut. 22:11, for example, the prohibition against *mixing* wool and linen is understood to be limited to the prohibition against mixing *wool and linen*. (Mishnah Kilayim, 9.1)

5. The *prat u-clal* principle provides that when a specification is followed by a general rule, all that is included in the general applies; according to this principle, the preceding particulars are taken as merely illustrative examples of the general.

An example of this principle can be found in Exod. 22:9, where the phrase "ox, donkey, and sheep" is understood to mean "any kind of animal."

6. The *clal u-frat u-clal* principle provides for a general rule's being followed by a specification, and then again by a general rule, and determines that the law is applicable to only such cases which are similar to the specification. According to this principle, the particular between the two general terms is to be extended only to that which is similar to the contents of the particular.

An example of rabbinic application of this principle can be found in the interpretation of Exod. 22:8 which both extends and limits the "ox, ass, and sheep, etc." to "*moveable* property of *intrinsic* value."

7. The *clal she hu tzarich l'frat u'ferat she hu tzarich l'clal* principle modifies rules 4 and 5. It provides that when a general rule requires an explicit specification for the sake of clarity, the general rule is not then limited to the specified particular; on the other hand, when a specification requires a generalization for the sake of clarity, the generalization does not have an all-embracing effect.

An example of this principle may be found in rabbinic interpretation of Lev. 17:3.

8. The *kol davar she hayah b'clal ve-yatzah min ha clal lelamed lo lelamed al atzmoah yatzah, elleh lelamed al ha-clal coolo yatzah* principle is a modification of rule 5 and provides that when a particular case that is included in a general law is singled out to instruct concerning something new, it is singled out not only to teach concerning its own case, but is to be applied to the whole of the general law.

An example of this principle may be found in rabbinic interpretation of Deut. 22:1-3.

9. This principle modifies rule 4 and provides that when a particular case that is included in the general law is singled out to add another provision similar to the general law, it is singled out in

order to lessen, and not increase, the severity of that provision.

An example of this principle may be found in rabbinic interpretation of Exod. 35:3.

10. This principle provides that when a particular case that is included in a general law is singled out to add another provision which is unlike the general provision, it is singled out in order, in some aspects, to lessen, and in others to add to the severity of the provision.

11. This principle provides that when a particular case that is included in a general law is singled out with a new stipulation, the provisions of the general law no longer apply to it, unless the Torah expressly states that such is to be the case.

12. This principle provides for the meaning of a passage's being deduced from its context or from a subsequent passage.

An example of this principle may be found in the rabbinic interpretation of Exod. 16:29.

13. This principle provides that when two biblical passages contradict each other, the meaning can be determined by a third biblical text which reconciles them.

According to rabbinic interpretation Lev. 23:14 (on seventh day bring offering, then eat) reconciles Exod. 13:6 (seventh day, unleavened bread) and Deut. 16:8 (sixth day, unleavened bread).

There are additional rabbinic rules or principles of interpretation which are similar to some of Rabbi Ishmael's principles but not exactly the same as his. These, however, give an idea of how the Rabbis went about interpreting the texts, and how it is, by the application of different principles to the same texts, that different Rabbis could legitimately differ in their interpretations of specific texts. Talmudic Studies embraces the results of the application by the Rabbis of these principles of interpretation to the biblical texts.

The Christian Bible: Assumptions as to its Nature and its Appropriate Interpretation

Traditionally, Christians shared with Jews the assumption that their sacred texts were divinely inspired; the Christian Bible "is" the Word of God. The authors of the texts, including Moses who was believed to have authored the Pentateuch, and Isaiah, Jeremiah, Matthew, Mark, etc.—who were believed to have authored those books which bear their names—were also believed to have been divinely inspired. The canonical Bible, as written text, was the primary bearer of revelation.

Like the Jews, Christians held to the closest of connections between their sacred texts and the divine. However, in contrast to traditional Jewish assumptions, Christians accorded later commentary and interpretation of the texts only a secondary status, privileging the written, which had been determined to be canonical and normative, over later commentary.

Because traditional Christians assumed that Jesus, the Christ, represented the fullness of revelation, those texts which record his life and message, and the lives and teachings of those who first came to believe in him, were privileged; the texts which had been produced before the coming of Jesus were included in Christian canonical literature, but were interpreted only insofar as they shed light on the divine plan of creation and advent of Jesus.

As an unspoken consequence of the assumption that the biblical texts were divinely inspired, traditional Christians assumed also the literal accuracy of the texts, though they sought to interpret them in ways which would provide the *sensus plenior*, or fuller sense of their meaning.

The Christian Bible: Methods of Interpretation

The authors of the New Testament developed methods for interpreting the Old Testament which were later used by patristic and medieval commentators to interpret the entire Christian Bible. Since these are more familiar to a predominantly Christian audience than the rabbinic methods of biblical interpretation, I will merely summarize them.

1. Prophecy and fulfillment

An outstanding example of this method of interpretation may be found in Matthew 1 and 2. In addition to the genealogy which establishes Jesus as Son of David, tracing his lineage back through the exile, the monarchy, Abraham and then to Adam, the chapters quote at least five passages from the prophets--from Isaiah, Micah, Hosea, Jeremiah, and the prophet Moses--and assert that particular events surrounding Jesus' birth took place in order to fulfill the word of the prophets. Though Luke 24:44-48 are more general, they accomplish the same purpose, with Jesus declaring to his disciples that everything written about him in the Law of Moses and in the prophets and in psalms was bound to be fulfilled.

2. Allegory

Allegory may be found in Galatians 4:21-27 where Paul parallels the two wives of Abraham, Hagar and Sarah, to the old and new covenants, respectively. The Genesis narrative is here provided with additional referents. In a similar fashion Origen's two-volume commentary on the book of Jeremiah applies that which is said of the prophet Jeremiah to Jesus. The Lord knew him before God formed him in the womb; and before he was born God consecrated him and appointed him a prophet to the nations (see Jer. 1:5).

3. Typology

Using this method, interpreters see the first human, Adam, as a type of the new human, Jesus (e.g., 1 Cor. 15); the lawgiver Moses is seen as a type of the new lawgiver, that is, the giver of the Beatitudes, Jesus (e.g., Matt. 5); and just as Moses lifted up the serpent in the desert, Jesus, the Son of Man would be lifted up (i.e., Jn 3:14). The children of Jacob came to be seen as a type of the children of God, Israel as the Church, the Church as the new Israel. The Solomonian and Herodian temples, as dwelling places for the Name of God, were types of the person of Jesus, in whom the fullness of God dwelt (i.e., Jn. 2) and of Christian believers, who themselves became temples of the Spirit (e.g., 1 Cor. 3:16).

4. Symbolism

Interpreting both things and events as *symbols* was common among the New Testament writers and later commentators of the Christian

Bible. A few examples will suffice. The vine of Israel, first introduced in Isaiah 5, is reintroduced as the vine of the community of the disciples of Jesus in John 15; the shepherd/king of 2 Samuel 7 who became the shepherd/king/God in Ezekiel 34 is reintroduced as the shepherd/God in John 10. The bride and groom of the Song of Songs, transformed perhaps into Jesus and his followers in John's gospel, is even more explicitly symbolically transformed in St. Bernard's commentary on the Canticle.

The Qur'an: Assumptions as to its Nature and its Appropriate Interpretation

The Qur'an, itself eternal and uncreated, is divinely authored and inspired. It is understood to be God's perfect and final guidance which Muhammed received directly from God. As a consequence of these assumptions, Muslims believe that any change in the literal text is an interpretation, including even the *translation* of the text into other languages.[9]

The Qur'an: Methods of Interpretation

From early on, Muslims have sought to determine how to apply the Qur'an to every aspect of life. The example of the prophet Muhammed, as reported in the Hadith, that is, the sayings or traditions of the prophet transmitted through a trustworthy chain of reporters, provided the primary sources for interpreting the law of the Qur'an. Because it is a fundamental Qur'anic principle that all life is governed by God's decrees, the interpretation of the Qur'an is closely connected to the development of Islamic law (*Sharia*). Although the law was organized and systematized by Islamic scholars, Muslims believed that it was not created by them, but that it emerged out of the community's striving to bring all aspects of life into harmony with God's design.[10]

Traditional Qur'anic exegesis may also be illustrated by comparing Sunni commentary on Suras 3:41, considered the acme of Qur'anic exaltation of Mary. "Then the angels said: O Mary, truly God has chosen you and purified you and chosen over the women of mankind." Al-Tarabi, a ninth century Sunni exegete, expands the phrase, "truly God chose you" to read, "truly He selected you and elected you for obedience to him." Al-Tarabi understands Mary's purification in a non-physical sense, insisting that "it is not Mary's body which is purified but her religion which is cleansed of the doubts of normal female religious behavior." Al-Zamakhshaari, an early twelfth century commentator, comments by expansion, "Truly God chose you" means "he chose you at the time when he received you from your mother and nourished you and selected you for an exalted mark of esteem." "He purified you" is expanded to mean, "He purified you from impure actions and from the disparagements which the Jews attributed to you." Al-Razi, a later twelfth-century exegete, connects Mary's divine selection to her mother's prenatal dedication of her to God's service. "God chose her" means that God accepted her consecrated status despite her being a female. Al-Razi understands the phrase "He purified you" in both a physical and spiritual sense: "God both cleansed her from unbelief and blameworthy behavior and he purified her physically from any contact with men and from menstruation." Rashid Rida, a late nineteenth and early twentieth-century Sunni commentator, interprets "God chose her" to mean "God's acceptance of her consecration to divine service in the Lord's house, the only woman to be granted such an honor." God purified her "from menstruation, so that she would bring no defilement to the temple."[11]

THE MODERN PERIOD

Tanakh: Assumptions and Methods of Interpretation

Religious Jews were reluctant to let go of their assumption about the divine authorship of the Tanakh. In fact, in most synagogues today, Reform as well as Orthodox, the reading of the texts is followed by their interpretation according to the teachings of the Rabbis, that is, according to traditional rabbinic methods. The Enlightenment, however, persuaded many Jews against divine authorship of the texts, and some, against their being divinely inspired.

The modern methods of biblical study which have been most acceptable to Jewish scholars include archaeological study in connection with the texts and various forms of literary criticism. Neither method is surprising. The archaeological sites have been accessible to those Jews who either live in Israel or have been highly motivated to travel there. Moreover, the attention which traditional rabbinic interpretation paid to the texts has been redirected, but the texts themselves continue to be the subject/object of Jewish study.

The Christian Bible: Assumptions and Methods of Interpretation

The Enlightenment not only challenged divine authorship of the texts, it called into question the very meaning of inspiration. Beginning in about 1800 the literal accuracy of the Bible could not be presumed. The theory of evolution challenged the creation account and scientific method has challenged the many accounts of direct divine intervention in a manner not explainable by reason alone, including miracles. Christians were forced to rethink the locus or loci of inspiration and to try to find rational explanations for the contents of their Bible. That which might previously have been judged mysterious and inscrutable was now considered to be rationally implausible and contradictory.

In response to the challenge presented to the Bible by the Enlightenment, believers developed methods of interpretation which now come under the umbrella heading of historical criticism. They include tradition criticism, source criticism, form, and redaction criticism. Their development was based on the assumption that all of the contents of the Bible can be rationally explained as to human origin--if only we get at the history which produced the texts and the meaning which the original authors intended to convey. I will not detail these methods of interpretation further, only point out that their integration into certain Christian communities was long delayed--Catholicism for one--and that the understandings of the texts which historical criticism produced were incorporated into Christian worship only limitedly and then, with mixed success.

The Qur'an: Assumptions and Methods of Interpretation

As much for political and economic as for religious reasons, the effects of the Enlightenment were delayed among Muslims. When they did eventually infiltrate, and the process continues though they were embraced wholeheartedly by some (because they were associated with prosperity), they were eventually understood to be associated with Western cultural and economic imperialism. Consequently these efforts of the Enlightenment have been deliberately but selectively rejected. Under Western/modern influence, many Islamic women in Iran ceased wearing the *chadur* or veil, but chose later to don it again, at the time when they were choosing to support the revolution which brought the Ayatolla Khomeini to power. The same habits of dress characterize many Muslim countries though often the practice is involuntary on the part of women. Many analysts believe that the women of Iran did not consider returning to the *chadur* a religious decision but a political one, and that they fully expected (to be able) to shed the *chadur* after the revolution if they so wished.[12] That is to say, the Enlightenment had, in fact, affected their religious consciousness. Nevertheless, to my knowledge, at no point did the effects of the Enlightenment so affect Muslims that they ever either challenged or rejected their assumption that Mohammed received the Qur'an from Allah.

That interpretation of the Qur'an itself has been affected by modern consciousness may be seen in the doctoral dissertation of Amina Wadud Muhsin, entitled *Women in the Qur'an: The Absence of Sex-Role Stereotyping in the Text*.[13] Wadud Muhsin tries to determine the Qur'anic intent with regard to the role of women. She distinguishes between what she calls the universal category of verses, which includes all the basic postulates of Islam, and a restricted category which, she says, consists of the verses with wording so precise that their only literal application must be to the particular circumstances in existence at the time of the revelation. (This approach differs from traditional interpretations which, she points out, were all written by men, and which, she believes, often contained sexist conclusions and opinions.)

THE POST-MODERN PERIOD

The Tanakh: Assumptions and Methods of Interpretation

In *The Slayers of Moses* Handelman details how modern Jewish literary theorists have rocked the foundations of traditional Jewish biblical interpretation, Among these theorists she names Sigmund Freud, Jacques Lacan, Jacques Derrida, and Harold Bloom. Time here does not allow for even a concise treatment of the contributions of each of these men--I doubt that I could make a concise treatment clear--and it probably allows for only a limited treatment in a course. Nevertheless, Handelman's book shows skillfully how these "slayers of Moses" work in ways which uncannily bring them back to their roots.

The Christian Bible: Assumptions and Methods of Interpretation

The assumptions of the Enlightenment have been challenged by Christians in the post-modern period. Such challenges, when brought to bear on the interpretation of the Christian Bible, have taken the form of deconstruction, reader-response criticism, and various liberation theologies. Emphasis has shifted from an effort to discover what the original author of a text intended it to say to the reader's making meaning in the process of interaction between reader and text. In addition, it is now recognized that the social location of the reader is a significant factor in the production of meaning. Furthermore, it has become evident that all texts carry within themselves elements which deconstruct what the texts *seem to have been constructed* to communicate.

The Qur'an: Assumptions and Methods of Interpretation

There are those who would argue that the Islamic resurgence is post and not pre-modern; that position is not totally without merit. However, as regards the Qur'an and its interpretation, I do not think that Islamic assumptions about it or Islamic methods of interpreting it can, as yet, be seen to have a post-modern perspective.

CONCLUSION

This investigation has been based on the premise that our curriculum needs to change. At the present time the College of the Holy Cross has only two courses in its religious studies department which are taught comparatively, the "Introduction to World Religions" and the "Introduction to Prophetic Religious Traditions" mentioned above. The latter, quite frankly, is not taught very often. In contrast, we have several sections of the "Introduction to Old Testament," even more sections of the "Introduction to the New Testament," several courses in various aspects of systematic theology, several courses in Christian ethics, and a few courses in non-Christian religions. What this exercise has led me to propose is the development of additional courses comparatively. Because my own area of expertise is the modern interpretation of the first part of the Christian Bible (only in the modern period with the assumption of total objectivity have we presumed to equate the Hebrew Bible and the Old Testament), I have tried to explore teaching the sacred scriptures of the three traditions comparatively. To assumptions and methods of interpretation, I would, of course, add selected readings from the actual texts, though in translation. What I would hope to gain from teaching in this way is a greater assurance that my subtext does not prejudice the Christian scriptures in such a way as to render students ignorant and intolerant of traditions different from their own. I do not believe that this approach will relativize the importance of the Christian scriptures. In fact, it will contextualize the Old Testament for Christian students in a way which has not been done since the advent of modern scholarship.

NOTES

[1]Quoted in Susan A. Handelman, *The Slayers of Moses: The Emergence of Rabbinic Interpretation in Modern Literary Theory* (Albany: SUNY, 1982), p. 27. See also *The Mishnah*, trans. by Herbert Danby (Oxford: Oxford University, 1933).

[2]Handelman, p. 27.

[3]Handelman, p. 31.

[4]Handelman, p. 41.

[5]Quoted in Handelman, p. 27.

[6]The interpretive principles given here are *halakic*. To complete the picture one needs also to pursue the development of *haggadic* interpretation. See, for example, Jacob Neusner, *Invitation to Midrash: A Teaching Book* (San Francisco: Harper & Row, 1989), and Hermann L. Strack, *Introduction to the Talmud and Midrash* (New York: Meridien Books, 1959).

[7]Rules 1 through 3 and the applications indicated in this paper may be found in Handelman, pp. 52-59.

[8]Rules 4 through 11 which deal with "the general and the particular," and rules 12 and 13 which deal with "determining meaning through context" have been taken from the Appendix to *The Slayers of Moses*, pp. 225-27.

[9]F. E. Peters, in his *The Children of Abraham: Judaism/Chrsitianity/Islam* (Princeton, NJ: Princeton University, 1982), p. 108, points out that Mohammed Pickthall calls his translation *The Meaning of the Glorious Koran*, "though the translation is actually quite literal." See also Peters' *Judaism, Christianity, and Islam: The Classical Texts and Their Interpretation* 3 vols. (Princeton, NJ: Princeton University, 1990) for a comprehensive comparative study of the three traditions.

[10]Theodore M. Ludwig, *The Sacred Paths: Understanding the Religions of the World* (New York: Macmillan, 1989).

[11]These examples have been taken from Jane Dammen McAuliffe, *Chosen of All Women: Mary and Fatima in Qur'anic Exegesis* (Abstract of doctoral dissertation defended at the Pontifical Institute of Arab and Islamic Studies, Rome, 1981).

[12]Heidi Izadi-Marshall, "Women in the Iranian Revolution," an unpublished paper produced in conjunction with a course at the College of the Holy Cross, Spring, 1992.

[13]Doctoral dissertation published at the University of Michigan, 1988.

SOCIAL AND RELIGIOUS PLURALISM

AND THE

CATHOLICITY OF THE CHURCH

Terence L. Nichols

INTRODUCTION

In this paper I shall argue that both social and religious pluralism, although widely celebrated as goods, are fraught with potentially serious problems. Social pluralism if carried too far, threatens to dissolve the commitment to public virtue and the common good which binds society together. Religious pluralism can be problematic in that it poses a theological problem for Christians and especially for Catholic Christians: namely, how can we hold that the fullness of revelation is given in Jesus the Christ and hence that Christian values ought to be normative, while at the same time maintaining an attitude of tolerance and thoroughgoing openness to non-Christian religions and viewpoints? These two problems are interrelated. I shall approach the problem of religious pluralism by sketching out a theology of non-Christian religions based on the notion of the catholicity of the Church. I will then suggest that this model has important implications for the problem of social pluralism as well.

THE PROBLEM OF PLURALISM

Social Pluralism

Social pluralism is today widely thought to be a desirable condition. In particular, it is prized on college and university campuses. We do not prize a student body or faculty which is too homogeneous; we want ethnic diversity, cultural diversity, gender diversity, religious diversity, and so on. In this we expect the universities to mirror the larger society.

America today is highly pluralistic, perhaps one of the more pluralistic societies in history. I recall reading a few years ago that some dozens of languages were spoken in the Los Angeles school district alone. Recently, however, a number of authors have called attention to a dark underside of social pluralism. We hear of a return to "tribalism" both in the schools and in society. We have become, in the words of the authors of *Habits of the Heart*, a "culture of separation," in which individuals and groups place their own private good ahead of the common good of the whole people. Our culture is fragmented both at the popular level and at the intellectual level of the university. Nearly lost are the old civic republican and biblical traditions, which fostered a commitment to the common good, a public sense of values, and a common notion of truth, all of which functioned to give society a unifying center and purpose. According to *Habits of the Heart*, the present culture of separation, if it becomes dominant, will either collapse from its own inner incoherence, or, more likely, be replaced by an authoritarian state which will supply the unity lacking in the culture itself.[1]

Richard John Neuhaus argues a similar thesis in *The Naked Public Square*. Pluralism, he thinks, is "often used to argue that no normative ethic, even of the vaguest and most tentative sort, can be 'imposed' in our public life."[2] The result is the "naked public square": a public forum stripped of all normative values, since values, like religions, are regarded as private affairs, and one ought not "impose" one's values on another. Questions of value are no longer questions of good and evil, right and wrong, truth or untruth; rather they become questions of factions and interest groups, and, at bottom, questions of power. Neuhaus argues that this is a profound change from the vision of the founding fathers, which was based on the republican and biblical traditions, both of which assumed that the cultivation of public virtue was essential for the wellbeing of society and the state. The republican tradition, indeed, looked to the biblical and religious tradition for the maintenance of public morality. Neuhaus quotes John Adams as saying "We have no government armed with power capable of contending with human passions unbridled by morality and religion. Our constitution was made only for a moral and religious people. It is wholly inadequate for the government of any other." [3] Loss of public virtue means that the public square is left a vacuum, open to takeover by nihilists, or by state totalitarian forces, or both. Neuhaus himself doubts that normative public ethics of any kind can be restored without being grounded in religious and biblical authority. But, he argues, this does not entail a theocracy (which he thinks the fundamentalists favor), rather it means a theonomous culture, one in which "religious and cultural aspirations towards the transcendent are given public expression."[4]

Finally, I would mention here the late Alan Bloom. In his *The Closing of the American Mind* Bloom argues, first, that the atmosphere in which today's students live is one of moral and epistemological relativism. Truth, for almost all of them, is seen as relative. So are good and evil, which are scarcely ever debated. Rather, such objective ethical categories have been reduced to "values" which represent the subjectivizing of belief about good and evil. The consequence is a loss of any notion of a common good. And, "in the absence of a common good ... the disintegration of society into particular wills is inevitable."[5] The consequence is an atomized, nihilistic society in which passion for the true, the good, and the beautiful has been replaced with the power struggles of factions and interest groups.

This, then, is the problem of social pluralism. It is, first of all, an inescapable fact. We cannot return to the simpler, more homogeneous society typical of the past. But the radical pluralism of today's society poses a challenge: what basis is there for unity and integration in a society so pluralized? I agree with those who argue that without a strongly articulated common good, the disintegration of society into destructive factions, broken families, and atomized individuals is inevitable. We will have reached the Hobbesian state of a war of all against all, where unity will have to be imposed from without by a totalitarian government. I also agree with those who aver that such a common good cannot be constructed apart from religious traditions and institutions.

In a 1986 study entitled "Religion in American Public Life," the Brookings Institution argued that the morality necessary to sustain democracy could not come from secular value systems alone, but must come from religion. "In a highly mobile and heterogenous society like the United States, the values based on religion are even more essential to democracy than they may be in more traditional societies, where respect for freedom, order and justice may be maintained for some time through social custom or inertia."[6] But if public virtue and the common good must be based on religious teachings, the obvious question is, "Which religion?" For in a pluralistic society, we are also faced with a pluralism of religious traditions. It is to this problem I now turn.

Religious Pluralism

Religious pluralism is both caused by and contributes to social pluralism. For the founding fathers it was easy to assume that the religious basis for public virtue would be a Christian basis. But that is no longer so easy. We are now a nation of Christians, Jews, Muslims, Buddhists, New Agers, agnostics, and atheists. Furthermore, we are confronted with the phenomenon of privatization in religion. For many, perhaps most, Americans religion has become a matter of private opinion, but not of a truth or value which carries a transcendent and universal claim. (Christian fundamentalists and Muslims are perhaps the major exceptions to this.) This is a natural response to religious pluralism. But to the extent that religion has become privatized, its claims have only private, not public force. It is not in a position then to challenge the secular and utilitarian values, or even the nihilistic values (such as the violence prevalent in the media), which have moved in and occupied the naked public square.

But any religion which wishes to assert that its teachings and values derive from a transcendent source and therefore have normative and universal claims must deal with the problem posed by religious pluralism. Otherwise it will have no persuasive rejoinder to the query "Whose values? Why just yours? Why not theirs?"

One possible answer to this question is that of the Christian fundamentalists, who typically wish to argue that their religion alone is right, and that the nation's values ought to be based directly on the Bible. They make little provision for the truths or goods which might be found in other religious traditions. In addition, insofar as they are biblical inerrantists this group is committed to a position which rejects many of the most widely agreed upon conclusions of modern physical and historical science, thus driving a wedge between revelation and faith on the one hand and reason on the other. I agree with Neuhaus that such a stance tends to solidify opposition, in that it leads people to think that the only alternatives are a thoroughgoing secularism or a biblical theocracy like that of the Puritan colonies. Neuhaus writes, "By separating public argument from private belief, by building a wall of strict separationism between faith and reason, fundamentalist religion ratifies and reinforces the conclusions of militant secularism."[7]

At the other extreme is the position that all religions lead to God and that none innately contains more truth or is better than another. The

Christian teaching that Jesus the Christ was the unique incarnation of God is a myth. All religions are but differing yet equally valid ways of conceiving and approaching the one God who lies beyond human comprehension. The difference between them stems from differing cultural and historical conditions, not from the object of their worship. As John Hick, a notable proponent of this position, puts it in a paraphrase from the *Bhagavad Gita*, "Whatever path men choose is mine."[8]

For differing reasons, I think that both of the above positions are unacceptable to almost all Catholic theologians, as they would be to Catholic bishops, pastors, and educators. The second position explicitly denies one of the central teachings, held by most who call themselves Christians, that is, the uniqueness of the incarnation of God's Word, and hence of God's revelation, in Jesus the Christ. The first position, because of the antithesis it sets between faith and reason, and its conviction that there is no salvation, and little truth, to be had in non-Christian religions, or other readings of Christianity than its own, finds itself at odds with Catholic teaching. The *Constitution on the Church, Lumen Gentium*, for example, explicitly affirms that even those who have no explicit knowledge of God can be saved if, with the help of God's grace, they strive to lead a good life.[9]

In resolving the challenge set by religious pluralism, therefore, it is necessary to strike a middle course between fundamentalism and what is called in Catholic theology indifferentism, that is, the notion that it does not make any difference which religion one chooses. In the following pages I will sketch out a theology of non-Christian religions based on the notion of the catholicity of the Church. I will then apply that theology to the problem of social pluralism.

THE CATHOLICITY OF THE CHURCH

Catholicity is one of the four marks of the Church enumerated in the creed, which says the Church is one, holy, catholic, and apostolic. The meaning of "catholic" in this creedal sense is not easy to define. The term is not used in a theological sense in the Bible. Ignatius of Antioch is the first to use it, in a letter possibly composed before some books of the New Testament (*To the Smyrnaeans*, 8.2). Liddell and Scott's Greek-English lexicon defines *katholikos* as "general, universal," and the adverb *katholou* as "on the whole, in general, generally." The precise meaning of catholicity, as it develops in the Catholic, Orthodox, and

Protestant traditions, varies with time and denominational affiliation. Generally it means universal, both in space and time, but it also carries the meaning of qualitative wholeness, in the sense that any Church which does not hand on the wholeness of the revelation stemming from scripture and the tradition of the fathers, is not catholic.

I will here follow Avery Dulles' analysis in *The Catholicity of the Church*[10] and distinguish four aspects of catholicity. First, catholicity means participation in the fullness of God and revelation, as mediated to the Church through Christ and the Spirit. Dulles calls this "catholicity from above." If Christ is the one unique Mediator between God and man, and if the plenitude of revelation and grace is given through his life, teaching, death and resurrection, then it follows that any Church which does not adhere to this plenitude cannot be called catholic (this plenitude is especially an Orthodox emphasis).

Second, catholicity means a rootedness in the human and natural world and their aspirations. Dulles calls this "catholicity from below."[11] Grace, according to Aquinas, does not destroy or suppress nature, it heals and perfects it.[12] Human nature has an inherent openness and orientation to God, and in the saints this aspect of human nature is included, transformed, and perfected. Grace and nature operate together. This also applies to the natural creation itself, which will eventually be transformed and glorified as a consequence of the general resurrection (Romans 8:17-21). Thus those traditions such as the Jansenist and early Protestant, which denied the goodness of human nature and asserted, as Baius did, that all the acts of the pagans are sins, were to that extent deficient in catholicity. Finally, it is in this aspect of catholicity that we find the sacramental aspect of the Church, for the grace and revelation given from above is mediated through natural objects and persons.

A third aspect of catholicity, called by Dulles "catholicity in breadth," is a radical openness to whatever is true and valuable in every tradition. This aspect is explicitly affirmed in the Vatican II *Declaration on the Relationship of the Church to Non-Christian Religions, Nostra Aetate*, which says "The Catholic Church rejects nothing that is true and holy in these [non-Christian] religions" (§ 2).

A fourth aspect is the unity and identity retained by the Church even as it grows in differentiation and diversity through history. Dulles calls this "catholicity in length." He argues, that there is a real though imperfect participation of the Church in the presence of Christ from Pentecost to the Parousia, and that it is from this indwelling that the Church derives its identity, unity, and continuity through time. Nonetheless, different periods of the Church's history have their own distinctive characters, so that they are able to "complement and complete what has been initiated earlier."[13] The idea that the Church develops in differentiation and diversity while retaining its unity and continuity is an idea that Dulles finds in the great nineteenth century theologians Johann Adam Möhler and John Henry Newman. In their understanding of the development of doctrine they appealed to the analogy of organic growth, whereby plants and animals develop in internal differentiation while retaining unity. They also appealed to the analogy of consciousness, in which a new idea grows in differentiation and articulation while remaining a unified idea.[14] The unity, then, of catholicity does not mean uniformity, nor does its continuity mean immutability; rather it means differentiated and diversified unity.

Dulles sums up his understanding of catholicity, and that of Vatican II, as "reconciled diversity."[15] We would not be untrue to his thought if we paraphrased this as "reconciled pluralism."

THE CATHOLICITY OF THE CHURCH AND NON-CHRISTIAN RELIGIONS

This notion of catholicity has important implications for an understanding of the relation of the Church to non-Christian religions. My argument in brief is this. Although the fullness of revelation, and hence of catholicity, is only found in the Church, the understanding and articulation of that revelation develops through history. The fullness of revelation given in Christ is, as it were, given only in principle or in germ; the complete appropriation of that revelation, and hence of the Church's catholicity, will not be possessed by the Church until the eschaton. Thus it is possible that a given aspect or facet of revelation may be, at any given time, only partially developed in the church. But I will also argue that authentic revelation can appear in non-Christian traditions. This raises the possibility that the Church may encounter a real activity of the Spirit, a real revelation, which is imperfectly developed and understood in its own tradition, in a more fully developed and articulated form in another religion. Or it may encounter a real revelation which is *similar* to the revelation it already possesses (I will argue that this is often the case in ethical areas). In either case, if the Church is to be truly catholic she cannot ignore such workings of the Spirit, but should acknowledge and appropriate them through discernment and dialogue. I will base my argument on the texts of Vatican II.

Vatican II affirms that the fullness of catholicity, given in the Church of Christ, "subsists in" the Roman Catholic Church (*LG* § 8). Other baptized Christians are related to this one Church of Christ and participate in its catholicity through the Holy Spirit, to the degree to which they live by the authentic Christian heritage.

But the Council argues that non-Christians also are related to the Church. *Lumen Gentium* makes the following statement:

> Those also can attain salvation who through no fault of their own do not know the Gospel of Christ of His Church, yet sincerely seek God and moved by grace strive by their deeds to do His will as it is known to them through the dictates of conscience. Nor does divine providence deny the helps necessary for salvation to those who, without blame on their part, have not arrived at an explicit knowledge of God and with his grace strive to live a good life. Whatever good or truth is found among them is looked upon by the church as a preparation for the Gospel. (§ 16)

Thus, according to Vatican II, God's will can be known through conscience, and God's grace may be found working within non-Christian traditions. *Nostra Aetate* in speaking of Hinduism and Buddhism, confirms this:

> The Catholic Church rejects nothing that is true or holy in these religions. It regards with sincere reverence those ways of conduct and of life, those precepts and teachings which, though differing in many aspects from the ones it holds and sets forth, nonetheless often reflect a ray of that Truth which enlightens all. (§ 2)

Most observers believe that Vatican II made no explicit statement that supernatural revelation was present in non-Christian religions. But the statement that these religions often "reflect a ray of that Truth which enlightens all" seems to imply that there is authentic revelation in other religions. This reading is supported by the statements above which affirm that God's grace is operative in non-Christian religions, and that God's will can be known by non-Christians. Again, it is supported by *Nostra Aetate*'s affirmation that the Muslims "Adore the one God . . ." (*NA* § 3), which implies that God has been revealed to them as well as to Jews and Christians. Furthermore, the *Decree on the Mission Activity of the Church, Ad Gentes*, states that "God, in ways known only to Godhead, can lead those inculpably ignorant of the Gospel to find that faith without which it is impossible to please God (Heb. 11:6) . . ." (*AG*, § 7). Now faith, in Catholic theology, is a response to revelation, which is why it is salvific. But if those who have not heard the Gospel can have saving faith, it must therefore mean that some authentic revelation is also given to them. Finally, *Ad gentes* speaks of the "seeds of the Word," (an expression taken from John Henry Newman and Justin Martyr) as being present in other religious traditions (*AG* § 11).

Based on all this, I think it is legitimate to argue that Vatican II strongly implies, even if it does not explicitly state, that authentic revelation is given within non-Christian religious traditions. This immediately leads to a further question, namely "Is this revelation a mere reiteration of the revelation already explicitly given within the Christian tradition?"

My answer to this question is "No." Though the fullness of revelation is given potentially in Christ, the Church's understanding and articulation of the meaning of that revelation grows through the course of history. The statement of the *Document on Divine Revelation*, *Dei Verbum*, is pertinent here: "This tradition which comes from the apostles develops in the Church with the help of the Holy Spirit. For there is a growth in the understanding of the realities and the words which have been handed down" (§ 8). Again, the *Constitution on the Church in the Modern World*, *Gaudium et Spes*, after observing that the Church has learned much from its exposures to other human cultures and from the progress of science, states that in this way "revealed truth can always be more deeply penetrated, better understood and set forth to greater advantage" (§ 44). I think it therefore possible, even likely, that some aspects or facets of the revelation which are present in germ in the Christ event, but which are imperfectly or incompletely understood within the Christian tradition, may be encountered in a form more fully articulated, or articulated differently, in a non-Christian tradition.

An example might be Gandhi's teaching on non-violence, *ahimsa*, a teaching derived in part from the Christian gospels, but mostly from Hindu and Jain traditions. This teaching was subsequently appropriated by Christian activists such as Martin Luther King Jr. In retrospect we can see that this certainly was part of Jesus' own life and teaching, and was present in one form in the tradition of Christian pacifism, but its full political dimension remained to be developed by Gandhi.

Another example might be the Enlightenment insistence on human rights and the importance of religious freedom and toleration. This tradition stems in part from St. Thomas Aquinas, but was certainly imperfectly developed within the Christian tradition. Yet after its articulation by Enlightenment thinkers it has been incorporated (in a modified form) into virtually all Christian denominations. A third example is the developing consensus among Christian theologians of all denominations that environmental spoliation is not just imprudent, it is sinful, a violation of God's will, and that environmental stewardship is a virtue willed by God. Something like this view has been present in both the Buddhist and the native American religious traditions for centuries. It is significant that the major Catholic spokesman for this vision is Thomas Berry, a man some of whose earlier work was in Buddhist studies. This emerging Christian understanding has also been prompted by the scientific realization that we are facing impending ecological disaster. The truth that creation is good and is a gift of God to humanity, to be cared for and treasured, is certainly present in the earliest strands of both the Jewish and Christian revelation: "The Earth is the Lord's, and the fullness thereof" reads Psalm 24. But awareness of this has been overshadowed by the teaching that the creation exists for the benefit of humanity. This teaching in turn was magnified and distorted by the scientific and technological emphasis on resource exploitation which has dominated the last two centuries. Through its encounter with other religions, and with modern science, the Church is now appropriating in a more explicit fashion an understanding of the value of the creation in its theology and ethics. And this appropriation represents a development of its catholicity.

I wish to argue then that Christians must assume the possibility of some authentic revelation occurring within non-Christian religions and even within secular movements, and that this revelation may not simply duplicate the understanding of revelation already available in the Church. At the same time this does not mean that Christians should shirk their responsibility of criticizing what is obviously contradictory to the Christian revelation within other traditions. The practice of human sacrifice among the Aztecs, or of Suttee among the Hindus, to take extreme examples, were rightly condemned by Christians.

This means that a crucial part of the developing catholicity of the Church will involve the discernment and appreciation of what is true, good, and even revelatory within other religions (and secular movements), in short, of the truth to be found within religious pluralism. The Church will undoubtedly be changed in this process of encounter, and this change may be part of its gradual understanding and appropriation of the fullness of the revelation as it moves through history. In this perspective, the catholicity of the Church, present in germ in the original Christ event, will grow in differentiation and diversity (while still retaining its unity), precisely *through* the encounter with non-Christian religions. But the other religions may also themselves be changed, and may even incorporate Christian values without becoming formally converted to Christianity. An example of this might be the change in the Hindu attitude toward caste, a change brought about by Gandhi, partly as a result of his exposure to Christianity.

The encounter with religious pluralism is an historically crucial challenge to the catholicity of the Church. For the Church to reject what is true and holy, and perhaps revealed, in other religions, would be for it to close itself to some of the work of the Spirit, and to lose or limit its catholicity. Conversely, to embrace all aspects of other faiths in an indiscriminate pluralism and relativism would be to surrender the heart of the Christian revelation, the uniqueness of the incarnation and the mediation in Christ, and so to lose its catholicity in another way. Our best course is to understand catholicity as a creative tension between unity and diversity (or pluralism), continuity and growth, fidelity to the revelation of the past and openness to truth and value in other traditions. This notion of catholicity is not that of a static unity, but of a dynamic unity whose articulation will not be complete until the eschaton, when and only when, according to *Lumen Gentium*, the Church will acquire its full perfection.

IMPLICATIONS FOR RELIGIOUS AND SOCIAL PLURALISM

Traditionally, Roman Catholic dialogue with non-Christian religions and with secular movements has been based on natural law reasoning. Unwilling to admit that revelation might extend to other traditions, the Church argued that the natural law, at least, was available to all as a foundation upon which to erect common teachings on ethics, social morality and policy, etc. An example of this approach can be found in John XXIII's encyclical *Pacem in Terris*. I am much in favor of this approach, and think that with atheists and agnostics it may represent the only possibility for dialogue. But with respect to non-Christian religions I am suggesting a different approach. I suggest that authentic revelation exists in their traditions as well as the Christian, and that therefore we may have much to learn from them precisely about religion, and that this learning represents an extension of the Church's catholicity. I would further suggest that many of the ethical teachings in the great religions which are similar to Christian ethics may also flow from revelation rather than simply from human reflection on the natural law. It is true that, especially in the case of the Eastern religions, these teachings are based on a very different metaphysic. But the similarity with Christian ethical teachings is striking. Hinduism in its philosophical traditions and Buddhism, like Christianity, Islam, and Judaism, all condemn selfish aggrandizement at the expense of the public good, economic injustice, greed, individualism, materialism, consumerism, untruthfulness, stealing, violence, sexual promiscuity, and so on. Each of the great world religions would address a similar critique to modern Western consumerist societies, even while proceeding from a different metaphysical base. If Christians can admit that such teachings may flow from authentic revelation, then we have already admitted a large area of unity with other religions. We have pluralism, but also unity.

This has implications for the problem of social pluralism mentioned earlier. What we are seeking in society is very much what we are seeking in the Church, diversity within unity, that is, reconciled diversity or reconciled pluralism. In this respect the Church, if it be truly catholic, can serve as a model for social pluralism also. It can show that it is possible to preserve legitimate pluralism while retaining unity in essential matters. This is one meaning as I understand it of the notion that the church is to be a sacrament of unity in the world.

But in addition to this, the Church, if it recognizes the ethical teachings of other religions as flowing from a transcendent, revealed ground, is in a position to proclaim a notion of the common good and public value which is not narrowly Christian but which is universally recognized by most or all of the great religions. Such a proclamation will carry more weight than one based on natural law, and would go a long ways towards filling the present void of values in the public square. We cannot, of course, base legislation directly on the religious revelation. Rather, legislation is likely to be based on community moral standards and the common good. But it is precisely those standards and that good which need to be asserted in the public square, and which can provide a unifying center for common social action.

It may seem to be quixotic to hope for this kind of agreement among major religions. I am well aware that there are gray areas, such as abortion, where there is little agreement. But I would maintain that there is agreement in many, even most areas. The selfish individualism and rejection of the demands of the common good decried by the authors of *Habits of the Heart* is one such area. All major religious traditions place the welfare of the larger community on a par with, or ahead of, the private gratification of individuals. Another area of agreement is environmental responsibility. Recently a coalition of scientists and world religious leaders of many faiths called the Joint Appeal by Science and Religion for the Environment, brought together in Washington D.C. by Carl Sagan and James Park Morton, subscribed to a strongly worded statement mandating responsible stewardship of the environment. The fact of such common agreement between scientists and religious leaders is promising. On that hopeful note, I close.

NOTES

[1]Robert N. Bellah, *et al.*, *Habits of the Heart* (San Francisco: Harper & Row, 1985), p. 281.

[2]Richard J. Neuhaus, *The Naked Public Square* (Grand Rapids, Mi: Eerdmans, 1984), p. 146.

[3]Neuhaus, p. 95. Bellah et al also cite Washington's farewell address in which "he called 'religion and morality ' the 'indispensable supports [of] public prosperity.'" Washington doubted whether "morality can be maintained without religion." See p. 222.

[4]Neuhaus, p. 188.

[5]Alan Bloom, *The Closing of the American Mind* (New York: Simon and Schuster, 1987), p. 118

[6]Cited in the Los Angeles Times, Jan 24, 1986, p. 6.

[7]Neuhaus, p. 37.

[8]John Hick, "Whatever Path Men Choose is Mine," in John Hick and Brian Hebblethwaite, editors, *Christianity and Other Religions* (Philadelphia: Fortress, 1980), p. 171ff.

[9]*Lumen Gentium*, § 16.

[10]Avery Dulles, *The Catholicity of the Church* (Oxford: Clarendon, 1985), chapter 2.

[11]Dulles, chapter 4.

[12]St. Thomas Aquinas, *Summa Theologiae*, I, 8, ad 2.

[13]Dulles, p. 92.

[14]Dulles, p. 100.

[15]Dulles, p. 24.

INTERRELIGIOUS TENSION:
A PSYCHOLOGICAL PERSPECTIVE

Frederick Keck

Why is there prejudice, persecution, war and attempted genocide in the history of relations between the great Western religions? One would expect otherwise. Judaism, Christianity and Islam all espouse the ideal of universal unity. In light of this, the elimination of interreligious tension should be a major concern for all genuine believers. But, the tension will not be resolved until it is understood at its deepest, psychological roots.

The taproot of the problem is this: tension arises when a religion repudiates a portion of human potential and then treats another religion as if the other embodied its own denied dark side. How does a religion come to externalize its own darkness onto another religion? How is this dynamic played out between the major traditions of the West? What does this psychological analysis imply for the resolution of interreligious tension? Answering these questions is the task of this paper.

PSYCHOLOGY OF INTERRELIGIOUS TENSION

Although best known for his thought on the individual psyche, C. G. Jung appreciates the intrinsic social quality of human existence. In fact, Jung himself extends his psychological analysis to the social order.[1] While he sometimes opposes individual autonomy to the "mass-mindedness" encouraged by society, Jung does not treat this opposition as absolute. He recognizes that most of the content of an individual's consciousness comes from society and that wholeness is achieved when the *collective* unconscious (which is the same in everyone) is integrated into consciousness. Christian Jungian writer John Sanford is quite emphatic about the importance of the social dimension of life: "Relating to others is part of the process of becoming whole. The whole personality extends beyond the boundaries of a person's individual psychological space and includes others."[2] Jungian psychology, therefore, can be appropriately employed to clarify what needs to change at the deepest level in order to achieve harmony between the religions. I will begin, then, by reviewing a few ideas from Jung's individual psychology.

Individual Psychology

A person's psyche, according to Jung, is divided into a bright region of consciousness and the dark region of the unconsciousness. The contents of consciousness—elements of identity, values, sensory perceptions, and functions such as thinking and feeling—are orchestrated into a coherent system by the ego. The ego system mediates consciousness and is the means by which an individual relates to others.

The ego's rational ability to differentiate is one of its basic powers. John Hitchcock describes it this way:

> Opposites arise when a unitary "content" [of the psyche] is given sufficient *energy*, so that it becomes, or can become, conscious. At the point of consciousness, the content splits in two, and the resulting contrast makes it visible.[3]

The rational capacity to discriminate opposites is, thus, a defining condition of ego consciousness, rather than simply a tool the ego has at its disposal.

It is essential to understand the "either/or" quality of ego functioning because it explains why consciousness is unavoidably one-sided. By one-sided, I mean that the ego constructs its system by selecting just one pole from each of the multitude of paired opposites presented to it. Basic categories such as "I versus not-I" and "good versus bad" guide the selection process. For the system to be rationally consistent, those qualities opposite to the ones the ego favors cannot be included. Qualities which are judged to be "not-I" or "bad" must be eliminated from consciousness, perhaps not as concepts, but certainly as viable options for that person's life. For instance, we have the concept of "cruel", but cruelty is regarded as bad. Most of us wish to think of ourselves as "kind" rather than cruel.

The distinctions perceived by the ego, however, do not change the psyche's essential wholeness. Unwanted capacities such as cruelty cannot simply be eradicated. They are, rather, pushed into a region of the unconscious called "the Shadow." Continual psychic energy must be exerted to maintain repression because Shadow elements possess energy which moves them toward conscious actualization.

In fact, developing a positive trait is like pulling one end of a rubber band whose other end is fixed in place. As the band stretches, energy is transferred which could ultimately enable the attached end to overcome its restraints. Similarly, the more a person deliberately perfects a talent or virtue, the more psychic energy is accumulated by its Shadow opposite. The more you strive to be kind to others, for example, the more energy is conveyed to your Shadow cruelty. At a weak moment, you may find yourself "snapping" at those you love as your dark side breaks free and rushes into conscious behavior.

Among the defense mechanisms used by the ego to repress material into the Shadow, the one which stands out in Jungian thought is projection. Here's how projection works. Say I repress anger toward my boss. If I turn things around so that I perceive *her* as angry at *me*, I am projecting. I may repress anger, in the first place, because I believe aggressiveness is wrong. If my boss is in a rage against me, then she is bad. I can oppose my Shadow aggression by righteously fighting her, rather than contending with this evil in myself. I may even feel justified in attacking my boss before she attacks me. Projection then serves as a cover under which my original anger may "leak out," perceived now not as aggression but as self-defense.[4]

Jung observes that successful projection requires a viable candidate. The person who receives it must have the right "hooks" or a projection will not stick.[5] So, for instance, my boss must actually be a fairly hot-tempered character to be a credible carrier of my projected anger.

Social Psychology

Jungian psychology is relevant to relations between the religions because individual consciousness has structural characteristics in common with monotheistic religious systems. Both are organized around a single focus: the ego in the case of the individual and God in the case of a religion. Also, both tend toward rational coherence and are therefore one-sided.[6]

Actually, the relationship between an ego system and a social system like religion is more than just one of similarity. The complex symbol system of any society is operative only to the extent that its symbols are consciously appropriated by the members. One's society provides a ready made system of identity and ego organization which is, at first, uncritically assimilated by the immature individual. In other words, a religious system forms a common layer in the conscious functioning of each of its constituents.[7]

Since the collective values and ideals of a religion are in the consciousness of its members, they cast a shadow in the unconscious of these individuals. Such a collective Shadow would consist of all traits, ideals and values opposite to those promoted by a particular religion. This is the line of thinking followed by Richard Rohr and Joseph Martos when they describe six elements of the Roman Catholic Shadow: uncatholic, ethnic, institutional, unscriptural, undemanding and consumeristic.[8] As Shadow qualities, these six tendencies are the exact opposites of what Catholicism explicitly promotes.

If a religion truly has a Shadow, it can also can engage in projection. John Sanford believes that, all too often, this is precisely what happens. He says:

> The more rigidly persons hold to certain dogmatic religious ideas, the more inclined they are to project their Shadows onto members of other religious groups whose varying opinions would have the disagreeable effect of inculcating doubt in them. . . . Since people under such circumstances are totally unconscious of their Shadows and of the mechanism of projection, terrible atrocities have been committed in the name of Christ without conscious guilt about it.[9]

There is nothing, short of its members' becoming more collectively self-aware, to keep a religion from seeking to purge its own hidden evil by struggling with another religion on which its Shadow is externalized. Here, then, is the deep root of interreligious tension.

PROJECTION AMONG WESTERN RELIGIONS

Do the religions of the West really have collective Shadows? Do they provide hooks suitable for carrying the Shadow projection of the others? An examination of Christianity's relationship with Judaism and with Islam will show that this is so.

Christianity Versus Judaism

The tension between Christians and Jews has manifested itself in a long history of anti-Semitic prejudice, pogroms and, in our own century, the near extermination of the Jewish people. How might we explain this impassioned opposition?

John Sanford suggests that Christianity actualizes "feminine"[10] qualities which were hidden in the Shadow of the "one-sidedly masculine" system of Judaism. Jesus is affected by the feminine, according to Sanford, most prominently in his ministry of healing, a ministry virtually nonexistent in the Old Testament. But, he sees the feminine influence on Jesus as more extensive. He says:

> [It] is shown not only in his qualities of intuition, concern for people, and relatedness, but in the close association Jesus had with many women (Mary and Martha, Mary Magdalene, the woman by the well of Samaria, etc.), which was an extraordinary thing for that highly patriarchal era.[11]

Further, belief in the infusion of divine spirit into physical matter, symbolized by the doctrine of the Incarnation, also indicates a shift toward the feminine in Christianity.

Theologian Rosemary Radford Ruether argues that the conflict between Jews and Christians stems, not from historical factors (i.e., past insults or injuries), but directly from doctrinal conflict over Christology. She writes:

> Anti-Judaism was the negative side of the Christian affirmation that Jesus was the Christ. Christianity claimed that the Jewish tradition of messianic hope was fulfilled in Jesus. But since the Jewish teachers rejected this claim, the Church developed a polemic against the Jews and Judaism to explain how the church could claim to be the fulfillment of a Jewish religious tradition when the Jewish religious teachers themselves denied it.[12]

According to Ruether, the core of the problem was that the Jews expected a sociopolitical Messiah, whereas the early Christians made Jesus' messianic role more inward and spiritual.

The revised Christian understanding of messiahship is more "feminine" than the Jewish. While the feminine element surfaces occasionally in the tradition of Judaism, especially in prophets like Hosea and Jeremiah, the Christian portrayal of a politically weak person like Jesus as the Messiah apparently went too far for the rabbis. The Christian sect provided the "hooks" on which Jewish leaders projected enough of their Shadow to justify expelling the Christians from the synagogues.

Afterwards, Christians retained their messianic understanding of Jesus. They believed he was the initiator of the new age in which Yahweh's promises, as announced by the prophets, are fulfilled. They regarded themselves as the sole heirs of all the good promised by God and dissociated themselves totally from Israel's history of failing to live up to YHWH's covenant. It took, in fact, nearly six hundred years for the church to institutionalize a routine way to deal with the continuing sins of its members because Christians really believed they had left sinfulness behind. So, in the new age, all that remained for the Jews who rejected Jesus to embody was the infidelity and sinfulness which YHWH's prophets had denounced.

After patristic theologians added their sharply disjunctive category of spirit-versus-flesh to the issue, Jews came to be seen as carnal, materialistic, unspiritual and, in general, evil. Ruether summarizes subsequent Jewish-Christian relations well when she says, "It was Christian theology that developed the thesis of the reprobate status of the Jew in history and laid the foundations for the demonic view of the Jew that fanned the flames of popular hatred."[13] The Jewish people, therefore, were made to bear the projected Shadow of Christianity.

Christianity Versus Islam

Of course, relations between Christianity and Islam have also been fraught with conflict. The Persian Gulf War is a recent example. As modern people, we may be inclined to believe that political and economic, rather than religious factors, are behind such conflict. But as noted Jungian analyst and author Robert Johnson observes:

> It seemed nothing less than a miracle that the Shadow projection between the United States and the Soviet Union had subsided, after years of the Cold War. Yet here is an example of what human creativity can do: we unconsciously picked up the energy released from this relationship and put the Shadow in another place!
>
> Only months later, we were engaged in another struggle, with terrifying technological power behind it. When the United States went to war in the Persian Gulf, once again we saw the rise of primitive psychology--with both sides projecting devils and demons onto their opponents.[14]

In their war-making rhetoric, President Bush and Saddam Hussein did paint each other as the embodiment of evil. This kind of rhetoric signals projection. Of what might the respective Shadows consist?

The United States, of course, is a modern secular state and stands for no particular religious doctrine. But, its culture is built on Christian values and prejudices, and a majority of its people are somehow Christian. Thus, the U.S. does provide hooks on which Muslims can project their collective Shadow.

In Islam, Allah is unconditionally singular, utterly transcendent and omnipotent.[15] In comparison, Christians seem to Jews and Muslims to flirt with polytheism in their doctrine of the Trinity and to diminish the majesty of God with their belief in the incarnation of God in Jesus Christ.[16] Faithfulness, understood as submission to Allah, is a major tenet of Islam. It is not difficult to see how Muslims could project the Shadow evil of infidelity onto Christians.

Furthermore, Islam requires that God's word be expressed in a system of law so that Muslims can concretize submission to Allah in every aspect of their lives, both personal and social.[17] For the Muslim, monotheistic universality means striving, by military means if necessary, to make sure every society conforms to the will of Allah.

Modern secular states do not share this theocratic outlook. Christianity can envision believers living out their faith in virtually any society. The modern separation of Church and state distances society from the influence of religion. Furthermore, nations like the U.S. not only tolerate but, within limits, encourage personal diversity and even dissent. To the Muslim, modern society appears faithless, chaotic and morally corrupt. Of course, these are some of the Shadow qualities of Islam. When Muslims passionately oppose modern nations, they are probably reacting to their own projected Shadow.

Modern nations, of course, also cast a Shadow. From its Christian and Enlightenment heritage, a modern society is likely to stress love, individuality and pluralism. Its Shadow would, therefore, include aggression, collectivism and intolerance of difference. Given the Muslim emphasis on power and social control, the Shadow of modernity can easily be projected onto Islam.

The emotional charge behind interreligious tensions such as anti-Judaism and the U.S.-Iraq confrontation indicates that conflict arises from sources other than reason. As in the case of the individual, the collective Shadow has energy to push its way up into consciousness. Just as the ego forcefully resists the Shadow, so the authorities of a social system resist the emergence of the collective Shadow. Not only is the coherence of the social system threatened by the content of the collective Shadow, but so are the personal security and social stability which it supports; hence the emotional charge.

Judaism, Christianity and Islam have all had to struggle with differences that arose from within their own religious communities, often in the form of sectarian subgroups. To name a few examples, Judaism had to deal with the Christians, the Karaites, the Kabbalists and the Hasids. Catholic Christianity had to deal with the Gnostics, the Protestants and Jansenists. Sunni Islam had to deal with the Sufis and the Shi'ites. All these movements may be understood as Shadow elements pushing their way into a religion's conscious collective life.

Often these eruptions from the collective Shadow occur during a period of history in which the religion has been undisturbed by outside forces for a long time. Opponents from the outside, on the other hand, offer the opportunity to rally the believers, who will put aside their differences and focus on their shared identity in order to fight the common enemy. Interestingly, Johnson speculates that modern societies need to engage in conflict with outsiders every twenty years. In each generation, it seems, there is a war which everyone claims they did not want.[18] Through war, not only is the Shadow opposed in its projected form, but energy is bled off so that the Shadow is too weak to emerge from within the society.

RESOLVING INTERRELIGIOUS TENSION

If the taproot of interreligious conflict is psychological in nature, the solution is also psychological. Interreligious tension and all its attendant ills will be undone when religious people withdraw their projections and own their own collective Shadow.

In the United States, for example, we Christians must face the fact that, despite our emphasis on love, support of the U.S. military as the greatest coercive power in the world manifests our aggressive tendencies. And, we must acknowledge that our individualism hides a high degree of conformity, as exemplified in our apparently unanimous support for the war against Iraq. We must also admit that, despite our more "feminine" tradition, we still maintain patriarchal structures in our civil and religious societies. Clearly, the remedy to conflict does not lie primarily in dialogue strategy or in theology, but in that transformation of consciousness which enables people to acknowledge the opposites within their religion and within themselves.

While this solution can be stated simply, we know how difficult it is in ecumenical and interreligious dialogue to reach agreement about similar beliefs. How much more difficult when beliefs seem to contradict. We also know that, even when the participants in dialogue come to agreement, they often find it impossible to convince their leaders and the believers back home. If interreligious tension is really to be overcome, conversion of consciousness must be experienced not only by their representatives but by a majority of a religion's adherents.

Further, resolution of the conflict between the religions requires that religious organizations be reformed to support and encourage psycho--spiritual growth among their members. For a whole religion to undergo such a transformation, however, a breakthrough in consciousness is required that seems almost unimaginable.

A New Consciousness

Yet Jung does imagine the kind of transformation of consciousness required when he describes the process of personality integration which he calls individuation. After a person has made his or her way in society, according to Jung, a new need arises, the need to form a relationship with one's unconscious. Among the first elements of the unconscious needing conscious attention are those of the Shadow. In order to cooperate in this new phase of development, however, the ego must take on a new attitude. Whereas, in the first phase of life, the ego was at the center, creating an identity and way of life out of the material presented by culture, the ego must now relinquish the totality of its control. In religious terms, the ego must be willing to "die" if the person is to "rise" to awareness of the deeper, non-rational contents of the psyche such as the Shadow.

Thomas Merton speaks of such a new level of consciousness as the key to interreligious harmony. Borrowing from Persian psychoanalyst Reza Arasteh, he calls on Christians to strive for "final integration" which, as he himself notes, is similar to Jung's thinking on individuation. Jung would approve of Merton's explanation of the self-transcendence that occurs in final integration--living "from an inner ground that is at once more universal than the empirical ego and yet entirely his own"[19]-- as an apt, if general, description of individuation.

However, Merton's thinking shares some of the limitations of classic mysticism. Mystical traditions often bear the scars of marginalization by their parent religions. The fruit of the mystical endeavor is often restricted so that it cannot disrupt the religious mainstream. Such is the price exacted for tolerance. Although Merton insists that in final integration what is best in all the limited forms of one's experience are retained and that creativity is released, he seems satisfied with the classical description of mystical experience in terms of "openness," "emptiness" and "poverty."[20] Limiting mysticism to private experience in the mode of imagelessness, however, is one example of how mysticism has been constrained. Contentless communion with God does not directly lead to the conscious recognition of the collective Shadow which must occur if the religions are to move toward harmony.

On the other hand, "the void" in traditional mysticism is, for Jung, populated by images often not found in religious culture, images which are spontaneously produced by the Shadow and the other archetypes of the collective unconsciousness. In addition, while Jung is aware that the emptiness described by the mystics often feels like death, he does not envision the actual annihilation of the ego. Rather, he thinks that the ego is relativized as it recognizes the Self or, in religious terms, God as the true center of the psyche. After this breakthrough, however, the ego is still needed to integrate unconscious imagery into consciousness. Because his vision is more detailed, Jung is in a position to guide work with imagery from the unconscious of which Merton is not even aware.

Nonetheless, their thought is similar enough that Merton's depiction of the consciousness characteristic of final integration is also true of individuation. In both formulations, the individual moves to a level of consciousness that transcends his culture and his limited ego identity. Describing a person living out of such consciousness, Merton says:

> He accepts not only his own community, his own society, his own friends, his own culture, but all mankind [sic]. He does not remain bound to one limited set of values in such a way that he opposes them aggressively or defensively to others. . . . He has a unified vision and experience of the one truth shining out in all its various manifestations, some clearer than others, some more definite and more certain then others. He does not set these partial views up in opposition to each other, but unifies them in a dialectic or an insight of complementarity.[21]

Thus, in Merton's mind, the key to the success of interreligious dialogue includes but transcends reason. The transcultural consciousness needed to get beyond interreligious difference is, precisely, the kind of consciousness associated with personality integration.

Transformed Religious Structures

The seeds of transcultural consciousness can be found in the mystical traditions within each of the religions. Merton suggests that assisting people to achieve final integration was, in fact, the original purpose for which monasticism was founded.[22] But Merton is distressed because it appears to him that the institutional side of the monastery and, indeed, of the whole Church takes a person only so far toward integration. Beyond a certain point, the organizational functions of discerning and channelling spiritual energy actually stifle the emergence of new consciousness.[23] This sort of thing occurs not only in Christianity but in the other religions as well. What is needed is not only a revival of mysticism, but a revival, specifically, of the image-rich, kataphatic kind of mysticism which was responsible for creating the religious tradition in the first place.[24]

Theologically, of course, God transcends everything human, even the collective unconscious. So, at some point in spiritual development, the absence of all images may be required for communion with God. But Jungian psychology suggests that, before this point is reached, there is still much imagery hidden in the unconscious with which believers must first deal in order to work out their relationship with God. And, perhaps, too sharp a contrast is traditionally made between apophatic and kataphatic spirituality. Ann and Barry Ulanov suggest that imagelessness is itself an image.[25]

One way a religion can encourage mysticism is by permitting, even welcoming, fresh interpretations of its symbols. Liberation theology, as a creative reinterpretation of Christian symbols, can be seen as a fruit of the kataphatic mysticism nurtured in the base communities of Latin America. But, just as air without oxygen will not support fire, the atmosphere created by authoritarian, chain-of-command style leadership is hostile to religious creativity. The role of religious leadership must be seen as the facilitation of individual development, not only when socialization is needed, but also when growth into a more personal, direct relationship with God is called for.

Support for mysticism could be institutionalized if the role of modelling spiritual growth were incorporated into a religion's definition of leadership. In addition, spiritual education, direction and support groups could be made available under official auspices, rather than leaving it to marginal movements to fulfill this need. Finally, decision-making structures could be created which, if not exactly democratic, would treat all members as important channels through which God's will for the religious community might be discovered.

Of course, the catch is that the role of religious leadership would have to be reformulated. Instead of preserving a pre-established order, leadership would mean continually creating order out of the vital, but somewhat chaotic experience of a religiously creative people. Leaders would, with the aid of the theologians, facilitate the settling of disputes and work to integrate innovation back into the religious system. Such a state of affairs would truly foster the growth of a kataphatic mysticism in individuals. The prerequisite for this kind of change, however, would be the willingness of leaders to accept the same relativization of their own importance as the individual ego undergoes individuation.

In regard to the withdrawal of projections and living with one's own Shadow, religious organizations can also offer support. Although much that is good is in the Shadow,[26] it is, psychologically, the source of human sinfulness. Since all Western religions call for the acknowledgement of one's own sinfulness, it can be said that, at least in regard to personal faultiness, the religions do encourage getting in touch with one's Shadow.

Jung appreciates this quality of religion because it provides an outside perspective from which modern society may be criticized. He recognizes religion's power to counterbalance the mass-minded conformity which makes destructive social systems such as Nazism and Communism possible.[27] But, Jung is not overly optimistic about religion because he sees it as imposing a mass-mindedness of its own.[28] Instead, he puts his hope in individuals who take up for themselves the task of entering into self-knowledge. Such individuals develop an independent standpoint from which the conventions of any social system may be criticized. As long as there is a critical mass of such individuals, Jung thinks, society will be safe from infection by Shadow elements such as occurred in Germany under Hitler.

It is at this point in his thinking, however, that Jung underestimates the social dimension of human life. Most people find it very difficult to stand alone against society. People generally feel a strong need to belong. Many balk at anything which tends to undermine their membership in important social groups. If there really are to be enough individuated people to prevent despotism in society and to counter interreligious conflict, some form of social belonging which provides support for the work of personality integration must be available. Merton and Jung are probably right when they say that religion has not provided a social context in which full human development is fostered. But, could religion not provide this in the future? Again, if individuals can let go of ego to admit the unconscious, perhaps religious authorities can let go of heavy handed social control and open up to the Transcendent speaking, in our age, through our collective Shadows.

Of course, the notion that a religious group functions in ways similar to an individual is absurd if the system is regarded abstractly, that is, if doctrine and ritual formulae are treated *as* the religion. Only when it is remembered that doctrine and ritual live just to the extent they are taken seriously by individuals can the psychological dimension credibly enter the picture. In the abstract, for example, if kindness is endorsed by a religious system, cruelty has no place in it. But, in the real world, for every good proposed by a religious system, there is its opposite in the Shadow of the concrete believer.

While maintaining traditional opposition to acts of sin, that is, to acting purely out of one's Shadow, the religions could also exhort their members to accept the Shadow as a given of the human condition. The same basic attitude could be extended to the collective life of the religious community. Just as individuals must accept the paradoxical existence of both Shadow and personal goodness in order to move toward wholeness, religious people as a group could be encouraged to acknowledge the collective Shadow even as they affirm the goodness of their religious institutions.

On the individual level, it is true, such comprehensive consciousness leads to inner conflict and to anxiety about sinful tendencies leaking out into overt behavior. It would be similar on the collective level. There would be ambiguity, intrareligious conflict and the demand for ongoing institutional reform. Although living with such tension is unpleasant, it is more fruitful to see the tension where it really is, rather than to project it outward. Furthermore, living with tension is the only way to prepare for a breakthrough to a deeper union with God in which the contrast of the opposites is transcended in a unified perception. As with the individual, in the end it is to be hoped that the collective Shadow elements of religion will be tempered by and eventually integrated with their already established opposites into a higher order synthesis.

Finally, a religious organization can also provide regular opportunities for its members to encounter, assist and dialogue with outsiders such as the poor and the members of other religions. As projections are withdrawn and the collective Shadow is faced, a deeper capacity to love others is released. Instead of causing enmity, consciously recognized Shadow elements deepen relationships with others by providing points of empathy and identification.[29] A religion should publicly stand for and evoke efforts to build human accord by institutionalizing such things as interreligious meetings, interfaith services and social justice programs through which newly liberated loving energy may flow.

Muslims, Christians and Jews all claim to have the full and final revelation of God. But, even if religion as a system is complete, the people are not. Christianity and Judaism express awareness of incompletion in the eschatological doctrine of the Kingdom. Thomas Merton puts it this way:

> The rebirth of man [sic] and of society at a transcultural level is a rebirth into the transformed and redeemed time, the time of the Kingdom, the time of the Spirit, the time of "the end" . . . this means entering into the full mystery of the eschatological Church.[30]

The fulfillment of religion is not a perfect system, but the passage of human beings through death into a new life whose ordering principle is the unpredictable mystery of God. In this sense, none of the religions are complete. Each must grow in mystical consciousness, learn to withdraw collective projections, integrate the collective Shadow and strive for genuine harmony with the other religions. A religion that refuses to change and develop not only adds to strife in the world, but also betrays the fullness to which it is called by God.

NOTES

[1]See, for example, Jung's *The Undiscovered Self* (New York: New American Library, 1958), p. 34.

[2]John Sanford, *Healing and Wholeness* (New York: Paulist, 1977), p. 119.

[3]John Hitchcock, *The Web of the Universe: Jung, the New Physics and Human Spirituality* (Mahwah, NJ: Paulist, 1991), p. 116.

[4]Jung notes that lack of awareness of evil deprives one of the power to deal with it; see Jung, p. 109.

[5]William Miller, *Your Golden Shadow: Discovering and Fulfilling Your Undeveloped Self* (San Francisco: Harper and Row, 1989), p. 56.

[6]Karl Jaspers, *The Origin and Goal of History* (New Haven: Yale University, 1953), pp. 1-77. See also William Thompson, *Christ and Consciousness: Exploring Christ's Contribution to Human Consciousness* (New York: Paulist, 1977), pp. 21f.

[7]Jung, p. 87.

[8]See *Why Be Catholic?* (Cincinnati: St. Anthony Messenger, 1989), pp. 37-67.

[9]John Sanford, *Evil: The Shadow Side of Reality* (New York: Crossroad, 1981), pp. 59-60. See also *The Undiscovered Self*, p. 114.

[10]I am convinced by feminist critics that the Jungian understanding of the "feminine" and the "masculine" as archetypal in the sense of being a given inscribed by God into the biology of males and females is mistaken. It is much more a matter of socialization than Jung was aware. See a good treatment of the issue in Demaris Wehr, "Religious and Social Dimensions of Jung's Concept of the Archetype: A Feminist Perspective," in *Jung and Christianity in Dialogue*, eds. Robert Moore and Daniel Meckel (New York: Paulist, 1990), pp. 112-39.

[11]Sanford, *Healing and Wholeness*, pp. 50-51.

[12]Rosemary Radford Ruether, *Disputed Questions: On Being a Christian* (Maryknoll, New York: Orbis, 1989), p. 57.

[13]Ibid.

[14]Robert Johnson, *Own Your Own Shadow* (San Francisco: HarperCollins, 1991), p. 28.

[15]Ninian Smart, *The Religious Experience of Mankind*, Third Edition (New York: Charles Scribner's Sons, 1984), p. 395.

[16]Ibid., p. 396

[17]Ibid., p. 429.

[18]Johnson, pp. 29-30.

[19]Ibid, p. 225.

[20]Ibid.

[21]Thomas Merton, *Contemplation in a World of Action* (Garden City, NY: Doubleday Image, 1973), p. 226.

[22]Ibid., p. 226.

[23]Ibid., pp. 227-29.

[24]On a practical level, letting go of conscious imagery is a necessary step in opening to the spontaneous symbolism of the unconscious. But then fresh imagery emerges which needs to be integrated into the conscious system of the ego and, eventually, into the social system of the religion.

[25]Ann and Barry Ulanov, *The Healing Imagination* (Mahwah, NJ: Paulist, 1991), p. 38.

[26]Jung, p. 119.

[27]Ibid., pp. 32-33.

[28]Ibid., pp. 30-31.

[29]See John Dourley, *The Illness That We Are: A Jungian Critique of Christianity* (Toronto: Inner City, 1984), p. 42. See, for example, Jung, p. 105.

[30]Merton, pp. 229-30.

Reconsidering the Relationship of

Sin and Death

Bernard P. Prusak

Christians have traditionally advanced as the theological reason for the universality of death the moral catastrophe of sin. The fact of sin has also provided theologians with certainty that the necessity of dying would never be abolished. Thus, Karl Rahner, having described death as simultaneously a natural and a personal event involving the whole human being, went on to affirm that the absolute nature of death is explained by sin:

> Since biology does not "really" know why all multicellular life, and especially man, dies, the only reason advanced to explain the indisputable universality of death is that advanced by faith--the moral catastrophe of mankind (Rom 5). And this theological basis itself provides the certainty that in all time to come the necessity of dying will continue to govern our lives, that we shall never be able to abolish death.[1]

Such theological certitude regarding the inevitability of death presupposes that death is the result of sin, a position which the Christian tradition has long accepted as a given. In the words of the Council of Carthage in 417, "If anyone says that Adam, the first human, was created mortal, so that, whether he sinned or not, he would have bodily died from natural causes, and not as the penalty of sin, let him be anathema." (Canon 1) The Council of Orange in 529 condemned anyone who held that "only the death of the body, the penalty of sin, was transmitted through one man to the whole human race, and not sin also, the death of the soul." (Canon 2) Session V of the Council of Trent in 1546 similarly insisted that "when God's command in Paradise had been transgressed Adam, the first human, incurred . . . death, which God had previously threatened to him, and with death came captivity under the power of him who thereafter had the imperium of death, that is the devil." (Canon 1)

Citing Romans 5:12, Trent also repeated the Council of Orange's condemnation of anyone who taught that "only death and punishments of the body were transmitted [from Adam] to all humanity, and not also sin, the death of the soul." (Canon 2)[2]

As Rahner also observes, if death is the consequence of the fall of the first man, this implies that, before sin, the first man was not under the necessity of dying. Yet, that does not mean that the first "man" in Paradise, had he not sinned, would have lived on endlessly in the bodily life of this world: "He would surely have had an end to his life; remaining in his bodily constitution of course, he would have brought this life of his from within to its perfect and full maturity. In other words, Adam would have brought his personal life to its perfect consummation even in his bodily form through a 'death' which would have been a pure, active self-affirmation."[3] Rahner explains that "this 'death' without dying, would have been a pure, apparent and active consummation of the whole man from within, without death in the proper sense, that is, without suffering from without any violent dissolution of the actual bodily constitution."[4]

Rahner accepts that death, *as we presently experience it*, is a consequence of the first sin. He grants that even before "Adam" there was death in the animal kingdom, and that even if there were no original or personal sin, humans would not have continued biological life in perpetuity in time:

> Even without sin man would have ended his biological, historical life in space and time, and would have entered into his definitive condition before God by means of a free act engaging his whole life. Death as we know it now, as part of man's constitution subject to concupiscence, in darkness, weakness and obscurity regarding its actual nature, is a consequence of sin.[5]

SIN AND DEATH IN THE HEBREW SCRIPTURES

Sin and death were interrelated in the Fall story of Genesis, where the expulsion of the man and woman from the garden does seem to suggest at least a lost opportunity for immortality.[6] Because he ate from the tree of the knowledge of good and evil, the *earthling* had to return to the dust from which he was formed. Sin appears to have brought the curse of death upon "Adam" and the "Mother of all living": the tree of life would no longer be accessible, because of the "cherubim" guarding the gates of Paradise. However, since Genesis does not explicitly say that the first humans were *created immortal*, or that they lost an *original* immortality through sin, some interpreters argue that the creation of the proto-humans included mortality, and "it is sin which makes it terrifying."[7]

Other passages of the Jewish scriptures did relate sin and death without reference to the notion that humans had lost immortality as a punishment for sin. Instead, sin was said to bring *premature* death to mortal human beings. Thus, in Deuteronomy, the choice was between life and prosperity or death and adversity. Those who observed the commandments of God could expect life and blessings. Those who turned away from God would receive death and curses.[8] Ezekiel warned that the person who sins shall die. However, because the Lord has no pleasure in the death of the wicked, they are encouraged to "turn from their ways and live."[9] Those who turn away from wickedness "shall save their life."[10] Proverbs reminded its readers that the wicked set an ambush for their own lives. Evil puts them on a path of darkness that leads to death, and to the shades in Sheol.[11] As the book of Job declared, "The godless . . . die in their youth, and their life ends in shame."[12] The Psalms acknowledged that after death there is no more hope, only the silence and oblivion of Sheol, the place of forgetfulness, where even God is not praised by those who have become *shadows* and dust.[13] However, the experience of centuries of foreign invasions and occupations, from the Assyrians in 721 B.C.E. to the Seleucids in 200 B.C.E., eventually made it necessary to explain why suffering and early death so often came to the innocent, while the sinful seemed to prosper in this life.

THE PSEUDEPIGRAPHAL LITERATURE

In the pseudepigraphal books written between 200 B.C.E. and 100 C.E. death was presented as a universal curse for sin. Unlike Genesis, the Ethiopic Apocalypse of Enoch, or I Enoch (written Second Century B.C.E.-- First Century C.E., and named for the righteous patriarch who died after *only* 365 years of life: Gen 5:21-24), explicitly said that humans were created immortal like the angels, "permanently to maintain pure and righteous lives. Death, which destroys everything, would have not touched them, had it not been through their knowledge by which they shall perish; death is (now) eating us by means of this power."[14] Humans lost their uprightness and immortality because of the many lessons about sorcery and astrology, about refining metals, about the secrets of cosmetics, ornamental jewelry, and sexual immorality, and about the art of making weapons and warfare, taught by the fallen *Watcher* angels who had descended to earth because of their lust for the daughters of men.[15] However, another stratum of I Enoch maintained that sin was not something "exported into the world," but was rather created by humans, who shall have to face the consequences of their actions in an afterlife: "And those who commit it shall come under a great curse . . . all your injustices which you have committed unjustly are written down every day until the day of your judgment."[16] The recurring theme of the entire work was that the righteous and the wicked will receive reward and punishment at the last judgment (an idea also found in Daniel 7:9-27 and 12:2 and in 2 Maccabees 7:9-23 and 14:46). One chapter even described the spirits of the dead waiting for the final judgment in separate places for the righteous and for sinners.[17]

In Jubilees (Second Century B.C.E.), Adam is the *first* to be buried in the earth having died prematurely at the age of nine hundred and thirty years (Gen 5:5). He died seventy years before the end of one world-year (1000 years), as predicted by the command in Genesis 2:17: "Of the tree of the knowledge of good and evil you shall not eat, for in the day that you eat of it you shall die."[18] According to Jubilees, the righteous Enoch was already led to the garden of Eden, where he is "writing condemnation and judgment of the world, and of all the evils of the children of men."[19] The Life of Adam and Eve (First Century C.E.) similarly maintains that Adam died when he was nine hundred and thirty years old.[20] For disobediently eating from the tree of knowledge, at Eve's urging, he no longer has access to "the oil of life from the tree of mercy."[21] Only in the last days will Adam again be allowed to take from the tree of mercy (or *of life*, according to the Apocalypse of Moses).[22]

As the notion of immortality gradually sank its roots into the soil of Judaism, the very *need* to die, rather than the manner or circumstances of death, was traced to sin. There was also a heightened sense of tragedy about death: it would never have been a necessity if the first human had not sinned. According to IV Ezra (late First Century C.E.), because Adam transgressed the one commandment laid upon him, God "appointed death for him and for his descendants."[23] In the Slavonic Apocalypse of Enoch, or II Enoch (Late First Century C.E.), death was said to have come to Adam "by his wife," since Eve, corrupted by Satan now said to be speaking through the serpent, led him into sin.[24] As a result, "after sin there is nothing . . . but death."[25]

The Syriac Apocalypse of Baruch or 2 Baruch (early Second Century C.E.) rhetorically asked what it profited Adam "that he lived nine hundred and thirty years and transgressed that which he was commanded." "The multitude of time that he lived did not profit him, but it brought death and cut off the years of those who were born from him."[26] "When Adam sinned . . . death was decreed against those who were to be born."[27] His descendants likewise sinned and trespassed after his death.[28] The presumption is that Adam's sin caused the loss of immortality both for himself and his descendants: "Adam sinned first and has brought death upon all who were not in his own time."[29] However, there is a trace of another, earlier line of thought, in which the effect of sin was a shortened lifetime rather than the very need to die: "For when he transgressed, *untimely* death came into being."[30]

THE DEUTEROCANONICAL BOOKS

In the deuterocanonical Wisdom of Jesus the Son of Sirach, death is presented as generally undesirable: "When one is dead he inherits maggots, and vermin and worms."[31] But it may not always be unwelcome. One who is dead "has left the light behind," but is also "at rest." Death is bitter to a prosperous person "at peace among possessions, who has nothing to worry about . . . and still is vigorous enough to enjoy food," but it is "better than a life of misery, and . . . chronic sickness." Since "it is better to die than to beg," death is welcomed by "one who is needy and failing in strength, worn down by age and anxious about everything . . . and [who] has lost all patience."[32]

In Sirach, the origin of death is again identified with sin, for which the blame is patriarchally assigned to *Eve*: "From a woman sin had its beginning, and because of her we all die."[33] Death and bloodshed and strife and sword . . . were created for the wicked.[34] Thus, reminded that they are "dust and ashes," all humans are called to set aside enmity and to be true to the commandments, remembering "the end of [their] life" and "corruption and death."[35]

Death is inescapable. "From the day they come forth from their mother's womb, until the day they return to [or *are buried in*] the mother [earth] of all the living," humans have "anxious thought of the day of their death."[36] According to the earlier, Hebrew text of Sirach 7:17, death is also final: "The expectation of mortals is worms." Thus, after death one lives *only* in the memory of others, through the persistence of one's good name, and through one's children.[37] The emerging concepts of personal immortality and eternal retribution would be reflected only in the later, Greek text for 7:17: "The punishment of the ungodly is fire and worms." As Daniel 12:2 had earlier (167-164 B.C.E.) proclaimed, "[m]any of those who sleep in the dust of the earth shall awake, some to everlasting life, and some to everlasting contempt."

The Wisdom of Solomon presupposed that humans were originally not subject to death: "God created us for incorruption, and made us in the image of his own eternity, but through the devil's envy death entered the world, and those who belong to his company experience it."[38] In its view, "God did not make death, and he does not delight in the death of the living. For he created all things so that they might exist; . . . For righteousness is immortal."[39] Therefore, even though all humans must die because of sin, the death of the righteous differs from the death of the wicked:

> The souls of the righteous are in the hand of God,
> and no torment will ever touch them.
> In the eyes of the foolish they seemed to have died,
> and their departure was thought to be a disaster,
> and their going from us to be their destruction;
> but they are at peace.
> For though in the sight of others they were punished,
> their hope is full of immortality.
> Having been disciplined a little, they will receive great good,
> because God tested them and found them worthy of himself;
> like gold in the furnace he tried them,
> and like a sacrificial burnt offering he accepted them.[40]

According to Wisdom, the death of the just man only seems to be a destruction or punishment. The Lord might even take up those pleasing to him while they are young, lest their innocence be corrupted by living among sinners, in the midst of wickedness: "Being perfected in a short time, they fulfilled long years, for their souls were pleasing to the Lord."[41] In Wisdom's Hellenized view, "a perishable body weighs down the soul."[42]

THE EPISTLES OF PAUL

Paul likewise assumed that death was the consequence of Adam's sin: in 1 Cor 15:21-22 he said "death came through a human being . . .

. all die in Adam"; and in Rom 5:12 & 17 he declared: "Just as sin came into the world through one man, and death came through sin, and so death spread to all because all have sinned . . . because of the one man's trespass, death exercised dominion through that one." Although the meaning of "death" in these passages included ethical or spiritual dimensions, physical death itself was likewise considered to be the result of sin. Paul seems to have shared the interpretation of Genesis 3 found in the pseudepigraphal and deuterocanonical writings: Adam lost immortality as the penalty of disobedience.

Jesus' obedience to the point of death (Phil 2:8), on account of which God exalted him, stood in contrast to Adam's disobedience punished by death: "Because of the one man's trespass, death exercised dominion . . . so one man's act of righteousness leads to justification and life for all."[43] Thus, like the book of Wisdom, Paul interpreted the death of the righteous as only a seeming death: "We will not all die, but we will all be changed . . . this mortal body must put on immortality," because death and the sting of death which is sin have been swallowed up in the victory of Jesus.[44] Paul believed that "though the body is dead because of sin, the Spirit is life because of righteousness. If the Spirit of him who raised Jesus from the dead dwells in you, he who raised Christ from the dead will give life to your mortal bodies also through his Spirit that dwells in you."[45] Christ Jesus "in the likeness of sinful flesh" has set us "free from the law of sin and of death" (Rom.8:2-3). A spiritual body, "the image of the man of heaven" will be raised after the physical body, "the image of the man of dust."[46]

The death of Jesus became an event in which Christians sought to share in order to gain eternal life: "For if [through baptism] we have been united with him in a death like his, we shall certainly be united with him in a resurrection like his."[47] As Paul exclaimed, "I have been crucified with Christ; and it is no longer I who live, but it is Christ who lives in me."[48]

CHRISTIAN WRITERS OF THE SECOND CENTURY

Some later Christians were not satisfied with being baptized into Christ's death. Ignatius of Antioch, in his epistle to the Christians at Rome, written about 110, requested that no one intervene to prevent his martyrdom, preferring instead that the wild beasts of the arena be coaxed so they might become a tomb for his body, leaving no part of it behind.

For only by being a sacrifice to God, imitating the passion of Jesus, would he truly become a disciple of Christ.[49] Ignatius believed that his sharing in the death of Jesus by martyrdom would bring a new birth, because, in spite of what appears, Jesus' death had abolished death.[50] In his view, the eucharist was itself the "medicine of immortality, and the antidote we take in order not to die but to live forever in Jesus Christ."[51]

Justin Martyr, writing about 155 to 165, presupposed that Jesus' death saved a humanity which "from the time of Adam had become subject to death and the deceit of the serpent."[52] His many references to the salvific value of Jesus' death reflected an established tradition.[53] However, Justin never explained how he understood Jesus' death to be salvific, nor fully integrated the cross into his emphasis on the *Logos*, the source of all life and wisdom in creation, become incarnate in Jesus who saves *as Teacher*.[54]

Tatian, writing ca. 170, said Adam lost immortality when he lost his initial fellowship with the *Logos*, because of his transgression.[55] He also held that the human soul is not in itself immortal but mortal. He granted that it is possible for it not to die: "If, indeed, it knows not the truth, it dies, and is dissolved with the body, but rises again at last at the end of the world with the body, receiving death by punishment in immortality. But, again, if it acquires the knowledge of God, it dies not, although for a time it be dissolved."[56] The "ultimate death" is punishment in immortality. Biological death is seen as a positive remedy for sin:

> And as we, to whom it now easily happens to die, afterwards receive the immortal with enjoyment, or the painful with immortality, so the demons, who abuse the present life to purposes of wrong-doing, dying continually even while they live, will have hereafter the same immortality, like that which they had during the time they lived, but in its nature like that of men, who voluntarily performed what the demons prescribed to them during their lifetime. *And do not fewer kinds of sins break out among men owing to the brevity of their lives*, while on the part of the demons transgression is more abundant owing to their boundless existence.[57]

Tatian seems to carry forward the theme already seen in the Wisdom of Solomon: death cuts short the influence of wickedness and the possibility of endless sinning.[58]

Theophilus of Antioch, writing about 180, held that God made Adam neither immortal, nor mortal by nature, but capable of both: "For God made man *free*, with power over himself."[59] If he had kept the commandment given in Paradise he would have received immortality as a reward and should have "become God." If he turned to death, by disobeying God, he would cause his own death. God would have been the cause of man's death only if he had created him definitively mortal; instead, Adam drew death upon himself by his disobedience. He was punished with expulsion from Paradise because he disobediently ate of the tree of knowledge, when God wished him, "yet an infant in age, [and] on this account as yet unable to receive knowledge worthily . . . to remain for some time longer simple and sincere."[60] However, Theophilus, like Tatian, did not consider death simply to be a punishment:

> God showed great kindness (*euergesian*) to man in this, that He did not suffer him to remain in sin for ever; but, as it were, by a kind of banishment, cast him out of Paradise, in order that, having by punishment expiated, within an appointed time, the sin, and having been disciplined, he should afterwards be restored . . . For just as a vessel, when on being fashioned it has some flaw, is remolded or remade, that it may become new and entire; so also it happens to man by death. For somehow or other he is broken up, that he may rise in the resurrection whole; I mean spotless, and righteous, and immortal.[61]

Even after sin, the God of mercy still gave humans the opportunity to obtain the gifts of resurrection and incorruption.[62]

Writing between 175 and 200, while Eleutheris and Victor were bishops of Rome, Irenaeus of Lyons echoed the Pauline theme that in Adam, who was disobedient, all came to suffer death, just as in Christ, who was obedient unto death, all hope for life.[63] In his *Proof of the Apostolic Preaching*, he said that Adam had been created immortal but became mortal, "melting into earth, whence his frame had been taken," by not keeping the command of God in the garden.[64] Irenaeus mitigated the gravity of the first sin, however, by emphasizing that it was committed while Adam was still a recently created "infant," with his discretion still undeveloped and childlike.[65] In keeping with that extenuating circumstance, he likewise presumed that perfection and the gift of immortality are qualities which humans are capable of acquiring only after a period of growth and development.[66] Thus, for Irenaeus, as for Tatian and Theophilus, death is not simply a punishment for sin. It is also a sign of God's mercy:

> He drove him out of Paradise, and removed him far from the tree of life, not because He envied him the tree of life, as some venture to

assert, but because he pitied him, [and did not desire] that he should continue a sinner for ever, nor that the sin which surrounded him should be immortal, and evil interminable and irremediable. But he set a bound to his [state of] sin, by interposing death, and thus causing sin to cease, putting an end to it by the dissolution of the flesh, which should take place in the earth, so that man, ceasing at length to live to sin, and dying to it, might begin to live to God.[67]

For Irenaeus, "the glory of God is a living [hu]man."[68] Citing 1 Cor 15: 54-55, he declared that Christ had vanquished sin which had rendered man subject to death and thereby deprived death of its dominion over men. Death is destroyed when the Lord vivifies humanity.[69]

INTO THE THIRD CENTURY

Tertullian, writing between 197 and 220, described death as "the complete separation of body and soul" which is never "so easy as not to be in some sense violent." In his view, death is not a natural result of human nature, because Adam had *not* been created with death as his destiny. Rather, death was the result of Adam's voluntary choice: "Had he not sinned, he would not have died."[70] "Entrapped by Satan into breaking God's commandment, Adam was given over to death, whereby he made the entire human race, contaminated from his seed, the carrier of his own condemnation."[71]

Cyprian of Carthage, in his treatise *On Mortality*, written during a plague in 252/3, portrayed human life as a struggle with evil.[72] Death was presented not as an ending but as a passage to immortality and unending joy, to which Christians should come without resistance. For why should they love a long life in the world which hated them?[73] In that light, Cyprian interpreted Genesis 5:24 to mean that God prematurely took Enoch (who had "walked with God" for three hundred sixty-five years) in order to rescue him from wickedness in the world; as the Wisdom of Solomon 4:10-14 teaches, those who please God are set free early lest they be polluted by the world.[74] He further concluded that the death of a Christian from the plague was a blessing for which one could congratulate oneself. It was like escaping before the collapse of an old house or like seeking the safety of a harbor before a storm in order to avoid shipwreck, since an *earlier* death spared one from suffering the disasters that would accompany the imminent collapse of the world.[75]

Clement of Alexandria, writing between 190 and 202, pictured death as a tyrant whom Jesus enslaved through his death and resurrection, thereby vanquishing the serpent who had first led man into disobedience, and turning sunset into sunrise, death into life.[76] God was not the cause of death; rather, Adam caused it by choosing what was forbidden.[77] In discussing martyrdom, Clement urged the enlightened or *gnostic* Christian to die easily, giving up the body like a warrior bravely dying in battle, without dread, and without being enfeebled or yearning to live.[78] In his view, all Christian *gnostics* are called, just as Adam was, to grow into or to develop an *adult* or mature practice of "passionless" obedience and virtue, which brings assimilation to the divine and immortality.[79]

Origen, Clement's successor in the school at Alexandria, did reflect biblical perspectives on death, especially in his later, more mellowed years,[80] However, in his *De Principiis*, written soon after 217, Origen's interpretation of death was colored by his position that God created bodies only after a pre-natal fall. He argued that God created a diversity of bodies to express tangibly the varying degrees of sinfulness among spirits who had fallen from an original perfection of oneness and sameness, through their misuse of freedom.[81] In that context, Origen interpreted death to be the change we must suffer, through which the diversity caused by sin is destroyed and the flesh of *fallen* bodies is transformed into a "spiritual," *risen* body.[82]

THE FOURTH CENTURY

Methodius of Olympus, who was martyred in 311, reacted against Origen's notion of a pre-natal fall, and argued that humans had bodies prior to sin. He also criticized Origen for supposedly teaching that only the "form" of the body will resurrect.[83] Contending that the body will co-exist with the soul in eternity, Methodius said that God clothed Adam and Eve with mortality, symbolized by the coats of skins (Gen 3:21), in order to destroy the sin which had arisen in their previously immortal bodies. God's love prescribed death for humans who had been created immortal, lest the flaw of sin be immortal and the blame eternal. Death is thus the process through which God lovingly recasts or remodels a human blemished by sin, melting away the sin, like a craftsman using fire to recast a damaged golden statue, or a potter who reduces a broken vessel to clay before remaking it.[84]

We have seen that the Wisdom of Solomon and Cyprian's *On Mortality* viewed an early death as God's way of protecting the righteous from the wickedness of the world. Methodius focused on death as God's way of putting an end to a human's sin, "lest man become a sinner for all eternity, and . . . be under eternal condemnation. And this is the reason why man, though he was not made mortal and corruptible, dies and his soul is separated from his body, in order that his transgression might be destroyed by death, being unable to live after he was dead."[85] As J. N. D. Kelly noted, for Methodius, "death, which was the punishment prescribed for Adam's disobedience, is also God's remedy for sin, since by destroying the body it makes possible the restoration of incorruption."[86] Walter J. Burghardt has suggested that Methodius may have discovered the thesis that death was God's remedy for sin, and a sign of God's love, in the works of Theophilus and Irenaeus.[87] Methodius, in turn, seems to have become a source for those who followed him.

During the fourth century, all three of the Cappadocians taught that death was God's remedy, lest humans sin forever; two also employed the kind of imagery used by Methodius. According to Basil of Caesarea, God did not create death; it came because of sin. However, like a potter remolding a flawed clay vessel before putting it into the kiln to harden, God did not prevent our dissolution lest our moral weakness should be preserved for ever.[88] Gregory of Nazianzus developed the same theme in his Epiphany (or *Theophany*) homily of 381 and in his Easter homily at Arianzus, where he lived in retirement after 383. Human death is not simply a punishment but rather an expression of God's mercy. For death cuts off sin, lest evil become immortal.[89]

In his *Catechetical Oration*, Gregory of Nyssa admitted that one who considered only the dissolution of the body might be greatly disturbed, and find it a hardship that this life should be dissolved by death. He also acknowledged that it is the extreme of evil that our being should be extinguished by the condition of mortality. However, Gregory then proceeded to emphasize that death is really the result of divine benevolence. Since sin, or the impulse to sin, have become mixed into the bodily constitution of a human, the body must be broken up and remolded, as a ruined clay jug might be pulverized and remade after being mischievously filled with molten lead. Death, which God put on the body like an external coat of skins (Gen 3:21), dissolves the material body (but not the soul) so that God may recast it through the resurrection, without any trace of evil. On the day of judgment, any evil that may have infected the soul will also be cut away, as a wart might be.[90] The same ideas, that death purifies humans from wickedness by melting sin away and that resurrection restores them to their pristine state of goodness, are also found in Gregory's *Funeral Oration on Pulcheria*, which consoled Emperor Theodosius and Empress Flacilla on the loss of their six year old daughter and only child.[91]

John Chrysostom's *Homily on Genesis* similarly treated death as a sign of God's love and mercy, not just as a punishment. Adam was exiled from Paradise lest his sinning become endless.[92] As Burghardt has observed, for many Greek Fathers "death is part not simply of the Fall but of redemption as well."[93] Modifying an earlier tradition which saw death as a punishment for sin, they came to see death as revealing not only wrath but love. Significantly, the interpretation of death as a remedy, rather than a punishment for sin, initially emerged among writers who maintained that Adam sinned while he was still in a state of infancy and in need of further growth and development.[94] In Irenaeus, the attenuation of death as a punishment was also joined to an image of God as one who mercifully desired to exonerate Adam, owing to extenuating circumstances, and then lovingly to save all humans in Jesus Christ.[95] What remained unquestioned and never modified was the position that death would not exist had there been no sin.

Although all three Cappadocians viewed death as a remedy for sin, only Gregory of Nazianzus presupposed that Adam had sinned while in a state of immaturity or simplicity, explaining that the Tree of Knowledge was really the "Tree of Contemplation," meant to be accessible only to those who had achieved a certain degree of maturity.[96] By contrast, Basil and Gregory of Nyssa gave a hint of the tradition of an exalted Adam, who was an image of archetypal beauty, and free of all sickness.[97] Probably influenced by the Cappadocians, Ambrose of Milan described death as putting an end to sin[98] and also portrayed Adam as a heavenly and blessed creature, free from all cares, even from the need for food, before the Fall.[99] Athanasius of Alexandria said that the first man was mortal by nature but enjoyed immortality as a "gift," along with freedom from trouble, pain, and care, which were all lost through sin. Only after the first humans disobeyed God's command did death gain a legal hold on humans.[100]

AUGUSTINE'S PERSPECTIVES

Augustine would describe Adam as an exalted and gifted person who was *able not to sin*, and who therefore should have fully appreciated the tragic consequences of his misuse of freedom through sinful pride.[101] He maintained that Adam had been created immortal in the sense that he was *able not to die* (rather than *not able to die*).[102] Although he had been able not to die, if he had not sinned, the sinful Adam was separated from the Tree of Life so that he would be able to die.[103] Because Adam's sin also vitiated the "seminal nature" of all his descendants (contained within his loins), all humans were henceforth shackled with the chain of death and justly damned.[104] Citing the book of Wisdom, Augustine did allow that a premature death might be a blessing for virtuous adults, since it enabled them to escape the wicked and to come to peace and rest: "This dissolution of the body is rest, not punishment, for the just and worshipers of God . . . when they are dissolved they are freed rather than destroyed. For that reason those who are faithful neither fear nor tremble at their dissolution . . ."[105] However, for unbaptized infants who had no personal sin, death was no blessing, but only a penalty inseparable from damnation. Because they were Adam's offspring and therefore bound up with "death and damnation," helpless infants who died without baptism were condemned to hell, although their suffering there would be less intense.[106]

Augustine's teaching that unbaptized infants who died were condemned to hell stood in stark contrast to the position of the Eastern writers who had spoken of death as a remedy for sin. John Chrysostom, his contemporary, said that the souls of children who died were "in the hand of God" (Wis 3:1), because they were not evil.[107] Gregory of Nazianzus had said that infants who died, "unsealed" by baptism but not wicked, would be neither glorified nor punished.[108] Gregory of Nyssa seemed open to the opinion that infants who die enter a state of blessedness. Granting that God might be curtailing sin by an early death, he pointed out that there could be no retribution for infants since they had not done good or evil. In his view, the premature death of an infant was not a misfortune, but neither was it on the same level as the death of persons who had purified themselves by a lifetime of virtue. He believed the happiness of the latter would be enhanced by the consciousness that God had used them to effect good.[109]

MEDIEVAL DEVELOPMENTS

Augustine's teaching that an unbaptized infant's death was *ipso facto* a damnation seems effectively to have smothered any future efforts to reinterpret death as a sign of God's mercy and love. Despite the fact that his opinion about unbaptized infants being condemned to hell did not find a *reception* in later Western theology (which instead opined that they went to a boundary place, or *limbus*, of natural happiness without the beatific vision[110]), death would be henceforth viewed primarily as a penalty, and not as a remedy. And no one questioned whether an infant's death had anything to do with sin in the first place.

Anselm of Canterbury's *Cur Deus Homo*, written between 1094 and 1098, simply presumed that Adam would never have died had he not sinned, and further presupposed that mortality did not belong to the *pure nature* of humanity.[111] Thus, Jesus was not subject to death because he had not sinned.[112] In choosing to suffer death by his free "obedience,"[113] he did what was not necessary, and thereby made infinite satisfaction for the sin of humanity.[114] Since he was not in debt to God, Jesus' death could satisfy for human sin, a thing that was impossible for sinful humans, because everything they had came from God and their death would simply be a just punishment.[115] Anselm never asked whether Jesus would have lived forever had he not been crucified, or whether he would have experienced the effects of aging, or whether his death was always biologically inevitable even if it had not been prematurely imposed. Neither did Thomas Aquinas, about two centuries later, raise any of these questions; he considered death and all the attendant defects of the body to be the punishments of original sin, and to be in accord with the punitive justice of God.[116]

CONCLUDING REFLECTIONS

In our time, it might be said that Rahner's positive interpretation of death as the culmination of freedom to create one's self-definition[117] has resumed the initiatives found in Theophilus and Irenaeus, but always amalgamated with the legacy coming from Augustine. For Rahner, death was not just a passive fate, the end of biological life which irrupts from the outside, but also an interior, active consummation, an ultimate fulfillment of all the free decisions which have formed the self during life.[118] He interpreted Jesus' death in that same light: it was not merely a passive event accepted in obedience but a human action which broke through emptiness, futility, and loneliness into an open, unrestricted relationship with the entire cosmos, the innermost part of the world.[119] Nonetheless, in Rahner's view, death "can only be experienced as the advent of emptiness, as the impasse of sin, as the darkness of eternal night (especially since the supernatural order is the real order in which there should be no death)." Death "in itself could be suffered, even by Christ himself, only as such a state of abandonment by God," although Jesus' obedient "yes" in the midst of his empty loneliness on the cross transformed death into "the advent of God."[120]

From his dialogue with the past theological tradition, Rahner concluded that death was part of "pure" human nature and that immortality was a preternatural gift. He further observed that the human with "conscious supernatural existentials" experiences death, not simply as an unavoidable consequence of finitude, but as unnatural, something alien to her or his being which ought not to be.[121] Rahner acknowledged his *reception* of that position from Augustine and those who followed:

> And if an Augustine and later the great scholastics too were thoroughly convinced that the present constitution of man with his concupiscentia and subjection to death could not be intelligibly interpreted except on the presupposition of a primordial Fall, i.e. if they felt that concupiscentia and death were very 'unnatural' and needed explanation (and this is the presupposition of the first affirmation); then it is possible that they were in the right, even if not every simple soul can verify this at every moment . . . The *fact* that they felt it to be unnatural is sufficient here.[122]

Although he *received* the position that death is unnatural and explicable only on the presupposition of a primordial Fall, Rahner subtly reinterpreted *how* death might be called "the penalty for original sin" and a "punishment." In his understanding, it was *not* that God made "a fresh, retributive intervention . . . imposing a penalty not intrinsically related to the sin itself." Rather human death is "primarily an expression and manifestation of the essence of sin in the bodily constitution of [a human], and as such, as a consequence, a punishment for sin." Humans have themselves made it that. The earthly reality of humans, "no longer or not yet completely permeated and transformed by grace," thus culminates not in "a purely transfiguring fulfilment," but in the darkness of death, which " 'really' ought not to be." For Rahner, "death (as a consequence of the actual human condition) is guilt made visible."[123] It is "the culmination of concupiscence . . . not only the expression and visible mark of [humanity's] alienation from God . . . [but] also, as a more careful examination of the doctrine of the New Testament on death (Rom 1:32; 7:9-10; 8:13; 6:16, 21, 23; 7:5; 8:2; James 1:15; and also

St. John) will incline one to admit, a consequence of grave, personal (and unforgiven) sins."[124] He admits that "[b]eneath the veil of darkness the very center of the phenomenon of death can differ profoundly from case to case."[125]

Besides reinterpreting how death could be called a penalty and punishment for sin, Rahner also rejected Augustine's pessimistic view of humanity as a "condemned mass" from which few will be saved, and instead expressed an optimism regarding the possibility of universal salvation.[126] He was pleased that Vatican II "buried" even the concept of *limbo*, by which theologians previously mitigated Augustine's teaching that unbaptized infants went to hell.[127] Beyond all theological constructs and opinions, Rahner ultimately put his trust in the victorious grace of a God who is infinite, unconditional love.[128] Rahner's concern to reinterpret *how* death might be called a punishment and penalty for sin was consistent with his *faith* in that kind of God. Yet, one might go even further.

The Gospels portrayed Jesus as distressed and sorrowful in the face of death (Mk14:33-34; Mt 26:37-38; [Lk 22:44]), and placed the prayers "My God, my God, why have you forsaken me?" (Mk 15:34; Mt 27:46) and "Father, into your hands I commend my spirit" (Lk 23:46) on his lips. In Rahner's understanding, Jesus "died our death": "if he really became like us in everything but sin, as the Epistle to the Hebrews says, then he became like us in death too and his death cannot be similar to ours merely in externals."[129] "Overwhelmed by a deadly feeling of being forsaken by God,"[130] the crucified Jesus, like every human, was confronted by the "radical powerlessness" and "darkness" of human death. In his full human freedom, he, too, had to renew once and for all his decision to trust in the Absolute Mystery of Love called God.[131] For Rahner, "it is precisely by its darkness that the death of Christ becomes the expression and embodiment of his loving obedience, the free transference of his entire created existence to God."[132]

As Walter Kasper put it, "Jesus' faith [in "the God with whom he felt uniquely linked"] did not give way, but he experienced the darkness and distress of death more deeply than any other man or woman. . . he experienced God as the one who withdraws in his very closeness . . . This extremity of emptiness enabled him to become the vessel of God's fulness."[133] In the words of Edward Schillebeeckx, the dying Jesus, in his "dark night of faith," "trusts in God [and] knows that he is still held in God's hand, even though there is no help that he can touch or feel, and in utmost emptiness will not let go of this hand." As the Fourth Gospel shows, "the deepest reality does not lie on the surface: Jesus [despite his helplessness and *apparent failure* as one rejected and condemned] was successful by virtue of his living communion with God, which is stronger than death." Thus, Schillebeeckx concludes, "God's transcendent overcoming of human failure is historically incorporated in Jesus' neverceasing love for God and [humans], during and in the historical moment of his failure on the cross."[134]

The 1980 Instruction of the International Theological Commission recommended transforming what was traditionally called "vicarious expiation" into an understanding of the cross as a "trinitarian event."[135] Rahner had himself significantly contributed to such a shift in theological understanding. As Jürgen Moltmann acknowledged in *The Crucified God*, "in Catholic theology, since 1960 Karl Rahner has understood the death of Jesus as the death of God in the sense that through his death 'our death [becomes] the death of the immortal God himself'."[136] Given his position that the Trinity of the economy of salvation [working in the world] is the immanent Trinity,[137] Rahner maintained that Jesus' death "expresses God as he is and as he willed to be in our regard by a free decision which remains eternally valid . . . Jesus' death belongs to God's self-utterance."[138] In other words, the fully human but sinless Jesus, "the image of the invisible God" (Col 1:15), distressed and sorrowful, in his *dark night of faith* on the cross expressed what the Triune God "is": a self-giving, *kenotic* Love (Phil 2:6-8), who in the Word become human truly shares the struggle of human freedom.[139] Moving along the path indicated by Theophilus and Irenaeus, such an understanding of the cross, in which the fully human death of Jesus expresses and manifests the *kenotic* God of mercy and love, seems to call for a reconsideration of the very language of penalty and punishment, so reinforced by Augustine.

The mysterious ambiguity of human death (which separates us from those we *love*) led the ancients to fear it and to connect it with sin. Admittedly, death continues to be a mysterious factor in human life, but we must have the courage to ask new questions about its origins and meaning. We must do that in relation to the God of unconditional love, who celebrates the return of those who are "lost" like a woman who celebrates finding an insignificant coin, as revealed by the Jesus who ate and drank with tax collectors and sinners.[140] If, as Rahner has suggested, death is the way such a God culminates our freedom, calling us to decide once and for all what we ultimately want to be, and, in Jesus, shares that *dark night of trust* with us, is it a moment of divine retribution and wrath, or a moment of hidden love?

NOTES

[1]Karl Rahner and Herbert Vorgrimler, "Death," in *Theological Dictionary*, ed. Cornelius Ernst, tr. Richard Strachan (New York: Herder and Herder, 1965), p. 115; also see Karl Rahner, "Death," in *Sacramentum Mundi, An Encyclopedia of Theology*, Vol. 2, ed. Karl Rahner, *et al.* (New York: Herder and Herder, 1968), p. 58.

[2]Conciliar texts in *Enchiridion Symbolorum Definitionum et Declarationum de Rebus Fidei et Morum*, ed. Henricus Denzinger and Adolfus Schönmetzer (Barcelona/Freiburg: Herder, 1965), No. 222 (Carthage, Canon 1), No. 372 (Orange, Canon 2), Nos. 1511 & 1512 (Trent, Canons 1 & 2).

[3]*On the Theology of Death* (New York: Herder and Herder, 1972; orig. 1961), p. 34.

[4]*Ibid.*, pp. 34-35.

[5]"Death," *Sacramentum Mundi*, p. 59.

[6]Gn 2:7 & 17; 3:19 & 22-24.

[7]See Lloyd R. Bailey, Sr., *Biblical Perspectives on Death* (Philadelphia: Fortress Press, 1979), pp. 36-39 & 129, n. 74; Otto Kaiser and Edward Lohse, *Tod und Leben* (Stuttgart: W. Kohlhammer, 1977), pp. 16-17.

[8]Dt 30:15-20. All biblical citations are from the *New Revised Standard Version, with Apocryphal/Deuterocanonical Books* , ed. Bruce M. Metzger (New York: Oxford University Press, 1989).

[9]Ezek 18:20-23.

[1]Ezek 18:27.

[11]Prv 1:18; 2:13-18; also see 7:27; 21:16; & 22:23.

[12]Job 36:13-14.

[13]See Ps(s) 6:5; 28:1; 30:9; 88:12; 115:17; 143:7. See also Is 38:18.

[14]1 Enoch 69:11; all citations of the Pseudepigrapha are from *The Old Testament Pseudepigrapha*, Vol. 1: *Apocalyptic Literature and Testaments*, and Vol. 2: *Expansions of the "Old Testament" and Legends, Wisdom and Philosophical Literature, Prayers, Psalms, and Odes, Fragments of Lost Judeo-Hellenistic Works*, ed. James H. Charlesworth (Garden City, N.Y.: Doubleday, 1983 & 1985).

[15]1 Enoch 8:1; 10:7; 65:6-8; 69:5-10.

[16]1 Enoch 98:4 & 7.

[17]1 Enoch 22:1-14.

[18]Jubilees 4:30; Gn 2:17.

[19]Jubilees 4:23.

[20]Life of Adam and Eve 45:1-3.

[21]Life 32:1; 33:3; 36:2 and 41:2; cf. Apocalypse of Moses 7:1-3; 9:3; 19:2-3 and 21:5.

[22]Life 42:1; cf. Apocalypse of Moses 28:1-4 and 13:2.

[23]4 Ezra 3:7.

[24]2 Enoch 30:17 & 31:6.

[25]2 Enoch 30:16.

[26]2 Baruch 17:3; cf. 19:8.

[27]2 Baruch 23:4; cf. 19:1.

[28]2 Baruch 19:3.

[29]2 Baruch 54:15.

[30]2 Baruch 56:6; cf. 17:3.

[31]Sir 10:11.

[32]Sir 22:11; 38:23; 41:1; 30:17; 40:28 & 41:2.

[33]Sir 25:24.

[34]Sir 40:9-10.

[35]See Sir 17:32 & 28:6.

[36]Sir 40:1-2.

[37]Sir 39:9; 41:11-13; & 44:10-14.

[38]Wis 2:23-24; cf. 12:1.

[39]Wis 1:13-15; cf. 1 Enoch 69:11.

[40]Wis 3:1-6; also see 4:16 and 5:15.

[41]Wis 4:10-15.

[42]Wis 9:15.

[43]1 Cor 15:54-57.

[44]Rom 5:17-18.

[45]Rom 8:10-11.

[46]1 Cor 15:44-49.

[47]Rom 6:5.

[48]Gal 2:19-20.

[49]*Epistle to the Romans* 4.

[50]See *Romans* 6; *Trallians* 2; *Magnesians* 5; *Ephesians* 19; *Smyrnaeans* 1.

[51]*Ephesians* 20; from *The Apostolic Fathers, Second Edition*, tr. J.B. Lightfoot and J. R. Harmer; ed. and rev. Michael W. Holmes (Grand Rapids, Mich.: Baker Book House, 1989), p. 93.

[52]*Dialogue with Trypho* 88; cited from *St. Justin Martyr*, tr. Thomas B. Falls, *The Fathers of the Church*, Vol. 6 (New York: Christian Heritage, 1948), p. 289; also see

Dialogue 91; 100; 116.

[53]*1 Apology* 32; 46; 50; 61; 66; *2 Apology* 13; *Dialogue with Trypho* 13; 40-41; 86; 89; 91; 95; 111; 134; 137; 138.

[54]See J. N. D. Kelly, *Early Christian Doctrines*, second edition (New York: Harper and Row, 1960) p. 170; L. W. Barnard, *Justin Martyr: His Life and Thought* (Cambridge: University Press, 1967), p. 122-25.

[55]*Address to the Greeks* 7.

[56]*Ibid.* 13; cited from *The Ante-Nicene Fathers*, eds., Alexander Roberts and James Donaldson; rev. by A. Cleveland Coxe (New York: Charles Scribner's Sons, 1899), Vol. 2, p. 70.

[57]*Address to the Greeks* 14; *The Ante-Nicene Fathers*, vol. 2, p. 71 (Emphasis is mine.).

[58]Wisdom 4:10-15.

[59]*To Autolycus* 2, 27; *The Ante-Nicene Fathers*, vol. 2, p. 105.

[60]*To Autolycus* 2, 25; *The Ante-Nicene Fathers*, vol. 2, p. 104.

[61]*Ibid.* 2, 26; *The Ante-Nicene Fathers*, vol. 2, pp. 104-105.

[62]*Ibid.* 2, 27.

[63]See *Against Heresies* (*Adversus Haereses*) 3,18,7; 3,21,10; 3,22,4; 3,23,1; 3,23,7; 4,22,1; 4,39,1; 5,13,3; 5,16,1-3; 5,19,1; 5,21,1; 5,23,1-2; 5,34,2.

[64]*Proof* 15; cited from *St. Irenaeus, Proof of the Apostolic Preaching*, tr. Joseph P. Smith, *Ancient Christian Writers*, No. 16 (Westminster, MD: Newman Press, 1952), p. 56.

[65]*Against Heresies* 3,22,4; 4,38,1-4; 4,39,2; *Proof of the Apostolic Preaching* 12 and 14.

[66]See *Against Heresies* 3,20,2; 3,22,3; 4,5,1; 4,38,2-3; 4,39,2; 5,6,1; 5,8,1; 5,12,1-3.

[67]*Ibid.* 3,23,6; *The Ante-Nicene Fathers*, vol. 1, p. 457; cf. *Proof of the Apostolic Preaching* 16.

[68]*Against Heresies* 4,20,7; *The Ante-Nicene Fathers*, vol. 1, p. 490.

[69] *Ibid.* 3,23,7; *Proof of the Apostolic Preaching* 31 & 33.

[70] *On the Soul* (*De Anima*) 52,1-3; cited from *Tertullian, Apologetical Works and Minucius Felix, Octavius*, trs. Rudolph Arbesmann, Emily J. Daly, & Edwin A. Quain, *Fathers of the Church*, Vol. 10 (New York: Fathers of the Church, 1950).

[71]*On the Testimony of the Soul* (*De Testimonio Animae*) 3; translation is mine.

[72]*On Mortality* 4 & 5.

[73]*Ibid.* 22 & 24.

[74]*Ibid.* 23.

[75]*Ibid.* 25.

[76]*Protrepticus* (*Exhortation to the Greeks*) 11.

[77] *Stromateis* 4,23; cf. 3,64.

[78] *Ibid.* 4,4.

[79] *Ibid.* 4,23 & 6,12.

[80]*Commentary on Romans* 5; cf. *Against Celsus (Contra Celsum)* 4,40.

[81]See *De Principiis* 2,1,3-4; 2,2,2; 2,3,3; 2,8,3; 2,9,2 & 6; 3,5,4-5.

[82]*Ibid.* 1,6,1-4; 2,10,1 & 3; 3,6,5-9; *Against Celsus* 5,18; 5,23; 7,32; 8,49.

[83]*On the Resurrection* 1,3; 3,1,2-5; 3,2,13; as enumerated in *The Ante-Nicene Fathers,* vol. 6, p. 364, 369-70, & 375-76.

[84]*Ibid.* 1,4 & 6-7; *The Ante-Nicene Fathers,* vol. 6, p. 365.

[85]*Symposium* 9,2; cited from *St. Methodius, The Symposium; A Treatise on Charity,* tr. Herbert Musurillo, *Ancient Christian Writers,* no. 27 (Westminster, MD: Newman Press, 1958), p. 135.

[86]*Early Christian Doctrines,* p. 183; also see p. 475.

[87]Walter J. Burghardt, "Eschaton and Resurrection: Patristic Insights," in *The Eschaton: A Community of Love,* ed. Joseph Papin, *The Villanova University Symposium,* Vol. 5 (Villanova, PA: Villanova University Press, 1971), p. 212.

[88]*Homily* 9,7 *(Quod Deus non est auctor malorum: MG* 31, 345-46).

[89]*Orations* 38,12 and 45,8.

[90]*Catechetical Oration* 8.

[91]*Pulcheria,* in the conclusion *(MG* 46, 875-78).

[92]*Homily on Genesis* 18, 3; or 18,8-10 in *St. John Chrysostom, Homilies on Genesis, 18-45,* tr. Robert C. Hill, *The Fathers of the Church,* vol. 82 (Washington, D.C.: Catholic University of America Press, 1990), pp. 8-10.

[93]"Eschaton and Resurrection," p. 216.

[94]Theophilus, *To Autolycus* 2,25; Irenaeus, *Against Heresies* 3,22,4; 4,38,1-4; 4,39,2; *Proof of the Apostolic Preaching* 12 and 14; as cited above in notes 60 and 65.

[95]See *Against Heresies* 3,23,3 & 5, and 4,40,3. Athanasius later said that the incarnation of Jesus was necessary in order that *man,* upon whom God had pronounced the sentence of death, might not perish: *On the Incarnation* 6.

[96]*Oration* 45,8.

[97]See Basil of Caesarea, *Homily* 9,6-7 *(Quod Deus non est auctor malorum; MG* 31, 343-44); Gregory of Nyssa, *Catechetical Oration* 6.

[98]*On the Sacraments* 6,17; *On Cain and Abel* 2,32 & 35; *Death as a Good* 4,15; *Explanation of Psalm 118* 18,3; *On Isaac or the Soul* 8,76.

[99]Ambrose, *Exposition on Psalm 118* 4,3; 7,8; 15,36; *Exposition of the Gospel according to Luke* 7,142; *Explanations (Enarrationes) of the Psalms* 43,75; *On Paradise* 24; 42; 63; *Epistles* 58,12 and 73,5.

[100]*On the Incarnation* 3-6.

[101]Augustine, *The Literal Meaning of Genesis (de Genesi ad litteram)* 8,25; 11,42; *Unfinished Work against Julian (Contra secundam Juliani responsionem imperfectum*

opus) 5,1; 6,22; *On Rebuke and Grace* (*de correptione et gratia*) 33-34; *City of God* 13,20; 14,11-13 & 17; *On the Merits and Remission of Sins* (*De peccatorum meritis et remissione, et de baptismo parvulorum*) 2,36; *On Marriage and Concupiscence* (*De nuptiis et concupiscentia*) 2,30.

[102]*The Literal Meaning of Genesis* 6,36 and *On Rebuke and Grace* 33-34.

[103]*The Literal Meaning of Genesis* 6,36.

[104]*On the Merits and Remission of Sins* 3,14; *Unfinished Work against Julian* 6,22; *City of God* 13,14; *Retractions* 1,13,5.

[105]*The Christian Life* (*De vita Christiana*) 5; cited from *St. Augustine, Treatises on Various Subjects*, ed. Roy J. Deferrari, *The Fathers of the Church*, vol. 16 (New York: Fathers of the Church, 1952), p. 18.

[106]*Enchiridion to Laurentius* 25-27 and 93; *Against Julian, the defender of the Pelagian heresy* 5,44; *Unfinished Work against Julian* 3, 199; *Epistle* (to Jerome) 166,10-25; *Sermon* 294,2-7; *On the Merits and Remission of Sins* 1,55.

[107]*Homily on Matthew* 28,3.

[108]*Oration* (on Baptism) 40,23.

[109]*On Infants Who Die Prematurely* (*De infantibus qui praemature abripiuntur*: MG 46, 161-92); English translation entitled *On Infants' Early Deaths* in *A Select Library of Nicene and Post-Nicene Fathers of the Christian Church, Second Series*, vol. 5, eds. Philip Schaff & Henry Wace (New York: Christian Literature Co./ Oxford: Parker, 1893), pp. 372-81. In his epiphany sermon, *On the Day of Lights, or On the Baptism of Christ* (*In diem luminum, In quo baptizatus est Dominus noster*: MG 46, 580-82), Gregory presumed that a new-born infant is free of all "charges and penalties".

[110]See Thomas Aquinas, *De Malo*, q. 5, a. 2-3; also cf. *Comm. in Sent.* II, d. 33, q. 2, a. 1 & 2; and *Comm. in Sent.* IV, d. 45, q. 1, a. 2 & 3 [*Summa Theologiae, Supplementum* III, q. 69, a. 6 & 7].

[111]*Why God Became Human* (*Cur Deus Homo*) 2,2 & 11. Anselm interprets the resurrection as a remaking or restoring of a human to what he or she would have been had he or she not sinned: *Ibid.* 2,3.

[112]*Ibid.* 2,10.

[113]*Ibid.* 1,9-10; 2,11 & 17.

[114]*Ibid.*, 2,6, 10 & 11.

[115]*Ibid.*, 1,20 & 25.

[116]*Summa Theologiae*, I,II, q. 85, a. 5, resp..

[117]"Death," p. 60; *On the Theology of Death*, p. 31; "On Christian Dying," *Theological Investigations*, vol. VII (London: Darton, Longman & Todd/ New York: Herder and Herder, 1971), pp. 287-92; "Ideas for a Theology of Death," *Theological Investigations*, vol. XIII (New York: Seabury Press-Crossroad Book, 1975), pp. 174-86.

[118]*On the Theology of Death*, pp. 30-31 and 38-41.

[119]*Ibid.*, pp. 61-66 & 71.

[120]*Ibid.*, p. 70.

[121]Karl Rahner, "The Theological Concept of Concupiscentia," in *Theological Investigations*, vol. I (Baltimore: Helicon Press, 1961), pp. 379 & 382.

[122]*Ibid.*, pp. 381-82.

[123]*On the Theology of Death*, pp. 48-49; also see 42-43.

[124]*Ibid.*, p. 50.

[125]*Ibid.*, p. 51.

[126]"The Abiding Significance of the Second Vatican Council," in *Concern for the Church; Theological Investigations XX* (New York: Crossroad, 1981), pp. 99-101.

[127]*Ibid.*, p. 101.

[128]*Ibid.*, pp. 101-02.

[129]*On the Theology of Death*, p. 57.

[130]"Dogmatic Reflections on the Knowledge and Self-Consciousness of Christ," *Theological Investigations*, vol. 5 (Baltimore: Helicon Press/ London: Darton, Longman & Todd, 1966), p. 207, also see p. 203.

[131]*On the Theology of Death*, pp. 61-62, & 70-72; "On Christian Dying," pp. 287 & 290-93; "Ideas for a Theology of Death," pp. 181-84.

[132]Karl Rahner, "Death," section 4: *"Christ's Death," Sacramentum Mundi: An Encyclopedia of Theology*, vol. 2 (New York: Herder and Herder, 1968), p. 61; also *On the Theology of Death*, p. 62.

[133]Walter Kasper, *Jesus the Christ* (London: Burns & Oates/ New York: Paulist Press, 1977), pp. 118-19.

[134]Edward Schillebeeckx, *Christ: The Experience of Jesus as Lord*, tr. John Bowden (New York: Crossroad, 1981), pp. 825 & 830.

[135]International Theological Commission, "Select Questions on Christology," (Washington, D.C.: United States Catholic Conference, 1980), p. 16 (section IV, C, 3.5).

[136]Jürgen Moltmann, *The Crucified God: The Cross of Christ as the Foundation and Criticism of Christian Theology* (New York: Harper & Row, 1974), p. 201; which cites Karl Rahner, "On the Theology of the Incarnation," *Theological Investigations*, vol. IV (Baltimore: Helicon/ London: Darton, Longman & Todd, 1966), p. 113.

[137]See Karl Rahner, "Remarks on the Dogmatic Treatise 'De Trinitate'," *Theological Investigations*, vol. IV, pp. 87-97.

[138]Karl Rahner, "Jesus Christ," section IV,F,6: *"Jesus' death as the death of God," Sacramentum Mundi*, vol. 3 (New York: Herder and Herder, 1969), pp. 207-08.

[139]See "Remarks on the Dogmatic Treatise 'De Trinitate'," pp.96-97; "On the Theology of the Incarnation," 114-18; "Current Problems in Christology," *Theological Investigations*, vol. I (Baltimore: Helicon Press/ London: Darton, Longman & Todd, 1961), pp. 155-63; "Christology within an Evolutionary View of the World," *Theological Investigations*, vol. 5, pp. 173-78.

[140]See Lk 15:8-10; Mk 2:15-17; Mt 11:16-19; Lk 7:31-34; 15:1-2.

PEOPLE OF THE BOOK:

BASIS FOR MUSLIM-CHRISTIAN DIALOGUE?

William Cenkner, O.P.

> O People of the Scripture!
> Why disbelieve ye in the revelations of Allah,
> when ye (yourselves) bear witness (to their truth)?
> —Qur'an 3.70

Several years ago two Muslim educators from Egypt met with me and a colleague at The Catholic University of America.[*] In a matter of minutes our conversation shifted from general religious education policy and practice to the role of our respective scriptures in our lives as teachers. The Muslims soon began to demonstrate their role with the melodious chanting of a passage from the Qur'an, followed by a spoken recitation of the same passage, a translation of it into English, and finally an explanation. My Christian colleague reciprocated by narrating a gospel story and concluded with a theological interpretation. Our visitors were surprised that we had neither quoted the gospel text in its original language nor performed a recitation of it before narrating and using it as a source of teaching. Long before our visitors left it was clear to me that as "People of the Book" my understanding and use of scripture was significantly different from theirs. It demonstrated to me the distinction between a recitation experience and a narrative experience.[1]

---

[*]This paper was first presented at a conference on "Dialogue for Muslim-Christian Friendship and Understanding," September, 1991, in Istanbul, Turkey, sponsored by the Council for the World's Religions. The International Religious Foundation who hold the copyright has given permission for its publication.

Passages from the Qur'an are taken from *The Meaning of the Glorious Koran, An Explanatory Translation*, Mohammed Marmaduke Pickthall (New York: Mentor, n.d.).

The phrase "People/Possessors of the Book" (*Ahl al-Kitab*) is not used in the Qur'an before the Meccan period and as such refers to Jews and Christians and only later to Sabeans and others. *Kitab* is generally understood to mean the Torah and the Psalms while *Injil*, used twelve times in the Qur'an, denotes gospel or good news.[2] "O People of the Scripture! Ye have naught (of guidance) till ye observe the Torah and the Gospel and that which was revealed unto you from your Lord." (Qur'an 5.68). Consequently, the scriptures of Judaism, Christianity, and Islam are understood in Islam as a revealed succession of divine guidance for the salvation of humanity. These scriptures emanate from a heavenly book, the "Mother of all Books," a hidden source, according to the Qur'an.[3]

SCRIPTURAL RELIGIONS

Is Christianity conscious of itself as a scriptural religion?[4] Primitive Christianity was a religion of the book in the sense that Hebrew scripture was that book. Jesus accepted Hebrew scripture as sacred and the early Christian community used it alone in worship. By the second century of the Christian Era gospels and letters were being read along with Hebrew scripture. The book tradition developed in the second and third centuries of the Christian Era as a response to the mystery religions whose texts were esoteric and held hidden meanings.[5] Wilfred Cantwell Smith has observed that Christian scripture constitutes the only instance in world history where one tradition incorporated the scriptures of another (in this case Judaism) within its own. It added things that were new, but made the old a part of and subordinate to its own writings.[6] By A.D. 367 Athanasius gave a complete listing of what became canonical literature. Jerome translated the Latin Vulgate from this listing, registering his preference for "Hebraica veritas" in the matter of the books of the Masoretic canon. By the fifth century of the Christian Era 27 books were generally accepted in the New Testament canon. This gradual and progressive history of a coherent and unified sacred book underlies the importance of the oral tradition and oral and aural sensibilities in its transmission.

The oral formation of Christian scripture is important in providing and helping to discover the context of the scriptural tradition. The oral transmission or actual use of scripture in Christian worship and education is the point this essay wishes to make. Although the Qur'an is fundamentally a "recitation" of God's literal word in worship and education, the Bible functions primarily as a narrative of God's interpretative word in worship and education. The distinguishing use of Christian scripture is in worship and as such is oral. Christian art and architecture, literature, and education, replete with phrases or images from the Bible, are further examples of a narration of God's interpretative word. It is only with the Protestant Reformation that Christians began to "speak" Scripture and Scripture began to saturate language. The notion of Christianity as a scriptural religion is best represented by Martin Luther and the traditions following him. Yet the book religion of the Reformers was still aurally perceived and orally transmitted, even with the onset of printing and the availability of the written text.[7] Luther and the Reformers, following St. Paul, continued the tradition that only when the gospel is preached is faith possible and a revelatory event present.[8]

A study of the tradition would demonstrate that the function of Scripture within Christianity has been diverse in practice and as a doctrinal norm in history and among the various branches of Christianity.[9] Yet the faith of the early Christian communities was focused upon the person of Jesus, encountered not in written or recited Scripture but in the preaching and experiences of those who gave testimony of their faith. The preaching of the written gospel transformed lives and created believing communities: faith resulted from hearing the spoken word, that is the interpretative word of Scripture, and oral testimony of the faith of another.[10]

MUSLIMS AS PEOPLE OF THE BOOK

Although the ancient Hebrews were the prototypical people of the book, the Qur'an is the prototypical book of scripture in both worship and thought.[11] Islam began as a scriptural religion: "In Islam the Qur'an is the Word of God made scripture."[12] The Qur'an, unlike Christian scripture, is not a gradual communal canonization of a text but a final and definitive revelation in the lifetime of one individual, the Prophet Muhammad.[13] It differs from all other scripture as the literal speech of God, eternal and uncreated, coexistent with God and prior to all created being. It is a writing (*Kitab*) that is a revelation (*tanzil*). But from the very beginning it was called a recitation, a *qur'an*, a reading, and in this sense primary importance is given to its oral transmission and aural presence.[14]

Not only is the authority and perfection of the text perceived in its recitation, but also the act of recitation (*tajwid*) is a reenactment of the revelatory event itself.[15] Recitation, as chanting or cantillation, makes beautiful and meaningful the living Word of God. As such it is experienced as the divine Word. The art of chanting is transmitted through oral tradition. Among Muslims and Christians, consequently, scriptural truth is orally conveyed. The calligraphic word of scripture, moreover, became the dominant expression and motif of Islamic art and culture.[16] In Christian art and literature, the narrative life of Jesus predominates.

Nonetheless, it is in worship and devotion that the Qur'an exhibits extraordinary power and blessings in the lives of people. An Indian Muslim leader once told his Christian friend, C.F. Andrews: "You will never understand this power and warmth of religion among us until you can feel in your own heart the poetry and music of the Qur'an *al-Sharif.*"[17] Attempting to grasp the role of the Qur'an in Muslim imagination, piety, family and social life, Wilfred Cantwell Smith observes: "The meaning of the Qur'an lies not in the text, but in the minds and hearts of Muslims."[18] The recitation of the sacred text brings one into the presence of the divine. In short, recitation internalizes scriptural truth, gathers and gives coherence to a community, while scriptural meaning permeates the affective and intellectual lives of believers.

SCRIPTURE AS WORD OF GOD

In modern times scripture is perceived as a reified written text, a documentary so to speak, while traditionally scripture is a relational term. It is scripture because it mediates divine revelation in the lives of a people. It is scripture to the degree that it relates to a community of faith and piety.[19] In theocentric religions scripture is the place where "God speaks" to people.[20] Christianity perceives a progressive revelation between Hebrew Scripture and the New Testament and the salvation history underlying the two testaments. Islam also perceives progressive revelation through the Torah to Moses and the other prophets, the Psalms to David, the Gospel to Jesus, culminating and finalizing in the Qur'an to the Prophet Muhammad. In each of these instances God "speaks" his Word in an encounter between the divine and human orders. In the Christian instance the divine encounter is in and through the person of Jesus Christ; in the Islamic instance the divine encounter is in and through the Qur'an, more specifically in and through quranic recitation.

H.M. Gwatkin draws the conclusion that "The Muslim idea of revelation gathers it up in a book, the Christian in a Person."[21]

The Qur'an functions in Muslim life as the person of Christ does in Christian life. Revelation for Christians is the person of Christ as God's Word and as the revelatory event; the Bible is a testament of that revelation. Revelation for Muslims is the event in which the Prophet Muhammad mediated God's literal Word in divine recitation, or *qur'an*s. Recent scholarship distinguishes between explicit mediation in the divine recitations and implicit mediation through the words and actions of the Prophet Muhammad.[22]

The Word of God in the Qur'an is uncreated and eternal, while the prophetic word (*Hadith*), the words and actions of the Prophet Muhammad, is created and temporal. The distinction between the divine word and the prophetic word was less defined in early Islam than in later history.[23] There is a significant difference between the sayings (*Hadith*) attributed to the Prophet and the tradition and those divine sayings (*hadith kodsi*) ascribed to God but not in the Qur'an. The latter were believed to have been received conceptually but not verbally by the Prophet Muhammad. Quranic chapters begin with the words, "God said"; the prophetic tradition begins with the words, "The Apostle of God said;" while the divine sayings (*hadith kodsi*) sometimes begin with the words, "God said in that which the Apostle of God related from His Lord." These brief observations point to three levels of revelatory experience: Qur'an, prophetic tradition, divine sayings. The divine sayings indicate that scripture is not exhaustive of revelation and, equally important, that the prophetic mission of the Prophet Muhammad shares in the revelatory event and experience. That is to say, the divine activity was a prophetic-revelatory event in which the Prophet Muhammad as messenger mediated God's explicit word in scripture.[24]

This may help clarify the contrast suggested between the Qur'an in Muslim experience and Christ in Christian experience. As the *Hadith* is a record of revelation in Islam, so the Bible is a record of revelation in Christian tradition. Scriptural inspiration is inherent to each. Each impinges upon the central revelatory events, respectively the Qur'an and Jesus Christ. This also overcomes the Christian obstacle of identifying Christ as merely prophet/messenger, but it does not resolve that fact as it occurs in the Qur'an.

The Swedish theologian Nathan Söderblom (d.1931) was one of the earliest Western scholars to suggest that the contrast between Christ and the Qur'an may be established on the Greek notion of *logos*, attributed to Christ.[25] The Qur'an would not necessarily conflict with the notion of Jesus as *logos* or even the *logos* becoming "flesh" but would find unacceptable the *logos* identified with God.[26] Likewise, Muslim faith would find incompatible the use of *logos* to clarify the reality of the Qur'an if it meant identification with God.

The above implies that Christ and the Qur'an are functionally and structurally similar: both are God's Word; both are a guidance and salvation for humankind; both offer spiritual power and a doctrinal basis for salvation; both heal, console, and sustain people in the course of life.[27] Christians have consistently used Western Christian theological realities to come to a better understanding of the contrast under discussion. The use of *logos* is but one example. The recitation of the Qur'an may be similar to what Christians call sacrament, although the term, as some have noted, is neither used by nor congenial to the Muslim.[28] Protestant Reformation thought which strongly supports the sacramental value in the proclaimed and preached gospel could aid an understanding of scripture in Islam. The divine presence experienced through quranic recitation has been contrasted to what Catholic Christians experience in the eucharistic presence of Christ.[29] Regardless of these attempts toward understanding by Christians, along with Muslim respect shown to Jesus as God's messenger, it has been observed that no practical results should be anticipated from Muslim-Christian dialogue concerning the theology or person of Jesus Christ.[30] When Muslims speak of Jews and Christians as people of the book, it is meant both as a respectful gesture and compliment on the one hand, and on the other the recognition of theistic believers who are clearly demarcated from nonbelievers.[31] The above contextualizes the question in the title of this essay: Is the phrase "people of the book" a basis for Muslim-Christian dialogue?

Precedents in Dialogue

The contemporary scholarship referenced in this essay has been the result of serious monologue with the scriptures of Islam and Christianity, and in some few instances it has resulted from significant dialogue. One such dialogue needs mention, namely, the *Groupe de Recherche Islamo-Chrétien (GRIC)*, meeting locally in Algeria, Beirut, Brussels, Paris, Rabat, and Tunis, and meeting annually between 1978-1982 either in Senanque, Tunis, or Rabat.[32] This dialogue brought to the surface thematic similarities, frequently with varying degrees of emphasis, between the two scriptural traditions. The partners to the dialogue realized that no single revelation exhausts the mystery of God and the ways of communicating God's word.[33] The initial task taken in the *GRIC* dialogue was to situate the scripture of the other in one's own perspective of revelation. Namely, how can I recognize the Word of God in the scripture of another? For the Christian it would require the sensibility to grasp some sense of the mystery of God in the Qur'an, so vivid in Muslim experience. For the Muslim, it would require the sensibility to grasp some sense of the mystery of God not only in the New Testament but also as experienced by Christians in the person of Jesus.[34] Such sensitivity would be necessary if religious dialogue is to be a sharing in the spiritual riches of the other. The *GRIC* dialogue prompted one participant to say:

> Personally, as a Christian theologian but without wishing to commit my Christian brothers, I have no hesitation in saying that the revelation of which Muhammad is the messenger is *a* Word of God, which addresses me in my faith. I do not say that the Qur'an is *the* Word of God, but I willingly say that the Qur'an contains a confession of faith in God that concerns me as a Christian and calls me therefore to consider Muhammad as an authentic witness of the God in whom I believe.[35]

The dialogic struggle for the Christian is to perceive the Qur'an as an authentic Word of God but also as fundamentally different from the Word in Jesus Christ.

Muslim participants in *GRIC* raised the question whether, from a Muslim perspective, the New Testament is an expression of the Word of God. They responded:

> Yes and no. Yes, to the extent that it contains the marks of the divine message transmitted by Jesus to the Jews, although it would be difficult to distinguish with any certainty between what Jesus really said and what he did not say. No, to the extent that if we do not accept the idea that the Holy Spirit inspired the authors of the New Testament, it is a human composition lacking in the authority of the Messenger. Anything derived from the testimony of Jesus' contemporaries or the traditions about him cannot be considered the Word of God.[36]

For Muslims, consequently, the Qur'an and the New Testament are not the same kind of writing because human interventions are invariably mixed with the authentic word in Christian scripture. These deviations (*tahrif*), alterations or falsifications are not consciously made but result from human mediation and consequent limitations in the text and its meaning.[37] It is the task of the Christian scholar in dialogue to determine whether the deviations (*tahrif*) are understood as the Christian tradition understands them.[38]

The *GRIC* dialogue offers evidence and a basis for Muslim-Christian discourse with sacred scripture. It also highlights attitudes for and goals in such conversations. Most significant are: (1) the need to possess an understanding of the other that the other recognizes as true; (2) the need to sense the mystery of God experienced by the other; (3) the need to develop a theology of revelation and the consequent meaning it gives to scripture that is acceptable and common to both Muslim and Christian.[39]

> O People of the Scripture! Come to an agreement between us and you: that we shall worship none but Allah, and that we shall ascribe no partner unto Him, and that none of us shall take others for lords beside Allah. And if they turn away, then say: Bear witness that we are they who have surrendered (unto Him).
>
> —Qur'an 3.64.

NOTES

[1]This is not to deny that the Qur'an has a narrative function. It is recitation and teaching, narrative and teaching. See Mircea Eliade, *Encyclopedia of Religion*, vol. 12, p. 157.

[2]Geoffrey Parrinder, *Jesus in the Qur'an* (London: Sheldon, 1965), p. 142. See *The Encyclopedia of Islam* (1960), vol. 1, pp. 264-66.

[3]*Encyclopedia of Religion*, "Islam," p. 308. Harold Coward, *Sacred Word and Sacred Text: Scripture in World Religions* (Maryknoll, New York: Orbis, 1989), p. 103.

[4]A provisional text for the Roman Catholic community titled *A Catechism for the Universal Church* (1990), n. 273 b, reads: "The christian faith is not, however, a 'religion of the Book.' Christianity is the religion of the 'Word' of God, 'not a written, dumb word, but of the incarnate and living word' (St. Bernard, *S. missus est hom.* 4.11; PL183,86)."

[5]William H. Graham, *Beyond the Written Word: Oral Aspects of Scripture in the History of Religion* (Cambridge: Cambridge University, 1986), pp. 122 ff. See, Coward, *Sacred Word and Sacred Text*, p. 37; Frederick M. Denny & Rodney L. Taylor, ed., *The Holy Book in Comparative Perspective* (Columbia, SC: University of South Carolina, 1988), pp. 37 ff.

[6]Wilfred Cantwell Smith, "Scripture as Form and Concept: Their Emergence for the Western World," in Miriam Levering, edit., *Rethinking Scripture: Essays from a Comparative Perspective* (Albany: State University of New York, 1989), p. 38.

[7]Graham, *Beyond the Written Word*, pp. 144, 150.

[8]Coward, *Sacred Word and Sacred Text*, pp. 75-76.

[9]W.C. Smith, "Scripture as Form and Concept," p. 53.

[10]Ibid., p. 37. See, Coward, *Sacred Word and Sacred Text*, p. 47.

[11]Graham, *Beyond the Written Word*, pp. 51, 79.

[12]Maurice Borrmans & R. Maston Speight, *Interreligious Documents I, Guidelines for Dialogue between Christians and Muslims* (New York & Mahwah, NJ: Paulist, 1990), p. 47.

[13]Graham, *Beyond the Written Word*, pp. 86 ff.

[14]Ibid., p. 79.

[15]Ibid., p. 100.

[16]Ibid., p. 86.

[17]Kenneth Cragg and R. Marston Speight, *Islam from Within: Anthology of a Religion* (Belmont, CA: Wadsworth, 1980), p. 11.

[18]Coward, *Sacred Word and Sacred Text*, p. 101.

[19]Levering, *Rethinking Scripture*, p. 152.

[20]Graham, *Beyond the Written Word*, p. 68.

[21]A.J. Arberry, *Revelation and Reason in Islam* (London: George Allen and Unwin, 1957), p. 10.

[22]William H. Graham, *Divine Word and Prophetic Word in Early Islam* (The Hague: Mouton, 1977), pp. 10 ff.

[23]Ibid., pp. 6 ff, 38 ff.

[24]Ibid., p. 10.

[25]Nathan Söderblom, *The Living God, Basal Forms of Personal Religion* (Boston: Beacon, 1962), p. 326.

[26]Paul J. Griffiths, edit., *Christianity Through Non-Christian Eyes* (Maryknoll, NY: Orbis, 1990), p. 109.

[27]Denny & Taylor, *The Holy Book in Comparative Perspective*, p. 97.

[28]Ibid.

[29]Graham, *Beyond the Written Word*, p. 87.

[30]Smail Balic, "The Image of Jesus in Contemporary Islamic Theology," *We Believe in One God: The Experience of God in Christianity and Islam*, ed., Annemarie Schimmel and Abdoldjavad Falaturi (New York: Crossroad/Seabury, 1979). It has been brought to the author's attention that Professor Mahmond M. Ayoub of Temple University is preparing a study on the person of Jesus from a Muslim perspective. A recent Muslim and Christian audience in Chicago, with five hundred attendees of whom over sixty percent were Muslim, listened to speakers lecture on "Jesus in the New Testament: Jesus in the Qu'ran."

[31]Levering, *Rethinking Scripture*, p. 31.

[32]See, Stuart E. Brown, tr., *The Challenge of the Scriptures, The Bible and the Qur'an*, Muslim-Christian Research Group (Maryknoll, NY: Orbis, 1989).

[33]Ibid., p. 73.

[34]Ibid., p. 90.

[35]Ibid., p. 71.

[36]Ibid., p. 85.

[37]Ibid., pp. 78, 86.

[38]Ibid., pp. 79-80. For example, Jesus as Son of God is perceived as *tahrif* because, seemingly, the Qur'an takes it literally as implying physical relationship between God and Mary. It is believed that Islam could tolerate a metaphorical interpretation of the phrase. Likewise, the Christian concept of God as a triad of Gods or tritheism, a frequent Muslim interpretation, is by no means the Christian understanding. Consequently, some of what are thought to be doctrines denied by the Qur'an are not genuine Christian understanding.

[39]Ibid., pp. 88-89. This is not to suggest a common theology of revelation, but a theology whereby commonalities can be shared while the uniqueness of each revelation in reality and understanding is recognized.

KARL RAHNER IN DIALOGUE WITH

JUDAISM AND ISLAM:

AN ASSESSMENT

Peter C. Phan

Among Christian theologians engaged in interreligious dialogue, Karl Rahner's theory of "anonymous Christians" or "anonymous Christianity," often labeled as an inclusivist Christian theology of religions (in contradistinction to the exclusivist and pluralist theologies), is by now so well-known among Catholic theologians and so thoroughly evaluated that it does not call for another exposition and analysis.[1] Besides elaborating this theology of non-Christian religions, Rahner was also personally involved in extensive and well-publicized dialogues with natural scientists (in the *Görresgesellschaft*), with Marxists such as Ernst Bloch, Milan Machovec, and Roger Garaudy (in the *Paulusgesellschaft*), and of course with non-Roman Catholic Christians.[2]

While Rahner's theology of religions and dialogical activities have been subjected to extensive scholarly scrutiny, little attention has been paid to his dialogues with Judaism and Islam, perhaps because in comparison with his other dialogues, these were much less frequent and did not produce a comparable number of publications. To fill this lacuna, I present in this essay some of Rahner's conversations with Jews, especially with Pinchas Lapide, on Judaism and Christianity, and his reflections on the affinities between the Christian theology of the Trinity and the Islamic understanding of the oneness of God. I conclude with an assessment of Rahner's views of Judaism and Islam in light of both his own theology and of current Christian theologies of these two religions.

RAHNER IN DIALOGUE WITH JUDAISM

In his introduction to Rahner's life and thought Herbert Vorgrimler notes that in the 1960s Rahner carried on conversations with Jewish theologians such as E.L. Ehrlich and F.G. Friedmann.[3] Rahner's exchange of letters with F.G. Friedmann was published in *Stimmen der Zeit* in 1966.[4] His extensive conversations with Pinchas Lapide have been published under the title *Heil von den Juden? Ein Gespräch* to which references will mainly be made.[5]

A word of caution may be in order on how to interpret Rahner's views of Judaism and its relationship to Christianity as expounded in the above-mentioned volume. First, in this dialogue, or perhaps more accurately interview, it is Lapide who set the agenda with his statements and questions. Hence Rahner was limited by the scope of the issues his partner in dialogue raised. He was obliged to react to them either with answers or at times with careful distinctions and clarifications. Secondly, even though Lapide covered a large number of important issues regarding the relationship between Judaism and Christianity, one cannot presume that these were those that Rahner himself would consider to be the most important or that he would accord the priority to them that Lapide did. Thirdly, given the time constraints of the interview, Rahner could not develop fully his positions on the issues raised by Lapide. Hence, to do justice to them one should not limit oneself to the text of the conversation but place them in the larger context of his theology. Finally, it is neither possible nor necessary to examine every issue discussed in the dialogue between Rahner and Lapide. I will therefore select some key themes for consideration around which I will organize the contents of these somewhat rambling and repetitive conversations.

Covenant and Election

Rahner and Lapide begin their dialogue with an explicit reference to Vatican II's teaching on the Church in relation to Judaism as found in section 4 of its Declaration on the Relation of the Church to Non-Christian Religions.[6] Rahner quotes the first part of article 4 of *Nostra Aetate* in which the Council highlights the fact that Christianity is deeply rooted in the religion of Israel and the spiritual ties that indissolubly link the two religions.

The Council's recognition of the fact that God has not revoked his covenant with Israel (see Rom 11:1-2; 29) and that Christians still "await that day, known to God alone, on which all peoples will address the Lord in a single voice and 'serve him with one accord'" (*Nostra Aetate*, 4) implicitly raises the question, which Lapide renders explicit, of whether the Christian mission to the Jews is not made superfluous. Related to this question are the issues of Jesus' role in salvation and his messiahship, to which I will return later. In answer to Lapide's question, Rahner replies that the fact that God's covenant with the Jews still continues does not exclude the possibility of God's further gifts, in this case, in Jesus: "A gift of grace not repented of and God's promise do not preclude the reception of further gifts of grace or a further historical development and execution of one of the old gifts of grace. Through the promise of the old covenant a more positive relationship of Israel to Jesus is not precluded. . . ."[7] And since for Rahner "all have sinned and need the forgiving grace of God, which is promised to us irreversibly and with historical clarity through the Jew Jesus in his cross and resurrection"[8] and since this message must be announced to all, Gentiles as well as Jews, the Christian mission to Jews is still necessary: ". . . all--including the Jews--are called and fundamentally obligated to confess explicitly this redemption through the cross of Jesus and the community of those who do that, called the Church of Jesus Christ, which should in principle envelop Jews and Gentiles."[9]

Rahner reiterates this duty on the part of Jews to acknowledge the saving role of Jesus for them also, when Lapide argues for the continuing validity of the Jewish covenant on the basis of their two thousand years of suffering in witness to their covenant with God: "Good. However I can now say: in exactly the same way you must acknowledge the passion of Jesus (no matter who caused it) as the great unprecedented crystallization and apex of the passion of Israel and from this accept Jesus also as your redeemer."[10]

At this point one wonders whether both Lapide and Rahner should not have drawn the differences between them more sharply by inquiring (1) whether it is possible and necessary to speak of God's covenant with the Jews as being fulfilled in the sense of its being superseded by Christianity, or, if not, (2) whether there is a single covenant with Christians simultaneously participating with Jews, in a unique ongoing covenant, with God, or (3) whether there are two different but complementary covenants given to humanity at Sinai and at Calvary respectively, or even (4) whether these covenants are but two of an undetermined number of covenants that God makes with humanity. Rahner's strong insistence on the universal role of Jesus in the history of salvation and on the obligation on the part of Jews to confess Jesus as their redeemer suggests that he is inclined to the first position or at most to the second, but definitely not to the third and fourth. The issues of election and covenant were not put to him, however, in these sharp terms, hence Rahner's answers to the above questions can only be deduced from his other related positions.[11] I will return to these issues later.

Faith in God: The Oneness of God and the Doctrine of the Trinity

Any theological conversation between Jews and Christians (and of course between Christians and Moslems, as we will see) cannot evade the issue of God's oneness and triune nature. It is only natural then that the dialogue between Lapide and Rahner should dwell for a moment on this topic. However, because Rahner's only essay in dialogue with Islam deals exclusively with the oneness and trinity of God, I will defer a substantive discussion of this theme to the second part of this essay. Let it suffice here to underline the following points.

First, Lapide readily accepts the triadic concept of God as expounded by Rahner. He acknowledges its compatibility with the Jewish understanding of God as implied in the theophany of God by the oaks of Mamre (Gen. 18) and in the expression "the God of Abraham, the God of Isaac, and the God of Jacob."[12]

Secondly, in his dialogue with Lapide, Rahner basically repeats the essential theses of his trinitarian theology, in particular his *Grundaxiom* that the economic Trinity is the immanent Trinity and vice versa (with which Lapide heartily agrees), his critique of the word "person" as applied to the Trinity, and his alternative proposal of "three distinct manners of subsistence."

Thirdly, while rejecting Wittgenstein's injunction that one should keep silent about matters whereof one cannot speak clearly, Rahner agrees with Lapide that we *have to* speak about God even though our speech about God must end up in silent worship. Nevertheless he demurs at the latter's contrast between head and heart, between reason and love, and insists on the necessity of judging between true and false theological statements.[13]

Jesus as the Universal Messiah?

One now reaches the heart of the dialogue between Lapide and Rahner; indeed the Jesus question occupies more than half of the conversation. The issues touched upon are: the Jewishness of Jesus, his messiahship, his role in the history of salvation, and the meaning of the Jews' refusal of Jesus.

Rahner gives a wholehearted agreement to Lapide's emphasis on the fact that Jesus was a Jew and that "the Jewishness of Jesus in no way exhausts itself in his biological flesh and blood, but rather manifests itself especially in his spiritual world and in the richness of his faith."[14] Granted the importance of Jesus' Jewishness for Christian theology and spirituality, the question remains: which elements of Jesus' Jewishness are *normative* for Christians today? That Jesus kept the Jewish calendar of feasts or kept his head covered or uncovered at prayer would obviously not be considered as normative for Christians. Rahner notes that certain things about Jesus can be normative for Christians, however, even though (1) on the one hand they cannot be deduced from the abstract idea of incarnation but are historically contingent (e.g., Jesus' preferential love for the poor) and (2) though, on the other hand, they did not belong to the Jewishness of the historical Jesus as such but can be deduced from his human nature in general (certain behaviors according to the laws of nature). Without elaborating on these kinds of normative elements and the theological criteria for identifying them, Rahner simply concludes that "in the Jewishness of Jesus I may once more distinguish, and must distinguish, between what simply belongs to this Jewishness and what is normative therein for me as Gentile Christian."[15]

Connected with the issue of the Jewishness of Jesus is the question of whether Jesus is the Messiah the Jews are expecting. This question is often cast in terms of waiting and praying for either the Messiah's advent or his return. As Lapide puts it: "For over two thousand years the Synagogue has prayed for the advent of the Messiah and for around nineteen hundred years the Church has prayed for the return of its redeemer."[16] Rahner agrees with Lapide that Christians are still praying and hoping for the "return" of Jesus but points out that the *parousia* is not simply a restitution to the same situation as that of Jesus. Rather it is the final self-communication of God: "I must stress once again: I hope for the final self-communication of God face to face. For me, that is the absolute future. That alone. Then the incomprehensible God, whom I cannot grasp absolutely, will be given as such. But then I will finally be accepted by him."[17]

But, Lapide retorts, if God's final self-communication is still outstanding, does this not mean that Rahner contradicts himself when he asserts in *Foundations of Christian Faith* that for him "the definitive self-

communication of God happened in Jesus Christ"?[18] Rahner replies that
Lapide has misunderstood him. He has not said that God has manifested
himself definitively in Jesus; rather, says he: "I must say: in Jesus is
given to me the irrevocable promise of the definitive self-communication
of God. I still await this self-communication itself, even if, as Paul says,
the 'earnest money' for it is already given to me in grace."[19]

Despite the different views concerning the identity of the Messiah
(or more precisely, as Lapide puts it, "[T]here is no Jewish "no" standing over against a Christian "yes", but rather a Christian yes to a humble
Jewish question mark"[20]) the common hope between Christians and
Jews in the final and absolute still-to-come self-communication of God
is for both Lapide and Rahner a source of unity for the followers of the
two religions in their witness of faith to "troubled atheists" and their
work to better this world.

Still, the extremely thorny question remains: What is the role of Jesus
in God's plan of salvation, especially vis-à-vis the Jews? While professing
respect for his partner in dialogue as "other" and for his faith commitment,
Rahner expresses his firm hope that Lapide may become a Christian: "So
you must indulge me (if I may formulate it so sharply) if I were still to
expect that you would be baptized in this present age."[21] In response
Lapide reiterates his refusal to accept Jesus as the Messiah of the Jews
or as the redeemer of a still unredeemed world, as well as his birth as the
incarnation of God. He acknowledges, however, that God has availed
himself of Jesus to bring about a step forward to redemption, at least
insofar as whoever accepts Jesus accepts also Israel's God.

In his turn Rahner points out that Lapide's positive description of
the role of Jesus is not very far from the Christian faith in the Incarnation: "[I]f I believe in Jesus in this way as the irreversible and victorious self-promise of God, I have already actually reached that which the
Church's theology of Incarnation teaches."[22] Rahner is careful to dispel
the mythological misunderstanding of the Incarnation as the act in which,
as Lapide puts it, "the creator of the universe shrank himself completely
into the human body of Jesus, in a manner of speaking, in order to
become totally flesh and blood."[23] He emphasizes that in Jesus God and
the creature remain different and unmixed, even if in total unity. The
scandal of the Christian faith lies, in Rahner's view, not in a christology
which includes the Incarnation (which, properly understood, is "an
almost self-evident matter") but in a Jesus-oriented christology.[24]

At this point it may be remarked that the issue of the role of Jesus in God's plan of salvation could have been made sharper had it been phrased by Lapide in terms of Christian mission to the Jews. The question can be formulated in this way: Is a Christian mission to the Jews essentially the same as that to the others? Or is it theologically and in principle different? If it is different, how should Rahner's expectation that Lapide be baptized be evaluated? We will come back to this issue.

The last significant issue in the dialogue between Lapide and Rahner concerns the possible significance of the Jewish "no" to Jesus as the Christ. As Lapide points out, the Church reacted to this Jewish no with a triple no of its own: it incorporated a no to the Jews on the part of Jesus into its Scripture, it radicalized this no by attributing it to God, and it added a no to Judaism on the part of Christianity. In contrast to this negative interpretation of the Jewish no to Jesus as the Christ, Rahner affirms that even though he himself says no to this no, he can "interpret this Jewish no to Jesus as the Christ as arising out of a positive relationship to God."[25] Rahner justifies this positive interpretation by appealing to the common Catholic doctrine that even an act that is not morally correct in and of itself can come from a subjective command of conscience pleasing to God.

But this invocation of the duty of an invincibly erroneous conscience to follow its own dictate still leaves unresolved the question of whether the Jewish no to Jesus can play a role in the history of salvation. As Lapide puts it somewhat playfully, is it true that, had the greater part of Jews contemporary with Jesus not rejected him as Messiah, the mission to the Gentiles would not have begun, and Rahner "and the Jesuits in Insbruck today would still be sacrificing horse meat to the mountain gods of Tyrol instead of praying the Hebrew psalms and paying hommage to the God of Israel"?[26] Rahner is led to agree with Lapide that Israel still has a redemptive function after Christ, at least in the ways described by Catholic theologian Franz Mussner in his *Tractate on the Jews*:

> The Jew is the continuing witness to God in the world and as such.
> . . . [T]he Jew is the continuing witness to the concreteness of salvation history. . . . The Jew does not allow the messianic idea to disappear from the world. . . . Israel is the world-historical witness for the not-yet of the divine will and resists the Christian pathos of eschatological time, truth, and judgment. . . . The history of humanity has become a holy history through Judaism. . . . The Christian needs the Jew . . . the Jew helps the Christian to retain his identity, for Israel remains the root of the Church.[27]

With this agreement on the positive significance of the Jewish no to Jesus as the Christ, all theological grounds for antisemitism are effectively removed. Still, should one further say that in the divine plan of salvation Jews and Christians are placed there by God as, in Lapide's words, "two fraternal opponents . . . necessary to scramble nearer the truth"? To this question Rahner gives his answer that can be regarded as a summary of his position regarding Judaism:

> I can grant all that--if it is not overlooked that as a Christian I recognize Jesus as the unsurpassable Messiah for all. On this question we still differ, and under such proviso (which must remain explicit), and only so, I can acknowledge a positive redemptive meaning and effect in the dialectical relationship between Jews and Christians. And so in an actual way this positive dialectical relationship is nevertheless something that for me should be superseded by a recognition of Jesus as the savior of the world, and thus also of the Jews.[28]

Thus ends the conversation between the Jewish and the Christian theologians. As indicated above, the differences between them could have been made sharper had questions been put differently. Furthermore, besides the issues of covenant and Christian mission, there are questions that would be central today in the Jewish-Christian dialogue that were not broached, e.g., the relationship between the two parts of Christian Scripture[29], the Holocaust *(shoah)* and its impact on Christian theology[30], the question of the state of Israel and the Palestinian people[31]. To some of these issues we will come back later, for now let us turn to the second partner of Rahner's dialogue, namely, Islam.

RAHNER IN DIALOGUE WITH ISLAM

In his conversation with Lapide, Rahner makes several references to Islam, especially to the lecture he gave to Muslims in Modling near Vienna on May 31, 1977, "Oneness and Threefoldness of God in Discussion with Islam."[32] As has been mentioned above, Rahner discusses the Christian doctrine of the triune God in reference to Jewish monotheism. However, it is only within the context of dialogue with Islam that he explicitly and extensively develops the implications of his own theology of the Trinity for the dialogue with non-Christian religions.[33]

Our concern here is not to expound Rahner's trinitarian theology as such but to examine how it may serve as a bridge for dialogue with the Islamic doctrine of the oneness of God. To begin with, Rahner confesses that he does not know much of Islamic theology, so that a real *dialogue* between him and Muslims is not possible. What he aims to achieve is to put forward only a few considerations on the relationship between Christian monotheism and the Christian doctrine of the Trinity so that an explicit discussion between Christians and Muslims on the doctrine of God will not be aborted because of preliminary misunderstandings of the Christian doctrine of the Trinity.

Christian Monotheism

Rahner points out, first of all, that "Christianity is primarily and not merely secondarily a monotheistic religion," that is, the belief in the one sole God is "the really basic dogma of Christianity."[34]

Secondly, this affirmation of the oneness of God is not primarily a metaphysical statement. Rather it is the conclusion derived from the experience of who God is in the history of revelation and salvation. In other words, for Christians, the statement on the oneness of God refers not to an abstract absolute, but to a *concrete* absolute, to "the God experienced concretely in his action on us, to the God of Abraham, Isaac, to the God of the prophets, the God of Jesus."[35]

Thirdly, since the one God is a concrete absolute, genuine religious experiences, wherever they occur, whether in Judaism or Christianity or Islam, reach one and the same God, so that in spite of diversities and apparent contradictions in the history of religions, there is a *universal* history of salvation. Hence the polytheistic tendency to refer different religious experiences to different absolutes must be resisted.

Fourthly, in this universal history of salvation monotheism as professed by Judaism, Christianity and Islam, because it is concrete, necessarily has an incarnational character, to use a Christian term. This incarnational character can of course take different forms such as a covenant, a particular person, or a book. Therefore, in Rahner's view, there is no incompatibility between Christian monotheism and monotheism as professed by either Judaism or Islam.

Christian Monotheism and Trinitarian Doctrine

But is there an incompatibility between Jewish and Islamic monotheism on the one hand and the Christian doctrine of the Trinity on the other? To answer this question a prior question must be settled, namely, what is the relationship between Christian monotheism and the Christian doctrine of the Trinity? If the latter doctrine is but an *addition* to the former, then the connection between Christian trinitarian doctrine on the one hand and Jewish and Islamic monotheism on the other can at best be tenuous.

Rahner's thesis on this question is that the Christian doctrine of the Trinity is a *radicalization* of Christian monotheism: "[T]he doctrine of the Trinity can and must be understood not as a supplement or attenuation of Christian monotheism, but as its radicalization, assuming only that this monotheism is itself taken really seriously as concrete monotheism based on the experience of salvation history which does not banish God in his oneness out of Christianity's experience of salvation history and into a metaphysically abstract solitude."[36]

In what sense is the doctrine of the Trinity a radicalization of monotheism? There are two explanations for this, the first of which is not given in Rahner's one dialogue with Islam but has been furnished elsewhere at great length.[37] Basically, for Rahner, the New Testament uses the word *ho theos* not only to indicate ("stand for" or "refer to" = *supponere*) but also to signify or mean (*significare*) God the Father. In other words, "God" in the New Testament does not mean "divine nature" (*divinitas* or *deitas*) but the Father of our Lord Jesus Christ, the concrete person who possesses unoriginately the divine nature and communicates it to the Son by eternal generation and to the Spirit by active spiration. In brief, "God" is the *fons trinitatis*. The Son and the Spirit are "God" insofar as they receive their "nature" from the act of self-communication of the Father.[38] In this way, the Father in the Christian trinitarian doctrine is no other than the one God of concrete monotheism, or to put the matter somewhat differently, the doctrine of the Trinity is the radicalization of Christian monotheism.

The second reason for Rahner's thesis is summarized in his formula that the economic Trinity is the immanent Trinity and vice versa. Christians, Rahner suggests, experience God in the history of salvation as the incomprehensible mystery called God the Father in two distinct modalities, namely, as origin, history, invitation, and knowledge in Jesus of Nazareth on the one hand and as future, transcendence, acceptance, and love in the Holy Spirit on the other. These two radically distinct yet unified modalities in which the one God communicates himself to humans in history and in their self-transcendence (the economic Trinity) are also the two modalities in which the one God, the Father, exists in God's inner self, namely, as Logos and as Holy Spirit (the immanent Trinity).[39]

Of course there is the danger that these two distinct yet unified modes of the self-communication of the one God can be misunderstood as (1) two distinct divine subjects in addition to God (hence the danger of tritheism) or as (2) two simply *created* modes in which the one God is present in history (hence the danger of abstract monotheism). Christian faith rejects both interpretations and affirms "that the one sole God as himself is close to man in two modes of factuality and that these two modes of factuality are themselves God,"[40] even though it cannot offer a higher rational synthesis of these two affirmations.

Thus, if Christian faith holds that the one unoriginated God called the Father has eternally in himself two modes of self-communication as Logos and Holy Spirit (the classical doctrine of "processions") and has communicated himself historically in Jesus of Nazareth as Word, and has likewise established himself as Spirit in the innermost center of intellectual creatures as their dynamism and goal (the classical doctrine of "missions"), then, Rahner argues, the doctrine of the Trinity is neither an amendment of nor a mere addition to Christian monotheism but rather its radicalization. Consequently it is fully compatible with Jewish and Islamic monotheism.

This being the case, Rahner is anxious to remove any language in trinitarian theology that might lead to misunderstanding. One of the possibly offending expressions is "three persons." Given the modern understanding of person as subject of self-consciousness in knowledge and freedom, it is only natural that upon hearing this expression one imagines that in God there are three distinct realities with reciprocal relationships or at least three reciprocally related centers of self-awareness[41]. Such understanding, however, is liable to the error of tritheism. In order to prevent this possible misunderstanding, Rahner proposes to speak of the one God subsisting in three distinct "manners of subsisting" (*Subsistenzweisen*).[42] One may quarrel with this way of speaking and reject it as too impersonal and not conducive to piety; Rahner himself was aware of this criticism[43] and retorted that such a charge is missing the point.[44] Be that as it may, the important point in the dialogue with Islam is that every care should be taken to avoid giving the impression that the Christian doctrine of the Trinity asserts that there are three "subjects" in God. Rahner points out that it is not absolutely necessary to use the expression "three persons" to present a correct doctrine of the Trinity, and that the word "person" is not used univocally when predicated of the three "persons" in God. As Rahner puts it:

At any rate we cannot be content to make use of any kind of blurred, indistinct concept of 'person,' continually in a process of historical development, when speaking about three persons in God, and then to assume that we have understood and correctly expressed the dogma of the Trinity. . . . Even an Islamic theologian may and must allow for the possibility that his denial of the Christian doctrine of the Trinity may be no more than a denial of a proposition that by no means expresses the content of that doctrine, since even a Christian theologian does not find it easy in his own thinking to avoid misunderstandings of the term 'person' which he is continually using.[45]

With these reflections Rahner is well aware that he has not carried out a *dialogue* with Islam; that would require a familiarity with Islamic theology which he admits he does not possess. What he has done is to show that on his understanding of the Trinity (which he claims to be quite orthodox) there is no contradiction between the doctrine of the Trinity and Islamic (and Jewish) monotheism. But if the doctrine of the Trinity is but a radicalization of monotheism, the question arises as to whether in their reflections on their own monotheism Jewish and Islamic theologians should not entertain a more open attitude toward the Christian belief in the Trinity.

CRITICAL REFLECTIONS

A fair assessment of Rahner's position on Judaism and Islam must take into account the limitations imposed upon him by the circumstances and literary genres in which he expressed his views (an interview and a lecture). I have already referred to these constraints as well as the issues which should have been broached (e.g., the theology of the covenant(s), the Christian mission to the Jews, the Christian interpretation of the Hebrew Scripture, the impact of the *shoah* on Christian theology, and the question of the state of Israel) so as to delineate Rahner's views more sharply and extensively. In this last section of the essay I will point out some of the strengths of Rahner's theology with respect to Judaism and Islam as well as aspects in which it could be further developed in light of contemporary Christian theologies of Judaism and Islam.

Common Ground Gained

One of the more salient features of Rahner's discussion of Judaism is the way in which he consistently applies his theology of "anonymous

Christians" to the issues of the role of Christ in the history of salvation and the significance of Judaism as a religion today. On the one hand he vigorously affirms the role of Jesus as the universal savior; hence his expressed desire that Lapide be baptized, even though it may sound offensive at first hearing, is entirely logical since one may and should wish to others what one considers to be an objective good.[46] On the other hand Rahner explicitly recognizes the saving efficacy of Judaism and even the positive redemptive function of the Jewish no to Jesus, though he hastens to add that such redemptive function is ultimately grounded in Jesus.[47]

Rahner's position is of course acceptable to neither exclusivists nor pluralists. For the former it unduly relativizes the universal necessity of an explicit faith in Jesus as the Christ for salvation; for the latter it still labors under excessive Christocentrism that smacks of arrogance and leads to a stalemate in interreligious dialogue. I myself would argue that Rahner's inclusivist stance is not only innocent of the charges of both exclusivists and pluralists but also better equipped than its two rival theories to carry out a dialogue with other religions.[48] I do think, however, that Rahner's position on the status of the Jewish covenant and the Christian mission to Jews still leaves something to be desired. Before turning to these themes I would like to single out two other aspects of Rahner's theology that make a significant contribution to the Christian dialogue with Judaism and Islam.

First, as regards the Jewishness of Jesus, Rahner clearly recognizes its fundamental importance for christology, a theological principle increasingly affirmed by contemporary biblical scholars and theologians.[49] He correctly points out that on the one hand not everything historical in Jesus' Jewish background is of binding value and on the other hand that something non-historical but deducible from Jesus' general human nature may be normative for Christians of today. It is regrettable that Rahner has not spelled out more explicitly criteria for making such distinctions; nevertheless his remarks are helpful for a discussion on the Jewishness of Jesus to counter both historical fundamentalism and ethical relativism.

Secondly, Rahner's trinitarian theology, which is shown to be a radicalization of Christian monotheism, will prove enormously helpful in making Jewish and Islamic theologians understand that there is no opposition between their monotheistic belief and the Christian faith in the Trinity. Whereas we are aware that Lapide reacts positively to Rahner's trinitarian theology from his Jewish perspective, we do not know how his

Islamic audience would receive his lecture. Nevertheless, if Rahner's dual affirmation that monotheism is the fundamental article of Christian faith and that the Christian doctrine of the Trinity is not an addition to but a radical deepening of Christian monotheism are both true, there is no reason to believe that Muslims will have insurmountable objections to the doctrine of the Trinity. Of course, the fact that Jesus is confessed by the Qur'an to be a "Spirit from God" (*ruhun mina' Llah*) and the "Word of God" (*kalimatu-Llah*) and that his titles include Messiah (*masih*), Prophet (*nabi*), and Messenger of God (*rasul*) does not make the Christian belief in his "divinity" acceptable to Muslims. Nevertheless, Rahner's reflections on the Trinity go a long way toward dispelling the suspicion, common among Muslims, that Christians worship three Gods (or even four, if Mary is included in the Trinity, as is often thought by Muslims).[50]

Steps Still To Be Taken

In his assessment of Rahner's dialogue with Lapide, Vorgrimler notes that "he carried on his discussion with the Jew Pinchas Lapide as an individual, in the light of the theology of Rahner, and not in the context of the Jewish-Christian conversation, which in the meantime had moved further on. That indicates that although he was asked about almost everything by outsiders, he was not up to date with all developments to the same degree."[51] Rahner could hardly be blamed for this lack of familiarity with contemporary developments in the Jewish-Christian dialogue or even in the conversations among the three Abrahamic faiths, given the enormous amount of literature on these complex issues. There are, however, two areas in which Rahner's view of Judaism would have been enriched or even modified in the light of current theologies operative in the Jewish-Christian dialogue.

The first concerns his understanding of the Jewish covenant. As has been mentioned above, Rahner was not explicitly questioned on whether it is still necessary and possible to speak of the Jewish covenant being "fulfilled" by Jesus in the sense of being superseded. As is well known, Christian theologians had long been operating under the category of *Heilsgeschichte* in which it customary to view the relationship between Judaism and Christianity in terms of promise (prophecy) and fulfillment. One of the implications of this "displacement" model is that Israel's election as the people of God and the covenant God made with Israel has come to an end and that the Church has replaced Israel. Rahner himself worked within this paradigm, especially in his theology of revelation, even if he did not hold the concomitant view that the continuing existence of the Jews is a sign of divine rejection and punishment.[52]

Recently, however, both theologians and the official documents of various churches have begun to question the validity of this position. In Christian-Jewish dialogue it is now customary to classify various Christian theologies of the covenant into three types: single-covenant, double-covenant, and multi-covenant perspectives.[53] The single-covenant view conceives of Jews and Christians as basically partners of an ongoing, integrated covenantal tradition lived out by each not so much in different contents as in different modes. In this view Gentiles can be saved only through linkage with the Jewish covenant, something made possible in and through the Christ event.[54] The double-covenant view emphasizes the distinctiveness of each covenantal tradition but insists that both are ultimately crucial for the complete emergence of the Kingdom of God.[55] The multi-covenant perspective regards the Jewish and Christian covenants as two among an undetermined number of covenants that God makes with different religious traditions among which none can claim universality and normativity for others.[56]

As has been pointed out above, Rahner's theology of religions would find itself in conflict with the third, multi-covenant perspective. But there is no serious difficulty to expand it beyond the now-discredited "displacement" model to include the single-covenant and even the double-covenant perspectives. There is no absolute contradiction between affirming in faith that Jesus Christ is the universal savior and affirming that being saved by Christ also means being inserted into the Jewish covenant with God which continues to be valid. Furthermore, Rahner's position on Judaism can avert two dangers inherent in these perspectives. The single-covenant perspective runs the risk of absorbing, albeit in a benign form, Judaism; this risk is countered by Rahner's explicit, though tepid, recognition of the continuing validity of the Jewish covenant. On the other hand, the temptation of the double-covenant perspective is to belittle the Jewish roots of Christianity; this temptation is avoided by Rahner's unambiguous recognition of the Jewishness of Jesus.

This expansion of Rahner's theology of Judaism, however, would require a modification of his view of the Christian mission to Jews, and this is the second area of concern. Recall Rahner's expressed wish that Lapide be baptized in the present age. The question is therefore: In what way should Christians give witness of their faith to Jews? Like the issue of covenant, the question of Christian mission to Jews has undergone a drastic evolution. Of course, forced conversion and proselytism in the pejorative sense of the term are now universally rejected. But the question remains: Does the universal missionary command given to the Christian Church include Jews among its targets? While still maintaining the obligation of the Church to bear witness to the saving work of Christ to all, including Jews, many churches have lately come to recognize an essential difference between "mission" to the non-Jewish people who are not yet Christian and "dialogue" with Jews. For instance, the Declaration of the Synod of the Evangelical Church in the Rhineland (1980) affirms:

> We believe that in their respective calling Jews and Christians are witnesses of God before the world and before each other. Therefore we are convinced that the church may not express its witness towards the Jewish people as it does its mission to the peoples of the world.[57]

A further step was taken by the Texas Conference of Churches (1982) when it affirms:

> In response to this movement of the Holy Spirit today, we believe that the desired and most appropriate posture between Christians and Jews today is one of dialogue.[58]

Clearly this new position is quite different from the view that the mission to Jews has a special salvific significance insofar as the conversion of Jews is the eschatological event that will bring the history of the world to its climax and the view that the mission to Jews and the mission to others are identical.[59] In this perspective Rahner's category of "anonymous Christians," whatever its merits in describing non-Jewish non-Christians from the Christian viewpoint, appears not to serve well to express the special relationship between Jews and Christians. Jews are not "anonymous Christians," rather they are, to coin another word, "co-partner Christians" just as Christians are "co-partner Jews."

With these criticisms I do not intend to belittle Rahner's enormous contributions to the Christian theology of religions in general and to the dialogue with Judaism and Islam in particular. It is indeed admirable that he was already engaged in dialogue with Jews and Muslims when such dialogue was not yet fashionable (and even risky). Amazing also is the fruitfulness of his systematic theology when it is brought to bear on such diverse issues as relations with Judaism and Islam.

NOTES

[1]Rahner's theory can be found in his "Anonymous Christians," *Theological Investigations* (=*TI*), vol. 8, tr. Karl -H. and Boniface Kruger (New York: Crossroad, 1982), 390-98; "Anonymous Christianity and the Missionary Task of the Church," *TI*, vol. 12, tr. David Bourke (New York: The Seabury Press, 1976), 280-94; "Anonymous and Explicit Faith," *TI*, vol. 16, tr. David Morland (New York: The Seabury Press, 1979), 52-59; "The One Christ and the Universality of Salvation," ibid., 199-224. The most comprehensive study of Rahner's theory is Nikolaus Schwerdtfeger, *Gnade und Welt. Zum Grundfüge von Karl Rahners Theorie der "anonymen Christen"* (Freiburg: Herder, 1982). The theory has been criticized from two opposite directions: for some (e.g., Hans Urs von Balthasar) it dilutes the uniqueness of Christianity; for others (e.g., Paul Knitter) it represents an imperialist imposition of Christian categories on non-Christian religions. For an able defense of Rahner's view see Gavin D'Costa, *Theology of Religious Pluralism: The Challenge of Other Religions* (Oxford: Basil Blackwell, 1986). For a discussion of exclusivism, inclusivism, and pluralism, see Alan Race, *Christians and Religious Pluralism. Patterns in the Christian Theology of Religions* (Maryknoll, N.Y.: Orbis, 1987); Gavin D'Costa (ed.), *Christian Uniqueness Reconsidered: The myth of a Pluralistic Theology of Religions* (Maryknoll, N.Y.: Orbis, 1990); Peter C. Phan, "Are There Other 'Saviors' for Other Peoples? A Discussion of the Problem of the Universal Significance and Uniqueness of Jesus the Christ," *Christianity and the Wider Ecumenism*, ed. Peter C. Phan (New York: Paragon House, 1990), 163-80.

[2]For a short account of Rahner's various dialogical activities, see Herbert Vorgrimler, *Understanding Karl Rahner. An Introduction to His Life and Thought*, tr. John Bowden (New York: Crossroad, 1986), 111-20. Rahner's lectures delivered at these meetings with natural scientists and Marxists have been published in various volumes of *TI*. For his ecumenical dialogue, see the important work he co-authored with Heinrich Fries, *Unity of the Churches. An Actual Possibility*, tr. Ruth C. L. Gritsch and Eric W. Gritsch (Philadelphia: Fortress, 1985).

[3]See *Understanding Karl Rahner*, 120.

[4]See "Unbefangenheit und Anspruch (zusammen mit F. G. Friedmann). Ein Briefwechsel zum jüdisch-christlichen Gespräch," *Stimmen der Zeit* 91 (1966) 81-97. Rahner's letter is found on pp. 92-97. Rahner's other early writings on Jewish issues include: "Einführung zu: A. Neher, *Dein verkannter Bruder. Ein Jude sieht uns Christen* (Freiburg i. Br.: Lebendige Kirche, 1961), 3-5; "Bekenntnis zu Jesus Christus," in: J. J. Schultz (ed.), *Juden, Christen, Deutsche* (Stuttgart, 1961), 149-58.

[5]Originally published in 1983 by Matthis-Grünewald-Verlag, Mainz and translated into English by Davis Perkins. Published by Crossroad, New York in 1987 under the title *Encountering Jesus--Encountering Judaism. A Dialogue* (=EJEJ). These two conversations took place in July and October, 1982 in the (Jesuit) University of Innsbruck, Austria. Pinchas Lapide (1922-) an Orthodox Israeli Jew, was on the faculty of Bar Ilan University in Israel and worked for the foreign service of the Israeli government before devoting himself exclusively to Jewish-Christian dialogue in Germany. His works include his earlier (1978) dialogue with Jürgen Moltmann on the Trinity published as *Jewish Monotheism and Christian Trinitarian Doctrine*, tr. Leonard Swidler (Philadelphia:

Fortress, 1981); *Israelis, Jews and Jesus* (New York: Doubleday, 1979); *The Resurrection of Jesus: A Jewish Perspective*, tr. Wilhelm C. Linss (Minneapolis: Augsburg, 1983).

[6]For a detailed history of this document (*Nostra Aetate*), see the commentary of John Oesterreicher in *Commentary on the Documents of Vatican II*, ed. Herbert Vorgrimler, vol. III (New York: Herder and Herder, 1969) 1-136. Rahner correctly notes that "the relationship of the Church to the Jews on the one hand and to non-Christian religions on the other should not be treated in one and the same document because these relationships are essentially different" (*EJEJ*, 4) It is well-known that the original intention of Vatican II was to deal with Judaism in a separate document, but because of the opposition of the Arab groups, it was finally decided to deal with Judaism together with other non-Christian religions in one and the same document.

[7]*EJEJ*, 7.

[8]Ibid, 9-10.

[9]Ibid., 10.

[10]Ibid., 16.

[11]It is true that at a later point in the dialogue Lapide does suggest that Rahner consider Christians as "incorporated" into the covenant people, as "co-citizens, co-heirs, and co-partakers of the promise," and not as "successor, usurper, expropriator, or even as heir of a still vital Israel." Still, he does not present the issue in terms of the number of covenant(s) as formulated above. To this suggestion Rahner simply replies that in spite of all that Paul has said about the relationship between Jews and Christians (Eph. 2:19; 3:6) "the final decisive question" is "whether Jesus is also the redeemer of the Jews and is recognized as such by them" (ibid., 59).

[12]See ibid., 3-32. For Lapide, the expression "the God of Abraham, the God of Isaac, and the God of Jacob" is shorthand for a triple way of experiencing God: God who leads the way (Abraham), God the guardian (Isaac), and God the combative angel (Jacob). Rahner, on the other hand, refers to the icon of Andrew Rublev as the classic artistic representation of the Trinity. For Lapide's more extensive discussion of Jewish monotheism and Christian trinitarianism, see *Jewish Monotheism and Christian Trinitarian Doctrine: A Dialogue by Pinchas Lapide and Jürgen Moltmann* (Philadelphia: Fortress, 1981).

[13]Lapide suggests that "what is written in burning devotion and with passionate love may contradict itself a hundred times over without diminishing its profound truth-content in the least" (*EJEJ*, 41). At a later point in the conversation, Rahner again rejects both Lapide's distinction between the logic of the head and the logic of the heart and his justification of this distinction on the basis of mysticism (especially that of Meister Eckhart). For him, the question is not so much the difference between head and heart as the acknowledgement by reason itself of its own limitations and that on its own principles: "For me human rationality only reaches its apex when it rejects as a false pretension the notion of itself as a final authority, and realizes that it must do so according to its own principles" (ibid., 45).

[14]Ibid., 51. For his part, Rahner points out that St. Ignatius of Loyola already had a considerable interest in the Jewishness of Jesus, especially his poverty. See ibid., 50-51.

[15]Ibid., 56. The question is of course as old as Christianity itself, as the discussion at the so-called Council of Jerusalem (see Acts 15) attests. Paul's polemics against Judaism betrays similar concerns, even though in his polemics Paul was, as Rahner frankly admits, "is often simply un-Christian" (ibid., 53). The same issue lies behind the various attempts at defining the "essence" of Christianity.

[16]Ibid., 68.

[17]Ibid., 71. For an extensive study of Rahner's understanding of the beatific vision, see my *Eternity in Time: A Study of Karl Rahner's Eschatology* (Selinsgrove: Susquehanna University Press, 1988), 142-49.

[18]*EJEJ*, 72. Lapide does not refer to any particular text in *Grundkurs des Glaubens: Einführung in den Begriff des Christentums* (Freiburg im Bresgau: Herder, 1976). ET by William V. Dych: *Foundations of Christian Faith: An Introduction to the Idea of Christianity* (New York: Seabury, 1978). Perhaps the clearest text is found in *Foundations*, 204-05 where Rahner argues that God's offer of forgiveness and divine life to humans is "final," "irrevocable," "unsurpassable" in Jesus. Therefore Jesus can be said to be the "absolute and eschatological savior."

[19]*EJEJ*, 72. In fairness to Lapide it must be said that Rahner does use the word "definitive" to describe God's offer of himself in Jesus and Jesus' acceptance of this offer. See, e.g., *Foundations*, 202. Nevertheless he misunderstands "definitive" to mean completed and ended, whereas for Rahner it simply means "irrevocable" and "unsurpassable." The future dimension of promise still remains.

[20]*EJEJ*, 79.

[21]Ibid., 82. This may sound arrogant on Rahner's part, but he himself grants Lapide the right to expect Rahner, from his Jewish conviction, to renounce his faith in the Incarnation.

[22]Ibid., 84

[23]Ibid.

[24]See ibid., 85.

[25]Ibid., 98.

[26]Ibid., 100.

[27]Ibid., 102 *passim*. Franz Mussner's work has been translated into English with an introduction by Leonard Swidler as *Tractate on the Jews: The Significance of Judaism for Christian Faith* (Philadelphia: Fortress, 1984).

[28]*EJEJ*, 109.

[29]See, for instance, Gerard S. Sloyan's still very useful *Is Christ the End of the Law?* (Philadelphia: Westminster, 1978); Samuel Sandmel, *Anti-Semitism in the New Testament?* (Philadelphia: Fortress, 1978) which maintains that anti-Semitism is neither an essential nor an irremovable element of Christianity; Rosemary Radford Ruether, *Faith and Fratricide: The Theological Roots of Anti-Semitism* (New York: Seabury, 1974) in which the author argues for the controversial thesis that anti-Semitism emerged in the New Testament as the "left hand of Christology"; John Oesterreicher, *Anatomy of Contempt* (South Orange, NJ: Seton Hall University Press, 1975) which rejects Ruether's thesis; *Anti-Semitism and the Foundations of Christianity*, ed. A. T. Davies (New York:

Paulist, 1979) which also reacts to Ruether's thesis; Leonard Swidler, Lewis John Eton, Gerard S. Sloyan, and Lester Dean, *Bursting the Bonds? A Jewish-Christian Dialogue on Jesus and Paul* (New York: Paulist, 1990); Helga Croner, Leon Klenicki and Lawrence Boadt (eds.), *Biblical Studies: Meeting Ground of Jews and Christians* (New York: Paulist Press, 1980); Richard Rousseau (ed.), *Christianity and Judaism: The Deepening Dialogue* (Scranton: Ridge Row Press, 1983).

[30]See, for instance, Charlotte Klein, *Anti-Judaism in Christian Theology*, tr. Edward Quinn (Philadelphia: Fortress, 1978); Eva Fleischner, *Judaism in German Christian Theology* (Scarecrow, 1975); John Pawlikowski, O.S.M., *The Challenge of the Holocaust for Christian Theology* (New York: The Anti-Defamation League of B'nai B'rith, 1980); idem, *What Are They Saying About Christian-Jewish Relations?* (New York: Paulist Press, 1980), 129-41; Elizabeth Schüssler Fiorenza and David Tracy (eds.), *The Holocaust as Interruption: A Question for Christian Theology. Concilium* 175 (Edinburgh: T. & T. Clark, 1984).

[31]See Otto Maduro (ed.), *Judaism, Christianity & Liberation: An Agenda for Dialogue* (Maryknoll, NY: Orbis, 1991); Naim Ateek, *Justice and Only Justice: A Palestinian Theology of Liberation* (Maryknoll, NY: Orbis, 1989).

[32]The original title is "Einzigkeit und Dreifaltigkeit Gottes im Gespräch mit dem Islam," published in *Schriften zur Theologie*, XIII, ed. Paul Imhof (Zürich: Benziger, 1978), 129-47. ET by Edward Quinn: *TI*, XVIII (New York: Crossroad, 1983), 105-21.

[33]For Rahner's trinitarian theology, see his *The Trinity*, tr. Joseph Donceel (New York: Seabury, 1974). Other helpful writings are: "Theos in the New Testament," *TI*, tr. Cornelius Ernst, I (London: Darton, Longman & Todd, 1966) 77-102; "Observations on the Doctrine of God in Catholic Dogmatics," *TI*, tr. Graham Harrison, IX (New York: Seabury, 1972) 127-44. For critical studies of Rahner's trinitarian theology, see M. de Franca Miranda, *O misterio de Deus em nossa vida: A doutrina trinitaria de Karl Rahner* (Saõ Paolo: Ed. Loyola, 1975) and "La teología trinitaria de K. Rahner," *Estudios Trinitarios* (Salamanca) 21:1-2 (1987), 7-168.

[34]"Oneness and Threefoldness of God," *TI*, vol. 18, 107.

[35]Ibid.

[36]Ibid., 109.

[37]See his "Theos in the New Testament," *TI*, I (London: Darton, Longman & Todd, 1961), 79-148.

[38]For a critique of Rahner's thesis, see Robert Warner, "Rahner on the Unoriginate Father," *The Thomist*, 55 (October 1991) 569-93. For a critique of Warner's critique, see my "Reflections on 'Rahner on the Unoriginate Father'," *The Thomist*, forthcoming.

[39]For Rahner's detailed exposition of this axiom, see *The Trinity*, 83-103.

[40]"Oneness and Threefoldness of God," 117-18.

[41]See *The Trinity*, 103-109.

[42]See ibid., 109-15. For a critique of Rahner's proposal, see Lawrence B. Porter, "On Keeping 'Persons' in the Trinity: A Linguistic Approach to Trinitarian Thought," *Theological Studies* 41, 3 (1980), 530-48.

[43]This line of criticism has been advanced by Walter Kasper. See his *The God of Jesus Christ*, tr. Matthew O'Connell (New York: Crossroad, 1984), 287-88.

[44]See *EJEJ*, 35: "Thus the reproach of Walter Kasper -- that one cannot pray to three modes of subsistence -- seems to me to miss the mark."

[45]"Oneness and Threefoldness of God," 114-15.

[46]By the same token Rahner also recognizes that other religionists have an equal right to wish that he be of whatever religious persuasion they believe to be objectively true, even though he himself is convinced that that religious persuasion is objectively not the right one. Thus, in his conversatin with Keji Nishitani, the Japanese philosopher and head of the Kyoto Zen Buddhist school, Rahner was asked how he would feel if he were to be called an anonymous Zen Buddhist. He replies: "Certainly you may and should do so from your point of view; I feel myself honored by such an interpretation, even if I am obliged either to regard you as being in error or to assume that, when correctly interpreted, being a genuine Zen Buddhist is identical with being a Christian rightly understood at *that* level properly and directly intended by such statements. Of course, in terms of objective and social awareness, it is indeed clear that neither a Buddhist is a Christian nor is a Christian a Buddhist." See "The One Christ and the Universality of Salvation," *TI*, tr. David Morland, XVI (New York: Seabury, 1979), 219 (translation emended).

[47]See *EJEJ*, 101.

[48]See my "Are There Other Saviors for Other Peoples?" in *Christianity and the Wider Ecumenism*, ed. Peter C. Phan (New York: Paragon, 1990), 163-80 and "Gott als Heiliges Mysterium und die Suche nach 'Gottes-Äquivalenten' im interreligiösen Dialog," *Zeitschrift für Missionswissenscaft und Religionswissenschaft* 3 (1990), 161-75. For an able defense of Rahner's position, see Gavin D'Costa, *Theology and Religious Pluralism* (Oxford: Basil Blackwell, 1986), 80-116 and for a recent elaboration of a Christian theology of religions along Rahnerian lines, see Jacques Dupuis, *Jesus Christ at the Encounter of World Religion*, tr. Robert Barr (Maryknoll, NY: Orbis, 1991).

[49]See the recent study of John P. Meier, *A Marginal Jew* (New York: Doubleday, 1992); Harvey Falk, *Jesus the Pharisee* (New York: Paulist, 1985) in which Jesus is shown to be close to the views of the Beth Hillel school of Pharisees and controverting those of the Shammaites; John Pawlikoski, O.S.M., *Christ in the Light of the Christian-Jewish Dialogue* (New York: Paulist Press, 1982) and *Jesus and the Theology of Israel* (Wilmington, DE: Michael Glazier, 1989), 48-70 in which Pharisaism is taken to be the key to christology; Pinchas Lapide, *The Sermon on the Mount*, tr. Arlene Swidler (Maryknoll, NY: Orbis, 1986) in which Matthew 5 is studied from a Jewish point of view; Bernard Lee, *The Galilean Jewishness of Jesus* (New York: Paulist Press, 1988); Leonard Swidler, *Yeshua: A Model for Moderns* (Kansas, MO: Sheed and Ward, 1988); James H. Charlesworth, *Jesus Within Judaism* (New York: Doubleday, 1988) in which the historical Jesus is studied in the light of recent archeological discoveries.

[50]For guidelines for dialogue between Christianity and Islam, see M. Borrmans (ed.), *Interreligious Documents: Guidelines for Dialogue Between Christians and Muslims* (New York: Paulist Press, 1990). For a journal dedicated to Catholic-Muslim issues, see *Islamochristiana*, published by the Pontifical Institute of Arabic Studies in Rome. For recent works on Christian-Muslim dialogue, see A. Schimmel and A. Falaturi (eds.), *We*

Believe in One God (New York: The Seabury Press, 1979) and Richard W. Rousseau (ed.), *Christianity and Islam: The Struggling Dialogue* (Scranton: Ridge Row, 1985).

[51]*Understanding Karl Rahner*, 121.

[52]See *Foundations of Christian Faith*, 164-70, in particular 168. In his article "Bekenntnis zu Jesus Christus," in: J. J. Schultz (ed.), *Juden, Christen, Deutsche* (Stuttgart, 1961), 151, Rahner terms Jesus "the finisher of the Old Testament." Parallel to this *Heilsgeschichte* theology of the covenant is the contrast (found mainly in continental Protestant thought) between Jewish legalistic pietism and the Christian gospel of freedom and grace. See a critique of this trend in Charlotte Klein, *Anti-Judaism in Christian Theology* (Philadelphia: Fortress, 1978), 39-91.

[53]See John Pawlikowski, *What Are They Saying About Christian-Jewish Relations?* (New York: Paulist Press, 1980), 33-67 and *Jesus and the Theology of Israel* (Wilmington, DE: Michael Glazier, 1989), 15-47.

[54]Pawlikowski argues that this position is held, of course with varying nuances, by Monika Hellwig, Marcel Dubois, Cardinal Carlo Martini of Milan, Michael Remaud, Pope John Paul II among Catholics; Berthold Klappert, Peter von der Osten-Sacken, Paul van Buren, A. Roy Eckardt, and J. Coos Schoneveld among Protestants. Among official Church documents which tend toward this position are to be noted the Vatican's *Notes on the Correct Way to Present the Jews and Judaism in Preaching and Catechesis in the Roman Catholic Church* (June 24, 1985) [available in *In Our Time: The Flowering of Jewish-Catholic Dialogue*, ed. Dr. Eugene J. Fisher and Rabbi Leon Klenicki (New York: Paulist, 1990), 38-50]; The Synod of the Evangelical Church of the Rhineland's *Towards Renovation of the Relationship of Christians and Jews* (January 1980) [available in *The Theology of the Churches and the Jewish People: Statements by the World Council of Churches and Its Member Churches* (Geneva: WCC Publications, 1988), 92-94].

[55]This position is held by Gregory Baum, Clemens Thoma and Franz Mussner among Catholics, and James Parkes and J. Coert Rylaarsdam among Protestants.

[56]This is the position of John Hick, Paul Knitter, and Rosemary Radford Ruether.

[57]*The Theology of the Churches and the Jewish People*, 93.

[58]Ibid., 97. It must be pointed out, however, that churches of a more evangelical stripe continue to affirm strongly the obligation to evangelize the Jews. See, for instance, The Willowbank Declaration on "The Christian Gospel and the Jewish People" (1989) and the Consultation on Jewish Evangelism of The Fourth International Lausanne Committee On World Evangelism at Zeist, The Netherlands, 1991 in: James A. Scherer and Stephen B. Bevans (eds.), *New Directions in Mission & Evangelization 1: Basic Statements 1974-1991* (Maryknoll, NY: Orbis, 1992), 306-14.

[59]For an overview of the issue of Christian mission to Jews, see Martin Cohen and Helga Croner (eds.), *Christian Mission--Jewish Mission* (New York: Paulist, 1982). Important in this discussion is the interpretation of Matthew 28:19, "Make disciples of all the *ethnē* (nations)." Daniel Harrington, S.J. and Douglas Hare have argued that "nations" should be understood in a Jewish context as referring to *goyim*. See their "Make Disciples of All the Gentiles," *Catholic Biblical Quarterly* 37 (1975), 359-69.

GOD AND CREATION IN JUDAISM AND ISLAM:

A PROPOSAL FOR DIALOGUE

Anne M. Clifford, C.S.J.

> Let mutual love continue.
> Do not neglect to show hospitality to strangers,
> for by doing that some have entertained angels without knowing it.
> --(Hebrews 13: 1-2)

In this exhortation the obvious allusion is to the story of Abraham's hospitality to the three strangers at Mamre in Genesis 18. At Abraham's bidding his visitors share a festive meal under a terebinth tree. The three are God's messengers who give to Abraham and Sarah words of promise and hope. As a result Abraham and Sarah are changed by this meeting, never to be the same.

The three religions that trace their lineage to Abraham could benefit from a Mamre experience, a meeting place in which mutual dialogue with respect and love is the goal. I envision this dialogue as one in which the objective is not to convert the other to one's own position, but rather to seek a better understanding of the other, as other.

If a dialogue between Jews, Muslims and Christians were to be initiated, what would be the topics for the first session? God and creation seem to be logical foundational topics with which to begin because 1) they are so basic to each religion, and 2) belief in one God who is Creator of the earth and the people who inhabit it discloses an inherent claim for universality.

This essay is envisioned as the first session of a dialogue between Jews and Muslims on God and creation, in which an interested Christian listens with a stance that takes to heart the exhortation of Hebrews to mutual love in hospitality to strangers.

CRITERIA FOR THE DIALOGUE

An interreligious dialogue is more than a haphazard conversation among believers from different traditions. Criteria are needed that help to keep the conversation well focused. In a recent essay Jacob Neusner outlined three helpful criteria for inter religious dialogue: 1) each party concedes the integrity of the other; 2) each party proposes to take seriously the position of the other; and 3) each remains open to the possibility of conceding the legitimacy of the other's view.[1] In his essay, Neusner called for a Jewish-Christian dialogue that would honor these criteria. It seems to me that his criteria would also be appropriate for a dialogue between Jews and Muslims in which a Christian might participate as a active listener.

The proposal to put myself, a Christian, in the position of listening to Judaism and Islam on God and creation is not meant to imply that dialogue can only take place between two parties. *Dia*-logue obviously does not mean two (the Greek prefix is *diá* and not *di*-) in contrast to *mono*-logue which clearly means only one speaker. Dialogue is discourse about common topics *through* (*diá*) which new understanding is gained. This means that as an active Christian listener, I must be willing to attend to the questions and assumptions of my own religious horizon, and try, as far as is possible, to bracket them in order to hear, really hear the others speak from their own horizons.

Dialogue, in the sense in which I am using it here, must obviously be built on Neusner's first criterion: respect for the integrity of the other as other. Judaism and Islam are two distinct religions that belong to the monotheistic family of religions. The term "Judaism" is difficult to define. Often Judaism is treated as a generic term applied to the religion of Israel or to the religion practiced by Jews.[2] However, since Judaism is so closely related to the people of Israel, within Jewish law being Jewish is a kind of citizenship. According to Rabbinic teaching, one is ethnically a Jew if one is born of a Jewish mother. This remains true even if one does not actively engage in the religious practices of Judaism. In contrast, Islam can be more directly defined; it is the religion brought from heaven through Muhammad. Islam, a term that appears in the Quŕan,[3] literally means "surrender" or "submission" [to God]. It is the religion practiced by Muslims. While the majority of people in the Arab states are Muslims, Islam is not associated closely with a particular nationality group, as is Judaism.

I have referred to Judaism and Islam as members of a family of religions, not to diminish their autonomy, but rather to stress that on many
levels these religions are similar. Both place a great deal of emphasis on
divine revelation. The primary source for the beliefs of Judaism and Islam
about God and creation, and about their identities as Jews and Muslims,
is God's inspired word. Judaism and Islam rely on revelation as the means
whereby God makes the divine will and purpose known to human creatures. Although, strictly speaking, revelation cannot be identified exclusively with the Tanakh or the Qur'an, for Judaism and Islam these sacred
texts provide the core of revelation.[4] Their authority rests with God but
the agents that brought the sacred books into being are human beings, holy
prophets. Because Jews (and Christians with them) look to revealed texts,
the Qur'an terms Jews (and Christians) *ahl al-kitab*, "People of the Book"
(Sura 2: 109-113 and *passim*).

Second, Judaism and Islam trace their geographic origins to the same
part of the world, the Middle East. Judaism and Islam (and Christianity,
as well) have developed, after two points in their common history, in close
contiguity with one another. Judaism and Islam not only share a common
region of origin, they also trace their origins to the remote figure,
Abraham/Ibrahim who is believed to have lived around 1750 B.C.E. Both
religions share a vision of a God of promise that can be traced to Abra-
ham/Ibrahim, a prophetic figure who personally received a special call
from God. This call required of him great trust in God. It is this trust,
modeled after that of Abraham/Ibrahim, that is the core of both Judaism
and Islam. From the perspective of their common monotheism, the
importance attached to divine revelation, their shared geographic birthplace and the common link to Abraham/Ibrahim, the metaphor of a family
is not inappropriate for these two religions.

All that said, respect for the integrity of each religion demands that
some significant differences be noted. While the common historical link
to Abraham/Ibrahim is significant, it is important to draw attention to a
major historical difference in their advent that separates them. One of the
reasons why Judaism is not easy to define is that Judaism has no obvious
and clearcut starting point. Some Jews trace Judaism's beginnings to
Abraham and God's promise of land (Israel) and progeny. More commonly, Jews look to Moses and the events that surround the Jews' deliverance from slavery and the sacred Sinai covenant as the origin of Judaism.
Ancient tradition holds that Moses was the author of the first five books
of the Tanakh, known as the Torah. The significance of Moses for

Judaism is kept ever before the Jews in one of the lines of scripture that Jews are expected to learn in earliest childhood so that it may be recited daily: "Moses charges us with the Torah; it is the heritage of the congregation of Jacob" (Deut. 33:4). Still others, however, trace modern Judaism to the Rabbinic movement which began in the first century after the Roman destruction of the temple.[5] It is this movement that gave Judaism the Mishnah and Talmud, which together constitute a supplement to Tanakh in the form of commentary and a second revelation from God. The difference in opinion among Jews themselves is owing to the fact that Judaism evolved by gradual stages that span long periods of time and in different geographic localities.

In contrast to Judaism, Islam has an obvious beginning with the prophet Muhammad (570-632 C.E.). The religion of Israel can be described as, in some sense, the parent of Islam because Islam in the Qur'an claims the revelations made to the patriarchs and prophets of Israel. Muslims, however, argue that Judaism's way of presenting Abraham and the other prophets of God and God's law is corrupt. Muslims contend that the biblical texts of the Jews (and the Christians) are a composite of human fabrication and God's inspired word. The Qur'an, since it was recited by God's angel to Muhammad verbatim and since it is a later revelation, abrogates (*naskh*) Tanakh and replaces it. Jews, in rebuttal, have argued that it is not possible for God to change the divine decree and dispensation once given; a change of mind is impossible for God.[6] What is curious about this argument is that Judaism, a religion that emerged through a long history, argues against Islam for ahistorical reasons. The historical books of the Torah and Nevi'im, although not history in the sense of factual chronological accounts, is salvation history that celebrates God's ongoing revelation to the people of Israel as their history evolves. As time passes, it does appear that earlier law such as that given to Jacob is superceded by a later law given to Moses. In contrast, Islam, a religion which traces its beginnings to 610 and a twenty-two year period of recitations (*qur'an*) of Gabriel (Jibril) to Muhammad, is not concerned with historical development at all. In compiling the angel's recitations, Muhammad was obviously not concerned with the historical succession of key figures and prophets, but rather with the unity of Allah's message. This message transcends history, regardless of when and how it was proclaimed.[7] Similarities in revelation are due to their common divine source; differences occur where Judaism (and Christianity) departed from the original revelation of God.

This is one example among many that highlights the tension that constitutes the "otherness" of Judaism and Islam. Over the centuries much attention has been given to what divides Jews and Muslims, resulting in conflict over rival claims to land and to political and economic hegemony.

Turning to Neusner's requirement that in dialogue the positions of the other be taken seriously, I recognize that I must be attentive to the fact that I am looking at the religions of Judaism and Islam as a Christian "outsider." As a Christian, I must guard against subjecting the autonomy of Judaism and Islam to criteria from within Christianity which these religions exclude or hold to be unimportant. Failure to do so will block the possibility for true dialogue.

One point that must be given attention immediately is the way in which Christianity views religion and theology versus the ways Judaism and Islam view them. Christians have at times spoken of religion in terms of creed, code and cult. Emphasis is often placed, however, on theology, a second level reflection that gives more attention to doctrines that explain beliefs than to ethics and worship. This is so because in the history of Christianity denials of beliefs have led to dogmas and doctrines that have become central to Christian self-identity. In contrast, Jews tend to speak of Judaism not so much as a religion of creeds, but as a way of life centered on the study of Torah and its revered commentaries, beginning with the Talmud and guided by *mitzvot* or sacred commandments. In a similar vein, although Islam has beliefs, theological doctrines do not play a central role in the way most Muslims perceive Islam. As the term implies, Islam focuses on submission to God's will. The term "Muslim" means one who submits to God. A Muslim is more concerned with worship of God and obedience to God, as a source of peace, than with specific doctrines. In this regard, Islam is closer in spirit and practice to Judaism than to Christianity. Especially as it has developed in the West, Christianity stresses doctrinal clarity and understanding. Judaism and Islam put more emphasis on religion as a way of life and a ritual patterning of that life under God's guidance. There is a great sense of security in both religions in maintaining proper worship and following divine guidance by "commanding the good and forbidding the evil," as the Qur'an puts it.[8]

The third criterion calls for each party to concede the legitimacy of the other's viewpoint. Obviously, the best an outsider can hope to achieve in applying this criterion is to present the perspectives of Judaism and Islam as accurately and in as balanced a way as possible. My primary interest in setting up a dialogue between Judaism and Islam on God and creation is to uncover the commonalities in the perspectives shared by these religions. What is to follow should be regarded as a preliminary, session in what should be a much more lengthy dialogue.

GOD IN JUDAISM AND ISLAM

Not only are the two religions radically monotheistic, the names for God in each are closely related. In Judaism a common name for God is *El*, an ancient name for divinity that occurred throughout the Fertile Crescent. *El* and *Elohim* are frequently found in the Tanakh. *El* has the same root as the Arabic *ilah*, which when combined with the definite article, *al*, becomes *Allah*, the name for God found in the Qur'an.[9]

In addition to the generic *El* and *Elohim*, Judaism has other names for God. The most sacred is the not to be pronounced name *YHVH*, revealed to Moses on Mt. Horeb (Exodus 3:15).[10] Because not spoken from the sixth century B.C.E. onward, *YHVH* presents God as essentially unknowable. God is also called by many other appellations chiefly *Adonai* (Lord), spoken when *YHVH* appears in the text, *El Shaddai* (God the Almighty), *El Elyon* (God Most High), etc. These names do not present God in the essence of godhead, but rather represent the various effects of God upon Israel as God's chosen people. In addition, there are numerous narrative images for God presented in biblical narratives and in the Psalms that highlight God's activity and functions in the history of Israel. Images such as that of a warrior King (Ps. 136), a concerned Shepherd (Ps. 23), a Mother giving birth (Deut. 32:18), all of which imply that God is a person and is to be related to as such.

Very importantly, the variety of names and narrative images do not detract from the most central belief of Judaism: God is one. This belief gradually emerged among the Jews early in their history[11] and has united all Jews regardless of culture or denomination. The belief that God is one is affirmed by Jews in the *Shema*, Israel's most prominent confession of faith, which opens with these words: "Hear, O Israel, the Lord our God, the Lord is One" (Deut. 6:4).[12]

The proper response of the Jew to the one God is expressed in the verse that follows. "You shall love the Lord your God with all your heart and with all your soul and with all your might" (v. 5). How is one to love God? Over the centuries Jewish commentators have explained this love in a variety of ways; some center more on actions, others more on contemplation. An ancient Midrash maintains that the best way to express love for God is for Jews to conduct themselves in a manner that makes God beloved by others.[13] Following this interpretation, it is by attention to the *mitzvot*, God's sacred commandments, that the Jews, as well as others, will be aware of the One in whose name they are performed. Each *mitzvah* done in the right spirit is an act of love for God. Citing medieval commentators such as Bahya ben Asher and Moses Maimonides, Steven Harvey argues that the traditional normative way in Judaism is that "one loves God by reflecting on his Torah, coming to comprehend him, delighting in him and ultimately leading others to do likewise."[14]

The *Shema* holds a position of importance in Jewish practice unparalleled by any other verses of Tanakh. It is recited daily, morning and evening, by many Jews and affirms the exclusive fidelity of Jews to God as one. But what does "one" mean? First of all, it means that there is only one God, not many, as the pagan religions that surrounded biblical Israel supposed. So, on one level, the *Shema* is a protest against idolatry. The full significance of this protest cannot be grasped unless the question-- What were the idols of paganism against which Judaism protested? --is raised. Neusner points out that in the worship of the pagan neighbors of the Jews, worldly phenomena were deified. Manifestations of nature were treated as aspects of "a mysterious supernatural vitality."[15] Judaism's monotheism affirms that God is transcendent over nature; God created the world and is completely different from it. The God of Israel has no myth of birth, nor is God subject to nature or any primordial reality.

Implied in the word "one" of the *Shema*, is a further and very far reaching idea, which was reflected on theologically by Jews in the middle ages. Although Jews have not often engaged in formal theology, in medieval Spain Jewish intellectuals influenced by Christian and Muslim thinkers did. The most highly regarded Jewish thinker of this period is Moses Maimonides (1135-1204) who presented Judaism with a list of doctrines, the "Thirteen Principles of Faith."[16] Although Judaism has never developed a formal consensus on Maimonides' principles, this is the most widely recognized list of doctrines among Jews. The first five principles deal directly with God. The second principle affirms the "unique unity of God. Not only is God one, but the oneness of God is unlike any other. God is not merely less than two, but one in a unique way."[17]

In commenting on the phrase "one in a unique way," Louis Jacobs argues that the meaning is not merely that there is only one God. Rather, Judaism is saying that God being God can only be one. God is alone brought everything into existence. God, as Judaism understands God, is

not a being among others. God is the only Being and Source of all that
is.[18] It logically follows, therefore that belief in God as uniquely one is
closely related to belief in God as the Creator of the universe. On the
basis of the analysis of Neusner and Jacobs, it seems fitting that in the
daily morning service the recitation of the *Shema* prayer follows two
berakhot (blessings), the first of which is a lengthy blessing for creation.
This prayer begins with these words: "Praised be You, O Lord our God,
King of the universe, Who form light and create darkness, who make
peace and create all things."[19]

In the tradition of Judaism, all prayer and worship is called service
of the Creator. This service also encompasses the whole range of activities
that constitute a Torah way of life: reading the Torah, observing the
mitzvot, and leading a good ethical life in one's home and the public
arena.

Like Judaism, Islam adheres strictly to belief in one God. Muslims
give witness to this belief in a confession of faith called the *Shahadah*:
"There is no god but Allah and Muhammad is the Messenger (or Proph-
et/Apostle) of God." The *Shahadah* is for Islam what the *Shema* is for
Judaism. The daily recitation of the *Shahadah* is the first of Islam's "Five
Pillars." The two independent clauses of this simple confession have
enormous significance for Islam. Muhammad grew up in a world in which
tribal loyalty to a plurality of gods was the rule. The purpose of his
prophetic message on behalf of God was to terminate idolatry and establish
the worship of God (Allah) alone. This is clearly expressed in Sura 22
of the Qur̓an. In the context of directives about the ritualized slaughter
of animals for food, the Muslim is reminded: "Dedicate yourselves to God
and serve none besides him" (31) . . . "Your God is one God; to Him
surrender yourselves" (34).

Faith in one God and in the absolute unity of God is a doctrine that
is central to Islam. It requires more than mere intellectual assent. The
Muslim is directed to make God "One" by means of daily prayer and
devotion and by refusal to compromise this belief.[20] The centrality of
belief in one God is emphasized not only in the *Shahada*, it is also the
emphasis in the opening Sura of the Qur̓an, the *Fatihah*:

> In the Name of God the Compassionate, the Merciful,
> Praise be to God, Lord of the Universe [or of Creation],[21]
> The Compassionate, the Merciful, Sovereign of the Day of Judgment!
> You alone we Worship, and You alone we turn for help.
> Guide us to the straight path,

The path of those You have favored,
Not of those who have incurred Your wrath,
Nor of those who have gone astray.[22]

The *Fatihah* is an exhortation which sums up the essence of the faith of the Qur̄an. This prayer begins by recalling the greatness of God, a pattern repeated at the beginning of each Sura with the exception of the ninth. According to the second of the "Five Pillars," Islamic law requires that the *Fatihah* be recited five times daily in the standing position. In a very real sense, no prayer, whether in public or private is complete without the recitation of the *Fatihah*. All Muslims are obliged to memorize it in Arabic.[23]

Additional verses that Muslims are required to memorize in Arabic are those of Sura 112, the *Al-Ikhlas*, often referred to as the "Chapter of the Pure Religion."[24] These verses, which are believed to be one of the earliest revelations of God to Mohammed, focus on the uniqueness and oneness of God to whom the Muslim is to surrender his/her life:

In the name of God, the Merciful, the Compassionate
Say: God is One, the Eternal God.
He begot none, nor was He begotten.
None is equal to Him (1-4).

In this brief recitation found in the final chapters of the Qur̄an, the oneness of God is explained with emphasis on the fact that nothing is comparable to God. God has no son, no father, no brother, no wife, no sister and no daughter. In God's unity, God is conspicuously unique.[25]

The name Allah occurs some twenty-five hundred times in the Qur̄an;[26] this is the "Supreme Name" for God. But in addition to the name Allah, says a *Hadith*, a sacred tradition from the Prophet: "Verily, there are ninety-nine Names for Allah."[27] Among the ninety-nine Names are names for God directly revealed in the Qur̄an and others derived indirectly, plus a few non-Quaranic traditional names. The Names highlight God's attributes. Included among them are names for God that explicitly relate to creation such as those found in Sura 59:24: "the Creator, the Originator, the Modeler." In addition to these are "the Giver of Life" (Sura 30:50) and "the Provider" (Sura 51: 57).

Islam does not believe that any of these epithets can capture the essence of God because they are functional. The names of God describe God's activity; they do not define God's nature. The names have to do with relationship--God's to us of sovereignty and ours to God of submission.[28] The primary way to express the submission owed to God is in worship. Through liturgical prayer, Muslims, both individually and collectively, give God the glory and praise that is proper and due. For God alone is the Mighty, the Wise One (Sura 59:26).

By way of summary, belief in One God in Judaism and Islam is not significantly different. In both religions, confessions of faith and public prayer make belief in one God absolutely central. The God of Islam is the same God to whom Jews pray. Like Judaism, Islam has no myth about the birth of God. God is not dependent on any primordial reality; nothing in creation is comparable to God. For this reason, both Judaism and Islam ban images or representations of God. Neither Judaism nor Islam claims to know God in God's essence. God is known through God's activity and through human responses to God. Jews express this response as love, a love closely tied to the study of the Torah and the observance of the sacred *mitzvot*. Muslims typify their response as submission to God's will guided by the Qur'an and by the *Sunnah* and *Hadith*, the sacred traditions ascribed to Muhammad. In the view of most Muslims, Islam is not a new religion.[29] There is definitely truth to that claim in that Judaism and Islam both believe in one God, the same God, although each religion specifies response to God differently. To this Christian outsider there does not seem to be a great deal of disparity between love of God embodied in obedient observance of the Torah and submission to God's will as it is revealed in Islam's holy books.

CREATION IN JUDAISM AND ISLAM

On a theoretical level, it is possible to speak of God in Judaism and Islam without also speaking of creation, because God does not need creation to be God. God's creation of the universe by free act is a religious belief that Jews and Muslims share. Creation, it would seem, can be approached in a narrow and in a wide sense. In the narrow sense, creation can be conceived of as the divine activity whereby the world begins to exist. Here creation refers to the beginning of a world which God initiated. In the wider sense, creation can be discussed in terms of a continuing God--world relationship without specific reference to world origins.

The treatment of creation in Judaism and Islam provided below will focus, for the most part, on the biblical Torah and on the Qur'an because they are the primary sources for normative Judaism and Islam. Within the scope of this essay, it is not possible to do more. It is good to bear in mind, however, that Judaism has numerous texts that focus on creation in the Torah, the Nevi'im[30] and the Khetuvim,[31] written in different genres and in different historical circumstances. The narratives found in the initial chapters of Genesis will be the focus here because of their significance for Judaism and because their influence appears evident in the Qur'an.

A preliminary point of clarification is necessary. When speaking of the beginnings of creation, Christians often immediately bring to mind the doctrine *creatio ex nihilo*, which in modern times has been interpreted as a claim about a singular event in the distant past in which the world originated.[32] While *creatio ex nihilo* is accepted by both Judaism[33] and Islam, teachings on the *historical* genesis of the world have not been a major concern in these two religions. The Torah and the Qur'an speak of the beginning, not of history, as such, but of the world as distinct from God in God's transcendent unity.

The Torah begins with a poetic prologue in which the existence of God is taken for granted. In this text from the Priestly tradition of the Babylonian Exile period, God's creative activity unfolds in a six day process culminating in a seventh day in which God rested. A common English translation of the first line is: "In the beginning God created the heavens and the earth, the earth was a formless wasteland" (Genesis 1:1-2).[34] However, an alternate translation: "When God began to create the heaven and the earth, the earth being unformed and void" is also found in Jewish Bibles.[35] Such a variation in translation reflects an emphasis on the "chaos" out of which the Creator brings life and order.

The emphasis on order is substantiated in a remarkable rabbinic passage that argues that before God came to create the world, God first looked into the Torah, which existed even before the creation of the world, much as an architect consults a blueprint before beginning to build.[36] This tradition makes it clear that creation in the narrow sense of the beginnings of the world cannot be separated from creation in the broader sense of the God--world relationship. The rabbinic teaching that God consulted the Torah when creating the world is a metaphorical way of saying that the world is so constituted that it fits with the teachings of the Torah. By implication, when Jews observe the laws of the Torah, they are in tune with the Creator's order and are advancing the Creator's purpose for creation. A Torah way of life, therefore, may be said to have cosmic significance.

The Genesis 1 text builds to a climax on the sixth day with the creation of the first humans, who, male and female, are made in God's own image and likeness (1:26-27). These words of description reflect the Torah's abiding wonder over humanity's special stature in creation. Men and women have a special dignity because they bear the imprint of the Creator. Marveling at the powers of humans, the Psalmist refers to them as "little less than the angels" (Ps. 8:6). Interestingly, Genesis 1 says six times that God found creation "good," but after human beings, male and female, were created God found it "very good."

The narrative, of course does not end here. A seventh day follows on which God rested. For Judaism, this seventh day is the Sabbath. Built into the very structure of the universe, this day is a memorial to God's work of creation and the mark of Judaism's sacred covenant with God. Jews do not interpret this day of rest on God's part as implying that God needed rest. Leo Trepp points out that the meaning lies deeper: "God ceased to make the world all by Himself; henceforth people are his co-workers."[37] People carry on God's work during the six days of labor, but on the seventh, they rest and re-create themselves spiritually for the work that lies ahead. In a sense the Sabbath is a day set aside as the divine seal on the universe. The Sabbath day of rest provides order for human commerce and a constant reminder of God's sovereignty as creator.

The text of the Quṙan, in contrast to the Tanakh, does not begin with a creation narrative but with the *Fatihah*. However, this exhortation to faith contains a reference to God as the Lord of Creation. This is typical of the Quṙan; the subject of creation is not addressed in a continuous narrative line in the manner of Genesis but is often simply alluded to, frequently to support or illustrate another point. There seems to be good reason to conclude that Islam is less concerned with creation in the narrow sense of the beginnings, than with creation in the broad sense of the God-world relationship.

For its major creation themes the Quṙan appropriates material from the Genesis accounts of Judaism but gives them a unique slant.[38] Islam includes creation in six days in numerous passages of the Quṙan. For example, Sura 7:54 states:

> Your Lord is God, who created the heavens and the earth in six days and then ascended his throne. He throws the veil of night over the day. Swiftly they follow one another. It was He who created the sun, the moon and the stars, and made them subservient to His will. His is the creation, His the command. Blessed be God, the Lord of the Universe.

The Qur'an also makes allusions to the Genesis 1 account of creation in Sura 10:3; 11:7; 25:59; 32:4; 50:38; 57:4. In these passages, God is regarded as having created the heavens and the earth and all that is in them in six days. What happened on each day is not specified in these passages. In an additional passage, it is stated that in the first two days the heavens and the earth received their form, while the remaining four days were devoted to the creation of their contents (Sura 41: 8-9). Summarily, it is asserted that the creation of seven heavens took place in two days (Sura 41: 11-12).[39] From the variations in the texts, it would seem that the Qur'an is not particularly interested in the details of the beginnings of creation. In regard to the creation of the seven heavens, it is quite possible that the Qur'an is taking over a standard belief long held by pre-Islamic Arabs.[40]

Interestingly, the Qur'an points out that the notion of "day" in the "six days of creation" is not to be taken literally. God's day may be a thousand years by human reckoning (Sura 32:5). Elsewhere, the Qur'an indicates that God created the heavens and earth in six "periods" (Sura 50:38). From these passages, one may conclude that the length of time seems far less important than God's creation of the universe in an orderly fashion.

In contrast to Judaism, Islam does not teach that God rested after creating the universe. God needs no rest like humans and animals. God is absolute life and is free from such needs. The Qur'an states: "God: there is no God but Him, the Living, the eternal One. Neither slumber nor sleep overtake Him. His is what the heavens and the earth contain . . . "(Sura 2:255). As a result, Muslims do not observe a Sabbath day of rest as do Jews. Friday is a day for congregational prayer, known as "the Day of Assembly," but not a day of rest from work. The lack of a Sabbath day of rest in no way means that creation does not play a central role in Islam. Islam teaches that everything is created to worship and serve God in veneration. Adoration, service of God in the true sense of the word, is the meaning of creation (Sura 51:56-7). Annemarie Schimmel points out that this is symbolized by the word of the primordial covenant of *alast*. This covenant is to be realized and manifested in the life of every individual, and even in the life of nations. The command is also intended for the lower ranks of creatures: for stones, plants and animals which, like the angels, are constantly occupied with worship, expressing their praise and adoration in silent eloquence by their whole being and action.[41]

In references to the "six days of creation," the creation of humans is not mentioned. However, in the first revelation of God to the Prophet Muhammad, God is revealed as the creator of humanity:

> Recite: In the name of your Lord who created--
> created man out of a blood-clot.
> Recite: Your Lord is the most Bountiful One, who by the pen,
> taught man what he did not know (Sura 96:1-5).

This text has a parallel in Sura 40:67-68:

> It was He who created you from dust, then from a little germ, and then from a clot of blood. He brings you infants into the world; you reach manhood, then decline into old age (though some of you die young), so that you may complete your appointed term and grow in wisdom.

The reference to creation from dust has an obvious relationship to Genesis 2:7: "The Lord God formed *ádamah* (the earthling) from the dust of the earth.[42] This first earthling was placed in the garden of Eden and given the charge to name all the other earth creatures. In the interest of providing a suitable helpmate for the earthling, God cast him into a deep sleep and from his rib fashioned a woman. Now there exists *ish* and *ishsha*, the pair known by the names Adam and Eve.

In the Qur'an, the first man God created is also called Adam, who is listed among the prophets. He is the first human to appear either in heaven or on earth. Sura (2:30) depicts Adam as created as the *khalifa*--viceregent[43] or deputy of God on earth. Sura 15:29 indicates that God breathed into the first human God's own spirit. Sura 95:4 declares that God created human beings in the best of molds or stature, details missing from the earlier text. In Sura 2, Adam is created after the angels and is taught by God the names of all things and the knowledge of their properties (Sura 2:30-31).[44] As the first recipient of the divine message, he becomes the lord of the names and named things. For this reason Adam is superior to the angels, who cannot recall the names when asked. It would seem that the special spirit of God given to Adam is a faculty of God-like knowledge.

The angels were directed to pay homage to Adam. All do, except *Iblis* (Satan), who proudly refused. It is *Iblis* who will become the enemy of humans. About this time God created a mate for Adam from a rib on his left side. She is Hauwa (Eve).

In Genesis 3 the story of the fall is told. Satan in the form of a serpent tempts Eve, who in turn tempts Adam. As a result of their sin,

God punishes the first pair: Eve will know great pain in childbirth and be ruled by her husband; Adam shall work hard and earn bread only by the sweat of his brow. Both are driven from the garden of Eden (Gn 3:16-24). The story of the fall in the Qur̓an differs from that in the Torah. It is Adam and not Eve who is tempted by the devil, but his action is not a willful transgression (*ithm*); rather it is a fault (*dhanb*) (Sura 2: 35-39). According to this text, woman is not the first to yield to the temptation of Satan; she is not portrayed as the cause for the fall as in Judaism and Christianity. However, there is some ambiguity in the Qur̓an on this point because there is also a text which indicates that Adam and Eve were both led astray at the same time (Sura 20: 115-24). It would seem, therefore, that the fall was a collective and not an individual act. In any event, Eve, not being the first sinner, has not meant that Muslim women have fared better than Jewish women in their respective religious societies. Historically, the positions of Jewish and Muslim women, as of Christian women, have been marked by secondary status and lack of equality.[45] B o t h religious societies are affected by texts that contain laws that are obviously defined by males. Laws in the Torah describe in great detail women's status in the family structure of Judaism and delineate male rights over women's sexuality. These laws assume the passivity of women. Laws concerning the virginity and adultery of women are clearly patriarchal as Deuteronomy 22:13-21 makes evident. This text allows for a married woman, who cannot prove that she was a virgin prior to her marriage, to be stoned to death on her father's door step.

Male dominance is certainly no stranger to Islam, either. The Qur̓an contains texts that promote the submission of women to their husbands. Sura 4:34 states:

> Men have authority over women because God has made one superior to the other, and because they spend their wealth to maintain them. Good women are obedient. They guard their unseen parts because God guarded them. As for those from whom you fear disobedience, admonish then and send them to be apart and beat them. Then if they obey you take no further action against them. God is supreme high.

The Qur̓an, however, is not without ambivalence where the status of men and women is concerned. There are several verses that can lead the reader to conclude that women and men are equal before God. Believers, male and female, are guardians of one another; they enjoin good and evil, perform the prayer, give alms and obey God (Sura 9:71). Whoever does good deeds, whether the person is male or female, and is a believer shall be rewarded (Sura 4: 124, 16:97 and 40:40). Obviously, to do full justice to the understanding of men and of women as creatures of God in Judaism and Islam would require another full dialogue session!

The Quṙan presents the fall of the first human(s) as a story of God's mercy and human repentance. In Genesis 3 the first act of disobedience brings with it punishment and hardship. In contrast, the Quṙan teaches that after Adam disobeys God, he repents. God responds by extending to Adam his mercy and guidance (Sura 20:122). The paradigm for sin and repentance in Islam follows this pattern: Adam turns from Satan and returns to God; Adam repents and God forgives. The return means that a Muslim submits to God by following God's will. Submission, of course, is given expression in the recitation of the *shahadah*, which affirms the absoluteness of God. In a sense, it places the Muslim back in the garden of Eden.

The perspectives on creation, especially human creatures, in Genesis and in the Quṙan are more difficult to summarize than the perspectives on the "One God." One thing that the two have in common is that both are passionately theist: an ordered world is fashioned by a transcendent Creator. Aside from that evident fact, in the creation texts of Judaism and Islam, common symbols such as the six days of creation, are found. However, as the analysis above illustrates, there are differences in the manner in which these symbols are presented and interpreted. In addition, the Quṙan presents details that Genesis 1 does not have. For example, the creation of the seven heavens in the Quṙan are not mentioned in Genesis, but do appear in rabbinic literature.

If we turn to the way God created the first human pair, we also find commonalities. Both Judaism and Islam share the mythological account of God's forming the first human from the dust of the ground and breathing into this creature the breath of life (Judaism) or spirit of God (Islam) and of the woman being made from the rib of the first human creature. There are differences, however, in how the God--human relationship is depicted. Judaism presents the human as created in God's own image and likeness (Gn. 1:27); an idea not explicitly expressed in the Quṙan. This text is often interpreted to imply that humans act as God's representatives and are capable of entering into a covenant relationship with their Creator. In this relationship they find delight in loving God with their whole heart, mind and strength. The opposite of delight is sin, which is the failure to be obedient to the requirements of the sacred covenant relationship specified in the *mitzvot*.

The closest parallel in Islam is likely the human gifted with "the spirit of God" which, when combined with the notion "viceregent," points: 1) to the God-like knowledge given to the first human creature manifested in the ability of humans to "name" creation, and 2) to the responsibility of humans to submit in prayer to the God who chose to reveal the Divine Names. Failure of a believer to submit to God is the penultimate sin; an offense which can be forgiven as long as the sinner calls upon God in hope.Deliberate unbelief in God (*al-kufr*), especially in the form of blasphemy, is the most serious of sins. God cannot forgive this sin because the sinner denies God and is without gratitude for the gifts of life and divine revelation. There is nevertheless a remedy even for this most serious of all offenses: turning to the truth of God.[46] So great is God's mercy and compassion.

CONCLUSIONS

It has been the modest goal of this essay to identify the content of an initial dialogue session between Jews and Muslims on two topics basic and central to each: God and creation. I have tried to present the information on the way each treats these topics in their sacred texts as accurately and as impartially as is possible for an outsider. In the process it has become clear that Judaism and Islam share much in common in their beliefs and prayer practices about God and creation, and in how they embody those beliefs in their daily lives. But there are also basic differences that are indeed worthy of respect. Dialogue can be a risky business, if each participant is not willing to try to understand the other from within the other's terms. Having consulted Jewish and Muslim exposition of these points, I have nonetheless found this to be a difficult task. It is probable that I have not achieved a proper understanding. Engagement in this exercise, however, has been an opportunity for me to appreciate more deeply the enormous plenitude of God.

It would seem that if dialogue among Jews, Muslims and Christians is to be successful, it must be entered in the spirit of Abraham, who so graciously welcomed guests into his tent at Mamre (Gn. 18:1). His welcome was lavish; as a friend of God he treated his visitors as "friends of God." The premise for this exercise may be idealistic, but not, it is hoped, unrealistic, for nothing is too wondrous for God (cf Gn. 18:14).

NOTES

[1] Jacob Neusner, "There Has Never Been a Judaeo-Christian Dialogue--But There Can Be One," *Cross Currents* 42 (1992): 3.
For my purposes here, I have changed the order in which Neusner listed his criteria. See also his *Telling Tales: Making Sense of Christian and Judaic Nonsense. The Urgency and Basis for Judeo-Christian Dialogue* (Louisville: Westminster/John Knox, 1993).

[2] Nicholas de Lange points out that Hebrew for a long time had no equivalent for the usual Christian meaning of "Judaism," as a religion. See de Lange's *Judaism* (Oxford: Oxford University Press, 1986), p. 4. Jacob Neusner devotes a whole chapter of a recent book to explain why it is so difficult to define "Judaism." He suggests to be a Jew means to argue about what being a Jew means. In the concluding section, he offers his own definition: "Judaism consists of the religious tradition enshrined in the holy books and expressed in the holy words, deeds, way of living and principles of faith subsumed under the word *Torah*. In *The Way of Torah* (Belmont, CA: Wadsworth, [fourth edition] 1989), p. 28.

[3] The name for the religion revealed to Mohammed appears in the Quṙan at the time of the prophet's farewell pilgrimage: "Today I have perfected your religion for you and I have completed My blessing upon you, and I have approved *Islam* for your religion" (Sura 5:5).

[4] For more on revelation in Judaism and Islam (and also Christianity) see chapters 1 and 5 of Francis E. Peters, *Children of Abraham. Judaism, Christianity and Islam* (Princeton: Princeton University, 1982).

[5] Neusner, *The Way of Torah*, pp. 9-18.

[6] Jacques Waardenburg, "World Religions as Seen in the Light of Islam," in *Islam: Past Influence and Present Challenge*, ed. Alfred T. Welch and Pierre Cachia (Albany: State University of New York, 1979), pp. 255-56.

[7] Abdoldjavad Falaturi, "Experience of Time and History in Islam," in *We Believe in One God*, ed. Annemarie Schimmel and Abdoldjavad Falaturi (New York: Seabury, 1979), pp. 65-68.

[8] Frederick Mathewson Denny, *An Introduction to Islam* (New York: Macmillan, 1985), p. 98.

[9] Ibid., p. 19. For the sake of emphasizing the common roots of the name for God in Judaism and Islam, I will use the English term "God," unless it is clearly inappropriate to do so.

[10] W. Gunther Plaut concludes that YHVH in Exodus 3:15 derives from the "*ehyeh-asher-ehyeh*" of v. 14. He notes the mystery that surrounds this name, which becomes the distinguishing name by which Israelites call their God. *Ehyeh* is the first person singular of the verb "to be." However, the tense is not clear; it could mean "I am" or "I will be." Jewish literature offers a variety of explanations of "*ehyeh-asher-ehyeh*." The majority of authors argue that the tense for *ehyeh* is future and interpret it to mean: "I will be what tomorrow demands," that is, God will respond to human needs. Others, such as S. R. Hirsch, argue that it means God will be what God wants to be, thus the emphasis is on

the autonomous freedom of God. Plaut argues that this name is an aspect of God's freedom to conceal His essence, and hence "*ehyeh-asher-ehyeh*" must remain ever elusive. W. Gunther Plaut, *The Torah, A Modern Commentary* (New York: Union of American Hebrew Congregations, 1981), pp. 404-06.

[11]According to Louis Jacobs, from the time of the sixth century B.C.E. at the latest God was conceived of as the One Supreme Being. See Louis Jacobs, "God," in *Contemporary Jewish Religious Thought. Original Essays on Critical Concepts, Movements and Beliefs*, ed. Arthur A. Cohen and Paul Mendes-Flohr (New York: Charles Scribner's Sons, 1987), p. 291.

[12]The Shema, which is to be recited twice daily, consists of two primary paragraphs, Dueuteronomy 6:4-9 and 11:13-21. Alternate translations of the Shema are found in various editions of the Torah. The translations underscore the difficulty in rendering the Hebrew word *echad* which occurs in Deut. 6:4 without punctuation and without a verb. As a result, *echad* has been translated as "is one," "alone," and "unique." W. Gunther Plaut, *The Torah, A Modern Commentary*, p. 1369.

[13]Plaut, p. 1370.

[14]Steven Harvey, "Love," in *Contemporary Jewish Religious Thought*, p. 560.

[15]Neusner, *The Way of Torah*, p. 11.

[16]Moses Maimonides wrote the *Moreh Nevuchin, The Guide for the Perplexed*, in which he brought teachings of Judaism into dialogue with Aristotle's philosophy. For a helpful treatment of Moses Maimonides' use of Aristotle in explaining belief in God, the Creator, see Herbert A. Davidson, *Proofs for Eternity, Creation and the Existence of God in Medieval Islamic and Jewish Philosophy* (New York: Oxford University, 1987).

[17]Cited in Stephen M. Wylen, *Settings of Silver, An Introduction to Judaism* (New York: Paulist Press, 1989), p. 31.

[18]Louis Jacobs, *The Book of Jewish Belief* (New York: Behrman House, 1984), p. 15.

[19]Philip Birnbaum, *Daily Prayer Book* (New York: Hebrew Publishing Co., 1977), p. 72.

[20]Denny, *An Introduction to Islam*, p. 92.

[21]Kenneth Cragg points out that *Rabb al-alamin*, which appears in the *Fatihah* is the most often repeated of Islam religious terms (p. 75). He goes on to point out that this proclamation of Islam signifies the awakening of humanity to the total, inalienable, indivisible Lordship of God over heaven and earth (p. 79). See *The Event of the Qur̄an. Islam in Its Scripture* (London: George Allen and Unwin, 1971).

[22]*The Koran*, translated with notes by N. J. Dawood (London: Penguin, [1956], fifth revised edition, 1990). In the "Introduction," Dawood indicates that "Lord of the Universe," may also be translated "Lord of the Creation," p. 3. All subsequent passages cited from the Qur̄an are taken from this translation in comparison with Maulana Muhammad Ali, *The Holy Qur̄an. Arabic Text, English Translation and Commentary* (Lahore, Pakistan: Ahmadiyyah Anjuman Isha'at Islam, 1973).

[23]Cyril Glassé, "*Fatihah*," in *The Concise Encyclopedia of Islam* (San Francisco: Harper and Row, 1989), p. 123.

[24]Andrew Rippin and Jan Knappert, ed. and tr. *Textual Sources for the Study of Islam* (Totowa, NJ: Barnes and Noble, 1986), p. 35.

[25]This passage condemns the pre Islamic belief in goddesses (*al-Manat, al-Lat, al Uzza*) as daughters of Allah. Badre D. Kateregga, *Islam and Christianity, A Muslim and a Christian in Dialogue* (Grand Rapids, MI: William B. Eerdmans, 1980), p. 2. It also underscores the distinction between Muslims and Christians who believe in Jesus Christ as the son of God. According to Denise Masson, Muslims rejected the divinity of Christ because it was interpreted by them as a form of *"Trithéisme."* See *Monothéisme Coranique et Monotheisme Biblique, Doctrines comparées* (Paris: Desclèe de Brouwer, 1976), pp. 51-52.

[26]John L. Esposito, *Islam, The Straight Path* (New York: Oxford University, [revised edition] 1991), p. 23.

[27]According to Badru Kateregga, this prophetic tradition is reported by Abu Huraira. See *Islam and Christianity*, p. 3.

[28]Kenneth Cragg, *Muhammad and the Christian, A Question of Response* (Maryknoll, NY: Orbis, 1984), pp. 102-03.

[29]John L. Esposito argues that Muhammad did not establish a new religion, rather he brought a reformation in the form of a call to total submission to Allah. See *Islam, The Straight Path*, p. 14.

[30]Several of the prophets refer to creation; see especially Isaiah 40:25-26 and Jeremiah 27:5.

[31]See especially Ps. 104, Prov. 8:22-31 and Job 38.

[32]David Kelsey, "The Doctrine of Creation from Nothing," in *Evolution and Creation*, ed. Ernan McMullin (Notre Dame, IN: University of Notre Dame, 1985), p. 180.

[33]See the non-Tanakh 2 Maccabees 7:28, the first text in which "creation from nothing" appears. It is debatable, however, whether this text is really a creation text per se. During the persecution of Antiochus IV (167-168 B.C.E), a mother of seven sons used the term to encourage them to remain strong in the face of martyrdom. In this context *creatio ex nihilo* ought to be interpreted as creation out of chaos. She is insisting that the bones and ashes of the just can be revived by God.

[34]*Genesis, The First Book of the Bible*, interpreted by Benno Jacob, tr. Ernest L. Jacob and Walter Jacob (New York: KTAV, 1974), p. 1.

[35]Plaut, *The Torah*, p. 18. Jon D. Levenson reflects extensively on this alternate translation in developing an interpretation of Genesis 1 which stresses God's activity in creation as bringing order out of chaos. The alternate translation also provides him with a basis for his refutation of *creatio ex nihilo*. See *Creation and the Persistence of Evil, The Jewish Drama of Divine Omnipotence* (San Francisco: Harper and Row, 1988), p. 5 and pp. 121-27.

[36]Jacobs, *The Book of Jewish Belief*, p. 23 and Wylen, *Settings of Silver*, p. 23.

[37]Leo Trepp, *Judaism, Development and Life* (Belmont, CA: Wadsworth, 1982), p. 285.

[38]For a now classic analysis of the Jewish foundations of Islam in the Qur'an from a Jewish standpoint see Abraham Geiger, *Judaism and Islam*, 1st ed. 1898, Prolegomenon

by Moshe Perlman (New York: KTAV, 1970).

[39]Although the Torah does not speak of the creation of seven heavens, there are inumerable references to the creation of the heavens in rabbinic sources.

[40]W. Montgomery Watt, *What Is Islam?* (London: Longmans, Green, 1968), p. 33.

[41]Annemarie Schimmel, "Creation and Judgment in the Koran and in Mystico-Poetical Interpretation," in *We Believe in One God*, ed. Annemarie Schimmel and Abdoldjavad Falaturi (New York: Seabury, 1979), p. 155.

[42]Plaut includes *âdamah* in his commentary and translates it as the "earthling"; therefore, the term can include males and females. *The Torah*, p. 29.

[43]Kateregga, indicates that Muslim scholars are not fully agreed on what *Khalifa*, which he translates as "viceregent" means. Some claim that it means that humans have a certain God-likeness. But the orthodox belief suggests that humans have no God-likeness, for God is absolutely transcendent; see *Islam and Christianity*, p. 15.

[44]The Quranic universe consists of three realms: heaven, earth and hell. The world is inhabited by human beings and spirits (angels, jinn who inhabit the subtle world, and devils) who are called to obedience to the one, true Allah, the Lord of the Universe. Angels serve as the link between God and human beings. Created out of light, immortal and sexless, they function as guardians and messengers. Between angels and humans are jinn (cf Western "genies"). Jinn were created from fire instead of earth. They can assume visible form and can be friendly or hostile to humans. Finally, at the opposite end of the spectrum from God is *Iblis* or Satan. See John L. Esposito, *Islam, The Straight Path*, pp 26-27.

[45]For a more in depth treatment of this topic I recommend: Judith Plaskow, *Standing Again at Sinai. Judaism from a Feminist Perspective* (New York: Harper and Row, 1990), Riffat Hassan, "An Islamic Perspective," pp. 93-128, in *Women, Religion and Society. Studies on the Impact of Religious Teachings on Women*, ed. Jeanne Becher (Philadelphia: Trinity Press International, 1990) and Freda Hassain, ed., *Muslim Women* (New York: St. Martin's, 1984).

[46]Glassè, "al-Kufr," pp. 241-42 and "Sin," p. 372 in *The Concise Encyclopedia of Islam*.

SIMONE WEIL:

JUDAISM, CHRISTIANITY, AND ISLAM, AND

TODAY'S FEMINIST CRITIQUE OF PATRIARCHY

Richard J. Beauchesne

Without transforming Simone Weil into a contemporary feminist, this article argues that aspects of Weil's critique of Judaism, Christianity[1] and Islam underscore several contemporary feminist assessments of mainstream religions especially where power and warrior gods are seen as a function of patriarchy.[2] The article does not discuss Weil's relationship to her own Jewishness, or her ambiguous attitude vis-à-vis other persecuted Jews, nor contemporary Jewish positions vis-à-vis Weil. Rather, it focuses on some of the few but provocative passages in her work where Judaism[3] and Islam[4] are jointly mentioned, and points out how the combined references allow for a discussion of Weil's critique of Christianity.[5]

WEIL AND FEMINISM IN FRANCE IN THE EARLY 1900S

Simone Weil's formative years as a youth (she was born in 1909 and died in 1943) belong to the early 1900s in France which, in the feminist movement of the age, contrasted the "woman-child" [*femme-enfant*] with the "women-boy" [*la garçonne*,[6] the feminine form of *garçon*]. Such a contrast, in turn, translated for the early 1900s a perennial view of woman as "woman-angel" [*femme-ange*] or "woman-devil/demon" [*femme-démon*].[7] Within that context and time, it was thought that if women were to dress as men, as George Sand did during the previous century, women's emancipation would be at hand. Maïté Albistur and Daniel Armongathe argue in their *Histoire du féminisme français* that between 1890 and 1920 avant-garde movements in France were ready to sacrifice women to men as women's virile heroes and masters.[8]

About Simone Weil (within the 1900-20 French feminist, historical context), I refer to Mary Dietz's observation in her book, *Between the Human and the Divine: The Political Thought of Simone Weil*. Dietz describes the relationship between young Simone and her mother:

> For [Simone's] mother, masculinity denoted more than gender. It was indicative of worldly achievement, success, and 'advancement' in both personal and social terms. [In a letter to a friend, Madame Weil wrote:] "I shall always prefer the good little boys, boisterous and sincere as I see them coming out of the Lycée Montaigne. And I do my best to encourage in Simone not the simpering graces of a little girl but the forthrightness of a boy, even if this must at times seem rude."[9]

Madame Weil's persuasion about her daughter Simone might explain why the Weil family referred to Simone as Simon (the masculine form), and why, as a young woman, she herself preferred "tailored, masculine clothes and for a period of time actually signed her letters to her parents 'your respectful son.'"[10] One can only speculate whether, later in life, she knew of the activities of the great French feminist, Nelly Roussel (1878-1922)[11] or the response of Valentine de Saint-Point,[12] *Manifeste de la femme futuriste* (1912), to the futurist Filippo Tommaso Marinetti's anti-feminist *Manifeste du Futurisme* (1909).[13] Did Weil know about *La Fronde* (the slingshot)--"the first feminist daily directed, administered, edited, and produced uniquely by women . . . . [f]ounded in 1897 by Marguerite Durand, [with] an initial press run of over 200,000."?[14] We do not know.

The fact is, however, that Weil's own writings against power and warrior gods might be regarded as her response to Marinetti who, in his *Manifeste*, exalted both male power and war. He wrote: "We wish to glorify war--the only cleansing agent of the world--militarism, patriotism, the destroying activities of anarchists, the beautiful ideas that kill, and contempt for the woman [feminist] . . . . [all the things that] get in the way of man's progress [characterized by] courage and heroism."[15] Similar ideas are found in André Malraux's *Anti-Mémoirs* in which he states: "[F]acing death was the illuminating experience [for the male] analogous to childbirth for the female.' Or as Mussolini put it during the thirties: "War is to man what maternity is to woman."[16]

POWER, WAR AND PATRIARCHY, AND FEMINISM TODAY

Carol Christ, among today's feminists, clearly connects power and war-gods with patriarchy. She writes:

I do not attribute war to the male nature, nor do I argue that women are incapable of warlike action, but I do believe that as feminists we must examine the equation of "manhood" and power with war that has been the legacy of patriarchal cultures . . . . Patriarchy and large-scale war arose together, *although not by simple cause and effect* . . . . [with] warlike invaders during the second, third, and fourth millennia B.C.E. The warlike Zeus was the God of these patriarchal peoples.[17]

It should be noted that Dr. Christ does not reject "female power," as symbolized in the goddess, "symbol of life and death powers, of waxing and waning energies in the universe, and in [women] themselves."[18] What she rejects is male power symbolized in God, symbol of domination and warlike behaviors, the God of Exodus, the Warrior God. God so conceived, according to Christ, must not be appealed to as symbol for feminist theology.[19]

Rosemary Radford Ruether also connects power and wargods with patriarchy. Referring to the idol of masculinity, she writes:

[I]t claims all the earth as the creation and domain of the father-rule. It monopolizes the image of God, claiming God can only be spoken by the name of Patriarch, can only be imaged in the image of Father-rule. God is sovereign, King, Warrior, God of Power and Might, who magnifies the rule of the powerful and abases the degradation of the lowly, who give the scepter to the mighty and teaches the little ones of the earth to cower in fear and self-hatred. . . . Men are the proper and fitting image of this mighty God, especially powerful men--rulers who command, warriors who kill, judges who punish. . . . To see them is to see God. To obey their word is to obey the Word of God. To criticize their power . . . is to rebel against God.[20]

Furthermore, according to Ruether, clericalism, "the transformation of ministry from mutual interaction with community and its transformation into hierarchically ordered castes of clergy and laity,"[21] itself is a function of patriarchy, since the relationship between clergy and laity is symbolically represented as one between the all-knowing father and the helpless child.[22] The power in question here relates specifically to sacramental ministry, where the all-knowing father possesses the powers necessary to redeem and sanctify the helpless child.[23] Power here means control on the part of the clergy (symbolically "husband") over a disempowered laity (symbolically "wife"), not only spiritually but also personally and socially, resembling the power of men over women in married life.[24]

SIMONE WEIL: JUDAISM, ISLAM AND CHRISTIANITY ON POWER

A first Weilian reference to Judaism and Islam questions any divine revelation in religions that lack belief in the incarnation. "Does a revelation imply an incarnation" Weil asks? She answers: "It was not so implied in Israel's revelation or that of Islam."[25] Here, Weil's point is that in a religion where incarnation exists there equally exists the antidote to creation; namely, decreation. In Weil, creation, incarnation and what Weil refers to as "decreation" all imply kenosis (an emptying out).[26] Thus, in creation, "God [empties] himself of his divinity [power]," Weil asserts, "and [fills] us with a false divinity,"[27] that is, human power. Through the incarnation realized in Jesus, "[God] emptied himself [s'est vidé] of his divinity by becoming [human], then [through his passion, he emptied himself] of his humanity by becoming a corpse (bread and wine), matter."[28] And through decreation, we, as humans, respond to God by emptying ourselves of power and thus become equal to God in "emptiness."[29]

Through the act of creation--the emptying out of God's divinity which in creatures becomes a false divinity or power--God becomes submitted to necessity, "that network of relationships [causes and effects] permeating the world of matter . . . ."[30] In humankind, creation translates itself as absolute power: the power of the "I" (deprived of goodness) that calls itself *to be* more and more regardless of others. Correlatively, creation means the progressive diminution of the divine as power tempered by goodness; at the same time, creation means the progressive increase of power as supreme, devoid of goodness--to the point that eventually progress as power is equated to goodness. (One comes to believe that what is referred to as "progress"--the ever-expanding self--is necessarily good.)

As a result, according to Weil, creation is not God's sacrament of goodness--that is, the physical reality capable of revealing the ultimate goodness that is God. For her, decreation would be the sacrament of God's goodness. As for creation, it is sacrament of God's abdication. Hence, as Creator, God is not all-powerful.[31] On the one hand, "God, in creation, by allowing the existence of other creatures, refuses to be everything";[32] God abdicates. On the other hand, we as creatures, the more we insist on being more, so much the more does God abdicate his divinity within us. Although Weil still refers to divinity in God as power, in God power is good because it is tempered by goodness; for the true God does not command in all places where He has the power to do so.[33] "Those religions that represent divinity as commanding everywhere [*part-*

out] it possesses power are false."[34] In true religions, divinity in God--
even as power--obeys goodness, the essential attribute of God. All other
divine attributes (including that of power) are secondary.[35] Thus God is
primarily all goodness and love which "rather than . . . streaming through
the natural order to us as light through a window pane . . . [makes us]
transparent as a window pane for God's love to pass through us to other
creatures."[36] Thus, in creatures God's goodness and love translate themselves as grace in the uncreated part of the soul. According to Weil, the
soul has two parts: created and uncreated. She explains:

> God asked us: "Do you want to be created [*read*: do you want more
> and more power]?" And we answered yes. At every instant [God]
> continues to ask us, and at every instant we answer yes. Except for
> a few people whose soul is divided in two; while a good portion of
> the soul says yes, a point of the soul exhausts itself in shouting
> suppliantly: no, no, no! In imploring [thus], this point enlarges itself,
> [and] becomes a spot [*tache*] which one day invades the entire soul.[37]

As a result of a kind of spiritual osmotic process--the uncreated part of
the soul "passing into" the soul's created part--the soul's created part
becomes "uncreated" or "decreated." At that point, "gravity" is outrun
by "grace." Thus, in the midst of our experience of power submitted to
necessity (an experience of the created part of the soul, an experience of
gravity), we, God's creatures, experience the desire for the good (an
experience of the "uncreated" or "decreated" part of the soul, an experience of grace). Such a desire is depicted by Weil as related to *un point
d'éternité dans l'âme* (a point of eternity in the soul).[38]

   In *La connaissance surnaturelle*, Weil writes: "God gave to his finite
creatures this power to transport themselves into the infinite."[39] In *Attente
de Dieu*, she writes: "Through the veil of the flesh, we receive from
above 'presentiments' of eternity, which are sufficient to remove all
doubts."[40] She also speaks of an "orientation by which God presses us
toward him [*l'orientation qu'il nous imprime vers lui*]."[41] Thus, to
counteract the "false deity (power) "incarnated" in us through creation
and in order to imitate God's refusal to be everything, there exists within
us the possibility of the "act of decreation." Decreation allows us to make
place for the divine. It is the human response to the divine process of
creation. Decreation is creation in reverse and is modeled upon God's
incarnation in Jesus Christ: "Adam," writes Weil, "made us believe that
we were [viz., that we possessed being]; Christ has shown us that we are
not [viz., that we do not possess being]."[42] Decreation, not creation,

transforms us into the image of God the Creator,[43] and, therefore, is the sacrament of God.

Thus "to reproduce [within ourselves] God's initial abdication means to refuse to be [as well as] to destroy a part of [ourselves]."[44] That part of ourselves must be the one which truly belongs to us; namely, our free will, which Weil equates with power or false divinity. For our free will is creation. And "[t]hat which is creation from the point of view of God is sin from the point of view of the creature."[45] Weil adds: "God's sacrifice is creation; man's sacrifice is destruction"[46] or decreation, which is the acceptance of our creatureliness by a person's "consenting to lose one's whole existence," one's autonomous self,[47] which for Weil is the human quest for power. "Consenting to lose one's whole existence" as power is precisely what "incarnation", which includes Jesus' passion, means. In *Simone Weil: Waiting on Truth*, Patricia Little explains:

> God before creation was more perfect than God having created, since before the creative act He was totally self-sufficient. The independent self-contemplation of the Creator is destroyed by the coming into existence of another being, creation, and the resulting diminution of God is the cause of His suffering. The suffering Christ on the Cross is hence only a reflection of the primordial suffering occasioned by man as the contradiction between what he desires and what he is, between his aspirations to goodness and his submission to necessity.[48]

According to Weil, the incarnation is related specifically to Christianity[49] untainted by Judaism. For, "[t]o teach us that we are non-beings" or ("powerless"), in Jesus, "God made himself non-being"[50] (read: powerless). As stated above, in Jesus, "[God] emptied himself [*s'est vidé*] of his divinity by becoming [human], then [through his passion, he emptied himself] of his humanity by becoming a corpse (bread and wine), matter."[51] Dr. Patricia Little, a Weil scholar, explains:

> [Humankind]'s response to God, decreation replying to creation, amounts to an almost necessary reciprocity, a symmetry indicative of Simone Weil's need in this, as in many other areas of her thought, to restore a balance that has been disturbed by the assertion of the autonomous self. Examples abound: the creature, by allowing itself to be created, preferred itself to God. It redeems itself by asking God to destroy it.[52] Or again, God abdicated his divine omnipotence and "emptied" himself. By abdicating our limited human power, we become equal to God in "emptiness."[53]

SIMONE WEIL: JUDAISM, ISLAM AND CHRISTIANITY ON
WAR AND WARRIOR GODS

The above considerations of Weil's views regarding the meaning of incarna-
tion, creation, and its counterpart, decreation, should clarify the meaning of a
second Weilian reference to Judaism and Islam jointly: "No one goes to God the
Creator and the Almighty without passing through God *EMPTIED OF HIS
DIVINITY* [the Christian God in Jesus]. If one goes to God directly, it then is
Jehovah [the Jewish God] or Allah, the one in the Qur'an,"[54] not the Christian
God [the Trinity] known through Jesus.[55]

According to Weil, to choose to go to God without mediation is to accept
a God who is present in a collectivity rather than in individual persons. To that
effect, a third Judaic/Islamic passage in Weil argues:

> There cannot be any contact between man and God as from one person
> to another except through the person of the Mediator. Apart from him,
> the only way in which God can be present to man is in a collective,
> a national way. Israel, at the same time, and at one stroke, chose the
> national God and rejected the Mediator. It is possible that Israel may
> from time to time have sought after genuine monotheism. But it always
> fell back upon, and could not do otherwise than fall back upon, the
> tribal God . . . . Islam is an illustration of the same law. Allah, in the
> Qur'an, is also the God of the armed Bedouins.[56]

Mediation is necessary for one to have access to God in order to avoid
idolatry.[57] In *La connaissance surnaturelle*, Weil asserts: "Israel has the
idea that by taking God as a national deity, it was absolutely assured of
victory. Israel made God the object of its idolatry."[58] Patricia Little
explains that the process of social divinization is, according to Weil,
idolatry--a view which, according to Little, does not quite fit the traditional definition: to adore things other than the true God. Weil expounds her
meaning this way: "To know divinity only as power and not as good, that
is idolatry, regardless of whether people have one God or many."[59]

The divinization of one's nation--with the correlative idea of a people
elected or chosen by God--equates God's will with a concept of history
which is linear rather that circular. Such a linear view allows one to
consider all progress as necessarily good, as God's will. Such a divinization of history--as happened in Israel--is fundamentally self-adoration.[60]
It led the Hebrews to take as "their idol, not something made of metal
or wood, but a race, a nation, something just as earthly. Their religion
is essentially inseparable from such idolatry, because of the notion of the
'chosen people.'"[61]

Even Christianity falls prey to social idolatry where it requests, as an act of faith, the "unconditional and global assent to all that the Church has taught, teaches and will teach."[62] For here the Church establishes itself as a terrestrial god, which is the equivalent to the national God of Judaism or to the incarnation in Wotan of the Germanic soul as Hitler believed[63]--a criticism of the Church which brings us to a fourth Weilian Judaic/Islamic passage, this one prefaced by the following strident remark: "Totalitarianism is an *ersatz* form of Christianity." Weil explains the origins of totalitarian Christianity by appealing to Judaism with a reference to Islam:

> Christianity became a totalitarian, conquering and destroying agent because it failed to develop the notion of the absence and non-action of God here below. It attached itself as much to Jehovah as to Christ, and conceived of Providence after the style of the Old Testament. Israel alone was able to resist Rome, because it resembled Rome;[64] and so it came about that the newly-born Christianity was contaminated by Rome before ever it became the official religion of the Empire. The evil wrought by Rome has never been truly repaired . . . . The same is true in the case of Allah, but to a lesser degree, because the Arabs have never become a state.[65] The sort of war of which he is the God is the razzia.[66]

The notion of the absence and non-action of God in the world relates directly to Weil's concept of creation explained previously; namely, that per se (regardless of how one conceives of God), creation is not God's sacrament or expansion but God's abdication. Hence, as Creator, God is not allpowerful.[67] "God, in creation, by allowing the existence of other creatures, refuses to be everything."[68] By creating, God submitted himself to the laws of necessity and therefore reduced himself to the status of absence and non-action of a powerful God in history. God's absence and non-action within creation, however, translates itself essentially as inspiration and love (God the Son and God the Spirit) in the midst of the necessary (God the Father/Creator)--the Christian concept of the Trinity, to be discussed below.

What Weil objects to is a Christian notion of Providence--as she sees it--rooted in Judaism[69] (and Islam); namely that of a powerful, warrior God acting in history, one that implies God's presence in history to the point of identifying an almighty God with history itself. Weil's assumption is that Rome would have accepted the religion of Judaism--with its equation of God with history--had it not been for its nationalistic flavor:

[A] nationalistic religion cannot be passed on from one people to another as a garment, [Weil remarks. So what did Rome do instead?] [T]he Romans took over the non-national form of the Jewish religion, that is, the Christian form. The Jewish religion--with its addendum: the transfer of Israel's privilege to the baptized gentiles [that of identifying the powerful God and history as enfleshed in the "chosen people"] was perfectly suited as a religion for the Roman Empire. [*Vide*] the Old Testament, plus Saint Paul's passages on the transfer of the Covenant, and "go teach all the nations." That is why the Old Testament was preserved.[70]

Then followed Augustine's *City of God* which, according to Weil, executed a new transfer: "[First, under the Romans], [t]he Empire succeeded to Israel [in its Christian form] and [then, with Augustine], the Church succeeded to the Empire"[71]; and Christendom succeeded to Christianity. As a result, "the unrootable [Jewish] nationalism perverted the order of Christ, and Yahweh, the Lord of the armies [the warrior God], under its Christian disguise, conquered the terrestrial globe."[72]

Nonetheless, as explained above, God's absence and non-action within creation (as opposed to the identification of the almighty God with history) translates itself essentially as "inspiration" and "love" (symbolized in God the Son and God the Spirit) that prevail in the midst of "necessity" (symbolized in God the Father/Creator); hence, the Christian concept of the Trinity, which a final Weilian, coupled reference to Judaism and Islam examines. The latter brings out the quandary raised by the confusion that exists between, on the one hand "what is good"[*le bien*] and on the other "power" [*nécessité*].[73] Weil believes that the dilemma can be solved only through the Christian notion of God as Trinity. She states: "God conceived exclusively as one and not as two (therefore three) compels [people] when [they imagine God as Creator] to confound "the necessary" [power] and "the good." Israel. Islam. . . ."[74]

According to Weil, the Spirit (within the Christian concept of God as Trinity) forms the connection between the Father and the Son, a connection which is essentially the expression of love and goodness (the kiss), which for her constitutes the essence of God. In relation to creation, it is this connection, the expression of pure goodness and love, which Jesus, as the Inspirer, mediates between the Father as Creator and the Spirit as Goodness and Love. Such a God experienced as Trinity, according to Weil, allows the good not to be confused with the necessary. For as Father, God is Creator and submitted to necessity. As Son, however,

God is Inspirer, and as Spirit, God is the Mediator between the two [that is, between the necessity of creation and the inspiration of love and goodness], which, for Weil, means: "God as author of the necessary. God as author of the beautiful. God as author of the Good. Father, Word and Spirit." Weil explains that "[t]he beautiful is the necessary which, whilst remaining in accordance with its own law and with it alone, obeys the good." Thus, within the Trinity, "the Spirit [as love] forms the connexion between the Father and the Son." But as the Trinity relates to the world, "the Son [as the inspirator of love in the midst of the necessary] forms the connexion between the Father and the Spirit."[75]

In an article entitled *"L'ordre de la charité chez Pascal, chez Péguy et chez Simone Weil,"* Alain Vinson in reference to the theologian François Varillon asks the following question about the Trinity: "Why three Persons, and not two?" In a reference to Augustine, Vinson quotes Varillon: *"Videt illa illum; videt ille illam; amorem nemo videt.* (She sees him; he sees her; no one sees love . . . .") Varillon continues: "In the Trinity, the Holy Spirit is Love itself: Love of the Father for the Son, Love of the Son for the Father. A mutual kiss."[76]

CONCLUSION

At issue for some among us--throughout this article--might have been the following questions: Are Weil's views on Judaism, Christianity and Islam historically accurate or are they ideologically construed? Are they perhaps a mixture of both? Whatever is the answer, I believe that there is something in Weil which lies beyond both history and ideology. It is the function of symbolism in religious stories that glorify deities connected with power and war, which today several feminist theologians relate to patriarchy.[77] Referring to Clifford Geertz, Carol Christ explains that; "[S]ymbols act to produce powerful, pervasive, and long-lasting moods and motivations in the people influenced by them."[78] Weil has much to say about religious myths of power and war and about their "powerful, pervasive, and long-lasting moods and motivations in the people influenced by them." She argues that the human perception of powerful deities as warrior gods acting in history leads humans to identify their respective gods' merciless demeanor with history itself, their own.[79] A connection, however, that Weil does not make is one that many among today's feminists make; namely, that history shows that power and war are functions of patriarchy, which in turn, I believe, has a symbolic meaning;

namely, that both women and men can be patriarchal. Patriarchy is essentially an attitude based on a domination/submission approach to relationships, although historically it was given birth by males sustained by their warrior gods.[80]

The *liaison dangeureuse* between patriarchy and deity (Judaic, Christian and Islamic) had already been exposed in 1949 by another Simone; namely, Simone de Beauvoir. De Beauvoir wrote then: "Man enjoys the great advantage of having a god endorse the code he writes; and since man exercises a sovereign authority over women it is especially fortunate that his authority had been vested in him by the Supreme Being. For the Jews, Mohammedans and Christians among others, man is master by divine right; the fear of God will therefore repress any impulse towards revolt in the downtrodden female."[81] This, fortunately, has not been the case. Patriarchy in its many forms has been unmasked by numerous contemporary feminist theologians. Perhaps no one has done so more graphically and poignantly than Rosemary Radford Ruether in *Women-Church*:

> We are Women-Church, not in exile, but in exodus. We flee the thundering armies of Pharaoh. We are not waiting for a call to return to the land of slavery to serve as altar girls in the temples of patriarchy. No! We call our brothers also to flee from the temples of patriarchy; we call our brothers Maurice Dingman and Frank Murphy and George Evans; Raymond Hunthausen and Charles Buswell and Tom Gumbleton [U.S. bishops], and even our brother Karol Wojtyla and all our fathers and sons and husbands and lovers, to flee with us the idol with flashing eyes and smoking nostrils who is about to consume the earth . . . . We call our brothers to join us in exodus from the land of patriarchy, to join our common quest for that promised land where there will be no more war, no more burning children, no more violated women, no more discarded elderly, no more rape of the earth. Together let us break up that great idol and grind it into powder; dismantle the great Leviathan of violence and misery who threatens to destroy the earth, plow it into the soil, and transform it back into the means of peace and plenty, so that all the children of earth can sit down together at the banquet of life.[82]

NOTES

[1]According to Dr. Diogenes Allen, Stuart Professor of Theology at Princeton and a Weil scholar, Catholicism was the only form of Christianity Weil knew. Dr. Allen writes: "[Weil's] brother André once told me that [Weil] had no contact with any other form of Christianity than [that of] Catholicism . . . . (But she did attend a Black Baptist Church in Harlem--to be with oppressed people)." Dr. Allen continues in his letter: "I expect her contact with Fr. Perrin [Weil's spiritual director] was the biggest reason Catholicism was important to [Weil]" (personal letter, dated 8/17/91). The reference to the Harlem Baptist Church--which Weil attended every Sunday while in New York--is in Simone Pétrement, *Simone Weil: A Life* (New York: Pantheon, 1976), 478. [On the same page in Pétrement, Weil complains to her mother after attending Mass in a New York Catholic church: "Have you ever seen anything like it! You pay to get in."] Dr. Eric O. Springsted of Illinois College and President of the American Simone Weil Society writes: "As to why [Weil's] penchant for Catholicism, there aren't any references [in Weil's writing] which suggest that she ever considered the issue of 'which denomination.' People have speculated on it. I especially remember some discussions about why she didn't move towards Eastern Orthodoxy, since its Platonism would seem rather compatible. Perhaps it was too esoteric and she didn't see choosing a religion or denomination so much as a personal choice of faith, as seeing it intimately bound up with the history and lives of a people. Thus Catholicism would come rather naturally to her, although she did have exposure to Protestantism such as [with] de Rougemont. But she only had one or two brief comments on Protestantism" (personal letter, dated 7/30/91). Dr. Patricia Little--of St. Patrick's College (Maynooth) and also a Weil scholar--writes concerning Weil's interest in Catholicism: "I personally think the attitude to the sacraments, and the nationalistic aspect are crucial there" (personal letter, dated 10/18/1991). Weil herself writes:

> By saying that the Catholic religion is true and the other religions false, one does an injustice not only to the other religious traditions but to the Catholic faith itself, by placing it on the level of those things which can be affirmed or denied. The intelligence needs to have complete liberty, including that of denying God: it follows from this that religion is related to love and not to affirmation and denial" (*Notebook*, I, 242, in *Notebooks* [London: Routledge & Kegan Paul, 1956], tr. Arthur Wills).

[2]See Carol P. Christ, "Feminist Liberation Theology and Yahweh as Holy Warrior: An Analysis of Symbol," in Janet Kalven and Mary L. Buckley (eds.), *Women's Spirit Bonding* (New York: Pilgrim, 1984), 202-12. See also E. Jane Doering in a presentation given to the American Weil Society, May 1992 (Mount Saint Mary's College, Los Angeles), "Simone Weil: A Woman's Voice." In the introductory paragraph, Doering states: In her notebooks Simone Weil declares, "Je ne suis pas féministe." [Doering comments:] How could she [Weil] declare this so adamantly when swirling all around her were discussions about women's suffrage? The small journals, in which she published her first essays [10 in all in *Révolution prolétarienne*] printed many persuasive articles supporting women's issues. Hers has to be a conscious choice because she lived a life guided by rational choices. To reflect, to understand and then to act was the constant concern in her life.

[3]Regarding Weil and Judaism, see David Minton (formerly Raper), "La critique weilienne de la conception de Dieu dans l'Ancien Testament," *Cahiers Simone Weil*, III, 2 (juin, 1980), 111-24. For other references regarding Weil and Judaism: in the same issue of CSW, see Jean Riaud, "Simone Weil et l'Ancien Testament," pp. 75-97; Gilbert Khan, "Limites et Raisons du refus de l'Ancien Testament par Simone Weil," pp. 98-110; Rolf Kuhn, "L'iconoclasme levé ou la vérité par l'image (Rôle du judaïsme et de la christologie chez Simone Weil pour la critique de la représentation)," pp. 125-40; "Extraits de lettres d'Alex Derczansky à Wladimir Rabi sur Simone Weil et les Juifs," pp. 143-45; in CSW, X, 3 (sept, 1987), "La Tradition mystique juive et Simone Weil," 189-295; in CSW, VI, 1 (mars, 1883), Martin Buber, "Bergson et Simone Weil devant Israël," pp. 46-54; in CSW, IV, 2 (juin, 1981), "Simone Weil, la résistance et la question juive (un entretien entre Marie-Louise Blum et Wladimir Rabi)," 76-84; in *Christianisme Social*, 64, 8-9 (août-septembre), L. et M. Benaroya, "Simone Weil et le Judaïsme," 577-587. See also Gilbert Kahn (ed.), *Simone Weil: philosophe, historienne et mystique* (Paris: Aubier Montaigne, 1978), esp. M. Broc-Lapeyre, "Les Hébreux" (1re partie, ch. 3, Le probleme du judaïsme), 123-34; et P. Giniewski, *Simone Weil ou la haine de soi* (Paris: Berg International, 1978), critique by W. Rabi and G. Kahn in CSW, I, 2 (sept. 1978), 30-42. See also CSW, De Simone Weil à la question juive, XIV, 4 (décembre 1991).

[4]I am grateful to Dr. Patricia Little (in a letter, dated 10/28/91) for Weil's references to Islam such as found in *Cahiers* II (Paris: Plon, 1972), 261 and 296, and in III (Paris: Plon, 1974), 222; to Allah, as in II, 183 and III, 134; and to Muhammad, such as II, 188. Dr. Little has also provided me with bibliography of Weil and Judaism.

[5]See, for example, what Weil wrote in 1940 to the French Minister of Public Education regarding the October 3, 1940 statute concerning the Jews: "The Christian, French, Hellenic Tradition is mine; the Hebrew tradition is foreign to me." (Pétrement, *Simone Weil*, 392.) In 1941, Weil wrote: "I consider the statute concerning Jews in a general way as being unjust and absurd, for how can one believe [referring to herself] that a university graduate in mathematics could harm little children who study geometry by the mere fact that three of his [sic in Pétrement's English translation] grandparents attended a synagogue"? (Pétrement, *Simone Weil*, 444)

[6]In 1922, a novel appeared entitled La garçone written by Victor Marguerite "[qui] s'est signalé . . . . comme un homme à idées d'avant- garde, simplistes et généreuses, féministes notamment." Monique Lerbier, the heroine, expresses the thesis of the author. "[She] has the qualities of a male celibate who is happy to be so: a lucrative and independent trade, *la garçonnire*, a car (at a time when even for males [owning one] was a privilege], [and] love without children. [Monique Lerbier] symbolizes a certain kind of feminine youth who wears very short hair (*à la garçonne*), knee-length skirts, [has] a wasp-waist, with no foundation garment, a barely discernible bosom, [who] smokes cigarettes and who, in the final analysis, 'virilizes' its body like its thoughts" (Jean Rabaut, *Histoire des féminismes français* [Paris: Stock, 1978], 276-77).

[7]Maïté Albistur and Daniel Armogathe, "Du futurisme au surréalisme, la resurgence des mythes de la femme," *Histoire du féminisme français, de l'empire napoléonien à nos jours* (Paris: Éditions des Femmes, 1977), 2, 586. (About this book, the authors claim: "Quinze siecles de l'histoire d'une protestation aussi ancienne que la pensée, une histoire tour à tour sereine et passionnée, grave et légre, besogneuse et festive, une histoire

arrachée aux pesanteurs des mythes, des doutes et de la mauvaise foi..." (Back Cover).

[8]Albistur and Armogathe, 586 ["Les traditionalistes comme Maurras y voient un signe certain de décadence, tandis que les mouvements d'avant-garde comme le futurisme ne sont pas loin de sacrifier la femme au héros viril, son matre."] In "De la vieille fille à la garçonne," *Autrement*, "Célibataires," 32 (mai, 1981), 222-30, Michelle Perrot, offers a positive interpretation of la garçonne. She writes: [F]emmes inconnues, indociles qui avez préféré les risques du célibat à la sécurité d'ennuyeux mariages, femmes créatrices de liberté, je vous salue . . ." (230). The reference directly refers to unmarried women and includes *la garçonne*.

[9]Dietz (Totowa, NJ: Rowman & Littlefield, 1988), p. 6. (Mme. Weil's quote is in Simone Pétrement, *Simone Weil: A Life*, tr. Raymond Rosenthal, [New York: Pantheon, 1976], 27.)

[10]Dietz, *Between the Human and the Divine*, p. 7 where one reads: "Mme. Weil induced Simone to accompany her to the opera and 'Simone agreed to have made for her not an evening gown but a tuxedo--a jacket and suit in black cloth, the jacket being similar to that of a man's suit'" (Pétrement, p. 28 / Dietz, p. 7.).

[11]Albistur and Armogathe, *Histoire du féminisme français*, 2, "Un féminisme intégral: Nelly Roussel," pp. 569-75.

[12]Valentine de Saint-Point wrote the following verses in Pomes d'orgueil/1908 (see Albistur and Armogathe, *Histoire du féministe français*, 2, 587) in an attempt to differenti-ate herself from *la femme-ange-enfant*:

Femmes enfants, en proie aux attendrissements,
Qui sans sensation ne goûtez pas la vie,
Qui jouez tous sans en avoir envie,
Je n'écris pas pour vous, pour vos amusements?

[13]Albistur and Armogathe, 586-587.

[14]See Margaret Collins Weitz, *Recent Writings on French Women* (Boston, MA: G.K. Hall, 1985), 8.

[15]Albistur and Armogathe, 586-587.

[16]Mary Condren, "Patriarchy and Death," in *Women's Spirit Bonding*, 185-86.

[17]Carol Christ, "War and Peace," 205, in Kalven and Buckley (eds.), *Women's Spirit Bonding*.

[18]Carol Christ, "Why Women Need the Goddess," in *Laughter of Aphrodite: Reflection on a Journey to the Goddess* (San Francisco: Harper & Row, 1987), 117.

[19]In this context, see "The Shekinah: The Feminine Face of God in Judaism," 242-48, in Gadon, *The Once and Future Goddess*. It should be noted here that some feminists do not reject "warrior gods". See for example, Karen McCarthy Brown, "Why Women Need the War God," in *Women's Spirit Bonding*, 190-201.

[20]Rosemary Radford Ruether, *Women-Church: Theology and Practice of Feminist Liturgical Communities* (San Francisco: Harper and Row, 1985), 69-70.

[21]Ruether, *Women-Church*, 75.

[22]Ruether, *Women-Church*, 76.

[23]In 1971, Bishop C. L. Meyers, opposing the ordination of women stated that the Episcopal Church priesthood was a "masculine conception." "A priest," he affirmed, "is a 'God symbol' whether he likes it or not. In the imagery of both the Old and New Testament God is represented in masculine imagery. Christ is the source of Priesthood. The Sexuality of Christ is no accident nor is his masculinity incidental. This is the divine choice." (San Francisco *Chronicle*, October 25, 1971, quoted in Stone, *When God Was a Woman*, p. ix. [See also five years later, the same point is made in the "Vatican Declaration: Women in the Ministerial Priesthood," Origins, 6, 33 (1977), 519-624, translating *Inter Insigniores, Acta Apostolicae Sedis*, 69 (1977), 98-116.] The Declaration affirms that the [Catholic] priest must bear a "natural resemblance" to Christ, a resemblance which would not exist in the Eucharist "if the role of Christ were not taken by a man" (*Origins*, 522).

[24]Ruether, *Women-Church*, 75-89. In addition to "male" sacramental power, Ruether refers equally in this chapter to male power both in theology and Church governance. Regarding the former, a woman friend of mine and political scientist at the University of Vienna told me that during the 1950s she had consulted with Karl Rahner about her taking a minor in theology. Rahner responded that sacred theology could not be reduced to the status of a minor. Theology could only be a major. However, it was not appropriate for my friend to major in theology because "du bist eine Dame," Rahner explained.

[25]Simone Weil, *The Notebooks of Simone Weil*, tr. Arthur Wills, II (London: Routledge & Kegan Paul, 1956), 351. [*Cahiers* II, 261.]

[26]"Dieu a abandonné Dieu. Dieu s'est vidé. Ce mot enveloppe à la fois la Création et l'Incarnation avec la Passion" (Weil, *La connaissance surnaturelle* [Paris: Gallimard, 1950], 68).

[27]Weil, *La connaissance surnaturelle*, 91 [author's trans]. The "umbrella" category for Weil is not creation but "abdication." Again in *La Connaissance surnaturelle*, p. 91, she wrote: "La création et le péché originel ne sont que deux aspects, différents pour nous, d'un acte unique d'abdication de Dieu. Et l'incarnation, la Passion sont aussi des aspects de cet acte [d'abdication]."

[28]Weil, *Notebooks*, I, 283. [II, 183.]

[29]Weil, *The First and Last Notebook*, 297. In Little, "Simone Weil's Concept of Decreation," 4.

[30]Little, *Simone Weil*, 55. Here, Little refers to Weil's *Pensées sans ordre concernant l'amour de Dieu* (Paris: Gallimard, 1962), 35. See also Weil, *Cahiers* II, 67-8.

[31]Weil, *First and Last Notebooks*, tr. Richard Rees (London: Oxford University, 1970), 120 and 297.

[32]J.P. (Patricia) Little, "Simone Weil's Concept of Decreation," p. 3, a presentation given during the American Weil Society Symposium, College of Wooster (Ohio), May 1991.

[33]Weil, *Attente de Dieu* (Paris: Fayard, 1966), 130.

[34]Weil, *Attente de Dieu*, 132.

[35]Weil, *Pensées sans ordre*, 47, referred to in Little, *Simone Weil*, 56.

[36]Diogenes Allen, "The Concept of Reading and the Book of Nature," p. 28, a presentation given during the Simone Weil's Philosophy of Culture symposium, College of Wooster, May, 1991. In Weil, see *Gravity and Grace*, Gustave Thibon (ed.), tr. Emma Craufurd (London: Routledge and Kegan Paul, 1972), 35-36. See also Weil, *First and Last Notebooks*, tr. Richard Rees (London: Oxford University, 1970), 132.

[37]Weil, *La Connaissance surnaturelle*, 168.

[38]Weil, *La pesanteur et la grâce* (Paris: Plon, 1948), 121. In *La Connaissance surnaturelle*, 92, Weil writes: "God gave to his finite creatures this power to transport themselves into the infinite." ("Dieu a donné à ses créatures ce pouvoir de se transporter dans l'infini.") And in *Attente de Dieu*, Weil writes: "Through the veil of the flesh, we receive from above 'presentiments' of eternity, which are sufficient to remove all doubts" (71). Again on p. 214, she speaks of "an orientation by which God presses us toward him [l'orientation qu'il nous imprime vers lui]."

[39]Weil, *La Connaissance surnaturelle*, 92. ["Dieu a donné à ses créatures ce pouvoir de se transporter dans l'infini."]

[40]Weil, *Attente de Dieu*, 71.

[41]Weil, *Attente de Dieu*, 214.

[42]Weil, *La Connaissance surnaturelle*, p. 175. In the same volume, see references to hunger, especially pp. 249-54. Weil states: "Faire mourir de faim la partie périssable de l'âme, le corps étant encore vivant. Ainsi le corps de chair passe directement au service de Dieu" (p. 252). Weil is not writing about suicide--the physical killing of the body. Again in *La Connaissance surnaturelle*, she writes: "Le sacrifice de Dieu est la création; celui de l'homme est la destruction. Seulement l'homme n'a le droit de détruire que ce qui lui appartient; c'est-à-dire non pas même son corps, mais exclusivement sa volonté" (168-69). See also, Judith Van Herik, "Simone Weil's Religious Imagery: How Looking Becomes Eating," in *Immaculate and Powerful: The Female in Sacred Image and Social Reality*, Clarissa W. Atkinson, Constance H. Buchanan & Margaret R. Miles (Eds.), (Boston, MA: Beacon, 1985), 260-82.

[43]Weil explains: "Every man, seeing himself from the point of view of God the Creator, should regard his own existence as a sacrifice made by God. I am God's abdication. The more I exist, the more God abdicates. So if I take God's side rather than my own I ought to regard my existence as a diminution, a decrease. When anyone succeeds in doing this, Christ comes to dwell in that person's soul. As regards myself, I ought to repeat in the opposite sense the abdication of God, I ought to refuse the existence that has been given me, to refuse it because God is good. As regards other people, I ought to imitate God's abdication itself, to consent not to be in order that they may be; and this in spite of the fact that they are bad" (Weil, *First and Last Notebook*, 213).

[44]Little, "Simone Weil's Concept of Decreation," 3.

[45]Weil, *First and Last Notebook*, 211.

[46]Weil, *First and Last Handbook*, 212.

[47]Weil, *First and Last Notebook*, 217.

[48]Little, *Simone Weil: Waiting on Truth* (New York: St. Martin's, 1988), 56.

[49]The God of Christians, according to Weil, is not a God of power. She wrote: "[T]his is not so [that he is a God of power] for the God of the Christians" (*Cahiers* II, 66--in Minton, "La critique weilienne," 114)--this I believe to be a reference to the 1952-55 edition of *Cahiers*.); namely, a supernatural God unlike YHWH, who is a natural God. Israel's God is a heavy God, associated to the physical laws of matter, the descending movement of gravity (see a discussion of *Kabod* (glory of God) in Minton, "La critique weilienne," CSW, p. 114.). *Leur Dieu [celui d'Israël] était lourd* (*Cahiers* II, 28, in Minton, 114).

[50]Weil, *First and Last Notebook*, 218.

[51]Weil, *Notebooks*, I, 283. [*Cahiers* II, 183.]

[52]Weil, *First and Last Notebook*, 123.

[53]Weil, *First and Last Notebook*, 297. In Little, "Simone Weil's Concept of Decreation," 4.

[54]Weil, *Notebooks*, I, 283. [*Cahiers* II, 183.]

[55]See Weil's description of Judaism deprived of mediation or incarnation, Weil, *Cahiers* I (Paris: Plon, 1970), 229-233.

[56]Weil, *Notebooks*, II, 581. [*Cahiers* III, 222.]

[57]Also connected to the idea of time and crucifixion. See Minton, 118. Also related to metaxu, "[e]very representation which draws us toward the non-representable. Need for metaxu in order to prevent us from seizing hold of nothingness instead of full being" (*Notebooks*, I, 233).

[58]Weil, *La connaissance surnaturelle*, 222.

[59]Weil, *Pensées sans ordre*, p. 48. In Little, "Le refus de l'idolatrie dans l'oeuvre de Simone Weil," CSW, II, 4 (décembre, 1979), 199.

[60]Weil wrote: "On ne faisait pas de statues à Jéhovah; mais Israel est la statue de Jéhovah. On a fabriqué ce peuple, comme une statue de bois, à coups de hache" (*Cahiers*, I, 233).

[61]Weil, *Letter to a Priest* (London: Routledge and Kegan Paul, 1953), 16. [*Lettre à un religieux* (Paris: Gallimard, 1951), 15. In Little, "Le refus de l'idolatrie," 202, where the idea of the divinization of history--which for Weil is idolatry--is very clearly explained.]

[62]Weil, *La connaissance surnaturelle*, 82.

[63]Weil, *La connaissance surnaturelle*, 136. In Little, "Le refus de l'idolatrie," 207-08.

[64]See in *La pesanteur et la grâce*, Weil's view of Rome and Israel. "Rome, c'est le gros animal athée, matérialiste, n'adorant que soi. Israël, c'est le gros animal religieux. Ni l'un ni l'autre n'est aimable. Le gros animal est toujours répugnant" (162). [Le 'gros animal' in Weil--as she found it in Plato--is any collectivity (see for example in *La pesanteur et la grâce*, 160]. See also Little, CSW, II, 4 (décembre, 1979), 208+ and Weil, *Letter to a Priest*, 78+.

[65]This comment reflects the world's geographical situation of the late 'thirties and early 'forties.

[66]Weil, *Notebooks*, II, 505. [*Cahiers*, III, 134.]

[67]Weil, *First and Last Notebooks*, 120 and 297.

[68]Little, "Simone Weil's Concept of Decreation," 3, a presentation given at the American Weil Society symposium, College of Wooster, May 1991.

[69]In Weil, *La pesanteur et la grâce*, 161-70, one can read Weil's view on Israel. For example she wrote:

> Dieu a fait à Moïse et à Josué des promesses purement temporelles à une époque où l'Egypte était tendue vers le salut éternel de l'âme Les Hébreux, ayant refusé la révélation égyptienne, ont eu le Dieu qu'ils méritaient: un Dieu charnel et collectif qui n'a parlé jusqu'à l'exil à l'âme de personne (à moins que, dans les Psaumes)? . . . Parmi les personnages des récits de l'Ancien Testament, Abel, Enoch, Noé, Melchisédech, Job, Daniel seuls sont purs. Il n'est pas étonnant qu'un peuple d'esclaves fugitifs, conquérants d'une terre paradisiaque aménagée par des civilisations au labeur desquelles ils n'avaient eu aucune part et qu'ils détruisaient par des massacres--qu'un tel peuple n'ait pu donner grand-chose de bon. Parler de 'Dieu éducateur' au sujet de ce peuple est une atroce plaisanterie (166-67).

[70]Weil, *La Connaissance surnaturelle*, 172.

[71]Weil, *La Connaissance surnaturelle*, 172.

[72]*La Connaissance surnaturelle*, p. 173. See Riaud, "Simone Weil et l'Ancien Testament,' CSW, III, 2 (juin, 1980), 75-97, esp. 95. In *The Notebooks*, I, 228-29, Weil wrote: "The Roman Empire had destroyed the religions in the oikoumene (except the Jewish) at the moment when Christianity appeared. The Jews alone resisted the State religion. But they were destroyed in A.D. 70. Christianity inherited from all these religions. It only took root in the Roman world (and not even in the whole of the Roman world because of the Mohammedan religion.) [And yet Russia, Armenia, Ethiopia . . . ."]

[73]See Little, *Simone Weil*, "The Good and the Necessary," 53-66.

[74]Weil, *Notebooks*, II, 379. [*Cahiers* II, 296.]

[75]*Notebooks*, II, 379. [*Cahiers* II, 296.] Notice: there are two other joint references to Judaism and Islam; *Cahiers* I, 229 and 232-33 [first ed. p. 162]; see CSW III, 2 (juin, 1988), Gilbert Khan, "Limites et raisons du refus de l'Ancien Testament par Simone Weil," 104; also *Cahiers* II, 188 (*Notebooks*, I, 287). Regarding the Trinity in Weil, see Patrick Sherry, "Simone Weil on Beauty," 12-17, a presentation given at the American Weil Society Philosophy of Culture symposium, College of Wooster, May, 1991.

[76]François Varillon, *The Humility and Suffering of God* (New York: Alba, 1983), 80-81. [French: *L'humilité de Dieu* (Paris: Centurion, 1974), 107- 108.] In *Cahiers Simone Weil*, see Alain Vinson, "L'Ordre de la charité chez Pascal, chez Péguy et chez Simone Weil," XIV, 3 (septembre, 1991), 139-240).

[77]For example, Merlin Stone, *When God Was a Woman*, (San Diego/New York/London: A Harvest Book, Harcourt Brace Jovanovich, 1976); Elinor W. Gadon, *The Once and Future Goddess* (San Francisco: Harper and Row, 1989); and see above references to Carol Christ and Rosemary Radford Ruether.

[78]Christ, "Feminist Liberation Theology and Yahweh as Holy Warrior," 205.

[79]An example regarding the deity's almighty demeanor as identified with history is the following which might "evoke racist claims about divinely apportioned lands to particular peoples. Thus Menachem Begin allegedly stated: 'Nobody has the right to tell me whether I can stay in Judea or Samaria, since this right is given to me by God the Father of Abraham, Isaac and Jacob'" (quoted in Charles Davis, "The Political Use and Misuse of Religious Language," *Journal of Ecumenical Studies*, 26, 3, (Summer 1989), 483. It should be noted here that Weil also argues that the result of the identification of power and war with the deity--which translates itself into the human conduct of power and war--is humans wielding power that eventually destroys not only other humans but also the possessors of power. But this is the topic of another paper. See for example the theme of Weil's *L'Iliade ou le pome de la force* (ET Mary McCarthy, *The Iliad; or The Poem of Force* [Wallingford, PA: Pendle Hill, 1962, c1956]), where

> the real hero of the Iliad . . . is force, that force which turns men into inanimate objects. Sometimes it kills, sometimes death is delayed, but always it turns a man to stone . . . , and the person wielding force behaves exactly as if he were confronted with an inanimate object . . . . The particular genius of the Iliad, however, is to have portrayed the protagonists not as masters and slaves, conquerors and conquered, but as all being equally subject to force. No one possesses force in the end, even those who have the illusion of doing so (Little, *Simone Weil*, 60).

[80]See quoted above: "I do not attribute war to the male nature, nor do I argue that women are incapable of warlike action, but I do believe that as feminists we must examine the equation of 'manhood' and power with war that has been the legacy of patriarchal cultures . . . . Patriarchy and large-scale war arose together, *although not by simple cause and effect* . . . . [with] warlike invaders during the second, third, and fourth millennia B.C.E. The warlike Zeus was the God of these patriarchal peoples" (Christ, "War and Peace," in Kalven and Buckley (eds.) *Women's Spirit Bonding*), 205.

[81]Simone de Beauvoir, *The Second Sex*, quoted in Stone, *When God Was a Woman*, p. viii. In *Simone Weil: A Modern Pilgrimage* (Reading, MA: Addison-Wesley, 1987), Robert Coles observes: "At only nineteen, [Simone Weil] had passed the entrance examination of the prestigious École Normale Supérieure; it is a well-known fact that she scored highest on that examination, and that the second highest score was received by a student also named Simone--last name: de Beauvoir" (p. 8). Although both Simones took the same Normale's entrance exams at the Sorbonne, it appears that de Beauvoir met Weil only once. In *Mémoires d'une jeune fille rangée* (Paris: Gallimard, 1958), de Beauvoir writes: "[Weil] intrigued me because of the great reputation she had of being intelligent and of her bizarre way of dressing [*accoutrement bizarre*]. . . . I managed one day to approach her . . . . She declared in a harsh tone that one thing only mattered today on earth: the Revolution that would give [food] for everyone to eat. I retorted no less peremptorily that the problem was not to make everybody happy but to find a meaning to their existence. She eyed me from head to foot (*elle me toisa*]: 'It's easy to see that you have never gone hungry,' she said. Our relations stopped there" (236- 37). See also Pétrement, *Simone Weil*, pp. 51-52. A conservative newspaper of the time referred to Weil as a "red virgin of the tribe of Levi, bearer of Muscovite gospels" (in Coles, *Simone Weil*, 9).

[82]Ruether, *Women-Church*, 73-4.

Judaism's Influence upon

the Syriac Christians

of the Third and Fourth Centuries

Frederick G. McLeod, S.J.

The Syriac-speaking church has fascinated Western theologians over the centuries. Though little is known for certain about its origins, we do possess sufficient extant works from the third and fourth centuries that allow us to make some fairly reasonable hypotheses. What is particularly interesting about the early Syriac church is that it confronts us with some notable major differences in approaches, emphases, and practices than those we find surviving among the Greek and Latin Fathers of the same period. This paper intends to explore one area that has especially intrigued scholars over the past century--the number of parallels between the Syriac writings of the third and fourth centuries and Jewish literature.

This question of parallelism has led to a lively scholarly debate as to whether the Syriac-speaking Christians are in fact relying upon Jewish sources and, if so, what sources and to what extent. As is evident, this is a critically important issue. For if the Syriac-speaking Christians living outside the Roman Empire have faithfully preserved a *direct* line with the authentic early Judeo-Christian[1] tradition, then we have at hand an independent source for investigating the original apostolic kerygma before it underwent alterations and, according to some,[2] suffered a radical transformation by those imbued with Greek philosophical thought. This is the issue we wish to examine.

We will begin our inquiry with a brief sketch, highlighting who the Syriac-speaking Christians are we are concerned about and what we know of early Syriac Christianity. After this, we will present the opinions of those who hold that the Syriac church was tightly bound to rabbinical traditions, even in the fourth century when both sides were engaging each other in bitter polemics. After this, we will balance this view of a direct dependency by examining the arguments of those who disagree--in varying nuanced ways--with this position. At the end, I will offer my own opinion

and broach for the reader's consideration how Aphrahat's way of contending with the Jews of his day can serve as a model for Christian-Jewish-
Islamic dialogue today.

WHO ARE THE SYRIAC-SPEAKING CHRISTIANS?

We can view the Syriac[3] world of the third and fourth centuries
from a number of different perspectives. Geographically, it stretched in
a band bounded west to east from the Mediterranean coast to the Persian
Gulf and from north to south by the borders of Armenia and the Arabian
peninsula. Politically, it was divided into two very different regions,
whose frontiers were constantly shifting like an incoming and outgoing
tide, depending on which army, the Roman, Parthian, or Persian, was
victorious at that moment. The usual line separating the Roman Empire
from the other two[4] was roughly the border between present-day Syria
and Iraq. The two regions remained fairly constantly under Roman/Byzan-
tine and Parthian/Persian control until both sides were defeated by Islamic
forces in the seventh century.

In the western section, that part that remained for the most part under
Roman/Byzantine dominion, the leading urban centers such as Antioch
and Damascus, spoke Greek, with Syriac, an eastern Aramaic dialect,
holding sway in the countryside. In the eastern section, that part under
Parthian and Persian control, Syriac was the predominant language for
Christians, though Greek was doubtless known by many on both sides of
the frontier, particularly by those who were engaged in trade and diploma-
cy between the Roman empire and the Persian Kingdom. The two leading
Syriac-speaking Christians in the fourth century, Aphrahat and Ephrem,
whose works we will be basing our present conclusions upon, appear to
have been conversant only in Syriac, not in Greek.

Until the deathbed conversion of Constantine, the Syriac Christians
living under Parthian and Persian rule were treated tolerably well. After
this, the Sassanid kings (a Persian dynasty from the second to the seventh
century) began to regard them as pro-Roman, especially when the Byzantine emperors began to proclaim themselves as protectors of all Christians
without as well as within the empire. Eventually in the fourth century,
the Sassanid King Shapur II subjected them to a brutal persecution,
perhaps abetted--though the evidence is inconclusive[5]--by the Jewish
community. Afterwards, the east Syriac-speaking Christians were extremely circumspect in their ecclesiastical dealings with the west, in order not

to offend their Persian rulers. This fostered an attitude of independent self-determination that later made it much easier for those east Syriac Christians living in the Persian empire to break definitively with the western church over its condemnations of Theodore of Mopsuestia and Nestorius. These are the Syrians whom we now wish to consider.

The Early Origins of the East Syrian Christians

Our present historical knowledge about the origins of those Christians living in the eastern section under Parthian and Persian control is, as we have noted earlier, cloaked in obscurity. The few sources[6] we now possess appear to be based upon legendary material. Syriac scholars differ as to whether these writings contain some nuggets of truth, for example does the account in the *Doctrine of Addai* about a Christian missionary sent by Jesus to Edessa and staying with a Jewish merchant have some factual basis? However, it seems certain that a Christian community did exist in Seleucia-Ctesiphon (an area northwest of Babylon) around the end of the first century and that there were Christians living near the Euphrates during the second century.[7] The discovery of Syriac inscriptions on graves on the island of Kharg supports the view that some form of Christianity or the Mandaean heresy had spread as far as the Persian Gulf by the third century.[8]

As regards the center of the east Syriac Christians, H.J.W. Drijvers[9] argues for Edessa (now the Turkish city of Urfa) which, until it fell under Roman-Byzantine control in A.D. 216, belonged to the kingdom of Osrhoëne. He believes that missionaries spread from here to evangelize those living farther to the east. Robert Murray objects to this view. He maintains that the faith emphases of the east Syrians cannot be adequately explained as coming from the melting-pot of Edessa. He opts for Adiabene, a state situated to the east of Osrhoëne, as the initial source of the east Syriac Christians dwelling outside the Roman Empire.[10] Since his position has, as we will see, a major bearing on the topic of this paper, we need to pause and consider Murray's speculations on the origins of this branch of Syriac-speaking Christianity.

Murray conjectures that the legendary account in the *Doctrine of Addai* relating the conversion of King Abgar of Edessa at the hands of Addai, one of Jesus' seventy disciples, may actually be a garbled memory[11] about an event that the Jewish historian Josephus makes mention of in the first century. Josephus proudly reports the manner in which the royal family of Adiabene was converted to Judaism.[12] This seems to have lasted as a Jewish kingship until it was overthrown by the Emperor Trajan in the second century. Later it became a vassal state under Parthian control. It seems safe to assume that throughout this turmoil, there remained a sizeable Jewish community in Adiabene. Murray believes that it was to this community that Christian missionaries originally came from Palestine (perhaps in flight from Roman vengeance after the Jewish revolts in A.D. 70 and 132-35) and began to make converts. If so, this would suggest that the original Christian community was a breakaway movement from Jews living in Adiabene.[13] F. Rieliet, like Murray, is of the opinion that Edessa was evangelized at the end of the first century by Judeo-Christians coming from Adiabene.[14] At a later date, perhaps around the fifth century when the *Doctrine of Addai* seems to have been written, the inhabitants of Edessa wove the distant memory of a first-century royal conversion at Adiabene into their own historical record. They would have done so in order to strengthen their ecclesiastical standing by claiming that their city was one of the first centers of Christianity.

While readily granting that such speculations are tenuous, Murray believes that other pieces of evidence are supportive. The first is archeo-logical. The typical church in Mesopotamia of that period had in the center of the nave a raised area called the "bema," from which the presiding priest conducted the liturgy of the Word. Because of its similarity to the bema in a synagogue, Murray sees this as buttressing his contention that the first Syriac Christians were of a Jewish background.[15] The second argument is the fact that the homilies of both Aphrahat and Ephrem reflect a tradition notably at variance with that of the Greco-Roman world, of which Edessa was then a part. If the east Syrians were converted by missionaries from Edessa, we should expect to find a much greater affinity between the two than what we have at hand.[16]

Murray notes too how the statutes of the famed theological school of Nisibis (founded by Narsai in the second half of the fifth century) are close to those of the Qumrân Community Rule.[17] For instance, the head of the Syriac school occupied the exegete's chair and was called a *rabban* (our "master"). Such a designation is similar to that employed in the Jewish schools and suggests some awareness, if not dependency, upon a Jewish model. It would seem highly unlikely that Jews would have followed a Christian educational pattern. More probably the first Christian converts continued a pattern they were familiar with and raised in--perhaps at Adiabene.

This brief historical overview has but one purpose: to show that there could be some plausible justification for asserting the existence of a bond between the early Syriac church and a Jewish community. This provides us with a background as we begin to consider the numerous literary parallels that scholars have singled out between Aphrahat and Ephrem and extant Talmudic literature. For us, the central--and **the** critical--issue to be examined is simply this: to what extent are these Christian and Jewish writings interrelated and, if it is the case, dependent upon each other.

THE SIMILARITIES BETWEEN SYRIAC AND JEWISH LITERATURE

Scholars began to attend to the presence of Jewish literary forms in the writings of Aphrahat and Ephrem in the last part of the nineteenth century. Interest began to be aroused when William Wright[18] published his critical Syriac text of Aphrahat's twenty-three homilies. Other scholars soon became involved when several of these homilies were translated from Syriac into western languages.[19] Salomo Funk was the first to examine scriptural passages common to Aphrahat and the Talmud, especially from the Pentateuch.[20] He concluded that Aphrahat's exegesis is completely dependent on the rabbinical traditions of Palestine and Babylon. Louis Ginzberg expanded further upon this by comparing and noting how Aphrahat's views concerning the soul, God, and divine retribution show not only that he is "a docile pupil of the Jews" but that "no [other] church father was ever so strongly influenced by rabbinical Judaism as this defender of Christianity against the Jews."[21]

Frank Gavin continued the study in his doctoral dissertation by examining Aphrahat's and rabbinical beliefs regarding creation, the fall, and death.[22] Though quite careful to acknowledge that Aphrahat's eschatology is closer to Philo's than to the Rabbis', he reached the conclusion that even a superficial examination of the large number of exact parallels in Aphrahat's thought and method with rabbinical literature reveals that Aphrahat is a "docile pupil of the Jews."[23]

A CRITICAL EVALUATION

In a critical, highly detailed response to these studies,[24] the Jewish scholar Jacob Neusner calls for caution. He especially challenges the previous conclusions that Aphrahat is relying upon rabbinical sources.[25] Since Neusner is so well versed in rabbinical matters, his main objection needs special attention. He begins by carefully examining the concepts, expressions, rhetorical devices in Aphrahat that have been presented as having significant parallels in rabbinic literature. At the end, he raises what is the central and decisive question regarding Aphrahat's close dependency upon rabbinical literature when he asks: "What do these parallels and commonalities prove?"[26] To answer this, he then turns to the exhaustive investigation of Morton Smith, his former teacher,[27] into all the different kinds of parallels and the conclusions that one can legitimately draw from each.

Neusner notes, for instance, that there are verbal parallels; parallels of idiom, of meaning, and of literary form; parallels too of parallelism and of association; and parallels that are either complete or have a fixed difference. He applies these distinctions to the parallelisms that have been cited and points out the flaws in the argumentation in their support or the cautions that must be observed in light of the evidence or lack of evidence at hand. A few examples will suffice. As regards the parallel between Aphrahat's word for Scripture *uraita* and the Talmud's *oraita*, Neusner observes that parallelism of this sort is to be expected in a region where Aphrahat and the rabbis spoke closely related Semitic dialects. One expects to find similar words for the same ideas, especially from two groups using the same Scriptures.[28]

Concerning the parallelisms where the same literary forms are found in Aphrahat's and the Rabbis' commentaries on Genesis and Exodus, Neusner holds that their significance is still an open question. But he strongly insists that we ought not assert in advance that this kind of parallelism indicates that Aphrahat had indeed received a rabbinical education.[29] Further proof is needed. He raises the same objection to the opinion that Aphrahat has set up a parallel between Christ and the church on the one hand and the Torah and Israel on the other, and that Aphrahat substitutes the former whenever he encounters the latter in a text. These kinds of parallel substitution, Neusner rightly insists,[30] can hardly be cited as evidence demonstrating a close, direct dependence of one upon the other.

Neusner wonders too why the writers in question manifest no interest whatever in exploring the possibility that there may be other reasons to explain the existing parallelisms. An instance would be the clear presence of a common tradition between the church and the synagogue. Simply to cite *targumim* (Aramaic paraphrases of the Old Testament) dating from the pre-Christian era and compilations from the medieval period without

addressing whether or not these have any meaningful bearing for Mesopo-
tamian Jews of the fourth century is, for Neusner, highly questionable.[31]
Nor have the writers on this question considered--unlikely as this would
have been--the possibility that it was not Jewish but rather Christian
thought that is the source responsible for these parallelisms.[32]

Neusner sums up well the inherent weakness in this kind of argumentation, when he writes:

> Parallels standing by themselves prove little. Many of the parallels
> drawn between Aphrahat and rabbinical literature prove not to be
> parallel at all. Some are so commonplace as to mean nothing to begin
> with, being little more than citations of the same Scripture in the same
> way. Indeed, if we compare the parallel comments on Scripture with
> the substantially larger number of components which are not parallel
> at all, and which stand in no polemical or exegetical relationship, and
> if we furthermore add to these the even larger number of Scriptures
> cited by Aphrahat on which the rabbinical tradition preserves no
> comment at all, we can conclude only one thing. Aphrahat and the
> rabbis had practically nothing in common, other than they lived in a
> single cultural continuum and believed in the same revelation.[33]

While rejecting the opinions of those who hold for a direct dependence of Aphrahat upon rabbinical[34] literature, Neusner does grant, as
his quote states, some sort of cultural contact. Of the three groups of Jews
who were living in Mesopotamia at the time of Aphrahat, namely the
inhabitants of Adiabene, Nisibis, and the descendants of the ten tribes in
Babylon, Neusner believes on the basis of historical and geographical
reasons that the Jews whom Aphrahat was most likely in contact with were
the descendants of the first century converts to Judaism at Adiabene.[35]
While these were indeed Jewish, Neusner has discovered nothing in his
studies to indicate that they had ever adopted the then Pharisaic form of
Judaism prevalent among the Jews in Babylon. He believes that it is more
than likely that the Jews at Adiabene followed their own sectarian variations.[36]

Robert Murray expands upon Neusner's view. After offering his own
speculations--which we have outlined above--on how the original east
Syriac-speaking Christian community had grown out of a Jewish back-
ground in Adiabene, he examines passages showing how Aphrahat and
Ephrem were both familiar with Jewish interpretations of the Hebrew
Scriptures. We see this exemplified and highlighted in the deft way that
Aphrahat weaves a paraphrase of Deuteronomy 20:1-8 with the story of

Gideon and the New Testament passages on spiritual warfare. For Murray, this points clearly to training in midrashic exegesis.[37] As another sign of this, he cites the conclusion that Sed reached after his careful study into Ephrem's paradise traditions that Ephrem's views reflect not a talmudic background but one revealing a primitive oral Torah.[38]

Murray too has analyzed Ephrem's method of scriptural exegesis and found it to be based on midrash and the application of haggadic (non-legal) materials of the Talmud that have parallels in rabbinic sources.[39] He believes that Ephrem's scriptural citations show that he is using an earlier version of the Peshitta (a free Aramaic paraphrase of the Hebrew Scriptures that was initially common to both the Jews and the Christians but later became for the Christians in Mesopotamia their Syriac edition) that contains "more readings in common with the targums[40] than the later standardized text has."[41] This is highly significant for two reasons. First, it suggests that the original targums written in Aramaic gradually underwent alterations as they were translated into local idioms, resulting in both an eastern as well as a Palestinian tradition of the Aramaic text of the Hebrew Scriptures. Secondly, it may explain why there are so many verbal parallels and differences between Aphrahat and Ephrem and later talmudic literature. They were all using a common source that was evolving in transmission.

Murray sees special significance in both Aphrahat's and Ephrem's designation of Syriac Christian ascetics as "sons of the Covenant."[42] Since these were all celibate, they would seem at first glance to be witnessing to an ascetical outlook that is Christian and not Jewish, as Judaism looks askance at celibacy. Murray notes that this view has undergone change with the discovery at Qumrân of a movement in first-century B.C.E. and C.E. Judaism in which the members called themselves "sons of the Covenant." While this group admitted married members, they also included an inner core of celibates who nourished a grandiose dream of taking part in an eschatological holy war.[43]

We must be careful not to exaggerate the weight of this similarity, but it does bear out Murray's contention that the ascetical practices detailed by Aphrahat and Ephrem concerning the "sons of the Covenant" were not alien to Judaism. It also suggests that a sectarian branch of Judaism, either the same as or similar to the one that existing at Qumrân, could have taken early root in Adiabene before Christianity appeared there. If so, this may explain why a life of celibacy as a way to encounter God in one's life would be attractive to the first Syriac-speaking Christians. This raises the problem, however, of who Aphrahat's target is in his defense of celibacy. If it is a Jew from Adiabene, one would expect that he would be familiar with a much earlier Jewish tradition favoring celibacy.[44]

CONCLUSIONS

What are we to conclude then from Jacob Neusner's and Robert Murray's critique? As Neusner has pointed out, we can only assume from the evidence we have at hand that the east Syriac-speaking Christians of the fourth century were distant cousins to--not direct dependents upon--the Rabbis of their day. The parallelisms cited simply do not prove the conclusion that has been drawn from them. Neusner's objection that the writers espousing a close dependency are yielding to parallelomania is justified. Yet Aphrahat's and Ephrem's frequent use of midrash and haggadic (non-legal) material from the Torah clearly indicates that they were at the very least heirs of a common heritage with the Jews of their day.

Murray has proposed a credible hypothesis on how this heritage could have been passed on. While rejecting the view that Syriac Christianity in the fourth century reflects a pure form of the Judeo-Christian faith espoused in Jerusalem--too many other forces would have cross-fertilized with this over the centuries--Murray still holds that it is likely that the origin of Syriac Christianity is the Jewish Christians who fled Roman wrath in the first or second century and sought refuge among the Jews in Adiabene. They then succeeded over a period of time in winning over some of these Jews to Christianity. The Jewish converts passed on their knowledge of and a devotion to their Aramaic version of the Hebrew Scriptures and their method of exegesis to the then growing gentile Christian group in Adiabene. Such an hypothesis helps to explain why Aphrahat's and Ephrem's writings reveal some similarities to the talmudic tradition but not with later orthodox rabbincal literature formalized in the sixth century at Babylon.

POLEMICAL CONTROVERSY

While Aphrahat and Ephrem manifest a dependency upon what appears to be a sectarian form of Judaism, we must also take note of the fact that the two communities were engaged in polemical disputes with each other.[45] Their negative and at times bitter remarks reveal--sadly--how far they had drifted apart. Since hostility of this sort would doubtless require time to reach such a state, this alone would suffice to reject the opinion that Aphrahat--who was not a Jew but a Gentile of Iranian descent--was a pupil of the Rabbis. But when and why did they split from one another?

If Murray is right, the separation would have begun some time in the first or second century. It would likely have accelerated after the conversion of Constantine when Christianity began to emerge as the predominant religious body in the Byzantine Empire. From then on, the split would have become a real concern, if not a threat, for the Jews in the fourth century, especially as more and more of the Syriac-speaking peoples turned to Christianity. For it would mean that the Jews could no longer dismiss Christianity as an insignificant and despised minority of whom no account need be taken. The Christians now enjoyed the backing of the Roman/Byzantine emperors who were frequently trying to extend their control over northern Mesopotamia.

Thus when the Persian King Shapur II began to oppress the Christians in the fourth century, some Jews may have seen this as a God-given opportunity to win back those of Jewish descent who had earlier or recently converted to Christianity, for Jews were not subject to Shapur's persecution. Aphrahat, therefore, may have been writing his anti-Jewish homilies with a twofold aim in mind: 1) to counteract those Jews trying to tempt Jewish Christians to escape possible death by returning to Judaism, and 2) to strengthen such Christians by proving from Jewish sources that Jesus was truly the Messiah and that Israel had been rejected in favor of the Christian church. Whether this hypothesis is true is only incidental, however, to the central point we wish to emphasize--that Aphrahat in his polemical joustings with his Jewish adversaries was well versed in their exegetical and argumentative methods.

Unfortunately we do not possess any Jewish counter-replies to Aphrahat and the bitter attacks by Ephrem. As Neusner observes, we have no historical evidence that the Jews of that period were even aware of the anti-Jewish homilies of the two men. If they were, they have simply responded as they usually did to any and all Christian claims--with silence or at most a reshaping of the symbolic or typical meanings that Christians found in Judaism's scriptural figures.[46] We have not the slightest indication from the Jewish side as to how the Jews regarded Christians in relation to themselves, especially on the question of whether they viewed the Syriac Christians as an offshoot from and a threat to their own community.

AN ECUMENICAL LESSON

The dispute between the two communities brings us to a final point that is relevant to the general theme of this convention: how ought those who profess to be descendants of Abraham react to serious religious disagreements among their communities? Jacob Neusner provides us with one answer to this in his work on *Aphrahat and Judaism* where he singles out Aphrahat as an exemplary model in this regard. After examining all the Church Fathers and Jews who wrote in the third and fourth centuries, he regards Aphrahat to be a unique theologian who "in developing his ideas, choosing Hebrew Scriptures to illustrate or demonstrate them, presenting reasons for the Christians' convictions...stands generally alone, original, inventive."[47]

What is especially impressive to Neusner is Aphrahat's rare ability not merely to argue in a balanced, reasonable way but to do so as a polemicist who has previously familiarized himself with the actually-held positions and arguments of his adversaries before he tries to respond to them. Rather than simply call up, as other Fathers have done, scriptural passages that Christians consider to be ironclad refutations of Jewish beliefs, or to introduce theological propositions that have no real interest for or impact upon Jews, Aphrahat uses materials that he and his Jewish adversaries regard as a common heritage, namely their Scriptures and history. In other words, he addresses the specific charges brought up by his adversaries and responds to them with arguments that they could understand and in a manner that reflects a keen sensitivity to how his words will be received.

Aphrahat stands out, therefore, as an historical, interreligious model for those who espouse Abraham as their common forefather. He emerges as a man willing honestly to speak up and assert what he is convinced to be right. But he does this in an informed way that is restrained, balanced, and sympathetic to the position maintained by his adversaries. Even when he opposes and rejects their views, he never descends into an anti-Judaic attack that repudiates all Jews without distinction. His preference is to win over, not to condemn. For he seems to be keenly aware of the truly radical changes that God's grace can accomplish in a community's as well as a person's life.

We too can learn from Aphrahat's informed and even tempered approach. He came of a community with a distinctive Jewish background-- as this paper has tried briefly to show and challenges our present-day attitudes and ways of dialoguing and disagreeing with those who believe as we do that Abraham is our common father. He instructs us to be not only open to but knowledgeable of the contents found in the Jewish and Muslim as well as the Christian holy books. We need--on all sides of the dialogue--to be mutually aware of and ready to respond to what each of us actually holds and argues for, rather than to what each of us believes and expects the other to be sympathetic to. The dialogue must be a genuine two-way street. Neusner's final enconium of Aphrahat as "the worthiest participant in the Jewish-Christian dialogue put forward in antiquity by either side,"[48] ought fittingly be attributed to us.

NOTES

[1]I think that it is important to observe the distinction that R. Murray makes in a footnote on p. 7 of his *Symbols of Church and Kingdom* (London: Cambridge University, 1975): '[the phrase, "Jewish Christian"] seems to me best kept to designate actual groups who combined Jewish observance with Christian faith, while "Judaeo-Christian" can appropriately be used more loosely to refer to the movements and elements in early Christianity which still reveal dominant influence of late [*sic*] Jewish thought forms."

[2]F. C. Burkitt believes that a knowledge of Syriac origins is critical for understanding the early evolution of Christianity and that it ought to have a serious impact on one's faith outlook. On pp. 6-7 of his *Early Christianity Outside the Roman Empire*, (Cambridge, 1899), he states: "Let me remind you in passing that this is not a merely literary question of *Quellenkritik*. On the contrary, it is the keystone of Protestantism. The one thing which historically justifies us in breaking with the Catholic tradition is this breach of continuity at the earliest period...in a word, we have a right privately to revise the judgments of the Church, mainly because the Church of the second century was so far removed in spirit and in knowledge from the life of Judaea in our Lord's day."

[3]Strictly speaking, "Syriac" refers to the literary language based on an eastern Aramaic dialect. It is sometimes used in this paper as signifying the people using this language.

[4]The Sassanid dynasty conquered the Parthians in the second century. For a brief contemporary survey of the relationship between the Roman/Byzantine Empire and the Sassanid kingdom, see Peter Bruns, *Das Christusbild Aphrahats des Persischen Weisen*, (Bonn: Borengässer, 1990), pp. 19-23.

[5]Cf. Jacob Neusner, *The History of the Jews in Babylonia* IV, (Leiden: Brill, 1969), pp. 26-27, for an evaluation of the evidence at hand.

[6]Such as the Chronicles of Edessa, Seert, and Arbela. For an evaluation of these works, see Bruns, *op. cit.*, pp. 10-17.

[7]See J.-M. Fiey, *Jalons pour une histoire de l'Église en Iraq*, in *Corpus Scriptorum Christianorum Orientalium* 310 Subs. 36 (Louvain: Secretariat du Corpus SCO, 1970), pp. 40-44.

[8]See M.L. Chaumont, "Les Sassanides et la christianisation de l'empire iranien au IIIe siècle de notre ère," *Revue d'Histoire des Religions* 165 (1964), 179; and also H.J.W. Drijvers, "Edessa und das Jüdische Christentum," in *East of Antioch* (London: Variorum Reports, 1984), p. 31.

[9]H.J.W. Drijvers, *op. cit.*, I "East of Antioch," p. 2; and VI "Early Syriac-Speaking Chrsitianity," pp. 170 and 173.

[10]Robert Murray, op. cit., p.9.

[11]See Murray, pp. 8-9.

[12]Murray, p. 9. We have no record of how long this Jewish kingdom lasted. Neusner believes it "likely that the royal family fled eastward during Trajan's invasion, and afterwards settled in Armenia. But if the conversion affected more than a few nobles, then some Jews must have been left behind." *Aphrahat and Judaism* (Leiden: Brill, 1971),

p. 148.

[13]Murray, p. 8.

[14]See F. Rieliet's entry on "Syriac" in the *Encyclopedia of the Early Church*, (New York: Oxford University, 1992).

[15]Murray, pp. 18-19. Cf. D. Hickley, "The Ambo in Early Liturgical Planning,"in *Heythrop Journal* VII (1966), 407-22.

[16]Even if F. Rieliet is correct in his view that Edessa was evangelized by Judeo-Christians from Adiabene, the divergence we detect between Edessa and Adiabene may be explained by the fact that the city of Edessa was exposed to several crosscurrents of theological thought that could over time have introduced changes in the simple, unsophisticated symbolic expression of the Christian faith introduced from Adiabene.

[17]See Murray, p. 24.

[18]I am indebted to Bruns and Neusner *op. cit.* for the reference to William Wright ed., *The Homilies of Aphraates, the Persian Sage* I: The Syriac Text (London, 1869). Bruns provides the most recent summary of Aphrahat's texts and translations.

[19]Translations are available in Joannes Parisot's *Aphraatis Sapientis Persae, Demonstrationes* in *Patrologia Syriaca*, Vol. II (Paris: Lutetiae Parisorum, 1907), pp. 1-489; Georg Bert's *Aphrahats des Persischen Weisen Homilien* (Leipzig, 1888); John Gwynn's selections (Demonstrations I, V, VI, VIII, X, XVII, XXI, and XXII) in P. Schaff and H. Wace's *A Select Library of Nicene and Post-Nicene Fathers* vol. 13 (New York: Christian Literature Co, 1898 and repr. Grand Rapids: Eerdmans, 1956); Jacob Neusner's selections (XI, XII, XIII, XV, XVI, XVII, XVIII, XIX, XXI, and parts of XXIII) in *Aphrahat and Judaism* (Leiden: Brill, 1971); and M.-J. Pierre's translations in *Aphraate le Sage Persan* Vols. 349 and 359 of *Sources Chrétiennes* (Paris: Cerf, 1988 and 1989). See Neusner *op. cit.* pp. 10-13 for an historical survey of how this question concerning Aphrahat's dependence developed.

[20]I am indebted to Neusner for the reference to Salomo Funk's *Die haggadischen Elemente in den Homilien des Aphraates* (Vienna, 1891), see especially pp. 9 and 53. For a bibliography of the early studies, see E. Lamirande, "Études bibliographique sur les Pères de l'Église et l'Aggada," *Vigiliae Christianae* 21 (1967), 1-11.

[21]The first quotation is from p. 664 col. b and the second from p. 663 col. b of Louis Ginzberg's article on "Aphrahat" in the *Jewish Encyclopedia* I.

[22]This was later published by Frank Gavin as a book, entitled *Aphraates and the Jews* (Toronto: AMS Press, 1923).

[23]Gavin, *op. cit.*, p. 58.

[24]For others who have written on this subject, see Jacob Neusner, *Aphrahat and Judaism* (Leiden: Brill, 1971), pp. 11-12.

[25]Neusner, especially pp. 150-95.

[26]Neusner, p. 153.

[27]Morton Smith, *Tannaitic Parallels to the Gospel*, in the *Journal of Biblical Literature*, Monograph Series, VI; also "The Present State of OT Studies," *Journal of Biblical*

Literature 88 (1969), 19-35.

[28]Neusner, p. 194.

[29]Neusner, p. 194.

[30]Neusner, p. 195.

[31]Neusner, pp. 148 and 154-55.

[32]Neusner, p. 154.

[33]Neusner, pp. 187-88.

[34]Neusner carefully distinguishes between Judaism and rabbinic Judaism on p. 155. He writes: "What is meant by Judaism? Gavin, not alone, sees 'Judaism' and 'rabbinic Judaism' as pretty much identical, and to him rabbinic Judaism is a monolith, unchanged and unchanging from some remote time in antiquity until the completion of the Babylonian Talmud and even later, medieval midrashic compilations. These conceptions obviously are false."

[35]Neusner, pp. 148-49.

[36]Neusner, p. 13. He is of the opinion that rabbis from Palestine set up schools in Babylon and Nisibis and imposed the oral as well as written Torah upon the Jews living there. The Jews at Edessa and Adiabene seem to have had no rabbinic schools. If one can judge from Aphrahat's remarks, they followed a kind of "Judaism based upon canonical Scriptures and little else" (p. 148). It is from among these latter that Christianity was able to make a sizeable number of converts (see p. 5).

[37]Murray, p. 15. Neusner is also impressed by Aphrahat's midrashic interpretations of Daniel 9 and the Grapecluster in Isaiah 65:8. See Neusner, p. 242.

[38]Murray, p. 10. The reference to N. Sed is to his article, "Les hymnes sur le paradis de saint Éphrem et les traditions juives," in *Le Muséon* LXXXI (1968), 455-501.

[39]Murray, p. 10.

[40]Neusner cautions that finding the same thought present in a targum and a Christian writer "may indicate only that targumic traditions and church traditions drew on the same antecedent materials. Nor is it to be taken for granted that the "targumim" are quintessentially Pharisaic-rabbinic" (p. 157).

[41]Murray, pp. 10-11.

[42]Murray, pp. 17-18.

[43]Matthew Black maintains that celibacy arose in this movement and subsequently in Judaeo-Christianity by an institutionalization of the sexual abstinence required for a holy war. See his article "The Tradition of Hasidean-Essene Asceticism: Its Origins and Influence" in *Aspects du Judéo-christianisme*, pp. 1932. The same kind of ascetical outlook is manifested in the sectarian Jewish writings found at Nag Hammadi.

[44]Drijvers believes that the Syriac emphasis on celibacy may have been determined more by the encratite ideals prevalent at Edessa in the third century.

[45]While Aphrahat is writing to Christians, he refers on occasion to an adversary, whom he variously calls a wise man, a scribe, a wise debater of Israel. Neusner observes that Aphrahat never indicates that his adversary is a rabbi and thinks that he may be, at least

in places, employing a literary device.

[46]Neusner, p. 244.

[47]Neusner, p. 242.

[48]Neusner, p. 244.

Sanctity of Life in Catholic and Jewish Thought: Convergence and Divergence

Patricia Talone

The first aim of interreligious dialogue, asserts Milwaukee Archbishop Rembert Weakland, is mutual respect. "This means more than toleration of differences."[1] It involves a positive attempt to understand and appreciate the other. It is important, Weakland maintains, in any dialogue to remember that no group is static or monolithic.

Currently, volatile moral discussion centers around human life issues, those at the beginning and end of life. Catholics, Jews and Muslims alike must be sensitive to each other's moral convictions as, together with other believers, they try to arrive at an ethical consensus on issues like abortion and euthanasia. Such dialogue demands, as the Milwaukee archbishop notes, utmost respect and willingness to listen to and understand similarities as well as differences among participants.

Human life topics have long played a central role in the present writer's theological inquiry, but a recent encounter with one of her college students compelled her to probe more deeply into Catholic and Jewish sanctity-of-life teaching. Paula was a non-traditional student, in her late sixties, auditing a medical ethics course because the topic vitally interested her. After the class discussed a unit on the biblical foundation for sanctity of life, Paula confided that she was a Jewish Holocaust survivor and that her war experience convinced her more than ever of life's value and our responsibility to support and sustain life. As the course continued, Paula argued eloquently and often for preservation of life for neonates, the elderly, and handicapped persons. Therefore, when she delivered an oral presentation calling for total freedom of choice in abortion, I expressed surprise at what seemed to be moral inconsistency. Motivated and puzzled by that encounter, I began dialogue with Paula, local rabbis, and Jewish health-care professionals in order to understand and appreciate both Jewish and Catholic ethical approaches.

THESIS

Religious explication of sanctity-of-life principles is in no way passé. Continued study and articulation of religious traditions remains a necessary component of the public debate about issues at the beginning and the end of life. Furthermore, even in areas where agreement may not be possible, as believing persons we must listen to and learn from one another. This paper explores the basis of the sanctity-of-life principle that Christians and Jews share. Because differences exist in interpreting and applying principles, it examines the specific issues of abortion and euthanasia so as to appreciate better the divergence of opinion in both the medical-moral and political arenas.

Given the differences between Jews and Catholics about end-of-life decisions, hospitals and health-care professionals should become aware of the teaching of each tradition. This is necessary to help physicians and patients understand the carefully crafted nuances of both religions because both abhor euthanasia while admitting that one need not do everything to forestall death.

WHAT IS MEANT BY SANCTITY OF LIFE?

Sanctity of human life is a spontaneous rather than a systematic term, arising from religious conviction that the human person is inviolable. Sanctity of life is implicit in the Hippocratic Oath by which a physician pledges to use all in his or her power to help the sick, to refrain from euthanasia ("[I will not give] a fatal draught to anyone if I am asked nor will I suggest any such thing") and abortion.[2] Western culture gradually strengthened the notion of sanctity of life. The expression itself gained wide usage in the ethical reflections of post-holocaust literature.[3] It was primarily Protestant theologians, Barth and Bonhoeffer among others, whose revulsion at the Third Reich's extermination tactics led them to proclaim the primacy of life's holiness. Barth, in *Church Dogmatics*, asserts that life deserves, "astonishment, humility, awe, modesty, circumspection and carefulness. . . ."[4] It seems that the sense of life's holiness remains so deeply imbedded in our moral imagination that only the possibility of the extermination of life forces us to articulate life's meaning.

The term "sanctity of life" does not find it's way into *The New Catholic Encyclopedia* of 1967 until its 1974 supplement. Apparently the term did not have wide Catholic usage until after the Roe v. Wade decision. Unfortunately, subsequent to that decision, the ordinary Catholic in the pew or even in the college classroom associates sanctity of life only with right to life for the unborn. Many Catholics do not connect the concept with the sanctity of life of the elderly, infirm, or handicapped, much less with issues like capital punishment or modern warfare.

Not all who uphold sanctity of life do so from a theistic perspective. Sociologist Edward Shils argues from a "natural metaphysic" that:

> the idea of sacredness is generated by the primordial experience of being alive, of experiencing the elemental sensation of vitality and the elemental fear of its extinction. Man stands in awe before his own vitality . . . the sense of awe is the attribution and therefore the acknowledgement of sanctity.[5]

Theologian Daniel Maguire likewise invokes experience, noting that "moral experience cannot be explained nor can we be true to our own experience if we do not accept the foundational role of our perception of the value of persons and their environment."[6]

Jewish Concept of Sanctity of Life

Judaism makes no attempt at a univocal teaching on sanctity of life, no appeal to a single, authoritative magisterial voice. Instead, Jewish ethicists appeal to the vast historical tradition of rabbinic teaching that applies religious thought to concrete, practical situations. What the researcher finds is definitely not "situation ethics," at least not in the pejorative sense of that term. This is because Jewish teaching recognizes some sacrosanct norms that flow throughout all of Hebrew thought—whether it be Orthodox, Conservative, Reformed or Reconstructionist.

The Hebrew Scriptures, particularly in their two creation narratives, provide the primary influence for Western culture's sanctity-of-life concept. In Genesis 1, God creates all things good and purposeful. Human beings stand at the apex of creation and have the highest value; all things are created for humanity's sake and are subordinated to us. Because we come from the hand of a loving Creator, we acknowledge that we do not own our lives, God does. Theologian Robert Nelson, in *Human Life: A Biblical Perspective for Bioethics*, declares that "the value of life is never independent or intrinsically cherishable by itself, for it always remains relative to the providential care and purposeful will of Yahweh."[7]

The high value placed on human life reflects our creation in the

image of God (Genesis 1:27; 5:1; 9:6) and the profound similarity between humans and their Creator.[8] Unlike later Christian scholars, most
modern Jewish theologians do not attempt to explain how humankind is
made in God's image. To be a person, many Jewish scholars tell us, is
to be an integral unity: the boundary between flesh and body remains indistinct and the concept of a body contrasted with a soul is completely
foreign.[9] Because an image imitates its original, the human made in God's
image is called to emulate the Creator, to walk in God's ways (Deut. 10:
12; 11:22; 26:17) and to be like God. To be alive is to receive life from
God; therefore it is incumbent upon each recipient of life to make life
holy, to "sanctify" life. This doctrine, called that of *Imago Dei*, profoundly influenced Christian thinking from the time of the Church Fathers.

Creation in God's image carries with it responsibilities. Each person
is "charged with preserving, dignifying and hallowing" life, not only one's
own, but also one's neighbor's.[10] J. David Bleich, in *Contemporary Jewish
Ethics*, quotes Rabbi Akiva ben Joseph who taught that the commandment
to love one's neighbor was the fundamental precept of the Torah. "Whoever sustains a single person," the Rabbi instructed, ". . . is as one who
sustains the whole world, and whoever destroys a single person is as one
who destroys the whole world; for every person bears the divine image,
and every person was created unique and irreplaceable."[11]

Judaism accords every human life the highest value, calling it
"absolute," "infinite," and "supreme." In Jewish law and moral teaching,
preservation of life precedes every other consideration. It is an absolute
good in its own right and not a good to be preserved in relation to other
goods.[12] The intrinsic value of life transcends the moral worth of the law
and of legal and religious observance.[13] Thus, the Jew is bound to
preserve life until the moment of death.

Bleich notes that even life accompanied by suffering is regarded as
preferable to death. "[P]reservation of life extends to human life of every
description and classification, including the feeble-minded, the mentally
deranged and yes, even a person in a so-called vegetative state." The
mitzvah of saving a life is neither enhanced nor diminished by virtue of
the quality of life preserved."[14] Most Jewish thinkers resist the term
"quality of life" because of life's intrinsic holiness. Nevertheless, as we
shall see later, when it comes to recognizing some practical quality-of-life
judgments, there are striking convergences between Catholic and Jewish
ethics in end-of-life issues.

Christian Concept of Sanctity of Life

The Christian concept of sanctity of life, like that of the Hebraic tradition, rests upon the Genesis account of creation. Christianity believes that human beings are made in the image of God and are part of the created order. What is not always so clear is exactly what the individual Christian understands by the phrase, "made in the image of God."

For an early Christian like Irenaeus of Lyons, we resemble God because Jesus became a man and dwelled among us, thus elevating our mortal state through his life, death and resurrection. For him, our perfection consisted in the union of soul with body, united in turn with the risen Christ. Human dignity resides in the flesh as well as in the spirit because the person had been fashioned after the Word who became flesh to dwell among us.[15] Unlike his Jewish predecessors, Irenaeus clearly distinguishes between body and soul, but unlike his gnostic contemporaries, the distinction does not represent a thoroughgoing dualism.

Augustine posited a necessarily sharp dichotomy between body and soul. The way we resemble God, he thought, is in our superior intellect. He stated that "the pre-eminence of man consists in this, that God made him to his own image by giving him an intellect by which he surpasses the beasts."[16] Aquinas, building on Augustine's thought, maintained that only intelligent creatures are made in God's image and that the body bears the image of God only in the "manner of a trace." The true image is properly reflected in the mind.[17]

Interpretations of Augustine and Aquinas have had both negative and positive effects upon contemporary Christian thought. Positively, one can recognize that life is more than simple bodily existence; it has a purpose. As Pius XII stated, "Life, health, all temporal activities are in fact subordinated to spiritual ends."[18] Negatively, some persons wrongly locate the essence of the human in functional rationality alone (measured by such criteria as intelligence tests or grade point averages and not necessarily including affectivity, relationality, ability to connect and integrate intellectual data). This assumes a hierarchical structuring that relegates those who do not possess an "adequate" reasoning skill to the lower strata of being. Children, the mentally handicapped, and the illiterate, not to mention women, are frequently treated as if they are not truly human—an abuse with striking ethical overtones for the treatment of the sick and dying.[19]

More contemporary theological depictions of humanity, as seen in Karl Barth, Karl Rahner and the Council Fathers in the *Pastoral Constitu-*

tion on the Church in the Modern World,[20] demonstrate that the human person is not a "soul" or a "body" but both at once; life itself is founded on the fundamental relationship between Creator and creature. To be made in God's image does not mean that the person *has* something, but that he or she *is* something.[21] This unitary view, refusing to locate the image of God in any particular attribute of the human, recognizes that our bodies, created by God, are indeed good. In fact, "holiness" can only be expressed in a bodily manner—as the sacraments of the Church "sanctify" the whole person within a believing and worshiping community. A unified understanding of human nature also protects those at the "fringe" or "lower rungs" of intellectual and physical capabilities. Since the whole person—body, soul and spirit—is human and in the image of God, all life—old or young, weak or strong, intelligent or mentally handicapped—is sacred and worthy of reverence and preservation.

Both Jewish and Christian sanctity of life teaching are grounded on the conviction that God is the Creator, that what God created is good, and that human persons are made in God's image and likeness. This ontological bond between creature and Creator provides the foundation for the belief that life is good, holy and worthy of care and protection. In fact, life is the highest good, without which we could not enjoy any other goods. Where Christians and Jews differ is in the application of this fundamental belief to concrete situations. For the sake of brevity, the rest of the reflections that follow will be limited to two current and passionately debated life questions, one focusing on the end of the life and the other on its beginning.

ISSUES AT THE END OF LIFE

Without doubt, euthanasia will be the most disputed medical-moral issue of the '90s and into the next millennium. This is not to say that moralists and politicians will ignore fetal or unborn life, but given technological advances, economic constraints, and the growth of the elderly population in the United States, issues at the end of life are already paramount in communal discourse. Both traditions have long heritages of reflection and articulation about end-of-life decisions.

Catholic Tradition

While Catholic tradition, has always recognized human life as sacred, it has not considered bodily or earthly life an absolute. It is relative to

God, the supreme good. Catholic theology avoids the extreme of "vitalism," the theory that holds that life must be sustained at all costs. Catholics have long affirmed decisions not to treat dying or chronically ill patients when treatment would prove useless or too burdensome to bear.

Catholic teaching consistently prohibits euthanasia. The 1980 Vatican *Declaration on Euthanasia* states:

> All crimes against life, including "euthanasia or willful suicide," must be opposed. Euthanasia is an 'action or an omission which of itself or by intention causes death, in order that all suffering may in this way be eliminated.' Its terms of reference are to be found 'in the intention and in the methods used.' Thus defined, euthanasia is an attack on life which no one has a right to make or request, and which no government or other human authority can legitimately recommend or permit.[22]

While there is a moral obligation to preserve life, there are times and circumstances in which that obligation ceases. The same document insists:

> Everyone has the duty to care for his or her own life and to seek necessary medical care from others, but this does not mean that all possible remedies must be used in all circumstances. One is not obliged to use either "extra-ordinary" means or "disproportionate" means of preserving life—that is, means which are understood as offering no reasonable hope of benefit or as involving excessive burdens.[23]

The distinction between ordinary and extraordinary means to preserve life builds on the scholastic distinction between affirmative and negative precepts of natural law.[24] Affirmative precepts command the carrying out of an action. Negative precepts prohibit an action judged to be intrinsically evil and must never be violated.[25] Therefore, direct, active euthanasia is not permitted for any reason. Affirmative precepts, however, have exceptions. They no longer bind when there is a proportionately grave reason for not complying with them. Accordingly, the affirmative obligation to preserve life does not bind when the means entail a disproportionately serious burden to the person.

Medical or technological means cannot be judged apart from the treatment of an individual patient. The terms ordinary/ extraordinary were first introduced into preservation of life discussions in the sixteenth century by Domingo Bañez who noted that the obligation to conserve life did not include extraordinary means involving great pain, anguish or undertakings disproportionate to one's state. Pius XII's 1957 teaching on this subject receives frequent ethical mention. In an address to an International Congress of Anesthesiologists, Pius maintained that our duty to prolong life has limits by stating:

> But normally one is held to use only ordinary means—according to circumstances of persons, places, times and culture—that is to say, means that do not involve any grave burden for oneself or another. A more strict obligation would be too burdensome for most men and would render the attainment of the higher, more important good too difficult. Life, health, all temporal activities are in fact subordinated to spiritual ends.[26]

While U.S. Catholic theologians over the years (Sullivan, Kelly, McFadden, McCormick) have interpreted the terms ordinary and extraordinary slightly differently, all recognize the importance of judging the means in relation to a particular patient and his or her physical, psychological, and social condition. The principles are relative to changing circumstances; and the patient's condition always co-determines the value of treatment.

Two questions arise when considering removing life-support or other treatment. First, is the treatment *futile*? That is, will it:
—cure the patient
—significantly prolong life
—offer palliation of pain or other comfort measures?
If not, then the treatment is considered futile and, therefore, extraordinary. Second, will the treatment cause grave or excessive burden on oneself or another? If this is so, then again the treatment is extraordinary and one may morally withhold or withdraw it. Note that if *either* of these conditions exists then one may legitimately decide to forgo treatment. Catholic tradition does not demand that treatment be *both* futile *and* burdensome.[27]

Whereas some secular ethicists deny any inherent difference in the distinction between killing and allowing to die, Catholic teaching maintains the distinction by applying the principle of double effect. While the direct killing of an innocent person is never morally right, allowing someone to die may, in fact, be a moral good. In the latter case, within a tradition that looks forward to union with God in heaven, one simply acknowledges the inevitability of death and permits nature to take its course. The administering of pain medications aimed to relieve a patient's suffering, while they may shorten the person's life, is morally good because the intention is to keep the person as comfortable as possible throughout the dying process, not to take the life.

Given this brief summary of Catholic teaching on end-of- life issues, one can see that Catholic moralists and bishops can argue convincingly that life support, even nutrition and hydration, may be removed from a patient if their administration is futile or if it involves a grave burden for the patient or others.

Jewish Tradition

Judaism has a "this-worldly" character in dealing with these questions, focusing on discharging one's duties to God and neighbor in the here and now of this life. Not surprisingly, its teaching is marked, as Rabbi Jakobovits notes in *Jewish Medical Ethics*, by a "relative sparsity of regulations on the inevitable passage of man from life to death."[28] Even during life's final phases consideration for the physical welfare of the patient remains supreme. Judaism urges every caution to ensure that last preparations for death should not aggravate the patient's condition nor compromise his or her will or ability to live.

Jewish thinking teaches that every moment of life, whether ten minutes or ten years, is inviolable and sacred in undifferentiated preciousness. Therefore, nothing may be done to hasten death. Life is God's, and no subjective considerations allow one to commit either suicide or homicide. This tradition, then, obviously prohibits euthanasia, whether direct or indirect. But Jews, like Christians, are not vitalists, in the sense of prolonging life at all costs. Their teaching is nuanced, taking into consideration the patient's condition, age, and general circumstances.

Particularly when dealing with dying patients, Jewish moralists recognize that demanding heroic measures often exacerbates the patient's condition, making the last days, hours, and moments of life more intensely painful than they might otherwise be. As with all moral judgments, religious persons carefully weigh the burdens and benefits of treatment. Rabbi Jakobovits observes that " . . . under certain carefully confined conditions, it [viz., the decision] might not require the physician to prolong the agony by artificial or 'heroic' methods, permitting him to withdraw such treatment in completely hopeless cases of lingering life."[29]

Similarly, J. David Bleich states that the *halacha* (the whole of rabbinic teaching, including Bible and Talmud) qualifies the obligation to prolong the life of the sick if a patient is in the throes of death. He carefully warns that not any terminally ill patient, but only one whom physicians judge to be days from death, meets this exception.[30] In his book, *Health and Medicine in the Jewish Tradition*, David M. Feldman notes that the Jewish law codes permit and even mandate the "removal of hindrances" to the "soul's departure." While one may not disconnect life-support systems to shorten life, one may do so to shorten the death process.[31]

Jewish ethicists, like their Catholic counterparts, disagree about the termination of food and hydration. Some authorities sanction the removal of medications or machines which only serve to prolong the dying process, so long as no natural means of subsistence (food, blood, oxygen) are withdrawn. Jakobovits believes that natural means to prolong life should continue until the patient dies.[32] Others see no obligation to maintain the life of a permanently comatose patient who has no hope of recovery, by medical treatment or the provision of food.

Summary of End-of-Life Issues

Some distinctions between Jewish and Catholic end-of-life analyses deserve mention because they are acted out each day in critical care units in hospitals throughout the country. First is the fact that Jewish moral thinking does not allow terminating life based on "quality-of-life" considerations, while the majority of Catholic moralists recognize that this is certainly one, although not the only, element to consider in end-of-life choices. Bleich maintains that "Judaism teaches that man is denied the right to make judgments with regard to quality of life. Man is never called upon to determine whether life is worth living—that is a question over which God remains sole arbiter."[33]

Second, Judaism recognizes that some forms of medical treatment are not mandatory, not because these treatments present a burden to patient or family, but because they are not part of an accepted therapeutic protocol. Going back to the Catholic distinction made above, Judaism recognizes that treatment may stop if it is futile, not if it is burdensome. Bleich observes: "The obligation to heal is limited to the use of drugs and procedures of demonstrated efficacy.[34] While Jews must use the full range of benefits science provides, they are not obliged to experiment with untried and unproven measures nor to use those treatments which are hazardous in the hope of effecting a complete cure.

Jewish persons should understand that, given the Catholic commitment to the afterlife, holding onto mere bodily existence when facing death does not represent an ultimate value. The Catholic asks: "What does this moment mean in light of eternity"? On the other hand, Catholics must understand that Jews may choose heroic medical treatments and procedures because every moment of life, even up to the last, holds infinite value.

ABORTION

Euthanasia challenges moralists into the next millennium. Yet, as various believing communities (including also the Muslim and Buddhist in this country), we have not solved the abortion dilemma. It is safe to say that we will go into the next century still torn as a nation by this rational question with its emotional overtones. Interreligious understanding and mutual respect remain absolutely necessary so that we may address this topic primarily in the realm of moral discourse.

Catholic Teaching

Catholic Church teaching on abortion, while nuanced, is nonetheless clear. The Second Vatican Council states that "from the moment of its conception life must be guarded with the greatest care, while abortion and infanticide are unspeakable crimes."[35] Over the years since Vatican II, particularly as abortion practices throughout the world became more lenient, there has been unanimity in the teaching of the popes and bishops on the right of the fetus to life from conception. They support the rights of mothers to life no less. Furthermore, they speak from the conviction that, as moral teachers, they must address what they consider a societal evil with the potential to erode our civilization.[36] While U.S. bishops assiduously argue for legislative reform about abortion, generally bishops' conferences in other countries argue for the internal conformity of their religious communities to Church teaching.[37]

With abortion, as with other medical-moral dilemmas, concrete cases are never as clear as ethical principles. While the mandate, "No direct killing of an innocent person," is the rule, there are sometimes exceptions to the rule. Catholic Church leaders have asserted that direct abortion is never permissible, even to save the life of the mother. The classic case mentioned in moral manuals of a former age cites the rare occasion when there are only two options: do nothing and both mother and child die, or abort and save only the life that can be salvaged. In the past, moralists would say "better two deaths than one murder," while today most moralists would say that the abortion in such cases could be indirect. They would apply the principle of double effect. The Belgian bishops, addressing such a case, said that "the moral principle which ought to govern the intervention can be formulated as follows: Since two lives are at stake, one will, while doing everything possible to save both, attempt to save one rather than allow two to perish."[38]

There is no doubt that the Catholic Church considers abortion the destruction of innocent life. The term murder carries with it a subjective connotation of deliberate and knowing, willful homicide. While the Church considers a direct abortion done in full human deliberation and freedom with full understanding of the evil involved to be equivalent to murder, it also recognizes that some abortions occur in human circumstances in which the word murder would not be an apt description of the subjective state of the person having or paying for an abortion.

Jewish Teaching

Jewish moralists distinguish between the moment when life begins (conception) and when life begins to be human. Most Jewish thinkers locate the beginning of human life at birth. This marks for them the time when the rights of the child equal the rights of the mother. Prior to that, "the mother's life takes precedence over the child's life as long as the child is a fetus in the womb. Once the child enters into the air, however, then the child's and mother's life take on equal value."[39] This is not to say that Jews do not recognize the indisputable embryological facts of individuation. They admit the beginnings and potential of life possessed by the fetus and therefore hold it in high moral esteem. Most Orthodox thinkers hold that preservation of life is the only reason to sacrifice the fetus. But nowhere in Jewish law does one find a connection between abortion and murder, which is the sin the Bible prohibits. Since the fetus is not yet a fully human being, destruction of the fetus is not murder.

The primary reason Jewish thinkers give to support a decision to abort is the health of the mother. Maternal health holds centrality in any discussion about abortion and would always override the fetus's right to life.[40] Religious law mandates the woman to preserve her own life and health. After all, her life is already established and she should not jeopardize its safety, while the child *in utero* may or may not survive the pregnancy and the birth process. To quote Dr. Fred Rosner, "When it's one life against another, you save the mother's life since human life is of infinite value."[41]

Orthodox rabbis permit abortion only in rare circumstances, but Conservative and Reformed rabbis may justify abortion by expanding the concept of maternal health to include emotional and mental well-being. The moral tradition urges the rabbi to engage the woman in serious moral consideration before she reaches such a decision.

If maternal indications may excuse abortion, fetal indications for abortion (genetic or neural-tube abnormalities) do not provide sufficient reason to abort since such a decision would be based on quality-of-life criteria.[42] Feldman, speaking from the Conservative tradition, observes that any considerations of relative quality of life must be rejected; all existing life is equally precious. However, when discussing quality of life for the fetus, he notes that some rabbis may interpret the possibility of fetal deformity as a severe mental anguish for the mother and therefore might justify abortion.

In all of Jewish writing, decisions to abort a potential human life are met with reverence for the mother and moral anguish for the potential child and for the ones making the decision. Nowhere does one find religious toleration of "abortion on demand." In fact, Feldman notes that abortion for "population control" is repugnant to the Jewish mind; nor is abortion for economic reasons admissible, since material considerations or career concerns are simply improper in this connection.[43]

Summary of Abortion Issue

The thorny abortion issue provides yet another challenge to interreligious understanding. While Catholics hold that direct abortion is the taking of life, traditional Catholic teaching recognizes that the word murder carries subjective connotations. The Church teaches that only those who knowingly and deliberately violate a value in bad faith engage subjective guilt. Therefore, according to Catholic teaching, it is improper to label those who do not engage in the subjective malice of such an act, murderers. Similarly, Jewish persons need to recognize that precisely because Catholics consider life sacred from conception, abortion—even to preserve the life of the mother—remains a serious offense against life.

A willingness to engage in moral dialogue over the abortion question provides a particularly delicate lesson for Catholics to learn from their Jewish counterparts. Some popular Catholic opinion assigns discussion of abortion to realms of discipline or indoctrination. In such an environment, authentic moral discourse cannot survive. Therefore, what some-· times happens is that Catholics give lip-service in the pews and even on picket lines to main-line "pro-life" activities and values while sadly failing to internalize the truly pro-life tradition about which they should justifiably be proud, or to inform adequately the consciences of the next generation.

CONCLUSION

Neither Jewish nor Catholic interpretations of sanctity-of-life maintain a strict biologistic notion of human life, but rather, continue to emphasize that life is God's gift and thus demands the utmost reverence and respect.

Catholicism's contemporary teaching about sanctity of life owes its force to the Hebrew scriptural account of the good creation and subsequent Jewish teaching about the meaning of creation in the image of God. Although practical application of the shared principles may vary, each tradition should know and esteem the other's long history of grappling with life and death issues.

As Catholics and Jews continue vital ecumenical dialogue both parties must continue to listen to the other, understand, respect and appreciate a shared heritage, each others' sacred history, and areas of common priority and concern. In a world which unfortunately places too little value on life's holiness we cannot afford to close the door on continued moral discourse within our own communities or across ecumenical lines. Too much is at stake.

NOTES

[1] Rembert Weakland, "Tasks Ahead in Catholic-Jewish Dialogue" *Origins* (30 April 1992):792.

[2] Hippocrates, *The Medical Works of Hippocrates*, trans. John Chadwick and W.N. Mann (Oxford: Blackwell Scientific Publications, 1950), p. 9.

[3] A.S. Duncan, G.R. Dunstan and R.B. Welbourn, eds., *Dictionary of Medical Ethics* (New York: Crossroad, 1981), p. 384.

[4] Karl Barth, *Church Dogmatics* III/4 trans. A.T. Mackay *et al.* (Edinburgh: T&T Clark, 1961), pp. 342-43.

[5] Edward Shils, "The Sanctity of Life," *Life or Death: Ethics and Options*, Introduction by Daniel H. Labby (Seattle: University of Washington 1968), p. 12.

[6] Daniel C. Maguire, *The Moral Choice* (New York: Doubleday, 1978), p. 84.

[7] J. Robert Nelson, *Human Life: A Biblical Perspective for Bioethics* (Philadelphia: Fortress, 1984), p. 66. See also *Encyclopaedia Judaica*, 11:235-36.

[8] David S. Shapiro, "The Doctrine of the Image of God and *Imitatio Dei*," *Contemporary Jewish Ethics*, ed. Menachem Marc Kellner (New York: Sanhedrin, 1978), p. 127.

[9] Nelson, pp. 68-69.

[10] J. David Bleich, "Karen Ann Quinlan: A Torah Perspective," *Contemporary Jewish Ethics*, p. 300.

[11] *Enyclopaedia Judaica*, 11:236.

[12]Bleich, p. 300.

[13]Immanuel Jakobvits, "Jewish Medical Ethics—a Brief Overview" *Journal of Medical Ethics* 9 (June, 1983):111.

[14]Bleich, "Karen Ann Quinlan," pp. 300-01.

[15]Maurice Jourjon, "The Image of God in Irenaeus," *Theology Digest* 32 (Fall, 1985):253-54. See, for example, Irenaeus, *Adversus Haereses* V.6.1.

[16]Augustine, *The Literal Meaning of Genesis*, 6,12,21, tr. John Hammond Taylor (New York: Newman, 1982).

[17]Thomas Aquinas, *Summa Theologiae*, tr. Marcus Lefébure (New York: McGraw Hill, Blackfriars edition, 1964), 1a, 93.

[18]Pius XII, "The Prolongation of Life" (24 November 1957) *The Pope Speaks*, 4/4 (1958):395.

[19]Douglas John Hall, *Imaging God: Dominion as Stewardship* (Grand Rapids: Eerdmans, 1986), pp. 108-09.

[20]Barth, *Church Dogmatics*, III, *The Doctrine of Creation*, Part 1, trans. J.W. Edwards, *et al.* (Edinburgh: T&T Clark, 1958), p. 184; Karl Rahner, "The Secret of Life," *Theological Investigations*, VI, tr. Karl-H. and Boniface Kruger (New York: Crossroad, 1982), p. 145.; Vatican Council II, *Gaudium et Spes*, ed. Austin Flannery (Collegeville: Liturgical, 1975), pp. 914-15.

[21]Douglas John Hall, *Imaging God*, 98.

[22]Congregation of the Doctrine of the Faith, "On Euthanasia," *Origins* 16/10 (14 August 1980):154.

[23]Ibid.

[24]The Vatican *Declaration on Euthanasia* indicates that the traditional terms, "ordinary" and "extraordinary" means to preserve life are no longer adequate in our highly medicalized society. The *Declaration* uses the terms "proportionate" or "disproportionate." Contemporary Catholic ethicists also evaluate means to sustain life according to "burden" vs. "benefit" ratio.

[25]See John F. Dedek, *Human Life* (New York: Sheed and Ward, 1972), pp. 127-28; Charles J. McFadden, *The Dignity of Life* (Huntington, IN: Our Sunday Visitor), pp. 146-49.

[26]Pius XII, "The Prolongation of Life," pp. 395-96.

[27]Pius XII and many subsequent Catholic theologians and bishops recognize that, in judging any means to be extraordinary one may take into account the burden not only to the patient but also to "others," notably to family members, care takers, and even in some cases, to society.

[28]Jakobovits, *Jewish Medical Ethics*, p. 119.

[29]Jakobovits, p. 11.

[30]Bleich, p. 302. Bleich does not clearly define "terminal," however and, as any oncologist will tell you, the term "days from death" is really rather elastic. Some Catholic

ethicists try to pin this down by saying that the patient must be two weeks from death, although accurate prediction of such a prognosis is next to impossible.

[31]David M. Feldman, *Health and Medicine in the Jewish Tradition* (New York: Crossroad, 1986), p. 95. Feldman reports a centuries-old rabbinic observation that one may remove a pillow from a dying patient even knowing that this will shorten his or her life because at this point what one is doing is "removing hindrances to the soul's departure."

[32]Jakobovits, *Jewish Medical Ethics*, p. 276.

[33]Bleich, p. 306.

[34]Bleich, p. 301.

[35]*Documents of Vatican II*, ed. Walter Abbott (New York: Herder and Herder and Association Press, 1966):256.

[36]The bishops generally do not get caught up in philosophical arguments about whether the fetus is a person, rather they view life as a continuum from the beginning, sometimes using terms like "person in the process of becoming."

[37]Richard A. McCormick, *Health and Medicine in the Catholic Tradition* (New York: Crossroad, 1984),pp. 128-29. James T. Burtchaell, *The Giving and Taking of Life* (Notre Dame: University of Notre Dame, 1989), p. 239, argues that abortion is one issue that will never be solved by law. He believes that to push the issue primarily to the legislative arena distracts the moral community from the discourse and teaching which are its proper responsibility.

[38]McCormick, p. 130. Given pre-natal technology available in all first-world countries today, the kind of scenario here described is so rare as to be almost non-existent.

[39]Scott Aaron, "The Choice in 'Choose Life': American Judaism and Abortion," *Commonweal* (28 February 1992):15. Aaron paraphrases the *Mishny, "Ocholot,"* 7. 6. It reads: "If a woman is in hard travail, the child must be cut up while it is in the womb and brought out member by member, since the life of the mother has priority over the life of the child; but if the greater part of it is already born, it may not be touched, since the claim of one life cannot override the claim of another life." Aaron acknowledges that religious discussion of abortion remains far from the ordinary Jewish man or woman who does not usually think of the issue in religious terms.

[40]Feldman, p. 80.

[41]Aaron, p. 16.

[42]Feldman, p. 92.

[43]Feldman, p. 90.

BIBLICAL HERMENEUTICS AND DIVORCE

Alice L. Laffey

When I received the announcement of a symposium on "Marriage and Divorce" entitled "From Covenant Relationships to Crisis Resolution: Scripture, Canon Law, Sexual Ethics, Feminism, Empirical Studies" under the auspices of the University of Dayton, I was tempted to volunteer to participate for several reasons. First, I am a Catholic--and the topic is to be approached as an "American Catholic issue;" secondly, I am a student, some would say scholar, of Sacred Scripture, with a doctorate in those studies from the *Pontificale Institutum Biblicum* in Rome; thirdly, I am a feminist. This Catholic, biblical feminist has been intuitively disturbed, since at least 1976 when I became a member of the Catholic Theological Society of America, that Catholic biblical scholars and Catholic theologians meet separately--as if the Bible and theology are appropriately studied as separate entities. (It is for this reason that I most respect the College Theology Society which is so structured that biblicists and theologians are brought together.) Finally, my intuition has been strongly confirmed both by Charles Curran who, when speaking to the members of the Catholic Biblical Association some years ago, strongly encouraged them to become involved in theological, including ecclesiological, issues, and Lisa Sowle Cahill's recently published Warren lecture at the University of Tulsa which asks "Is Catholic Ethics Biblical? The Example of Sex and Gender"[1]

I am a post-Enlightenment Catholic whose biblical training was, for the most part, historical-critical and later, canonical-critical; moreover, as a feminist, I bring to both Catholicism and biblical study a hermeneutics of suspicion. As I proceed through this paper, you will notice the interaction of these influences.

SPECIFIC OLD TESTAMENT TEXTS WHICH DEAL EXPLICITLY WITH HUMAN SEXUALITY, MARRIAGE AND/OR DIVORCE

Three texts from the book of Genesis have been interpreted as referring to the divine creation of human sexuality and the consequent procreative potential of men and women. These include the priestly Gen 1:27-28 which reads: "So God created humankind in his image, in the image of God he created them; male and female he created them. God blessed them, and God said to them, 'Be fruitful and multiply and fill the earth' . . . "[2] and its paraphrase in Gen 5:2 which introduces the genealogy of Adam. The third text, from the pen of the Yahwist, is Gen 2:24: "Therefore a man leaves his father and mother and clings to his woman, and they become one flesh."

Because ancient Israel possessed a patriarchal, polygamous culture, its laws were developed within that context. Deuteronomy 24:1-4 is one illustration:

> Suppose a man enters into marriage with a woman, but she does not please him because he finds something objectionable about her, and so he writes her a certificate of divorce, puts it in her hand, and sends her out of his house; she then leaves his house and goes off to become another man's wife. Then suppose the second man dislikes her, writes her a bill of divorce, puts it in her hand, and sends her out of his house (or the second man who marries her dies); her first husband, who sent her away, is not permitted to take her again to be his wife after she has been defiled. . . .

After noting the lack of reciprocity in the law--it is directed to men, and only men could initiate divorce--it is important to acknowledge--although it may be difficult for contemporary women to see it--that this law actually protects Israel's women, who were the less powerful in the society; the law served to discourage men from dismissing their wives lightly. After she had been taken by another, which she would need to have done in order to secure material support, there was no having her back. From a patriarchal perspective, this second man had defiled the woman and for the first man to take back such "polluted goods" would be abhorrent to God.

Because of the relationship of priests to the temple, and their key role in postexilic Israel, they were not permitted to take as marriage partners women who had had sexual intercourse, regardless of whether they were widowed or divorced, victims of rape, or prostitutes (Lev. 21:14). Such a woman, though not a suitable marriage partner for a priest, if she were the *daughter* of a priest and had been widowed or divorced and, without offspring, returned to her father's house, could eat the food alotted from the sacrifices for the priest and his family (Lev. 22:13). Finally, the vow of either a widow or a divorced woman with which she had bound herself would be binding. This was in contrast to vows made by fathers' daughters or husbands' wives, both of which kinds of vows were made subject, for them to be binding on the women, to the approval of the respective males (Num. 30:9). From these laws one may conclude that although a divorced woman was not to be deprived of the food of priests, and although she was less subject to male control than her unmarried and married sisters, she was somehow unworthy of worthier men. One might also conclude from these provisions that divorce was not rare.

A patriarchal culture such as that which produced the texts of the Old Testament also established laws to prevent the forceful taking of one man's possession, that is, his woman, or one of his women, by another man. We are most familiar with Exod. 20:14 and Deut. 5:18, directed only to men incidentally, which read: "You shall not commit adultery," and Exod. 20:17 and Deut. 5:21 both of which prohibit a man from coveting his neighbor's wife. The consequences of violating the prohibition against adultery are laid out in Deut. 22:22: "If a man is caught lying with the wife of another man, both of them shall die, the man who lay with the woman as well as the woman. . . . " In this verse, whether or not the woman was taken against her will, and since she was the property of one man and taken by another, her penalty was death; she could not be taken back by the first man who had had her.

The following verses apply to a woman who is engaged but not yet married:

> If there is a young woman, a virgin already engaged to be married, and a man meets her in the town and lies with her, you shall bring both of them to the gate of that town, and stone them to death, the young woman because she did not cry for help in the town, and the man because he violated his neighbor's wife. . . . But if the man meets the woman in the open country, and the man seizes her and lies with her, then only the man who lay with her shall die . . . . (vv. 23-25)

The law provides that nothing shall be done to the young woman; the young woman had not committed an offense punishable by death since he had found her in the open country; the betrothed woman may have cried for help, but it is unlikely that anyone could have heard to rescue her (vv. 25-27). On the other hand, "If a man meets a virgin who is not engaged, and seizes her and lies with her, and they are caught in the act, the man who lay with her shall give fifty shekels of silver to the young woman's father, and she shall become his wife. Because he violated her he shall not be permitted to divorce her as long as he lives" (vv. 28-29). This last-case scenario, though with different endings, may be found in

Gen. 34, the biblical account of the rape of Dinah, and 2 Sam. 13, which details the rape of David's daughter Tamar. In both of those cases the women fare worse than marrying their rapists--if one can imagine anything worse.

The above laws are written from a patriarchal perspective; they are nevertheless *meant to protect the sacredness of human sexuality* which God created. Though it is inconceivable today that a woman should have to marry her rapist, in that culture the provision that he should be forced to marry and never divorce her would at least protect her from starvation.

THE OLD TESTAMENT'S USE OF MARRIAGE AS SYMBOL FOR GOD'S RELATIONSHIP WITH ISRAEL

Ancient Israel's patriarchal culture came to conceive of the relationship between YHWH and Israel in marital terms. Just as the husband was *ba'al*, that is, husband/master, over his wife--the Hebrew term *ba'al* implies either and/or both--so the Lord was *ba'al* over Israel (cf. Jer. 31:32). The eighth-century prophet Hosea is first credited with the use of this symbol. In the analogy he presents, with which we are all familiar, Hosea (read: the "Lord") is a loving, faithful husband who is betrayed by his adulterous and harlotrous wife, Gomer (read: "Israel"). Hosea (read: "Lord") remembers their early life together, a time of Gomer's (read: "Israel's") dependence on Hosea (read: "God") and their faithfulness to each other; Hosea (read: "God") longs for the return of such a time. In fact, in violation of Israelite law (Deut. 24:4 cited above), Hosea (read: "God") would even take back his unfaithful wife (Hos. 2:15-20). Jeremiah picks up on the marriage symbol when God addresses Israel, saying: ". . . I remember the devotion of your youth, your love as a bride, how you would follow me in the wilderness, in a land not sown" (2:2). In the following chapter we read: "If a man divorces his wife and she goes from him and becomes another man's wife, will he return to her? Would not such a land be greatly polluted? You have played the whore with many lovers, and would you return to me, says the Lord." (3:1); and a few verses later: ". . . for all the adulteries of that faithless one, Israel, I had sent her away with a decree of divorce. . . . " (v. 8). These instances, clearly conceived in a patriarchal culture, not only portray the male YHWH as superior but, in fact, depict his female wife Israel as unfaithful and evil.

Ezekiel picks up the theme of the husband-wife relationship, again portraying God as the faithful husband and the female as the unfaithful Judah (ch. 16). In chapter 23, though the relationship is not expressly that of husband and wife, it is the faithful male (read: "God") who stands in relationship to the two unfaithful and ungrateful sisters, Oholah and Oholibah (read: "Israel and Judah"). The author of Lamentations carries the husband-wife covenant relationship through the five chapters of the book, portraying the exiled people of Judah as God's widow, punished for her adultery and other unfaithfulness.

Referring to the exile, the author of Isa. 50:1 asks:

Where is your mother's bill of divorce
with which I put her away?
Or which of my creditors is it
to whom I have sold you?
No, because of your sins you were sold,
and for your transgressions your mother was put away.

These texts clearly establish that divorce by husbands of their wives and second marriages were acceptable in the culture of ancient Israel. Though polygamy diminished significantly, patriarchal prejudice remained strong. And the later author of Isa. 62:5 also uses the marriage metaphor, but in a way that declares Israel's restoration. The text reads:

For as a young man marries a young woman,
so shall your builder marry you,
and as the bridegroom rejoices over the bride,
so shall your God rejoice over you.

Before turning our attention to the New Testament, one last text needs to be considered. In Mal. 2:13-16 we read:

And this you do as well: You cover the Lord's altar with tears, with weeping and groaning because he no longer regards the offering or accepts it with favor at your hand. You ask, "Why does he not?" Because the Lord was a witness between you and the wife of your youth, to whom you have been faithless, though she is your companion and your wife by covenant. . . . Do not let anyone be faithless to the wife of his youth. For I hate divorce, says the Lord, the God of Israel. . . .

These verses were preceded by the following: "Judah has been faithless, and abomination has been committed in Israel and in Jerusalem; for Judah has profaned the sanctuary of the Lord, which he loves, and has married the daughter of a foreign god" (v. 11). From the context one may conclude that Malachi has literalized the husband (read: "God")-wife (read:

"Israel") metaphor to prohibit divorce of one's wife (now read: "covenant unfaithfulness"). Textual critics point out that the Hebrew of vv. 13-16 is very obscure, so that the translation is conjectured rather than certain. Historical critics hypothesize that many men of postexilic Israel may have been tempted to divorce their wives in order to marry--and be able to support--younger, more attractive foreign women. The prophet cautions against the practice of men divorcing their wives lightly.

THE NEW TESTAMENT: MARRIAGE AND DIVORCE[3]

The preceding texts are important for any adequate understanding of the New Testament texts regarding marriage and divorce. It is my contention that the culture of Jesus' time was also thoroughly patriarchal, even though Jesus himself called for a discipleship of equals. It is against this background that the relevant New Testament texts must be interpreted. The texts most often associated with a Christian/Catholic prohibition against divorce are Mark 10:2-9 and Matt. 19:3-9. Let us look at them in turn:

> Some Pharisees came, and to test Jesus, they asked, "Is it lawful for a man to divorce his wife?" He answeed them, "What did Moses command you?" They said, "Moses allowed a man to write a certificate of dismissal and to divorce her." But Jesus said to them, "Because of your hardness of heart he wrote this commandment for you. But from the beginning of creation, "God made them male and female." "For this reason a man shall leave his father and mother and be joined to his wife, and the two shall become one flesh." So they are no longer two, but one flesh. Therefore what God has joined together let no *man* separate."
> Then in the house the disciples asked him again about this matter. He said to them, "Whoever divorces his wife and marries another commits adultery against her; and if she divorces her husband and marries another, she commits adultery." (Mk 10:2-12)

Jesus is here portrayed as being "set up" by the Pharisees, given a no-win question. If he says divorce is acceptable, that would contradict the text in Malachi and his own demonstrated attitude toward women. If he says divorce is not acceptable, he contradicts Mosaic law. Jesus answers the Pharisees' question by acknowledging the patriarchy of ancient Israel, that is, the understanding that the husband could divorce the wife, but he challenges that patriarachy with an appeal to the creation of human sexuality. (It is for this reason that I do not agree with the New Revised Standard translation, "let no *one* separate" for even though the word is the generic *anthropos*, the context understands dismissal by a male.) I believe Jesus' response in the passage is to disallow the patriarchy traditionally associated with divorce. What God has joined together, *men* should not be allowed to separate.

When the setting changes and, more importantly, the dialogue partners change, Jesus challenges his disciples to reciprocal relationships in marriage, wife toward husband as well as husband toward wife. Since the husband's dismissal of his wife had been an expression of patriarchal "power over," one should not be surprised that Jesus rejects such an expression of patriarchy.

Turning our attention to Matt. 19:3-9, we find a text similar to, but not identical with, the Markan text. Matt. 19 reads:

> Some Pharisees came to Jesus, and to test him they asked, "Is it lawful for a man to divorce his wife *for any cause*?" He answered, "Have you not read that the one who made them at the beginning 'made them male and female,' and said, 'For this reason a man shall leave his father and mother and be joined to his wife, and the two shall become one flesh. Therefore, what God has joined together, let no man separate." They said to him, "Why then did Moses comand us to give a certificate of dismissal and to divorce her?" He said to them, "It was because you were so hard-hearted that Moses allowed you to divorce your wives, but from the beginning it was not so. And I say to you, whoever divorces his wife, except for unchastity, and marries another woman commits adultery. (vv. 3-9)

The text continues:

> His disciples said to him, "If such is the case of a man with his wife, it is better not to marry." But he said to them, "Not everyone can accept this teaching, but only those to whom it is given." (vv. 10-11).

The first part of the passage differs from the Markan text in the addition of the phrase "for any cause" to the Pharisees' question, in the order or reasoning by which Jesus answers it; and most obviously, in Jesus' allowing men to divorce their wives for unchastity. Obviously the text is addressed only to men, to the Pharisees, yes, but in reference to the Mosaic law, which was addressed to Jewish males. Just as Elizabeth Schussler Fiorenza traces in *In Memory of Her*,[4] the gradual patriarchalizing of Jesus' words and message, so I would submit here that Matthew's account is more patriarchal than Mark's. What we learn from it, however, is just how clearly historically-conditioned the text is.

When we turn our attention to the response of Jesus' disciples--that if such is the case, it is better not to marry--we have implicit evidence of the acceptability if not the pervasiveness of divorce and/or sexual intercourse with more than one woman, and further evidence of the patriarchal culture pervading the Matthean community which produced the text.

In Matt. 5:27, again directed to men, Jesus teaches: "You have heard that it was said, 'You shall not commit adultery.' But I say to you that everyone who looks at a woman with lust has already committed adultery with her in his heart." Note the text's effort to protect women, but also its lack of reciprocity. And in vv. 31-32 we read:

> It was also said, "whoever divorces his wife, let him give her a certificate of divorce." But I say to you that anyone who divorces his wife, except on the ground of unchastity, causes her to commit adultery; and whoever marries a divorced woman commits adultery."

This text also betrays a strong patriarchal perspective. It is directed to men--only the male can divorce--and though it limits the circumstances under which a man may divorce it accuses the woman of adultery, even if she has been wrongly divorced. Women were economically and socially dependent on men--as they still are throughout the world--and so she would have had to remarry had she been divorced. Because it also accuses of adultery the man who would marry a divorced woman, it would discourage men from marrying divorced women and thereby relegate a divorced woman, even if she had been wrongly divorced, to a life of dire material poverty and lack of social identity.[5]

1 Cor. 7:8-16 and vv. 36-40 are believed to have been written by Paul in light of an imminent *parousia*. In 8-16 he counsels that 1) those who are unmarried remain so unless they are not practicing self-control, in which case they should marry; 2) wives should not separate from their husbands, but if they do so, like the unmarried, they should not remarry; if they cannot practice self-control, they should become reconciled to their husbands; 3) husbands ought not divorce their wives.

Paul then goes on to counsel male believers and female believers who have unbelieving spouses who consent to remain with them, not to divorce them. On the other hand, if the unbelieving partner separates, Paul thinks that to be acceptable and the believer not to be bound to the other. The passage suggests that the unbeliever is made holy through his or her believing spouse, and their children are holy. Somehow unbelieving, like unchastity, can be grounds for separation and/or divorce.

In 36-40 Paul counsels a man who is not behaving properly toward his fiancee because his passions are strong (most likely, therefore, having sexual relations with other women), to marry his fiancee. But a man who is not having difficulty abstaining from sexual relations Paul counsels to keep his fiancee as a fiancee. Neither action is wrong--to marry or not to marry one's fiancee, but, according to Paul, the latter is better. In v. 39 Paul speaks literally about a wife's being bound to her husband as long as he lives, but being free to marry after he dies. Nevertheless, Paul's own opinion is that it is better if she refrain from marrying again. (Note that Paul does not speak of the man's being bound to his wife as long as she lives.) Taking these texts as a whole, one interprets Paul's counsel to be determined by the imminent *parousia*, but also by an effort to discourage promiscuity, and an ideal husband-wife relationship implicitly based on the symbol of the marriage relationship between Christ and the Church.

The author of the letter to the Hebrews at 13:4 comments only, "Let marriage be held in honor by all, and let the marriage bed be kept undefiled; for God will judge fornicators and adulterers."

THE NEW TESTAMENT'S USE OF MARRIAGE AS SYMBOL FOR CHRIST'S RELATIONSHIP WITH THE CHURCH

There are several other New Testament passages which must be considered, which use the marriage symbol analogously. The first is brief and occurs in 2 Cor. 11:2. Addresing the community of believers, Paul picks up on the marriage metaphor of the Old Testament when he says, "I am jealous for you with a divine jealousy; for I have betrothed you to Christ, thinking to present you as a chaste virgin to her true and only husband." Another passage occurs in Rom. 7:3-4. Paul is making the point that the law is binding on a person only during his lifetime, and that those who have died and risen with Christ are no longer bound to the law. The text reads:

> Thus a married woman is bound by the law to her husband as long as he lives; but if her husband dies, she is discharged from the law concerning the husband. Accordingly, she will be called an adulteress if she lives with another man while her husband is alive. But if her husband dies, she is free from that law, and if she marries another man, she is not an adulteress.

It is my contention that, in conjunction with the other relevant texts, this text deliberately uses the female, not the male, in the analogy. This would allow for the double standard, that a woman could not have another man while her husband was alive--consistent with the texts of the Old Testament--while nothing is said about men having other women.

A third text is one which too often, when read at weddings, is applied literally. It reads as follows:

> Wives, be subject to your husbands as you are to the Lord. For the husband is the head of the wife just as Christ is the head of the church, the body of which he is the Savior. Just as the church is subject to Christ, so also wives ought to be in everything, to their husbands. Husbands, love your wives, just as Christ loved the church and gave himself up for her, in order to make her holy by cleansing her with the washing of water by the word, so as to present the church to himself in splendor, without a spot or wrinkle or anything of the kind--yes, so that she may be holy and without blemish. In the same way, husbands should love their own wives as they do their own bodies. He who loves his wife loves himself. For no one ever hates his own body, but he nourishes and tenderly cares for it, just as Christ does for the church, because we are members of his body. For this reason a man will leave his father and mother and be joined to his wife, and the two will become one flesh. This is a great mystery and I am applying it to Christ and the church. Each of you, however, should love his wife as himself, and a wife should respect her husband. (Eph. 5:22-33)

Obviously the author of Ephesians has taken over the God, now Christ (read: "husband") and Israel (now Church, read: "wife") metaphor and is calling husbands to be like God, faithful to Israel, and calling wives to be faithful, like Church, to God. Because men are not God and Israel has not been faithful, the text's constructions are hortatory and imperative. No doubt men wrote the text, and men have been its interpreters. Should one be surprised, then, that the patriarchy latent in the text has been preserved, and the metaphor has been reduced to literal interpretation?

The first letter of Peter is considered a late text, and it is this judgment that must be taken into consideration as part of any attempt at its interpretation. By the time the letter was written, the patriarchal-hierarchical culture of the surrounding societies had all but silenced the more egalitarian tendencies associated with the example and preaching of Jesus, and the earliest New Testament writings. Consequently, the author of 1 Peter recommends docile submission to unjust suffering as a symbol of the unjust suffering which Jesus endured. In that context, he not only encourages slaves to submit to their harsh masters, but also wives to submit to husbands who do not act in accordance with the teachings of Jesus. 1 Pet. 3:1-7 reads:

> Wives . . . accept the authority of your husbands, so that, even if some of them do not obey the word, they may be won over without a word by their wives' conduct, when they see the purity and reverence of your lives. . . . Let your adornment be the inner self with the lasting beauty of a gentle and quiet spirit, which is very precious in God's sight. It was in this way long ago that the holy women who hoped in God used to adorn themselves by accepting the authority of their husbands. Thus Sarah obeyed Abraham and called him lord. You have become her daughters as long as you do what is good and never let fears alarm you.
>
> Husbands . . . show consideration for your wives in your life together, paying honor to the woman as the weaker sex, since they too are also heirs of the gracious gift of life--so that nothing may hinder your prayers.

This text has been used to establish "a gentle and quiet spirit," accompanied by obedience and submissiveness as attributes to be encouraged and admired in women, and to legitimate the diverse expressions of patriarchy which flow from identifying women as the weaker sex.

Other New Testament texts have to do with the relationship between husbands and wives in the resurrection. To the Saducees' question about who would be the husband of a woman who had had seven brothers consecutively as husbands during her lifetime, Jesus responds that "in the resurrection they neither marry nor are they given in marriage, but are like angels in heaven." (Matt. 22:23-32; Mk. 12:18-27; Lk. 20:27-40); the eschatological passage in Rev. 19:7,9 which reads: "Let us rejoice and exult and give him the glory, for the marriage of the Lamb has come, and his bride has made herself ready; to her it has been granted to be clothed with fine linen, bright and pure--for the fine linen is the righteous deeds of the saints. And the angel said to me, 'Write this: Blessed are those who are invited to the marriage supper of the Lamb'."

CONCLUSION

Now what does all this have to do with the crisis believed to be facing the contemporary Catholic Church with respect to marriage and divorce? My point, simply stated, is this. The prohibition against divorce is not a universal. Human beings become one in sexual intercourse, and the human procreation of that sexual intercourse is a new human being who is equally the product of both parents, but not separable into the work of each: the two become one flesh. The Markan community adapted the text from the Genesis creation accounts and incorporated it into their account of Jesus' message in order to portray marriage as ideally a mutual, reciprocal, interdependent relationship between a woman and man faithful to each other. This portrayal is consistent with Jesus' protection of society's powerless (in this case, women) and his advocacy of a discipleship of equals. In addition, it implicitly idealizes the relationship of Jesus and his Church.

The Matthean community also adapted the text from the Genesis creation accounts and incorporated it into its account of Jesus' message, both to diminish the expression of patriarchy which divorce represented in that culture and, most likely, to diminish the incidence of divorce itself. Though not particularly advocating a non-hierarchical, mutual relationship between marriage partners, the Matthean texts, by seeking to limit divorce, intended, I believe, to seek the wife's best interest.

The Ephesians text, as metaphor, is essentially subordinative in intent; unfortunately, however, as with much of our theology we have literalized the metaphor, although we could hardly have done otherwise in the patriarchal culture in which the text has been interpreted.

If we take historical criticism seriously and feminist criticism seriously, we can no longer appeal to the Bible to defend the traditional Catholic position on divorce. Just as one cannot defend the prohibition against women priests on biblical grounds, neither can one defend an absolute prohibition against divorce (such as has been done except for the "Pauline Privilege," and second marriages "in favor of the faith") on biblical grounds.

All of the texts were produced by men in a patriarchal culture and have been interpreted by men in patriarchal cultures. Just as medical researchers did heart studies on men and presumed that they applied to women also, and neglected breast cancer research since the disease is infrequent in men though it claims one out of nine women as its victim--in short, making men the norm of the human--so, too, texts produced by men and directed to men in a patriarchal culture have been universalized. Men, even those who have sincerely sought to interpret the texts from the perspective of gospel values, have interpreted the texts without paying sufficient attention to the real experiences of real women.

The prohibition against divorce may originally have been intended to protect the economically and socially powerless/dependent wife and the vulnerable children. In today's society--in some ways not greatly different from first-century Palestine--the restriction of divorce and even its prohibition *may* inhibit men from leaving their socially and economically dependent wives and families of many years for the physical attraction of younger females. On the other hand, the prohibition against divorce has, for many women, been the prison which has enslaved them and their offspring and sentenced them to lives of mental, physical and sexual abuse.

As late as the 1950s Catholic marriage manuals encouraged women to be obedient to their husbands; often priests counseled women to remain in their marriages in spite of the fact that they were being abused. The counsel came from a tradition of literal interpretation and universalized application of the biblical texts. Divorce is not ideal: it falls short of the ideal set forth in the covenant symbol of Christ and the Church. On the other hand, in the present historical situation and cultural context, it may be divorce and not its prohibition that serves to protect the *wellbeing of the less powerful* in the relationship--however they are less powerful and whoever they may be. Divorce, not annulment, may be every bit as much in keeping with fidelity to the gospel and Jesus' discipleship of equals as either its prohibition or its too narrow restriction.

NOTES

[1]Lisa Sowle Cahill, "Is Catholic Ethics Biblical? The Example of Sex and Gender." Warren Lecture Series in Catholic Studies, No. 20. The University of Tulsa, March 15, 1992.

[2]*Holy Bible. The New Revised Standard Version with Apocrypha.* (Nashville: Thomas Nelson Publishers, 1989). All biblical quotations in the article are taken from this edition unless otherwise indicated.

[3]See Raymond F. Collins, *Divorce in the New Testament.* Good News Studies 38 (Collegeville, MN: Liturgical, 1992) for a recent and comprehensive treatment, though his interpretation differs from mine at several points.

[4]Elizabeth Schussler Fiorenza, *In Memory of Her: A Feminist Theological Reconstruction of Christian Origins.* (New York: Crossroad, 1983).

[5]Two excellent insights regarding Matt. 5:30-31 came from respondents to a first draft of this paper. The first pointed out that the Matthean counsel against divorce is situated in the larger context of the Beatitudes passage. She noted the inconsistency--and implicitly, the patriarchy--which has led traditional biblical interpreters to consider most of the Beatitudes as ideals while applying this text literally. The other comment cited a commentary on the passage which enlarges the notion of "unchastity." My response to the comment was to guess that the commentator was wishing to enlarge allowances for divorce. His method of interpretation is to suggest that the text meant more than we now hear it saying. Though I sympathize with his approach, I do not think it takes seriously enough the patriarchy of those who produced the text in the first place.

ON *THE RESTRUCTURING OF AMERICAN RELIGION*

AN ANALYSIS AND CRITIQUE

Peter Huff

The publication of Robert Wuthnow's *The Restructuring of American Religion*[1] signals the permanent addition of a provocative voice to the discussion of religion's public role in contemporary American society. Much of the critical praise it has received suggests that the merits of the work may warrant its inclusion in the sociology of American religion's canon of classics. One measure of the book's current success is its prominence in the documentation supporting the arguments advanced in *The Good Society* (1991) by Robert Bellah and colleagues. Because of its largely favorable reception, the assumptions, arguments, and implications of Wuthnow's work invite continued analysis and criticism.

In *The Restructuring of American Religion* Wuthnow attempts to chart the volatile course of public religion in changing U.S. society from the Second World War to the present. The central thesis of the work concerns the polarization of the contemporary religious community into hostile camps of conservatives and liberals--a subject Wuthnow also treats in *The Struggle for America's Soul*.[2] Relying heavily upon the data of a 1984 survey conducted by the Gallup Organization and funded by Robert Schuller Ministries, Wuthnow maintains that the divisions of late twentieth-century American religion derive more from ideological disagreements over religion's proper function in democratic society than from traditional feuds contesting points of ecclesiology and theology. No longer is religious identity solely a matter of official membership, he says, but rather it depends upon participation in loose transdenominational coalitions geared toward specifically liberal or conservative ends. The "restructuring" he has in mind is the transformation of Andrew Greeley's "denominational society" into a reordered configuration of religious loyalties and prejudices only accidentally related to the conventional system of denominationalism. Drawing upon the terminology of anthropologist Mary Douglas, Wuthnow claims that since World War II American religion has experienced a radical shift in its "symbolic boundaries." From social demarcations negotiating differences among largely cooperative tribal denominations, the boundaries have been realigned to form a massive chasm separating partisan antagonists within the standing denominations.

Wuthnow attributes this shift of boundaries to a variety of forces internal and external to religious organizations. He identifies "fault lines" within the religious landscape, undetected at mid-century, which provided a precarious foundation for denominational life in the postwar decades. Among these "fissures" he treats the tenuous union of tenacious church loyalty with relative indifference to denominational heritage; the operative divorce of religious activism from the values that supported it; and the insecure link between bureaucratic denominational programs and individualized personal piety. Outside pressures that contributed to the restructuring of American religion range from the slipping prestige of the United States in world opinion to domestic social changes such as the rapid rise of a post-industrial culture of technology. Of special concern to Wuthnow is the effect that the expanding federal government had on religion in postwar society. During the economic boom and the Cold War scare, he contends, as the state extended its power into the private spheres of health care and education, the churches found themselves in the awkward position of protesting the state's intrusion into religious matters while simultaneously prodding the state to assume a greater role in social controversies over civil rights and public morality. The advent of interest-based parachurch groups Wuthnow perceives as a direct response to changing conceptions of the state's appropriate role in late modern society.

Wuthnow's stimulating study contains a variety of promising features. Its engaging thesis is enhanced by a well crafted prose style and enriched by an impressive command of source material. It resists popular theories of the secularization and privatization of modern religion, while ably balancing an investigation of religious practice with an interpretation of the social significance of belief. Though uneven in places, the work is a model of sociological scholarship distinguished by impeccable fairness and humane concern for religion in culture.

Wuthnow's project also raises a number of serious questions. Foremost is the problem of historical perspective. Wuthnow generously presupposes the accuracy of two portraits of the state of American religion and society prior to the alleged restructuring: H. Richard Niebuhr's *The Social Sources of Denominationalism* (1929) and Will Herberg's *Protestant-Catholic-Jew* (1951). The uncritical use of their authority to bolster Wuthnow's theory that a highly conscious affirmation of denominational identity characterized religious life until World War II obscures the fact that religious Americans throughout much of U.S. history have often combined an eclectic belief system with a tentative relationship to church bodies. Recent works such as Jon Butler's *Awash in a Sea of Faith* (1990) and Nathan Hatch's *The Democratization of American Religion* (1989) demonstrate that strict denominationalism rarely played a major role in American religion from the seventeenth century through the early national period. Mitigating Wuthnow's conclusion is his own admission that parachurch organizations exercised a vital function in antebellum nineteenth-century America and that the turn of the century witnessed the unprecedented creation of massive denominational structures. Employing Wuthnow's same evidence one could argue that the early twentieth-century obsession with denominations represents the real restructuring of American religion, while post-World War II developments indicate a return to a more traditional pattern of religious behavior.

Secondly, Wuthnow's work raises the issue of the relevance of sociological interpretation for the broader enterprise of religious studies. As the academic debate over method becomes increasingly sophisticated, the ability of social science research to achieve its aim of comprehending religion's social career warrants further scrutiny. To what degree, it may be asked, is the sociology of religion as a mode of inquiry subject to the judgments articulated by Alasdair MacIntyre and like-minded critics of the Enlightenment legacy? It is instructive to recall Niebuhr's misgivings concerning the limitations of his own accomplishment in *The Social Sources of Denominationalism*. In the preface to *The Kingdom of God in America* he writes: "Though the sociological approach helped to explain why the religious stream flowed in [the] particular channels [of ethnic, class, and regional interest], it did not account for the force of the stream itself."[3]

Thirdly, Wuthnow's main argument positing a schism of religious America into conservative and liberal factions regardless of denomination, while compelling, seems to overlook the deep ambivalence ingrained in the nature of religious commitment. It takes no stock of what southern poet Allen Tate called "modern unbelieving belief." Focusing particularly on the Catholic church, Eugene Kennedy and other journalistic observers have commented on the "two cultures of American Catholicism." Similarly, in a recent *Commonweal* article, theologian William Shea reflects on the "dual loyalties in Catholic theology." With language reminiscent of Wuthnow's, he describes the deep fissure dividing the Catholic theological community. "Catholic liberals and conservatives," he says, "have become practicing separatists." More importantly, though, Shea goes on to speak autobiographically of the contradictory allegiances that may exist in the mind of the individual theologian.[4] The nagging ambiguities that beset the uneasy conscience of the contemporary believer defy classification by the straitlaced categories of even the most complex opinion poll. Like the inter-subjective meanings discussed by philosophical anthropologist Charles Taylor, these aspects of contemporary religious experience "fall through the net of mainstream social science."[5] In the same fashion historian Henry May has recently criticized David Davis's characterization of the present as "a time when American culture is ominously divided between fundamentalists and secular humanists." According to May, "That seems to be what the fundamentalists themselves think. Most of the sound and fury does indeed come from these two camps, but there are still millions of Americans and even quite a few academic intellectuals who belong in neither of them."[6]

Another issue raised by Wuthnow's work concerns the place of the religious institution under a dislocated sacred canopy. Granting the validity of Wuthnow's thesis regarding the diminishing importance of denominationalism and the concomitant rise of religious interest groups, the restructured condition of American religion challenges theology to draft a viable ecclesiological strategy of response. Perhaps confirming Bruce Kuklick's suspicion that the social scientist in America functions as a quasi-theologian, Wuthnow provides his own provisional answers to the ecclesiological dilemma. His epigraph from T. S. Eliot's "The Rock"-- 11"And the Church must be forever building,/and always decaying,/and always being restored"--evokes the theological principle of *ecclesia reformata, semper reformanda*, intimating a theoretical framework for assessing the churches' role in the present restructuring, and in his recent book, *Rediscovering the Sacred*, Wuthnow even suggests that religious restructuring necessitates an American version of Old Testament nomadic ecclesiology. Today, he points out, religious Americans consider themselves "a pilgrim people whose tents must always . . . be in motion through the wilderness."[7]

Finally, Wuthnow's text raises the ever present problem of religious pluralism. Writing with a measured sense of urgency, Wuthnow views the supposed bifurcation of American religion with some alarm. Like Robert Bellah and Richard John Neuhaus, he betrays an obvious bias toward consensus. The purpose of his project, after all, is to contribute toward revitalizing "the role of American religion as a witness to the collective values that will keep the nation strong and yet free" (13). The crucial assumption, of course, is that there is only one way to affirm collective values. A public theology of pluralism, by contrast, would interpret religious rivalry as a condition favorable to social life. As historian Laurence Moore has observed, "The American religious system may be said to be 'working' only when it is creating cracks within denominations, when it is producing novelty, even when it is fueling antagonisms."[8] Bids for consensus, on the contrary, rarely steer America toward greater religious tolerance. A notorious example of this tendency is John Dewey's curiously intolerant performance in *A Common Faith* (1934). What Moore has called the "historiography of a desire," the dominant approach to American religious history well into the twentieth century, overemphasized the reality and necessity of consensus in national religious life, often overlooking the very sources granting American religion its distinctive vitality. Since Jefferson's "fair experiment," argu-ably, requires a degree of competition in public religious discourse, and since sectarian fervor, according to Wuthnow's own account, shows no signs of abating, the polarization of liberals and conservatives in the mainline denominations does not augur the threat of imminent stalemate in the religious future. Rather, if Wuthnow's thesis is correct, the restruc-turing of the familiar religious terrain, though discomforting some theologians, may in fact represent a revitalization of American religion.

NOTES

[1]Robert Wuthnow, *The Restructuring of American Religion: Society and Faith Since World War II* (Princeton, NJ: Princeton University Press, 1988).

[2]Robert Wuthnow, *The Struggle for America's Soul: Evangelicals, Liberals, and Secularism* (Grand Rapids,MI: Eerdmans, 1989).

[3]H. Richard Niebuhr, *The Kingdom of God in America* (1937; New York: Harper Torchbooks, 1959), p. ix.

[4]William M. Shea, "Dual Loyalties in Catholic Theology: Finding Truth in Alien Texts," *Commonweal* (31 January, 1992): 9-14.

[5]Charles Taylor, *Philosophy and the Human Sciences* (Cambridge: Cambridge University Press, 1985), p. 40.

[6]Henry F. May, "Religion and American Intellectual History, 1945-1985: Reflections on an Uneasy Relationship," *Religion and Twentieth-Century American Intellectual Life*, ed. Michael J. Lacey (Cambridge: Cambridge University, 1991), p. 21.

[7]Robert Wuthnow, *Rediscovering the Sacred: Perspectives on Religion in Contemporary Society* (Grand Rapids, MI: Eerdmans, 1992), p. 152.

[8]R. Laurence Moore, *Religious Outsiders and the Making of Americans* (New York: Oxford University Press, 1986), p. 208.

THE LIFE, SOCIAL THOUGHT AND WORK OF JOSEPH CASPAR HUSSLEIN, S.J.

Stephen A. Werner

1992 marked the fortieth anniversary of the death of Joseph Husslein, a largely forgotten but significant figure in American Catholicism. In the early 1900s he was a leader in Catholic social thought, in the 1930s and 1940s a leader in promoting Catholic literature.

Born in 1873, Husslein grew up in Milwaukee, Wisconsin.[1] He was graduated from Marquette College (later Marquette University) and in 1891 he entered the Society of Jesus at St. Stanislaus Seminary near St. Louis, Missouri. For several years he taught at Saint Louis University and was ordained a priest in 1905. In 1911 Husslein joined the staff of the Jesuit weekly *America* in New York. During the next eighteen years he wrote eleven books and hundreds of articles in Catholic journals on the Christian response to social problems. He attempted to reach a wide Catholic audience with his writings.

The encyclical *Rerum Novarum* (1891) of Pope Leo XIII (1810-1903) provided the foundation for Husslein's social thought; but the experiences of American Catholics also influenced him. Due to immigration the Catholic population in America mushroomed. Many Catholics suffered under the industrialization of the late 1800s and early 1900s. Workers often labored in unhealthy and dangerous factories for very low pay. Fearing these desperate workers would join the burgeoning socialist movement, the Catholic Church became involved in social problems.[2]

Several controversies, however, prevented Catholics from developing an American answer to social problems: the controversy over the writings of Henry George; the controversy over Catholic recognition of the nationwide union, the Knights of Labor; and the controversy over Americanism--how far Catholicism should adjust to American culture. Thus Husslein looked to *Rerum Novarum* for answers.

Husslein was one of several pioneers who applied Catholic teachings to the American setting, among whom John A. Ryan (1869-1945) was the most important and best known. Other significant figures were

Frederick P. Kenkel (1863-1952) of the Central Bureau of the Central Verein (an organization of German-American benevolent societies, located in St. Louis), William J. Kerby (1870-1936, a priest of the Archdiocese of Dubuque at the Catholic University of America and Trinity College), William J. Engelen, S.J. (1872-1937--at Saint Louis University), Peter E. Dietz (1878-1947, a labor activist priest who worked in Cincinnati, Ohio), and the Jesuit writers at *America*.

Husslein believed the Catholic Church had the answers to social problems. *Rerum Novarum* boldly made such a claim, "For no practical solution of this question (i.e., the alleviation of the condition of the masses) will be found without the assistance of religion and the Church."[3] Husslein applied Leo XIII's ideas under four main themes: an explanation of history, a critique of capitalism, a rejection of socialism, and Husslein's alternative, "Democratic Industry."

HUSSLEIN'S EXPLANATION OF HISTORY

Husslein answered the criticism often made by socialists that the Catholic Church neglected the poor and workers.[4] Pulling together the threads of Leo XIII's views of history, Husslein argued that the Church alone had advanced the cause of workers. Husslein surveyed history, starting with the Old Testament, to show true religion as the protector of workers. From the early Christian centuries to the middle ages the Church worked to abolish slavery, to humanize serfdom, and to protect labor. According to Husslein, the medieval guilds represented the high point of the Church's effort. Tragically, during the Reformation the guilds were destroyed and the moral teachings of the Church rejected. This led to the disastrous consequences of the industrial revolution under *laissez-faire* capitalism. Unfortunately, Husslein reshaped history around his polemical position, and in doing so, failed to treat history critically.

HUSSLEIN'S CRITIQUE OF CAPITALISM

Husslein vehemently attacked *laissez-faire* capitalism:

We still have men in business for whom there is but one industrial principle, and that is the law of supply and demand; for whom labor is but a commodity upon the market to be purchased at the lowest price and worked to the utmost limits that so they may procure through it the highest profits; for whom, in fine, all considerations urged for the need of adequate family wages, such as may suffice to keep the mother engaged in the care of her children amid the decent comfort of a happy home, are pure sentimentalism which has no place in business, commerce, and finance.

It is that class of men, devoid of practical Christianity or true religious principles--and let us hope their number is daily growing less!--which is the real menace of industry and civilization, far more than Socialism, Anarchism, or the whole Soviet regime of Bolshevism ever could possibly be. Such men, precisely, are the most responsible for all radical systems and labor revolutions that disturb the world.[5]

Husslein lamented the system of ethics that justified this:

Its law was summed up in the materialistic motto: "Business is business," which means that the considerations of humanity and religion may have their proper time and place, but must not be allowed to interfere with the interests of personal gain. A man might grind and crush the poor, pay starvation wages to labor and exact starvation prices for his products, and yet stand justified by the principles of this system. He might even, if he chose, be crowned as a philanthropist and public benefactor, to satisfy his craving for publicity. Such a code of morality was impossible in the Middle Ages.[6]

Husslein attacked the injustice of capitalism. In a typical article entitled, "The Message of Dynamite" on the bombing of the anti-union *Times* of Los Angeles in 1910 by radical unionists, Husslein condemned the bombing but then turned on business:

It is important however, that the crimes of capital be weighed in the same scales as the crimes of labor, and that the same Nemesis overtake them both. It is needless to enumerate the scores of industrial accidents, the poisoning, the crippling and premature death brought on by the neglect of capitalism providing the proper means of safety and sanitation where the need of them was sufficiently understood. Although such neglect was not always criminal, yet there are instances where the fatal results could have been worked out with almost mathematical certainty. Not infrequently the wasting diseases or sudden deaths due to manufacturing processes and conditions of labor could readily have been averted, but the remedy would have diminished to some extent the streams of dividends pouring into the overflowing reservoirs of wealth. Gold has proved more deadly to the human race than dynamite.[7]

In making his attacks on capitalism, Husslein fit the model of the Old Testament prophet who used the language of metaphor, hyperbole, and image to attack social injustice.

Husslein fought specific abuses such as child labor, unsafe factories, and unhealthy work conditions. Although he opposed what he considered radical elements in the feminist movement, Husslein called for equal pay for equal work for women and protection for women from dangerous occupations. Husslein also attacked sexual harassment in the work place.

Husslein's Rejection of Socialism

Husslein saw unrestrained capitalism as the source of socialism. Desperate workers suffering under the capitalist system turned to socialism. But Husslein rejected socialism, primarily because of its irreligion.[8] He believed that only true religion could solve the problems of workers. In particular he attacked socialist claims of neutrality toward religion. He quoted the Chicago Platform of the 1908 National Conference of the Socialist Party of America: "The Socialist Party is primarily an economic and political movement. It is not concerned with matters of religious belief."[9] Husslein called this statement a subterfuge, a tactical falsehood to attract members. "Let us, then, make no mistake. True *Christianity* and true *Socialism*, as here described, are forever irreconcilable."[10]

Husslein attacked and rejected revisionist or mitigated socialism which sought change through democratic and parliamentary means--promoting evolutionary socialism instead of radical, revolutionary socialism. Husslein cited Pius XI who stated, "No one can be at the same time a sincere Catholic and a true socialist."[11]

Husslein's Democratic Industry

Private property was the most developed argument in Leo XIII's *Rerum Novarum*. Yet the property argument proved difficult to apply. Apparently Leo XIII envisioned an agrarian or crafts economy and not a modern industrial economy when he called for a wider distribution of private property.[12]

Husslein attempted to salvage Leo XIII's insistence on private property as the solution to the social question by combining it with the pope's views on history. Thus Husslein applied the principles of the medieval guilds to modern worker cooperatives. Not a naïve romantic wanting to return to the middle ages, Husslein believed that guild principles such as the insistence on quality, worker control of enterprises, and regulations for fair prices were essential to bringing justice to modern economic systems. "It is clear that the guilds cannot be reproduced today precisely as they existed in the middle ages. . . . What we can and must copy is their spirit and motivation."[13] Husslein called his application of guild principles to modern economies, "Democratic Industry."

For Husslein, Democratic Industry involved five specific and concrete approaches: profit sharing, cooperative banks, cooperative stores, co-partnership, and co-production.[14] Husslein envisioned a mixed economy: cooperative industries alongside capitalist industries.

In profit sharing, the workers' receipt of a share of profits presupposed living wages for workers. Husslein considered this a positive step, but an inadequate solution to the industrial problem, since workers had no share in management of the business.

In cooperative banks or credit unions, workers and poor people could obtain credit when refused by commercial banks and escape usurious interest rates. Husslein described cooperative stores where members owned shares of stock in stores where they purchased goods at low prices. Cooperative stores eliminated middlemen who raised prices without providing tangible service to consumers.

In co-partnership, the fourth approach, workers owned a substantial share in voting stock and a reasonable share in management. Unions would still be necessary.

Finally, Husslein proposed co-production (also called cooperative production and cooperative ownership), in which workers owned and managed the businesses in which they worked. He saw this approach as voluntaristic, not socialistic, and based on private, not public, ownership.

Husslein believed that these cooperatives would benefit and protect workers, give them control over their lives, and stop the economic injustices of modern society such as shoddy products, market hoarding, price fixing, price gouging, and inadequate wages. Furthermore, Husslein thought that cooperatives could reach these goals without government intervention.

Husslein, possibly the most prolific American Catholic social thinker, wrote some five hundred signed articles, countless unsigned articles, and eleven books on social issues. His first book published in 1911 was *The Church and Social Problems*. *The Catholic's Work in the World*, published in 1917, provided a handbook for organizing Catholics, probably modeled after socialist handbooks.[15] It contained a chapter on religious conversion entitled, "Win my Chum week." An outstanding book was Husslein's

Bible and Labor published in 1924.[16] This book, unique in American Catholic thought until recent times, attempted to develop principles for social ethics from biblical--largely Old Testament--principles.

The bulk of Husslein's social writing ended with his book *The Christian Social Manifesto* which appears to be, for its time, the definitive American interpretation of *Rerum Novarum* and Pius XI's *Quadragesimo Anno*. Husslein based this book on his radio broadcasts of Catholic social teaching.

Husslein bridged the period between Leo XIII and Pius XI. In many points, by drawing out the implications of Leo XIII's thought Husslein anticipated Pius XI. Husslein received international recognition for his work.

A UNIVERSITY IN PRINT

In the early 1930s Husslein returned to Saint Louis University and founded its School of Social Service to train social workers. During the Great Depression many Catholic universities established similar schools. Husslein sought an organization to promote and develop Catholic social science and to train professional social workers. Husslein directed the school until 1940.

Husslein also had in mind a more daring project. In 1931 he founded "A University in Print," a collection of books to promote Catholic scholarship, published by Bruce Publishing of Milwaukee.[17] In Husslein's time the shortage of American Catholic literature and scholarship was widely lamented. There was a deliberate effort to create and encourage an American Catholic literary revival and to promote Catholic intellectual efforts.[18] Husslein desired to establish a university in print with books of biography, history, literature, education, the natural sciences, art, architecture, psychology, philosophy, scripture, and religion:

> It was to be a university for the people, a university for the men and women with intellectual interests, whether within college walls or outside of them, offering to all the best scientific and cultural thought of Catholic thinkers, scientists and literary men. Each work was intended to be the result of original research while at the same time presenting larger and more familiar aspects of the subjects treated. It was to be popular, but without sacrificing scholarship.[19]

Husslein envisioned "A University in Print" with a faculty of productive Catholic authors, their books as lectures, and the world as their student body. Although started in the Great Depression, the series grew rapidly. It included such authors as Hilaire Belloc and Fulton J. Sheen.

Husslein's "A University in Print" began with the first group of books the "Science and Culture Series." A year and a half later Husslein began the "Science and Culture Texts" series and in May 1934 Husslein started a third series: the "Religion and Culture Series."

Working without a secretary, Husslein edited over 212 books during a twenty-one year period. The series included Husslein's two-volume *Social Wellsprings* which provided English translations of the social encyclicals of Leo XIII and Pius XI. Also the series published several of Husslein's eight devotional books on such topics as the kingship of Christ, the biblical roots of Eucharist, and Thérèse of Lisieux.

All of Husslein's work flowed from his belief that the Church had the answers to social problems. Husslein labored throughout his life to disseminate Catholic teaching and to prove the viability of this belief. In his social writing and his founding of the School of Social Service at Saint Louis University he applied and promoted Catholic social teaching. In his "A University in Print" and devotional writing he promoted Catholic teaching and spirituality as the catalyst for social reform. Husslein's work represents a unique and important contribution to American Catholicism.

NOTES

[1]Several short articles describe the life and work of Husslein: *The New Catholic Encyclopedia*, s.v. "Husslein, Joseph Caspar," by E. J. Duff; Matthew Hoehn, ed., *Catholic Authors: Contemporary Biographical Sketches: 1930-1947* (Newark, N.J.: St. Mary's, 1957), 344-45; "Rev. Joseph A. [sic] Husslein," *The News-Letter--Missouri Province* 17 (February 1953): 139-41; George G. Higgins, "Joseph Caspar Husslein, S.J.: Pioneer Social Scholar," *Social Order* 3 (February 1953): 51-53; Walter Romig, ed., *The Book of Catholic Authors: (First Series)* (Grosse Pointe, Mich.: Walter Romig, 1942), 131-38. Archival material exists at the Jesuit Archives at 4517 West Pine, St. Louis, Mo. The most detailed study is Stephen A. Werner, "The Life, Social Thought, and Work of Joseph Caspar Husslein, S.J." (Ph.D. diss., Saint Louis University, 1990). The only recent writing on Husslein has been Peter McDonough, *Men Astutely Trained: A History of the Jesuits in the American Century* (New York: Free Press, 1992). This book incorporates a previous article by McDonough that discusses Husslein: "Metamorphoses of the Jesuits: Sexual Identity, Gender Roles, and Hierarchy in Catholicism," *Comparative Studies in Society and History* 32 (April 1990): 325-56. However it is this writer's opinion that McDonough does not accurately interpret Husslein or his writings.

[2]For general works on American Catholic social thought in the early 1900s see Aaron I. Abell, *American Catholicism and Social Action: A Search for Social Justice, 1865-1950*

(New York: Doubleday, 1960); Charles E. Curran, *American Catholic Social Ethics: Twentieth Century Approaches* (Notre Dame, Ind.: Notre Dame, 1982); and James E. Roohan, *American Catholics and the Social Question 1865-1900* (New York: Arno, 1976).

[3]Leo XIII, *Rerum Novarum*, 13; found in Joseph Husslein, *Social Wellsprings*, vol. 1 (Milwaukee: Bruce, 1949), p. 175.

[4]Husslein developed his views on history in three books: *Bible and Labor* (New York: Macmillan, 1924); *Democratic Industry* (New York: P. J. Kenedy, 1919); Joseph Husslein and John C. Reville, *What Luther Taught* (London: R. & T. Washbourne, 1918).

[5]Joseph Husslein, *The Christian Social Manifesto* (Milwaukee: Bruce, 1931), p. 44.

[6]Husslein, *The World Problem: Capital, Labor and the Church* (New York: P. J. Kenedy, 1918), pp. 37-38.

[7]Joseph Husslein, "The Message of Dynamite," *America* 8 (8 February 1913): 414.

[8]Husslein's attack on socialism permeates his writings but is clearly stated in *The Church and Social Problems* (New York: America, 1912).

[9]Husslein, *Church and Social Problems*, p. 25. See also pp. 25-31.

[10]Husslein, *Christian Social Manifesto*, p. 85.

[11]Pius XI, *Quadragesimo Anno*, 39; found in Husslein, *Christian Social Manifesto*, p. 314.

[12]Charles Curran, The Changing Anthropological Bases of Catholic Social Ethics," *The Thomist* 45 (April 1981): 307-308.

[13]Husslein, *Social Wellsprings*, I:190.

[14]Joseph Husslein, *The World Problem: Capital, Labor, and the Church*, (New York: P. J. Kenedy, 1918), pp. 203-31

[15]Joseph Husslein, *The Catholic's Work in the World* (New York: Benziger, 1917).

[16]Joseph Husslein, *Bible and Labor* (New York: Macmillan, 1924).

[17]Descriptions of Husslein's "A University in Print" can be found in Joseph Husslein, "A University in Print," *The Jesuit Bulletin* 15 (April 1936): 1-3, 8; Joseph Husslein, "A University in Print," *The Jesuit Bulletin* 26 (February 1947): 12-14; William Holubowicz, "University in Print: Science and Culture Series," *Sign* 21 (December 1941): 281-82; William Barnaby Faherty, *Better the Dream; St. Louis: University and Community, 1818-1968* (St. Louis: Saint Louis University), 298-300; and William Barnaby Faherty, *Dream by the River: Two Centuries of Saint Louis Catholicism, 1766-1967* (Saint Louis: Piraeus, 1973), p. 173.

[18]Arnold Sparr describes the attempt to remedy the lack of American Catholic literature in *To Promote, Defend, and Redeem: The Catholic Literary Revival and the Cultural Transformation of American Catholicism, 1920-1960* (New York: Greenwood, 1990).

[19]Husslein "A University in Print," *The Jesuit Bulletin* 15 (April 1936): 1.

$E = MC^2$ AND

"GOD WAS IN CHRIST

RECONCILING THE WORLD TO HIMSELF":

AN UNBRIDGEABLE CHASM?

Elizabeth Newman

For the most part, modern thinking about science and scientific knowing has moved away from the Cartesian-Newtonian worldview which imagines that nature, the world of facts, is a vast machine written in the language of mathematics. From this standpoint, real knowledge, which mirrors the "external" world, is objective, static and valueless. Indeed, perhaps, the two greatest scientific discoveries that have challenged this earlier worldview are Einstein's theory of relativity and Heisenberg's uncertainty principle. For these discoveries indicate 1) that the world "over against us" is not as fixed as previously imagined, that all points are relative to all others, and 2) that "the world of experience depends in part on variable features of us . . ."[1]

Such a shift in scientific epistemology has no doubt contributed to the growing interest in reconsidering the relationship between religion and science. An example is the recent University of Notre Dame-sponsored public TV discussion series entitled simply "Science and Religion." While the series is informative and offers some valuable insights, perhaps most valuable is its acknowledgement that there is no consensus on *how* to relate religion and science. Some panelists suggest that religion and science are not fundamentally at odds because they simply ask and answer different questions; others suggest that science relies upon concrete evidence which religious explanations lack. While I do not wish to deny the positive contributions of the debate, I do wish to suggest that this debate, like other similar debates, does not fully incorporate the radical shift in scientific epistemology reflected in the comments and discoveries of many great scientists themselves. The debate between science and religion continues to be, albeit less explicitly, a debate between the objective and subjective, fact and value, mind and body. These dualities, in part, issue from the assumption that one must *begin* with the dichotomy between religion and science and then figure out how to relate the two. The result of assuming the primacy of this dichotomy is the tendency to lapse into the, by now, old and familiar dualisms which regard science as real and intractable in a way that religion is not. While some of us may think these old dualisms between objective and subjective, "have been polemicized about until we are left in a state of near stupefaction,"[2] they nonetheless continue to haunt our imaginations. It seems obvious that "$E = MC^2$" (Energy = Mass x Speed of Light^2) or "$2+2=4$" is more objective and universal than the value-laden belief that "God was in Christ reconciling the world to himself." From the standpoint of the *apparent* durability and certainty of scientific and mathematical statements, religious statements appear to be more subjective, more relative and more adequately regarded as symbolic.

I wish to enter the ongoing interdisciplinary conversation by considering more closely our conception of language. Most broadly, my central question is: *is* there a place to stand from which we can claim that such a statement as "God was in Christ reconciling the world to himself . . ." is not inherently more problematic than the statement "$E = MC^2$" or "$2+2=4$"? To address this question, I will first explore in detail some previous attempts to relate religion and science. I will then look at how our notions of objectivity and subjectivity, often presumed by the language we use to describe science or religion, are shaped primarily by our visual sensibilities. Finally, I will seek to orient our imaginations toward an alternative framework, one in which such dualisms as mathematical fact and religious belief have no traction. To this end, I will consider how our perceptions of the world and ourselves differ when we allow not sight but speaking and hearing to inform our worldview, and most fundamentally lanaguage itself.

Exploring Previous Responses:
Horace Judson and Gordon Kaufman

It seems quite common today to reject the stereotypical picture of the dispassionate scientist objectively observing external phenomena. For example, Horace Freeland Judson, author of several books on scientific epistemology, quite wonderfully recounts the personal statements of

various well-known scientists which soundly contradict scientific ojbectiv-
ism. Judson relates the comments of Noble Prize recipient Joshua Lederberg, whose discoveries established the genetics of microorganisms.
Lederberg rather bizarrely describes his own scientific endeavors:

> One needs the ability to strip to the essential attributes of some actor
> in a process, the ability to imagine oneself *inside* a biological situation;
> I literally had to be able to think, for example, "What would it be like
> if I were one of the chemical pieces in a bacterial chromosome?"—and
> try to understand what my environment was, try to know *where* I was,
> try to know when I was supposed to function in a certain way, and
> so forth.[3]

Another well-known physical chemist whom Judson refers to "was
credited by his peers, who watched him awestruck, with the ability to
think about chemical structures directly in quantum terms—so that if a
proposed molecular model was too tightly packed he felt uncomfortable,
as though his shoes pinched."[4] Finally Judson describes mathematician
Henri Poincaré's intense efforts to make a mathematical breakthrough.
Realizing he needed to put his work behind him, Poincaré decided to go
on a geological excursion for several days. To his surprise, however,
Poincaré's work "found" him as he was carrying on a conversation while
boarding a bus. Poincaré states: "At the moment *when I put my foot on
the step, the idea came to me*, without anything in my former thoughts
seeming to have paved the way for it, that the transformations I had used
to define the Fuchsian functions were identical with those of non-Euclid-
ean geometry." Poincaré did not try to prove the idea, but went right on
with his conversation. "But I felt a perfect certainty," he wrote. When
he got home, "for conscience's sake I verified the result at my leisure."[5]

Clearly, as Judson rightly notes, these scientists and mathematicians
do not understand themselves as detached, passionless knowers! Judson
reminds us yet again, as Micheal Polanyi has done previously in his book
Personal Knowledge,[6] that 1) the scientist is not a subject removed from
the objects which she studies and 2) that all explicit knowing relies upon
the tacit absorption and incorporation of what in fact we are trying to
know. Like an actor or an artist the scientist dwells passionately and com-
mittedly in a particular world. Judson concludes that "passion is indispensable for creation no less in the sciences than in the arts." He further indicates that often when one listens to the personal, as opposed to theoretical,
comments from great scientists about how they come to know, comments
which Judson recounts quite wonderfully, the "scientific objectivism"

endorsed at times by our popular culture is usually soundly defeated.[7]

What is interesting, however, for my own investigations is that while Judson rightly notes a common thread amongst seemingly disparate kinds of knowing, he nonetheless maintains that science, above and beyond any other discipline, describes the world as it really is:

> The scientist enjoys the harsher discipline of what is and is not the case. It is he, rather than the painter or the poet in this century, who pursues in its stringent form the imitations of nature. . . . Here the scientist parts company with the artist. The insight must be sound. The dialogue is between what might be and what is in fact the case. The scientist is trying to get the thing right. The world is there.[8]

Judson's use of the words "harsh," "stringent," "in fact the case" all suggest that he still reserves for science a privileged place in our knowing about the world we live in. Although he states, and rightly, that scientific knowing resembles the knowing process in other disicplines, he nonetheless maintains that science deals with the real world in a way that the implied "softer" disciplines do not.

I have turned to Judson because I believe he exemplifies a fairly common confusion in the debate between science and religion. While on one level, Judson sees a continuity in all types of knowing, on a more basic level his imagination accords science the fullest reality. All that falls outside of the "harsh" scientific criteria, so Judson implies, does not describe the *real* world. We can see that Judson's earlier attempt to defeat the common notion of the detached objective scientist is itself defeated by his own ultimate endorsement of a picture of reality grounded in "what is in fact the case," the real in-itself. For his statement "the world is there" makes it sound as if we have no part in laying claim to that world. Judson presumes that "the real is just the way it is, whether known by some person or not."[9] His claim that the scientist, not the poet, deals with "what is in fact the case" implies a belief that observable facts are intractable in a way that values are not. It is precisely this picture of reality that has contributed to the rise of scientific objectivism which imagines the knower to be simply a nuetral, passive observer.

Given Judson's position, I imagine that he would believe that E=MC² describes quite soundly the "real world," while "God was in Christ reconciling the world . . ." is more inherently problematic. In stating this, I do not intend simply to indict Judson, but rather to use his thought as an example of what I believe is still a very common cultural belief, despite some protestations to the contrary: namely, that scienctific language describes objective reality in a way that religious language does not. This is because, as I shall discuss below, Judson assumes that the meaning of language derives from a correspondence theory of truth: language is true if it accurately corresponds to the existing state of affairs in the world.

Issues relevant to the relation between religion and science can be observed as well in the works of well-known theologian Gordon Kaufman. While I do not wish to deal with all of Kaufman's rich and wide-ranging thought, for the purposes of my thesis I do wish to focus on one aspect, namely his understanding of scientific and religious language. As recently as the 1991 National AAR Meeting in Kansas City, MO, Kaufman made a presentation entitled "Nature, History and God: Toward an Integrated Conceptualization," in which he called for the "symbol God" to be understood not in terms of content, i.e., father, creator, but in terms of the "evolutionary trajectory." In his book, *Theology for a Nuclear Age*, Kaufman explains more fully his position by stating that he relies, for his re-construction of the "symbol God," upon two criteria which he draws from traditional Christianity. First, the "symbol God" must serve a relativizing function, for "the mythic notions of God as creator, as sovereign lord of life and history, as judge of all the earth, were often used in the tradition to express this relativizing motif."[10] Secondly, the "symbol God" must serve a humanizing function because "God is seen as ultimately a humane being, a 'father' (to use the symbolism of the tradition) who loves and cares for 'his' children . . ."[11] The "symbol God" then, according to Kaufman, needs to be conceived in terms of "biological evolution and the eco-system, on the one hand, and the long process of human history and the diverse socio-cultural systems which it has produced, on the other."[12] Thus if we are to speak of God today at all, we must draw our symbols and images from these processes because 1) they both relativize and humanize us and 2) they are connected with contemporary experience.

That Kaufman regards all theological language as only symbolic or metaphorical is at once revealing of Kaufman's own thought and problematic. For Kaufman states that "at best, all of the concepts and images with which we seek to conceive God and to understand God are *only* analogies or metaphors, symbols or models, drawn from human experience and history; they are, therefore, never applicable literally."[13] Kaufman, here influenced by Immanuel Kant, holds that understanding cannot go beyond experience to define metaphysical Being which we call God. Our language cannot fully describe God or any metaphysical concept because we do not experience God directly. Kaufman notes that Kant's epistemology has today been largely confirmed in that "we now know that all our perception is heavily colored by the interpretive schemes carried in language and culture, that we never perceive objects immediately, uninterpreted by a conceptual framework created by the human imagination."[14] Given that language does not function to describe immediate experiences of God, Kaufman then claims that theological language functions to relativize illegitimate absolutes (or serves a "regulative use," in Kant's terminology), as noted earlier by Kaufman's emphasis on the need for theological language to relativize and humanize. Thus in Kaufman's framework, on the one hand, we have biological evolution and social history as *literally* real, and on the other, theological conceptions as *only* symbolic, since they cannot fully describe the "supernatural-in-itself."

Yet it is precisely while he is standing in the shadow of Kant that Kaufman displays a profound confusion about language. For in this shadow, theological language, since it cannot grasp or correspond to the "in-itself," suffers a loss. Kaufman implicitly assumes this loss when he writes: "When we are dealing with metaphysical or theological conceptions, then—with the 'world' or the 'whole,' with 'being' or 'reality' or 'God'—the ordinary truth-criterion of correspondence simply cannot be directly applied."[15] Because the "ordinary truth-criterion of correspondence" does not apply to theological language, that language becomes "only symbolic" and indirect. Yet for Kaufman where does the "ordinary truth-criterion of correspondence" directly apply? In his conceptual schema, language that is direct and literal, and thus corresponds, is found in the "phenomenal" sphere: science. Examples of such direct language in Kaufman's usage are "evolutionary trajetory," "biological evolution," and the "eco-system." In contrast, Kaufman suggests that in theology we must imaginatively construct our symbols and metaphors of God "drawn from ordinary experience but now used in quite extraordinary ways to develop an overall conceptual structure within which all else can be understood."[16]

At this point, we can see a subtle dualism operating in Kaufman's imagination between direct, scientific language and symbolic, religious language. Kaufman assumes that scientific language is primary (since it directly describes the phenomenal world) while religious language is a constructed part of our perception of things, derived from the more primary "evolutionary trajectory." Thus Kaufman can write that "God is here understood as that ecological reality behind and in and working through all of life and history . . ."[17]

Both Judson's implication that poetry and art do not represent the real world and Kaufman's claim that theological language is "only symbolic" reflect a fundamental dichotomy in their thinking about language, and consequently about reality. There is: 1) the literally real, as established by science, which relies upon the truth-criterion of correspondence, and 2) all that falls outside this primary reality, such as poetry and religion. In contrast to Judson, who holds that "the real world" is really discovered by scientists, Kaufman splits the real between our ordinary experience, the phenomenal world, and the metaphysical or noumenal world, which our language can never directly grasp. Nonetheless, Judson and Kaufman share similar assumptions about religious and scientific language, as suggested by Judson's elevation of scientific language as descriptive of the real world and Kaufman's notion of theological language as only capable of describing the supernatural symbolically and indirectly. These assumptions are so deeply ingrained in our cultural imagination that it seems commonsensical to describe scientific statements, such as $E = MC^2$, as real (Judson) or direct (Kaufman), and religious statements, such as "God was in Christ reconciling the world to himself," as only symbolic and indirect. Indeed to suggest otherwise seems, to some, counter-intuitive.

THE IMAGINATIVE WEIGHT OF VISION

Before considering an alternative to Judson and Kaufman's dichotomous descriptions, I would like first to consider how it is that their framework has achieved such imaginative weight. Kaufman is indeed right to point out that "all our perception is heavily colored by the interpretive schemes carried in language and culture, that we never perceive objects immediately, uninterpreted by a conceptual framework created by the human imagination."[18] Kaufman, however, overlooks how his own conceptual schema is influenced by a particular "interpretive schema carried in language and culture." I say this not in the attempt to free ourselves from interpretive schemas, but rather to free us from Kaufman's (and Kant's) schema so that we might imagine genuine alternatives. For the split between the noumenal and phenomenal is itself a particular schema heavily shaped by our *visual* sensibilites. Walter Ong notes that Kant concretized the tendency to deal with intellection by analogy with vision. Focused on sight alone, understanding is condemned to deal only with surfaces which have a "beyond" that it can never attain. "As soon as one sets up the problem of intellectual knowing in terms of a visualist construct such as 'phenomena,' the question of 'noumena' thus automatically arises."[19] The Kantian problem that our language cannot directly get at the "thing-in-itself " arises primarily from within a visual paradigm.

That Ong is right, and that Kant's (and Kaufman's) thought is deeply indebted to a visual conceptual framework, can be seen in Kant's understanding of space, a form which according to Kant springs from the subject. Interestingly enough, however, space is primarily visual: "the condition of the existence of any object for me."[20] Space is that in which *extended objects* exist. Within a Kantian framework, for example, there is no distinction between visual space and aural space.[21] While no doubt much brilliant analysis evolves from Kant's framework, at the same time such a schema heavily influenced by our visual sensibilities can lead us down blind alleys, such as I believe it easily does in our understanding of religious and scientific language.

Before moving to an alternative, I wish to consider more closely the influence of vision on our epistemological sensibilities. While Ong helpfully describes the influence of the (visual) written word on our cultural imagination, I wish, in light of the religion/science debate, to look at a particular scientific discovery, influential at the beginning of the modern era: the invention of the telescope, which Galileo himself referred to as an *occhiale*, his "eye-glass." Just as Einstein's theory of relativity and Heisenberg's uncertainty principle have been slowly making their way into our current epistemological convictions, so also did Galileo's invention gradually yet profoundly shape the cultural perceptions at the beginning of the modern era. Hannah Arendt in fact compares this invention to "the babe born in a manger," in that both were "something so unexpectedly and unpredictably new that neither hope nor fear could have anticipated [them] . . ."[22] For, in the cultural imagination, the invention of the telescope, among other things, verified scientifically the authority of sight as a means of knowing and of unlocking the secrets of the universe. Yet this was not just "seeing" this tree or that person, but rather the telescope gave us the imaginative capacity to see the world from the outside, as a god might. For the first time, men and women had the scientific capacity to release themselves from the "shackles of earth-bound experience" and achieve a universal and objective point of view. Galileo's discovery lent empirical confirmation to Copernicus' move from a geocentric (Ptolemaic) to a heliocentric worldview, "which lifted him from the earth and enabled him to look down upon her as though he were actually an inhabitant of the sun."[23] William H. Poteat elaborates on the power of this view: "In that mirror [of Copernicus] we beheld ourselves looking, *as spectators*, at our home, the earth, one planet among others, swinging with others in its orbital path, reckless of us, and imagined that we could now at last 'see ourselves even as already we are seen.'"[24] With its tremendous capability to discover new worlds, the telescope lent authority and imaginative power to a particular kind of vision: one in which we see ourselves from the outside, as an omniscient observer might.

Hans Jonas elaborates upon the powerful world-forming powers that vision has given us in his article "The Nobility of Sight," in which he describes how profoundly our deepest philosophical convictions are rooted in our sensory experience. Jonas, in fact, links epistemological objectivity to sight: "Only the simultaneity of image allows the beholder to compare and interrelate: it not only offers many things at once, but offers them in their mutual proportion, and thus *objectivity emerges preeminently from sight.*"[25] This contrasts radically with hearing, where the sound discloses "not an *object* but a *dynamical event.*"[26] Likewise with touch, the qualities sensed have "process character" and are essentially "time-entities." In addition to the notion of objectivism being rooted in sight, Jonas also states that sight "provides the sensual basis on which the mind may conceive the idea of the eternal, that which never changes and is always present."[27] In contrast, Jonas notes that in neither touch nor hearing is there a static present:

> To put it in Platonic terms, they are senses not of being but of becoming. Only the simultaneous representation of the visual field gives us co-existence as such. . . . The time thus taken in taking-in the view is not experienced as the passing away of contents before new ones in the flux of event, but as a lasting of the same, an identity which is the extension of the instantaneous *now* and therefore unmoved, continued present. . . .[28]

The leading virtues which Jonas attributes to sight are 1) simultaneity of presentation, which gives us the experiential basis of eternity, 2) dynamic neutralization, from which we derive objectivity, and 3) distance, which gives us the idea of infinity. This analysis, while powerful, is rightly qualified by Poteat, who states that Jonas is referring to our present "*picture* of sight, abstracted from actual seeing."[29] And it is important to note that this picture of sight is not natural or the same for all people everywhere. Rather our modern seeing is itself a learned skill shaped by history and culture.[30] In our modern era, the "visual virtues," which Jonas describes, are not to be denied their intellectual powers. Such a visualist picture of reality, however, has so captured our modern imagination that it is difficult to conceive how we might think differently. We can detect our enamoration with visualist criteria especially in the belief that the function of language is to mirror reality: language describes an already existing state of affairs, eternal and unchanging before our eyes. This, we believe, is what $2+2=4$ does, irregardless of whether people hold this to be true and irregardless of the circumstances in which this mathematical truth is made.

ORALITY AS AN ALTERNATIVE PARADIGM

In order to orient our imagination toward an alternative framework, I wish to turn to a way of thinking about language, knowledge and knowing that is primarily rooted not in our visual sensibilities, but rather derives from speaking and hearing. It is my hope that such a shift will enable us to move toward an understanding that language, instead of being an object representing other objects, is first and foremost an activity. Before we can debate whether a word directly or indirectly represents reality, language as activity points to the fact that we necessarily and acritically rely upon words to speak. This is significant because it challenges the notion that as knowers we are simply passive observers, a notion, as stated earlier, at work in Judson's description of the scientist as one who describes what "is and is not the case." Furthermore, such a paradigm shift shaped by orality rather than by our visual sensibilites enables us to understand that our words are not static objects, but rather, to use Jonas's language, "dynamical events" and "time-entities." From this alternative standpoint, meaning is not primarily derived from what words *stand* for, whether directly or indirectly, as Kaufman assumes in his reliance upon truth as correspondence. Rather with orality, and language as activity, meaning issues first and foremost from the variety of circumstances in which we use words. This shift is not meant to evade questions of truth and reality. In focusing on speaking and language as activity, however, and thus on the concrete circumstances we presuppose, it can no longer be the case that one set of truth criteria (from a correspondence theory of meaning), derived from one "circumstance" (a particular visualist picture of reality), should be lifted above all others. As the philosopher Ludwig Wittgenstein has said, "In different circumstances we apply different criteria. . . ."[31]

By incorporating the thought of the both Wittgenstein and Poteat, I will elaborate below on this alternative framework with an eye to addressing the following: what would be conceptually different in our understanding of the relationship between science and religion if we relied not upon vision but upon speaking and hearing to inform our notion of language and thus of reality?

Whereas Wittgenstein originally believed that propositions were true if they were *pictures* of reality, he later admits that he "had been forced to recognize grave mistakes"[32] in his earlier works. Attempting to move away from a "visual picture" of language, Wittgenstein claims that the language of correspondence or representation does not adequately capture the meaning of words. Rather "the word 'meaning' [itself] is being used illicitly if it is used to signify the thing that 'corresponds' to the word."[33] Wittgenstein, in his now well-known dictum, instead holds that the meaning of a word is its use in the language.[34] This shift indicates that Wittgenstein's later philosophical investigations are rooted in his grasp of language as that which issues from our dynamic speaking with one another, and from the grammar we necessarily adhere to in order to be able to speak and mean anything. From this standpoint, Wittgenstein describes language not as a visual countersign to silent thought, which we imagine the written word to be, but as an activity, or part of a "form of life." This focus on the dynamism of language, on language as activity, is captured by Wittgenstein when he writes: "Giving grounds, however, justifying the evidence, comes to an end—but the end is not certain propositions' striking us immediately as true, i.e. it is not a kind of *seeing* on our part; it is our *acting*, which lies at the bottom of the language game."[35]

In order to develop this point, Wittgenstein refers to words as tools,[36] upon which we actively rely and which we dynamically use in a variety of ways. Our words as tools enable us to take initiative, to set in motion particular worlds, and to disclose who we are before others.[37] With our spoken words, we usher in concrete worlds of meaning, whether we are giving a lecture on mathematics, preaching, gossiping or engaging in a lively conversation over dinner. Like our use of some tools, a saw for instance, some words, can be *hard* to say: for example, says Wittgenstein "as [these] are used to effect a renunciation, or to confess a weakness."[38] This notion of our speaking as an activity—as that which enables us to begin, to move, to appear as who we are before others—contrasts sharply with a visual perception of words as static entities or signs which

correspond (or do not correspond) to a world already there, whether noumenal or phenomenal. In a framework where words are imagined primarily as spoken and heard rather than as written and seen, words are not
signs but deeds. Wittgenstein reflects this conceptual shift when he suggests that a motto for the whole of his later philosophy might be Goethe's
phrase from *Faust*, "In the beginning was the deed."[39] Words are deeds
in the sense that by them we bring forth worlds of meaning, meaning
which is dependent upon the grammar and history of language, but nonetheless makes sense only in our particular and concrete situations.

In agreement with Wittgenstein, Poteat captures this alternative sense
of language when he states: "To use a word is *to speak*, that is quite
simply to actualize a potentiality of our lively mindbodies in their oral
aural setting, like pointing or walking or singing a tune."[40] Like Witten-
stein, Poteat connects speaking with acting, with actualizing: that which
makes our potential worlds actual or real. This is captured even more
forcefully when Poteat states:

> In my writing and speaking I make a world appear. I am more likely
> to see that this is so, if what I write or speak issues from an effort to
> formulate a novel or even just a difficult thought; but it is no less the
> case that the sentence 'snow is white' is true if and only if "snow is
> white" makes a world appear, brings forth for me what I know.[41]

This notion, that our speaking (as activity) brings forth a world, is quite
the opposite of Judson's claim that scientific language describes what
already is the case. Such a notion also contrasts with Kaufman because
"speech-as-world-creating" implies that religious language, with its
world-forming powers, is just as direct as scientific language, with its
world-forming powers. Poteat himself reiterates this claim in a number
of places. One of these is when he asks the rhetorical questions,

> But what would the *figurative* solemnization of a marriage be? . . .
> Would we say, "Well, all of the participants didn't mean what they
> said and did *literally*." Or is it rather that they *really, fully, unequivo-*
> *cally* meant what they said and did, only differently? Is Hamlet the
> figurative representation of an actual (historical) Prince of Den-
> mark?[42]

Poteat is here challenging the assumption that only *literal* langauge is
direct. This, as we saw earlier, is Kaufman's assumption: figurative or
symbolic language is *only* indirect, and thus religious language is indirect.
In Poteat's understanding of what language is and does, however, religious

language is as direct as any other language, only direct in a different way. In other words, religious langauge relies upon a different set of criteria to determine what counts as real, but nonetheless is as direct as any other linguistic usage. In fact, Poteat holds that in all circumstances in which we acritically dwell or rely upon language (which we necessarily do in all linguistic usage), a real world is called forth, whether this be religious or mathematical. It is only because our imaginations are immured by an essentialist view of meaning that we think otherwise.

Poteat is thus not operating out of a correspondence theory of meaning, in which the problem literal versus figurative arises. Rather Poteat understands meaning to be that which is generated out of our "lively mindbodies."[43] While it is beyond the bounds of this article to do full justice to this aspect of Poteat's thought, I do want to note that in rooting our language in our mindbodies, Poteat means by this that "language—our first formal system—has the sinews of our bodies, which had them first."[44] In other words, for Poteat language is structured like our mindbodies, which includes "our *lived* and *lively* being in the world prior to speech, which still bears traces of its primitive rootedness in this prelingual setting."[45] Thus, for Poteat, even our most abstract thought is generated out of our mindbodies, rooted as we are in particular times and places. This understanding enables us to situate Judson's and Kaufman's postition more clearly. For as we noted earlier, Judson's objectivism and Kaufman's reliance upon the "truth-criterion of correspondence" are generated or arise from a particular bodily way of seeing, itself influenced by, among other things, writing and the invention of the telescope. From within this framework, however, bodiliness is easily imagined to be incidental to our understanding of truth and meaning. In contrast, as discussed earlier, our way of seeing is itself a body-skill which we have learned, one of many ways we live and move "mindbodily" in the world. This lends support to the notion that other ways we are in the world—speaking, hearing, or touching, for example—are, like seeing, sources we can draw upon to both shape and inform our understanding of reality.

Yet the general claim that speaking is an activity, that in our speaking we bring forth worlds seems to leave the door wide open to charges of both relativism and solipsism, i.e., "I can mean whatever I want by my words." To the contrary, neither Poteat nor Wittgenstein in any way imagines that the individual can simply create the meaning of words *de novo*. Wittgenstein's argument against the possibility of a "private language" clearly displays his rejection of solipsism. Language, by definition, has shared meanings and judgments, as indicated by Wittgenstein in the following passage:

> Why can't my right hand give my left hand money?—My right hand can put it into my left hand. My right hand can write a deed of gift and my left hand a receipt.—But the further practical consequences would not be those of a gift. When the left hand has taken the money from the right, etc., we shall ask: "Well, and what of it?" And the same could be asked if a person had given himself a private definition of a word. . . .[46]

If meaning and language were entirely relative to ourselves alone—if language were private—we would not in fact have a language, which is by definition public. Words would have no traction, because meaning itself is learned and presupposes community. Wittgenstein applies this to mathematics: "Could there be arithmetic without agreement of those who calculate? Could a solitary man calculate? Could a solitary man follow a rule?"[47] It is, as Norman Malcolm points out, difficult to imagine a human being "who is always isolated without, unwittingly, endowing him in imagination with thoughts and ideas that are rooted in the learning of a common language."[48]

In addition to the charge of solipsism, Wittgenstein also defends himself against relativism[49] by introducing an interlocutor who says, "So you are saying that human agreement decides what is true and what is false?" Wittgenstein emphatically responds, "It is what human beings *say* that is true and false; and they agree in the *language* they use. That is not agreement in opinions but in form of life."[50] Here Wittgenstein is pointing to that which is *non-negotiable*, to a place where there is no logical space for the question of true or false, relative or absolute to arise. Our "*human* form of life"[51] is the condition of the possibility for us even to be able to talk about relativism or absolutism. In other words, the relationship we have to our first-order spoken and heard words is a logically necessary one and thus incommutable: not in the sense that our words correspond to an external logos, but rather in that we necessarily depend on our words and a shared meaning in order, by definition, to speak and hear. Without such dependency and acritical reliance, nothing could get said. Even when we make the assertion that "all is merely relative" we are relying upon a shared meaning which is itself not merely relative. Wittgenstein is here trying to get back to a truly *human* orientation for meaning and truth, one where thought is not "surrounded by a halo."[52] The notion that meaning is relative to a particular circumstance, to our particular usage in a concrete time and place, would not, for Wittgenstein, issue in the dissapointed belief that all we are left with is this lesser reality. Rather the misleading picture out of which this disappointed belief arises is one that, according to Wittgenstein, sublimes the logic of language and fails to acknowledge that speaking and knowing are human activities. So also, in contrast to solipsism and relativism, Poteat points to our reliance upon our bodies, our archaic history, our "world prior to speech" which mitigates the picture of a solipsistic self left hanging, disincarnate, in thin air, a self that has no place to stand to judge the truth bearing powers of different human worlds.

To return, however, to the notion that our speaking makes worlds appear: given that what is meant here is not solipsism nor relativism, can we still claim that a scientist, in her discoveries, no less than a poet, in his creative writings, *make* a world appear? Perhaps, it seems for poetry this is true. A great poem does create for its hearers a world; it possibly places its hearers in the world in a way that they have never been placed before. W. H. Auden, for example, writes in *"Musée des Beaux Arts"* about how well the Old Masters understood suffering, "how it takes place/ While someone else is eating or opening a window or just walking/ dully along. . . ." Certainly Auden's words, in the context of his poem, call forth a particular world of meaning. Yet scientific and arithmetic statements seem somehow different. After all, we are tempted to say, $2+2=4$ does not make a world appear, but rather describes an already existing independent state. We want to agree with Wittgenstein's interlocutor: "But mathematical truth is independent of whether human beings know it or not! . . . Even though everybody believed that twice two was five it would still be four."[53] Wittgenstein responds to his interlocutor by asking, "What would it be like for everybody to believe that?—Well, I could imagine, for instance, that people had . . . a technique which we should not call 'calculating.'[54] Wittgenstein's point relates to my own because he is suggesting that when we use "calculating" we mean something that involves, among other things, two plus two equaling four. When we speak of addition, this mathematical world is what we call forth and not some other. This is the mathematical world in which we dwell and upon which we rely. If we meant something else, that is, if we had a different calculus, our world would be different, and most likely we would act differently. (Says Wittgenstein: "Of course, in one sense mathematics is a branch of knowledge—but still it is also an *activity*.")[55]

Earlier, I stated that both Judson and Kaufman ultimately root their conception of the real and direct in a scientific worldview, as they under-stand it: "the world as it is," for Judson, for Kaufman, "the evolutionary trajectory."[56] As I noted, however, such a perception of the "real" has been shaped by a particular picture of seeing, itself influenced by the invention of the telescope. In contrast to this, I have stated that orality does not give us such perceptual grounds, for our spoken words are not visual objects over against us but are "tools" we rely upon to make worlds of meaning appear. From the standpoint of our speaking, language does not correspond to *the* real, thereby having only one essential meaning. Rather our lively oral/aural world indicates that we use the word "real" in a variety of ways, for example, "that was *really* a beautiful sunset," or "the earth *really* circles the sun." Both uses of the word "real" cohere and make sense in their given context; one is not a more authentic or di-rect use than the other. In a similar fashion, Wittgenstein referred to the variety of things we can mean when we say, "I can walk." For example, "I can walk, I mean I have time" but also "I mean I am already strong enough" or "as far as the state of my legs is concerned. . . ."[57] The reality or truthfulness of such statements holds, although different criteria are relied upon in each circumstance. In arguing against a correspondence theory of meaning, I am stating, following Wittgenstein, that one set of criteria should not devour all others for what counts as true and real. Indeed Wittgenstein warned against imagining that "there is some *totality* of conditions corresponding to the nature of each case. . . ."[58] Far from the most real world being only the scientific one, the worlds we call forth in our day to day lives are all real in that they place or orient us in particular ways. If we imagine that the real is already statically there, then we are again relying primarily upon a visual conception of reality.

In conclusion, I wish to claim that Kaufman and Judson, to be able to speak and write as they do, are tacitly relying upon their cultural and linguistic histories replete with stories, metaphors, symbols and deep memories which their "mindbodies" have absorbed. They rely upon this incorporation even to be able to distinguish between science and religion. If they did not rely upon this more primary reality, which means in part if they did not speak English, they would not be able to use the word "real" or "world" at all. When Kaufman, then, says religious language is "only" symbolic, he himself is ignoring all the ways particular cultural stories, symbols and metaphors have shaped his own thinking, even about the "evolutionary trajectory" itself. Michael Foster argues, for example, that only after the absorption of the Christian doctrine of creation was modern science possible.[59] While the entirety of Foster's argument is beyond the confines of this article, suffice it to say that Foster's thesis reflects the fact that the deep interconnection between religion and science, and their influence upon each other in our shared linguistic and cultural history, make it difficult to claim that one linguistic usage (scientific) is direct while another (religious) is only indirect and symbolic.

To return again to Joshua Lederberg, only through his actual reliance upon his bodily place—steeped in the scientific story and community, in its explicit and inexplicit rules, in its rich symbols, metaphors and memories—only by relying upon all this was he able to make the discovery he made. What was most real for Lederberg was not his mind observing a static world "in fact the case," but his ability to immerse himself, with his wealth of scientific wisdom, in the world of the chromosome. As he himself stated, "I *literally* had to be able to think . . . 'What would it be like if I were one of the chemical pieces in a bacterial chromosome'?" This imaginative feat, this placement, was Lederberg's most literal reality! It is what subsequently enabled him to make a new world appear, i.e., a world establishing the genetics of microorganisms. Such imaginative knowing feats are what enable us to make all our worlds appear.

From this standpoint, then, I wish to claim that religious statements, such as "God was in Christ reconciling the world to himself," are not less stringent (Judson) or direct (Kaufman) than mathematical or scientific propositions, such as $2 + 2 = 4$. For both uses are rooted in our incorporation of particular stories and metaphors drawn from a deep and complex linguistic and cultural history. Both statements *directly* get at "what is and is not the case" because both speak forth worlds in which we live and dwell, the full reality of which depends on our responsibly laying claim to those worlds. When we imagine otherwise, then a picture has indeed held us captive.

Finally, while my use of 2 Corinthians 5:19 is illustrative of religious language, it is not meant to be *merely* that. Rather in seeking to challenge the dichotomy between scientific and religious language, and the easy tendency to elevate scientific statements as more rigorous and direct, it has been my purpose to restore a balance by seeking to dissolve this dichotomy. I have attempted to do this by arguing that religious statements are as direct as scientific statements, and that both are rooted in our particular and historical ways of being in the world. By acknowledging that all our knowing is rooted in a place, my aim has been to establish a place for theological statements, such that a religious statement is no more inherently problematic than a scientific or mathematical one. For science and theology alike require of us not only "passionate attentivenss . . . the heartbeat of all serious investigation, but also an unending discipline in *learning how to speak.*"[60]

NOTES

[1]Clark Glymour, "Realism and the Nature of Theory," in Merrilee H. Salmon, *et. al.*, eds., *Introduction to the Philosophy of Science* (Englewood Cliffs, NJ: Prentice Hall, 1992), p. 128.

[2]William H. Poteat, *A Philosophical Daybook. Post-Critical Investigations* (Columbia: University of Missouri, 1990), p. 4.

[3]Horace Freeland Judson, *The Search for Solutions* (New York: Holt, Rinehart and Winston, 1980), p. 6.

[4]Ibid.

[5]Ibid., p. 8, my emphasis.

[6]Michael Polanyi, *Personal Knowledge. Towards a Post-Critical Philosophy* (Chicago: University of Chicago, 1958).

[7]Albert Einstein in fact advised more radically, "If you want to find out anything from theoretical physicists about the methods they use, I advise you to stick closely to one principle: don't listen to their words, fix your attention on their deeds," as quoted by James Loder, *The Transforming Moment* (Colorado Springs: Helmers & Howard, 1989), p. 46.

[8]Judson, p. 11.

[9]Ronald L. Hall, "Critical and Post-Critical Objectivity," unpublished paper, delivered at November, 1991 Polanyi Society, Kansas City, MO.

[10]Gordon D. Kaufman, *Theology for a Nuclear Age* (Philadelphia: Westminster, 1985), p. 34.

[11]Ibid.

[12]Ibid., p. 36.

[13]Ibid., p. 25, my emphasis.

[14]Gordon Kaufman, *The Theological Imagination* (Philadelphia: Westminster, 1981), p. 244.

[15]Ibid., p. 255.

[16]Ibid., p. 248.

[17]*Theology for a Nuclear Age*, p. 145.

[18]*The Theological Imagination*, p. 244.

[19]Walter J. Ong, *The Presence of the Word. Some Prolegomena for Cultural and Religious History* (New Haven: Yale University, 1967), p.74.

[20]Karl Jaspers, *Kant* (New York: Harcourt Brace Jovanovich, 1962), p. 20.

[21]For an elaboration of this point, see William H. Poteat, "Persons and Places: Paradigms in Communication," in James Waddell and F.W. Dillistone, eds., *Art and Religion as Communication* (Atlanta, GA: John Knox, 1974), pp. 175-241.

[22]Hannah Arendt, *The Human Condition* (Chicago: University of Chicago Press, 1958), p. 257.

[23]Ibid., p. 259.

[24]William H. Poteat, *Polaynian Meditations. In Search of a Post-Critical Logic* (Durham: Duke University, 1985), p. 302n.

[25]Hans Jonas, *The Phenomenom of Life. Toward a Philosophical Biology* (Chicago: Univeristy of Chicago, 1966), p. 144, my emphasis.

[26]Ibid., p. 137, my emphasis.

[27]Ibid., p. 145.

[28]Ibid., p. 144.

[29]Poteat, *Polanyian Meditations*, p. 58.

[30]Polanyi, *Personal Knowledge*, p. 96-99.

[31]Ludwig Wittgenstein, *Philosophical Investigations*, trans. G.E.M. Anscombe (New York: Macmillan, 1968), p. 66e, paragraph 164.

[32]Ibid., p. vi.

[33]Ibid., p. 20, paragraph 40.

[34]Ibid., p. 20, paragraph 43.

[35]Ludwig Wittgenstein, *On Certainty*, ed. G.E.M. Anscombe and G.H. von Wright, trans. G.E.M. Anscombe and Denis Paul (New York: Harper & Row, 1969), p. 28e, paragraph 204.

[36]*Philosophical Investigations*, p. 11, paragraph 23.

[37]Hannah Arendt points out that "to act, in its most general sense, means to take an initiative, to begin (as the Greek word *archein*, "to begin," "to lead," and eventually "to rule," indicates), to set something into motion . . ." in *The Human Condition* (Chicago: University of Chicago, 1958), p. 177. Arendt nuances this even more when she states action (speech) is not the beginning of something but of somebody.

[38]*Philosophical Investigations*, p. 146, paragraph 546.

[39]Here we see Wittgenstein's reliance upon the Hebrew *dabhar*, which means both word and deed, and consequently his reliance upon the Hebraic dynamism of the spoken word rather than the more static Greek *logos*.

[40]Poteat, *Philosophical Daybook* (Columbia, MO: University of Missouri, 1990), p. 29.

[41]Ibid., p. 112.

[42]Ibid., p. 7.

[43]Poteat says about the word "mindbody" that "this coinage and variations upon it . . . [have] provided me as I have written with the means for sustaining my grip, frequently awkward and precarious, upon my own central idea; and it has established for me as I have subsequently read the conceptual footing from which to explore that idea's many implications" in *Polanyian Meditations*, p.7.

[44]Ibid., p. 9.

[45]Ibid., p. 10.

[46]*Philosophical Investigations*, p. 94, paragraph 268.

[47]As quoted, in Norman Malcolm, *Wittgenstein: Nothing is Hidden* (Cambridge, MA: Basil Blackwell, 1989), p. 175.

[48]Ibid., p. 176.

[49]By relativism, I mean the belief that because we have no god's eye view of the way the world is, independent of us, we are only left with the lesser reality of people in different times and places saying different thing.

[50]*Philosophical Investigations*, p. 88, paragraph 241.

[51]This term is used by Stanley Cavell in *This New Yet Unapproachable America, Lectures After Emerson and Wittgenstein* (New Mexico: Living Patch, 1989), p. 44, my emphasis.

[52]*Philosophical Investigations*, p. 44, paragraph 97.

[53]Ibid., p. 226. Wittgenstein attacked G.H. Hardy for holding this view. Hardy had said, "Mathematical theorems are true or false; their truth or falsity is absolute and independent of our knowledge of them . . ." Wittgenstein replied that "[Hardy] conceived philosophy as a decoration, an atmosphere, around the hard realities of mathematics and science. These disciplines, on the one hand, and philosophy on the other, are thought of as being like the necessities and decoration of a room," as cited by Ray Monk in *Ludwig Wittgenstein. The Duty of Genius* (New York: The Free Press, 1990), pp. 329-330.

[54]Ibid.

[55]Ibid., p. 227.

[56]Kaufman, of course, distinguishes himself from Judson by giving primacy to a more dynamic worldview: not the world as it is, but the evolving world. This distinction, while important, does not undermine my analysis because both ultimately *weight* the metaphors, stories, symbols drawn from the "scientific" world over any other, including religion.

[57]*Philosophical Investigations*, p. 74, paragraph 183.

[58]Ibid.

[59]See Michael B. Foster, "The Doctrine of Creation and the Rise of Modern Science" in *Mind*, Vols. 43-45 (1934-1936). Stanley Jaki, in *The Road of Science and the Ways to God* (Chicago: University of Chicago, 1978), who has a similar argument, begins by asking why the ancient Greeks, despite their brilliance, continually went down blind alleys in their scientific inquiries.

[60]Nicholas Lash, "Contemplation, Metaphor, and Real Knowledge," unpublished paper, delivered at "Knowing God, Christ and Nature in the Post-Positivistic Era," Symposium, University of Notre Dame, April 14-17, 1993, p. 18, my emphasis.

"From the Most Ancient Times":

Lessons from Israel to the

Ninth Century Christian Aristocracy

Marie Anne Mayeski

At significant moments in the history of exegesis, Christian scholars have consulted Jewish experts to illumine their understanding of what Christians came to call the "Old Testament." Origen, the father of Christian exegesis, began the tradition. Jerome acknowledged his debt to the rabbis in both translations and exegetical work. Certainly Jerome's concern for the historical meaning of the text owes much to his rabbinic tutors, as it does to his long residence in the Holy Land. But scholarly research has not investigated in depth the slender evidence for contact between Jewish and Christian biblical scholars from Jerome's time until the twelfth century. Nevertheless, the Old Testament continued to be a major resource for doctrinal and ethical teaching during these centuries and, during the Carolingian period, bishops and court theologians placed a particular emphasis on Old Testament narratives as containing the blueprint for a Christian state.

John Michael Wallace-Hadrille, respected scholar of the Carolingian period, notes succinctly that, "When a Carolingian wanted a picture of how a God-directed king should behave, his attention was directed to the Old Testament. . . ."[1] He draws from the work of Alcuin, Rhabanus Maurus, Jonas of Orleans and from the Ordinals for the consecration of a King to demonstrate that the Carolingians rethought the problem of royal authority for their own day by a reinterpretation of the conduct of the kings of the Bible. This method of using the Jewish scriptures to address the concrete historical circumstances of a later day was, of course, deeply rooted in the theological method of the Christian tradition. The earliest theologians had used *typology* in both the writing and the interpretation of those texts that came to be included in the New Testament canon. Typology functioned prominently as well in the selection of scriptural readings for liturgical worship and became the foundation of all monastic interpretation and theology.

By "typology" I mean that basic theological insight by which an intrinsic and necessary relationship is perceived between an earlier, usually Old Testament, event (the "type" or "figure") and a later reality, either in the saving work of Christ as described in the New Testament or in the life of the people studying the text. Lawrence T. Martin, in an essay on Bede as preacher, underscores an important element in typological interpretation. "Unlike allegory in general, and unlike tropological or moral exegesis of the sort we find in many medieval preachers, typological exegesis takes the biblical event very seriously as an historical reality."[2] Typology does not ignore the historicity of either the Old or New Testament event. Rather, both are seen as points on a continuum of events understood as salvation history. There is a congruence between the earlier and the later events, precisely as historical, because God, who is the source and ultimate destiny of all human history, is necessarily consistent. However far some allegorical interpretation might have wandered from the historical meaning of the text, typology itself was founded on a particular theology of history. In its most proper use, typology respects and builds upon the historical meaning of Old Testament texts insofar as these were known to later readers: as paradigms of the Christian interpretation of history, Old Testament narratives remained nonetheless Jewish stories and models.

Typological history was celebrated in the liturgy. As and whenever the church moved from *lectio continua* to the selection of particular scriptures in a cycle of feasts, the events of Jewish history were placed in dialogue with major gospel events. Both together had their context in the living experience of the liturgical community. Salvation history, which began with creation and achieved a fullness in the mystery of Christ, continued to unfold in the life of the Church in all later centuries. Nowhere is this more clearly manifested than in the liturgy for the Easter Vigil. The readings take the believing community from creation through the call of Abraham, the Exodus, the moments of salvation proclaimed by the prophets up to the proclamation of the Resurrection of Christ. Then the reality signified by all of these readings is accomplished in the baptisms performed and celebrated by the community. One cannot read the catechetical instructions and homilies of Augustine, nor the works of Chrysostom or Cyril of Jerusalem, without feeling the full sweep of this understanding of history.

It is not to be wondered at that the monastic tradition of contemplation and biblical interpretation, fed as it was in the West by both the Roman liturgy and patristic exegesis, particularly the writings of Jerome, Augustine, Ambrose and Gregory the Great, should continue to develop within this understanding of human history. Each monastic community understood itself according to the paradigms presented by typology: the images of the "new Eden," the "garden enclosed," the "army of Israelites in the desert," the "apostolic community," and the "new Jerusalem" flow through the monastic texts as description and as ideal, ebbing and flowing into one another with the fluctuations of taste and times. But always, the monastic writers see their community as the continuation of the drama of salvation history. They use the ancient biblical texts as norms and guides in deciding monastic policy and in directing the day-to-day activities of the monastic community. That is the principle that guides their practice of *lectio divina*. They read the texts from the perspective of their lives and they understand their lives by the images and teaching of the text.

Seen in this perspective and against the background of this tradition, the work of the Carolingian political authors whom Wallace-Hadrille analyzes is seen as a variation upon a theme rather than a departure from it. The general and pervasive influence of such use of Old Testament texts is supported by the study of a text that stands somewhat outside the mainstream. The *Liber Manualis*, written by Dhuoda of Septimania in 842,[3] is outside the mainstream insofar as the author is without ecclesiastical office or authorization and is writing for her son, a very young magnate with a political destiny, but not yet bearing real political power. Her entire text is marked by methods of biblical exegesis which are drawn from liturgical experience, the monastic style of *lectio divina* and the study of the acknowledged masters such as Augustine and Gregory the Great. But in one section of her work, Book III, Dhuoda attempts a piece of political theory; her thought there bears a striking resemblance to the work of the better known authors discussed by Wallace-Hadrille. In that Book, she writes to her son, William to teach him the virtues necessary to an aristocrat who lives among the powerful at court. She also provides a small essay on the role of the political counsellor and its moral implications. In doing so, she draws heavily upon the Jewish scriptures with a deep conviction that not only personal morality, but more especially a Christian political ethic, can consistently be drawn from the saints and stories of "the most ancient days."

There is no real question of Dhuoda's possible dependence upon Jewish interpretations in her use of Old Testament texts. The Christian theological tradition had appropriated these from the beginning as its own. Dhuoda inherited this tradition and any interest in or knowledge of Jewish exegesis she may have had is undocumented. There is, however, one clear reference to the presence of Jews in her life and some historical data available about the situation of the Jews in her place and time that may be of some interest. In Book 10, Chapter 4 of the *Liber*, Dhuoda says,

> I acknowledge that, to defend the interests of my lord and master Bernard, and so that my service to him might not weaken in the March and elsewhere--so that he not abandon you and me, as some men do--I know that I have gone greatly into debt. To respond to great necessities, I have frequently borrowed great sums, not only from Christians but also from Jews.[4]

The presence of an episcopal mint at Uzès has caused some scholarly speculation. The minting of gold coins was such a rarity in the Carolingian empire that many historians speculate that the mint was permitted to continue operating in order to induce Spanish Jews to trade with Uzes, long a commercial center of some importance. Dhuoda's text is evidence that Jews were an accepted part of economic life. There are some indications that the situation of the Jews in southern France, as a whole, was marked by some tolerance and civic involvement. In 449, for instance, the Jewish community at Arles took part in the obsequies of the bishop St. Hilary, chanting psalms in Hebrew as they accompanied the bier in the funeral procession. They participated in a similar way in the entombment of Bishop Caesarius in 543. This must have been sufficiently general a custom to provoke the Council of Narbonne (589) to formulate Canon 9 which forbade Jews to celebrate funeral processions with the singing of psalms.[5] However, as late as the seventh century, a prominent Jew of Narbonne inscribed an epitaph to his three dead children using Hebrew characters. Such a public display of the Jewish religion argues a certain uncommon tolerance on the part of the bishops of the Narbonnaise.[6] This kind of tolerance seems to have marked the hierarchical church at Uzes as well. In 558, Bishop St-Ferréol experienced a kind of exile imposed on him by Childebert, King of the Franks, for having friendly intercourse with the Jewish community of that city. Apparently he had violated official policy by inviting them to share the hospitality of his table.[7] By the time of Louis the Pious, the situation had undoubtedly changed. The emperor himself, previously a resident of the south, took steps to protect the Jews, even against the wishes of the clergy.[8] But the presence of Jews and even their public expression of religious sentiment does not in any way indicate theological dialogue and, in any case, Dhuoda's thought is perfectly within the established Christian tradition.

Dhuoda's thought in Book III of the *Liber Manualis* can be divided, for purposes of discussion, into two themes. The first is the structure of Carolingian society as William experiences it, the second, the importance of fidelity to all the obligations which bind him in that, for her, divinely ordained structure. Dhuoda describes William's social life as a network of hierarchical relationships. In this hierarchy, the mandates of the divine will are foundational and without qualification: nothing may be done to violate one's obligation to God, the ultimate feudal lord. Among human authorities, Dhuoda affirms the absolute primacy of the father: only obligations to God may take precedence over obligations to one's father; all other obligations are contingent upon these. Dhuoda begins Book III, therefore, by laying out William's absolute duties to his father (under God) and his contingent obligations to Charles, his father's overlord and his own. At the end of Book III, she completes her description of the feudal hierarchy by describing in short, specific chapters William's responsibilities to the king's relatives, the nobility of various ranks, and the priests. In validating these obligations and in exposing the virtue of fidelity which they require, Dhuoda mines the wisdom of the Old Testament, primarily the narratives in Genesis and the Books of Kings, but also the wisdom literature; in these books, she finds striking parallels to the personal and political situations in her son's life.

In her analysis of William's obligation to his father, for instance, Dhuoda insists that William must *fear*, *love* and *be faithful* to his father in all things (III, 1, 3-5), but her admonition is not to a slavish or thought-less obedience. Quoting Sirach 3 and 7 (Ecclesiasticus in the Vulgate), she speaks first of the respect which comes to a father from a morally upright son: William is to receive his father in old age and not sadden him by a dissolute life. She thus indicates that the duty of obedience is paid, most importantly, in the currency of character. She also underlines Sirach's advice that a son not show contempt for a father who may grow weaker precisely as the former reaches the apex of his strength (III, 1, 17-19). With this simple biblical reference, Dhuoda points to the changing situation between father and son. William is now at court, in the very center of power, while his father Bernard is still in the field, subject to the vicissitudes of battle. Because of this placement William must not become arrogant but reflect even more deeply on the obligations he owes his father.

In attempting to motivate William to appropriate obedience, Dhuoda gives full play to her powers of persuasion. To reinforce her own arguments, she mines the wisdom of a variety of Old Testament books. She describes, for instance, the very real temptations by which William is surrounded, doing it in scriptural language and with the aid of models from the Bible. In Book III, 1 she urgently warns William to avoid two specific kinds of disobedience. She urges him not to grieve his father in his old age (Ecclus. 3:15) nor to inflict harm on his father, insulting his dignity (Deut. 27:16). From Sirach, she takes the reminder that without his father William would not have life (7:28); from Exodus, the promise that those who honor their fathers will be granted long lives (Exod. 20:12). The Pentateuch supplies curses for those who are unfaithful (Deut. 27:16 and Lev. 20:9) and reinforces the negative message gleaned from the examples of Absalom and the sons of Heli.[9] She sums up biblical evidence to conclude that all manner of evil befalls the disobedient child: envy, jealousy and disaster are their portion and, the ultimate irony, they lose all the material possessions which they sought by infidelity to gain.[10]

These biblical allusions are scattered like the lines of a refrain throughout the first two chapters of Book III. Then, as if supplying a coda, Dhuoda ends the section on filial obedience with a kind of catalogue of the wisdom of the patriarchs (III, 3). She culls from Genesis the stories of the faithful sons (Sem, Isaac, Jacob and Joseph) and piles up the list of blessings which they achieved through their obedience: prosperity; deliverance from sorrow; happiness; fortitude and the overcoming of temptation; a wife, children and riches; safety amidst the vicissitudes of life. In the composition of this catalogue, Dhuoda is careful to show how both worldly and spiritual blessings are given to loyal children. At the same time, in the story of the patriarch Joseph, she shows that the path of the obedient will not be without pitfalls. Joseph's way led, after all, through a very deep pit. But at the end, for him, there was the opportunity to rule in a *peaceful* kingdom. This, for Dhuoda, is the ultimate blessing, both spiritual and secular. Clearly, Dhuoda sees the Old Testament texts as containing the necessary practical wisdom for her own day and aristocratic circle.

It was not just the king who found his true ancestors in the historical books of the Jews. Other powerful Christians were also the spiritual descendants of the biblical characters of old. The Kingdom of God, for Dhuoda, began in Israel, was given a particular character in the New Testament, and continued in the Frankish kingdom of her day. So thoroughly does she rely on Old Testament texts that we cannot escape the impression that she interpreted her own times as particularly congruent with Old Testament times. Nowhere is this more true than when she seeks to understand and to ameliorate the civil strife and treacheries of the circles of the court.

In contrast to her explanation of William's obligations to his father, her chapter on his fidelity to his feudal lord is brief (Chapter 4), less intense, and more well organized. In this chapter particularly, Dhuoda demonstrates that she is as circumspect as she bids William to be. She begins, as always, with the simple admonition: serve your Lord in all practical matters with *prudence*, seeking not to "please the eye" but to preserve both true loyalty and the purity of body and soul. This is a most difficult balance, one to which she exhorts William throughout the chapter. On the one hand, William's service to Charles must be fixed, loyal and without reservation;[11] toward his lord he must always be true, alert, helpful and the first to step forward in service.[12] On the other hand, William must be truly prudent, considering not only what will serve the immediate purposes of the King, but what will also preserve his own conscience and the purity of his soul, as well as honor God who is the Lord of all.

The rationale with which Dhuoda supports her admonition is primarily practical and on the side of true and faithful service. William is to serve Charles because Charles has been chosen as lord by both Bernard and God (4, 2-3). Such fidelity to feudal obligations is the family tradition and honor. No one in his family was ever unfaithful, nor are they now, nor will they ever be (32-36). Though the words express confidence, their impassioned repetition reminds the reader of Bernard's recent equivocation and turns this affirmation into a warning, for Bernard as well as for William. Dhuoda stresses that society considers treachery reprehensible; she also hopes and prays that William's aristocratic family traditions will make it unthinkable. To the familial tradition, Dhuoda adds her reading of the theological tradition. Using Romans 13: 1-2, verses much commented on in the eighth and ninth centuries, Dhuoda points out that all office and power are given by God. Therefore William's service must be faithful, wholehearted and energetic (22-25). The teaching is clear and unqualified, but the array of biblical models which she gathers in support echo the moral tension inherent in her original admonition.

She cites the servant of Abraham sent to get a wife for Isaac, Joab, Abner and the other servants of David, as well as "many others in Scripture." On the one hand, the obedience of these models brought them material blessings and a good name "in the world." On the other they themselves underwent trials in their attempt to please their lords rather than themselves (14-19). From the narratives of Israel, Dhuoda draws the understanding that William must be prepared for the difficulties and moral ambiguities of feudal service as well as for its blessings. Faithful service is not a slavish fulfillment of royal commands. It is a *virtue* that must be learned and acquired. She therefore bids William to read both the lives and the sayings of the Fathers.

Her emphasis on the *lives* of holy ancestors is important. It is not just words of wisdom which William needs but the concrete example of lives which demonstrate practical prudence. William must study the ways in which successful predecessors negotiated the moral ambiguities of their own time so that he can, as she puts it, "learn in what manner and in what measure one ought to serve."[13] Measure is equally important as manner. Neither can be learned entirely in the abstract and so the lives of holy predecessors, especially in the colorful, historical narratives of the Old Testament, are important evidence. In the Jewish scriptures, particularly in the historical narratives, she finds models of filial obedience and of feudal fidelity, the two virtues she sees as essential to the creation of a true Christian kingdom among the Franks.

The second theme that Dhuoda develops in Book III of the *Liber Manualis* is the role of the royal counselor, its moral character, and the virtues both practical and spiritual that it requires. The royal counselor was an institution of great importance among the Frankish nobility.[14] In the political institution of the counselor, Dhuoda sees great possibilities for moral development and leadership, an opportunity for bringing the mandates of the divine will to bear on the practical politics of the day.[15] Her chapter on the Role of the Counsellor is a kind of expanded discussion of the virtue of prudence; to be a counsellor is to fill a political *office* in which the virtue of prudence may be both acquired and exercised. But it is an office that requires both maturity and Christian virtue. The opening sentence of Chapter 5 exposes the main outlines of her thought: "If at some time God leads you to such perfection that you are considered worthy to be called as a counselor among the magnates, consider prudently what, when, to whom and how you should speak so that what you say is worthy and to the point."[16] Note that only God can give the perfection required of a counselor; therefore the counsel to be given is of a higher order than worldly wisdom. For Dhuoda, the role of counselor is more than a political appointment; it is a vocation, not lightly to be taken on oneself. Her thought is consistent with that of the better known Hincmar of Rheims, author of the *De ordine palatii*. Hincmar had become a strong supporter of Charles the Bald after the death of Louis the Pious and himself crowned Charles emperor in 869. In 882, he wrote in the *De Ordine* that counselors are to be chosen only because they fear the Lord and have such faith that they will recommend nothing to the king except what promotes eternal life. Other human qualifications such as their friendship for or relationship with the king, their cunning or sophistry, are not to be considered. Hincmar distinguishes explicitly between the worldly wisdom which is inimical to God and the "just and correct wisdom" which can guide the ruler through the murky waters of human influences and temptations.[17]

This understanding of the spiritual character of the office of counsellor is a given for Dhuoda and one shared by her contemporaries. Her own emphasis, however, is on the manner of giving counsel. Virtuous advice may be given, but it is not authentic counsel unless it is effective, that is to say, unless it is accepted. The counsel expected from the true counselor, therefore, is that which is to the point, worthy (of divine approbation) and given with due regard to all the circumstances. She develops this idea by introducing a controlling metaphor from the world of the artisans, clearly demonstrating the essentially practical nature of her thought. Her model is the successful goldsmith, who considers all of the circumstances attendant upon the task. According to her such an artisan weighs the time of day, the temperature and the humidity to ensure the quality, permanence and beauty of the artifact being constructed.[18] Like goldsmithing, the giving of good counsel is an art and a craft. The word "gold" provides her with a key for selecting a supporting *catena* of scriptural passages from the books of wisdom. Intelligent advice, she says, is purer than gold or silver (III, 5, 20, citing Prov. 22:1).[19] The one who is zealous for divine practical wisdom can please both God and his Lord, but will be tested like gold in the fire (30, citing Ps. 11:7, et. al). Biblical allusions thus help her to play upon the image of the prudent goldsmith.

Additional citations further define and describe proper counsel with precision and reiterate the moral and spiritual horizon against which practical actions are to be taken. Explaining Sir. 32:24, she says that only the higher and nobler actions, those which are for the good of the soul, constitute good counsel (8-11). She refers to 2 Sam. 19:19 to explain that a virtuous counsellor will advise only those lines of action which are true and right under all circumstances (11-12). She thus distinguishes "good counsel" from simple pragmatism and speaks against the principle that the end justifies the means. The means themselves are to be tested by the virtuous counselor, and accepted only if they are consistent with the values of the ancient wisdom. It is significant that the scriptures from which she quotes so freely in her chapters on royal counsel are taken, by and large, from the books of wisdom. The wisdom of Israel, like that of its neighbors, was essentially practical; the Hebrew word "wisdom" was first used to designate the skill of the artisan. By extension, it came to denote the skill with which an office-holder fulfills responsibility and, ultimately, the craft by which a person designs a life of fidelity to Yahweh. In borrowing so heavily from the wisdom literature of the Old Testament, then, Dhuoda was giving to Jewish wisdom a meaning close to, if not identical with, its original meaning.

The role of counsellor as Dhuoda conceives it is not that of the isolated wise man. The goal of true counsel is nothing less than to achieve the kingdom of God; the road to that kingdom must be traveled in the company of colleagues who share one's faith convictions and one's struggles for virtue.[20] As Dhuoda understands it, the virtuous counselors of her own day are only the latest in a long and noble line. Therefore, she again reaches back for specific models to William's spiritual ancestors, the "first fathers" described in the Old Testament. She details Joseph's counsel to Pharaoh, Daniel's to Nebuchednezzar, Balthasar and others, Jethro's to Moses, Achior's to Holofernes (72-80). As she interprets their stories, these were counselors who achieved the marvelous moral and practical balance which she hopes that William can also attain. They did not abandon their own kin (is there a subtle plea here that William remember his family's fortunes?), they won freedom and prosperity for themselves and others on all sides and, especially, they preserved the integrity of their consciences. She does not hesitate to remind William that these counselors did not reach such great heights without having to undergo the test of suffering (a reprise of her gold-in-the-fire theme). Indeed, the Lord of the Kingdom welcomes them precisely as "sacrificial offerings."[21]

As a conclusion to her thought on the role of royal counselors, Dhuoda constructs yet another catalogue of biblical models. She comments on the bad example given by Achitophel who encouraged Absalom to rise against his father, David, and by Amann who advised Asuerus to destroy the sons of Israel (11-14). In contrast, she praises Doeg the Edomite (from the First book of Samuel) and Mordecai in the Story of Esther (15-16). Evil counselors (along with their kin) fell victim to the violence they had prepared for others, their "innocent brothers;" the good saved themselves and their own people through their wise advice (16-26). In this catalogue, Dhuoda emphasizes the social and political ties which bind a counsellor to those around him and to those who depend upon him. The evil counselors sought to destroy filial, familial and tribal bonds, in a greedy and envious quest for personal aggrandizement. They suffered justly when they fell, but they brought their families down with them. Doheg and Mordecai, on the other hand, saved others as well as their own people. From this litany of Jewish stories, Dhuoda concludes it is possible for a Christian noble to live more or less consistently in accordance with the divine will and to lead others to do so as well. It is to such a happy but difficult achievement that William is to direct his counsel.

For both the virtues appropriate to a Christian aristocrat and the political strategies appropriate to a Christian kingdom, Dhuoda of Septimania has recourse to the wisdom of the "most ancient fathers in the faith," that is, to the doers and writers of the Jewish scriptures. In making their wisdom her own, she continues in a long line of Christian biblical interpreters for whom the story of salvation began with Abraham and continued to their own day. She ignores neither the historicity of the texts themselves nor the specific texture of her own life. For her, Israel remains Israel and the particular treacheries which have overturned her own life are not to be ignored in the interests of a disembodied spirituality or eschatology. Dhuoda finds both the saving power of God and the vacillating fidelity of God's chosen people enacted in the entire sweep of biblical narrative as well as in the specific lives of her and her son. Since all these human events constitute, for her, a single salvific drama, she can write a script for William's salvation based on the stories of Israel's heroes and villains. Her son's role ended in tragedy, as she feared it might. We can only hope that her careful reading of the vicissitudes of Israelite history had prepared her for the unfortunate, inevitable dénoument.

NOTES

[1]*Early Medieval History* (New York: Barnes and Noble, 1975), p. 184.

[2]"The Two Worlds in Bede's Homilies" in T. L. Amos, E. A. Green and B. M. Kienale, eds., *De Ore Domini: Preacher and Word in the Middle Ages* (Kalamazoo, MI: Medieval Institute, 1989), 27-60. See also "Figura" by Erich Auerbach in *Scenes from the Drama of European Literature* (Gloucester, MA: Peter Smith, 1973), 11-98.

[3]For the historical context of this text, biographical information on Dhuoda, the details of the transmission of the text, and its literary character, see the critical edition by Pierre Riché, *Manuel pour mon Fils. Sources Chrétiennes* 225 (Paris: Cerf, 1975). An excellent English translation by Carol Neel is entitled *Handbook for William: A Carolingian Woman's Counsel for Her Son* (Lincoln and London: University of Nebraska, 1991).

[4]The quote is from Neel's translation, p. 100. Neel also translates Riché's note that "Dhuoda here gives the first extant testimony of the activity of Jews as moneylenders in the south of France," p. 144, n. 17.

[5]André Dupont, "Uzes pendant le périod du haut Moyen-Age," *École Antique de Nîmes* XXI (1940), 45.

[6]Michel Chalon, "L'inscription juive de Narbonne et la condition des Juifs en Narbonnaise à la fin du VIIe siècle," *Homage à André Dupont* (Montpellier, 1974), p. 51.

[7]P.Béraud, *Uzès, son diocèse, son histoire,* (Nîmes, 1940), 28-29. See also Dupont, p. 63.

[8]See Wallace-Hadrille, *The Frankish Church* (Oxford: Clarendon, 1983), "It may seem odd, then, that [Louis] should have been a notable protector of Jews--sufficiently to incense some of his southern clergy. His own deacon, Bodo, was converted to Judaism and fled to Spain, where he had a notorious debate with Albar, a convert from Judaism to Christianity. Jewish influence was plainly at work at or near the court. But it was in an economic sense only that Louis protected Jews, and this chiefly in the south where he was once at home. It did not affect his intensely religious outlook," p. 229.

[9]As Riché notes, Rhabanus Maurus had used the same biblical models to reinforce the same political and familial themes. See *Liber de reuerentia filiorum erga patres et erga reges. Monumenta Germaniae Historica*, Epist. 5, 403-05.

[10]III, 1, 20-47.

[11]"puram et certam illi in omnibus tene utilitatis fidem" III, 4, 8-9.

[12]"seniori ut praedixi tuo sis uerax, uigil, utilisque atque praecipuus" (4, 38-39).

[13]"Lege dictas uel uitas sanctorum praecendentium patrum, et inuenies qualiter uel quomodo tuo seniori debeas seruire atque fidelis adesse in omnibus" (41-44).

[14]Riché speaks, in his introduction, of the importance of this office in the ninth century. He points to the historical narratives which describe the work of the counselors: Thegan, *Vita Ludowici*, the *Annales de S. Bertin*, and Nithard and Hincmar's advice in *De ordine palatii*, ed. Thomas Grass and Rudolp Schieffer (Hannover, 1981), p. 25.

[15]Wallace-Hadrill, in discussing the moral teaching given to the Frankish kings, asks: "What was the difference, then, between the virtues of the just man and those of the just

king? It was difference of scale, mostly; any man might imperil the salvation of Christian society by injustice, but the king was likeliest to do so because he had entrusted to him a greater share of divine authority than had anyone else, and had the added responsibility of supervising authority delegated to those beneath him," *Early Medieval History*, p. 192. Dhuoda imputes the same expanded responsibility to the royal counselor, on whose advice the king might act.

[16]"Si ad perfectum te aliquando adduxerit Deus, ut ad consilium inter magnatos merearis esse uocatus, tracta prudenter quid, quando, cui, uel quomodo dignum et aptum possis exibere sermonem" (III, 5, 2-5).

[17]Hinkmar von Reims, *De Ordine palatii*, ed. Thomas Grass und Rudolf Schieffer (Hannover, 1980), Chap. 31, 507-533, p. 86-87.

[18](5, 13-17) This is one of the few, but illuminating, windows which she opens onto her everyday life. Since Uzes was the site of a Carolingian mint, Dhuoda may well have observed the artisans there.

[19]In these chapters on the role of counselor, her citations are most frequently from the wisdom literature of the Old Testament. At the very heart of that literature is the understanding that "the good life" is, indeed, one carefully crafted by a spiritual artisan, adept in the Torah as in the knowledge of the human heart.

[20]Here, Dhuoda echoes Isidore of Seville, a writer she recommends to William elsewhere. In *Synonyms* II, 44, Migne, *PL* 83. 855 C,D, Isidore recommends that those who would give good counsel must seek virtuous companions, "similes enim similibus conjungi solent."

[21]". . . ut aurum probatos sibi dinoscitur applicuisse, et uelut holocausti hostiam . . . "(84-86). The reference is from Wisdom 3:6: "Tanquam aurum in fornace probauit illos, et quasi holocausti hostiam accepti illos."

THE UNITY AND DIVERSITY OF AFFECTIONS: SCHLEIERMACHER ON WORLD RELIGIONS

Robert T. Cornelison

In 1799, Friedrich Schleiermacher anonymously published a series of addresses to those whom he described as the "cultured despisers" of religion.[1] This work has become one of the enduring apologetics for affective language about God. Unlike Jonathan Edwards and William James, both of whom executed phenomenological examinations of religious affections, Schleiermacher attempted to resuscitate religion in a world he viewed as becoming more and more religiously sterile. He ultimately wanted to find a way to cultivate religion in those who had denied the importance and validity of religion in the modern age.[2]

What I should like to explore in this paper is how Schleiermacher's understanding of religious experience and feeling gets played out in his discussion of the relationship among religions. I will be focusing primarily on his *Speeches*, but will also bring in some insights of Schleiermacher's later works, primarily his dogmatic treatment, *The Christian Faith*. The ultimate purpose of this examination is to see if there is something in Schleiermacher's thought which can be used as a basis for ecumenical dialogue in our times.

AFFECTIONS AND THE SEARCH FOR THE INFINITE

Schleiermacher was writing in an age full of ambiguities. The industrial revolution was altering the social and economic face of Europe[3], and Napoleon was looming on the immediate horizon. The religious terrain was also quite unsure. According to the Schleiermacher of the *Speeches*, the age had lost any sense of the infinite. To blame were two ways of viewing God which had become prevalent in his age: rationalism and moralism.

On the rationalist side, the Enlightenment had called "orthodox" religious belief into question by portraying much of what was considered religious as superstition. Reimarus and Lessing had found that most miracles could be explained away as natural occurrences.[4] The infinite had become reduced to mere natural experience which could be explained through human reason. For many, religion had become "a way of thinking, a faith, a way of contemplating the world."[5]

This perspective, in a sense, is a *Logos* theology, based on the idea that all of creation is constituted of reason (*logos*) and therefore has a reasonable character. It is reason itself which forms the unity for all the diverse elements of creation. Nature cannot be comprehended without God, yet God can only be known through nature. God is the highest form of rationality.[6]

The second way of approaching God which Schleiermacher takes to task is religion limited to the realm of morality. According to Schleiermacher, contemporary religion was also viewed as "a way of acting, a particular desire and love, a special kind of conduct and character."[7] As such it comes under the purview of morality understood as duty. Kant, in particular, espoused this view. According to Kant, the world is not only the place where we think, but more to the point, a place where we act. Religion, therefore, is to be found within the boundaries of "practical reason." Rather than view the moral law as binding because it is based in some religious *a priori*, Kant contends that the knowledge of God is the inference of moral reason. Religious beliefs are moral postulates. Morality inevitably leads to religion and religious faith becomes synonymous with recognizing all of our duties as divine commands.[8]

These two perspectives, either individually or in some sort of combination, formed the common understanding of religion in Schleiermacher's time. Schleiermacher, however, was dissatisfied with each of the approaches. In each, the infinite was somehow too restricted. On the one hand, the infinite was too quickly identified with rationality; on the other, it was identified with the moral law. For Schleiermacher, religion had little to do with science or morality. In a telling paragraph from the *Speeches*, he attempts to convince the cultured despisers that religion was not attempting to replace the hard-won science of the Enlightenment:

> In order to make quite clear to you what is the original and characteristic possession of religion, it resigns, at once, all claims on anything that belongs to science or morality. . . . Although you contend that nature cannot be comprehended without God, I would still maintain that religion has nothing to do with this knowledge.[9]

For Schleiermacher, neither rationality nor morality could lead us to the infinite because each denied the ultimate transcendence of the infinite. The true essence of religion, the true means of access to the infinite was to be found in the immediate experience of the infinite through *feeling* (*Gefühl*), *intuition* (*Anschauung*) and *sense* (*Sinn*). According to Schleiermacher:

> Religion is the immediate consciousness of the universal existence of all finite things in and through the infinite, and of all temporal things in and through the eternal. Religion is to seek this and find it in all that lives and moves. . . . It is to have life and to know life in immediate feeling. . . . In itself it is an affection, a revelation of the infinite in the finite, God being seen in it and it in God.[10]

It is this shift from religion as rationality or morality to religion as experience, feeling, intuition and sense, that is Schleiermacher's revolutionary turn. It is a thoroughly modern perspective which Schleiermacher claims can be made sensible to even the "cultured despisers" of religion. At the same time, it presents a view of religion which orthodox Christians can also recognize. We turn now to a more in depth explanation of the categories Schleiermacher uses.

For Schleiermacher, *feeling* is not mere emotionality as some commentators of his own time and ours seem to imply.[11] Rather, feeling is both the way in which we experience the infinite and the result of that experience. While feeling is the way in which we come to know the infinite, we only become conscious of the infinite through its operation upon us. What we feel is not the infinite but the effect of the infinite on us.[12] This act of feeling can be identified with consciousness (both self-consciousness and general consciousness) but probably is best understood as the undifferentiated experience of the unity of the world and all experiences in it.[13] In this sense, *Gefühl* is the way in which we experience the world and the way that the world discloses itself to us. Understood in this manner, to "know" the world is only possible when one first has the secrets of the world opened up through the religious apprehension of the infinite. Knowledge, therefore, demands a "religious apriori":

> To wish to have true science or true practice without religion, or to imagine it is possessed, is obstinate, arrogant delusion and culpable error. . . . What can man accomplish that is worth speaking of, either in life or in art, that does not arise in his own self from the influence of this sense of the infinite . . . ? Only when the free impulse of seeing and of living is directed toward the infinite and goes into the infinite, is the mind set in unbounded liberty. Religion alone rescues it from the heavy fetters of opinion and desire.[14]

For Schleiermacher, it is possible to understand the true nature of the diverse parts of reality only when one sees them in their connectedness and unity. This is only possible when one allows oneself to be apprehended by the infinite. The methodology of science operates through dissection and division and therefore cannot approach true knowledge of anything. Rather, it annihilates the universe while trying to construct it.[15] For Schleiermacher, feeling is what gives us immediate access to the world. Thus, feeling is primary; contemplation or scientific analysis is secondary.[16] The attempts of science to understand the world through observation, reduction and objectification come to naught for Schleiermacher because, to know an object, one must experience and participate with the object through union with it in feeling.[17] Consequently feeling is primary while conceptual thinking (*Begriff*) is secondary.

The process of disclosure and experience takes on a somewhat mystical character for Schleiermacher.[18] From his perspective, the experience of any object is in part determined by being grasped by that object. In being grasped by the object both the object and the person grasped by it become one. The object absorbs that which it grasps and that which is grasped absorbs the object. Then the object and the person being grasped again separate.[19] History, then, is merely the interaction of the infinite and the finite, the grasping and being grasped, the union and separation.[20] In this mystical approach, Schleiermacher has found the principle of identity which unites subject and object. Kant's critique of pure reason created a duality between the "thing in itself" (*Ding an sich*), and the "thing in phenomena" (*Erscheinung*). Schleiermacher believes that this dichotomy is a false one. Subject and object can indeed be understood as one because both are grounded in the unity of the infinite. Subject can truly know object because ultimately there is a "coincidence of opposites" in religious feeling. One can know an object truly through the immediate experience of it in feeling and intuition. This immediate feeling, however, is only possible when the subject is grasped by the object and the two become one.

Schleiermacher grounds this absorption and separation in human nature itself. For him, the human soul has two impulses: the desire to manifest itself as individual, and the desire to lose itself in the whole. In feeling, both of these impulses are held in tension. In being grasped by the infinite, one becomes absorbed, determined, changed. In the subsequent separation, the person's individuality is not only left intact but is strengthened by its contact with the infinite.[21] Individuality, therefore, is dependent on a prior unity and loss of self in the infinite.

Once Schleiermacher defines feeling as the essence of religion, he then goes on to delineate the content of that feeling. It is here that we can speak about religious affections in Schleiermacher in a true sense. The "core" religious affection for him, the affection from which all other affections can be derived, is openness to the infinite. In practical terms, this means that the infinite and finite are considered to be a unity, that oneness is the essence of the infinite. It means that religious feeling is first and foremost the human yearning for completeness and oneness. For a religious mind, the connection of infinite and finite makes everything holy.[22] In Schleiermacher's words: "The sum total of religion is to feel that, in its highest unity, all that moves us in feeling is one; to feel aught single and particular is only possible by means of this unity; to feel . . . that our being and living is being and living in and through God."[23] Such an affection underscores the fact that the human being lives from the power of the infinite. According to Schleiermacher: "The universe is ceaselessly active and is at every moment revealing itself to us. . . . Now religion is to take up into our lives and to submit to be swayed . . . as an exhibition of the infinite in our lives."[24] God, therefore, is present for humans as an awareness of the underlying unity of all individual experience. Thus the religious person must be passive and receptive to the infinite. It is a "surrender, a submission to be moved by the Whole that stands over and against man"[25] The whole religious life, therefore, consists in surrendering oneself to the infinite to be influenced and shaped by it.[26]

From this primary affection other affections grow; all of them, however, are based on the idea of the unity of the infinite and finite. From Schleiermacher's perspective, all affections, for that matter, all human activity, has the potential for being religious. If an activity reflects the infinite, then it is religious. Schleiermacher does contend, however, that certain activities reflect the unity of the infinite better than others. Interpersonal relationships, for example, take on religious character when they reach a level of such intimate union that one intuitively knows the other. Schleiermacher points to both friendship and love as a place where this can take place.[27] In deep friendship and in love, the two people involved have lifted their lives above the mundane into the realm of the infinite. The relationship is based on immediate feeling, sense and intuition. Lovers need not always speak their feelings because they intuitively know each other. Sometimes a nod or a look tells more than the spoken word. In fact, in his attempt to describe what this feeling or intuition of the infinite really is, he uses interpersonal, relational language, comparing it to an "embrace" with the infinite, "wedlock," a "kiss," to "lie in the bosom of the infinite."[28] To be a friend or a lover for Schleiermacher thus means to recognize the self and the other not only as part of the Whole, as the carriers of the infinite, but also as the reflection of the unity of the infinite. It is in this sense that Schleiermacher commented to Henriette Herz in a letter that he wished to "intuit her religiously," that is, he wanted to find the infinite in her.[29]

While interpersonal examples betray much about the nature of the infinite, it is in the fellowship of religious communities that the unity of the infinite is most succinctly expressed. When one has an intuition, sense or feel for the infinite, it operates on that person in two ways. In the first place, it reveals the interconnectedness of all that exists. In the second place, the individual becomes painfully aware that he or she, alone, can only reflect a minute part of the infinite. This reveals the inherently social nature of the religious person.[30] Because the infinite is ultimately inclusive, the individual must view oneself as a part of a greater, corporate whole. This does not mean, however, that the religious persons attempt to make the "other" like themselves. Rather, it means to be conscious of and to exhibit the interconnectedness of all that lives in the infinite. Consequently mutual communication and intimacy become central marks of the community.[31]

Most important for Schleiermacher, however, is that the sociality of the community must reflect the unity of the infinite it its own structure. It can only do that by overcoming dissension and sectarianism. In Schleiermacher's words,

> The visible religious society can only be brought nearer the universal freedom and majestic unity of the true church by becoming a mobile mass, having no distinctive outlines, but each part being now here, now there, and all peacefully mingling together. . . . The more everyone approaches the universe and the more they communicate to one another, the more perfectly they all become one. No one has a consciousness for himself, each has also that of his neighbor.[32]

It becomes obvious that for Schleiermacher, all rigid outline within the religious community should be and would be lost. Since fellowship is a primary mark of the religious community, a goal toward which the community strives, interconnectedness would produce a corporatism which smooths over and overcomes all differences.[33] It is at this point that we can make sense of Schleiermacher's view of world religions (he uses the term "positive religions").

RELIGION AND THE RELIGIONS

Given Schleiermacher's emphasis on the unity of the infinite and the need to reflect that unity in human structures, it would seem logical to believe that Schleiermacher would view the distinct positive religions as a negative development in human history. Indeed, Schleiermacher does admit that the divisions of the church which he so regretfully laments, and the divisions of the different religions are always found together and seem inseparable.[34] Plurality in one seems to be based in the plurality of the other. Nothing would be further from the truth, however. Rather than criticize the plurality of religions, Schleiermacher finds that they are the logical result of the diversity of feelings which the infinite produces in us. His argument is based on his understanding of the religious affections which develop in the individual.

As stated above, for Schleiermacher knowledge of the infinite through feeling and intuition entailed an absorption by the infinite and a loss of all individuality. That, however, was only one moment of the confrontation with the infinite. The second moment entailed the separation from the infinite and the transformation and strengthening of the individuality of the person through his or her union with the infinite. This process of producing a stronger individuality means that the piety of each individual, the constellation of affections which contact with the infinite produced and which links the person in the greater unity of the infinite with others, is a whole by itself. Religion thus creates for itself endless variety. While the person is somehow determined by the infinite, it is a determination which allows for absolute freedom and is the basis for a person's self-determination. It allows for a purely personal set of affections.[35]

Schleiermacher then adopts a similar model when speaking about world religions. In his time the so-called "cultured despisers" of religion had developed what is commonly known as a "natural religion." Its tenets include the following: 1. religion is based on rationality; its unity is a rational one; 2. because it is rational it can be understood and practiced by all people at all times; 3. to understand natural religion one must examine how it is practiced in the world; 4. tolerance is the required relationship among religions.

For these "cultured despisers," the individual historical religions represented everything opposed to natural religion. They were the source of chaos and conflict; they were constantly at war with one another. The individual religions were the seat of many of the irrational superstitions which the Enlightenment and its rationality had attempted to discard. There was an atavism about positive religions. The positive religions were inherently intolerant; the truth claims made by one religion became a vilification of the truth claims of others. Rather than permit and suffer these differences, the "cultured despisers" pleaded for a rational religion which could subsume the beliefs of all religions under the single banner of rationality.

It is against this attempt to unify all religions under rationality that Schleiermacher defends the plurality of religions. For him, the whole of religion is nothing more than the sum of the relations in which human beings become conscious of the infinite. Since all consciousness can theoretically be religious, there must be an infinite number of ways of manifesting that consciousness. In an individualist perspective, each individual would have his or her own set of religious feelings and intuitions; therefore each set would be a religion in itself.[36] In a communal perspective, it is more common for many people to have similar experiences of the infinite. These people would then associate together, sharing those experiences in a common life and form a religion. They represent only one set of experiences, however. Each set would represent a different religion.

Schleiermacher is clear that the experiences of the infinite which are ultimately formed into the different religions are so different that they cannot be subsumed into a single *Ur*-religion. In fact, the co-existence of the individual positive religions over the centuries points to the inability to unite the religions into a single religion. In Schleiermacher's words,

> It is evident that the different religious perceptions and feelings are not, in a determinate way, awakened by one another or interdependent. Now as each exists for itself, each can lead, by the most various combinations, to every other. Hence, different religions could not continue long beside one another, if they were not otherwise distinguished. Very soon each would supplement itself into uniformity with all others.[37]

For Schleiermacher, therefore, the diversity of religions is a necessary result of the multiplicity of ways in which the infinite can be experienced. To limit religion as a whole to rationality, or to a single set of affections is to do damage to the infinite itself. To participate in the infinite means to have one's own identity established. This occurs in a collective sense in the positive religions, where a specific set of experiences of the infinite has as much validity as any other set.

This is basically where Schleiermacher stops with his treatment of positive religions in his *Speeches*. The response to their publication, however, caused him to alter his perspective somewhat in his later writings. One of the more vociferous comments made about his *Speeches* was that they seemed to place Christianity on the same level as other religions. This seemed to relativize Christianity to a degree unacceptable to many of the pietists of his time. It is ironic, however, that this is precisely the strength of Schleiermacher's argument in the *Speeches*. For religion to be resuscitated from its rationalistic lethargy, the infinite had to be allowed to be infinite. The religious expression of the immediate experience of the infinite had to be as broad as possible to be able to correspond to the infinite itself.

The criticisms of his work prompted him to place Christianity in a dominant position, and Christ in a central position, among the various positive religions. In *The Christian Faith*, written in 1821, rather than emphasize the role of individuality as a result of communion with the infinite, Schleiermacher emphasized the monolithic unity of the infinite. This resulted in a hierarchy of religions based on the degree to which each seemed to reflect that unity in its religious consciousness. Schleiermacher made a specific affect, the feeling of absolute dependence, into the primordial and all-inclusive affect of religion in general. The degree to which each religion exhibits this consciousness determines its place in the hierarchy.

At the bottom of the hierarchy stands *idol worship* (also called fetishism), which marks the lowest level of human self-consciousness. In the religions that practice it, religious consciousness does not develop out of communion with the infinite. Rather, it arises from an interaction with nature.[38] In such perspectives, the divinity has no qualities of the infinite but rather is localized, limited and ineffective.

The next stage is *polytheism*. Here one climbs one rung further on the ladder of religious consciousness. For Schleiermacher, polytheism proper is present only when the local references disappear and the gods form a coherent plurality.[39] The difficulty with polytheism is that, although it does approach the infinite and does grant qualities of infinitude to its gods, it remains on the level of diverse affections and never reaches the unity which is the mark of the infinite.

At the top of the hierarchy stands *monotheism*. It and only it can do justice to the infinite. As we saw in the *Speeches*, true religious consciousness sensed the inherent unity of finite and Infinite. While a variety of religious affections were produced by such a unity, the sense of the Infinite did not allow them to remain on the level of plurality. They must immediately be superseded by a sense of their connection and unity. Monotheism is the form of religion which discovers, and holds on to, that ultimate unity. Once piety has reached the level of monotheism, it can no longer remain stationary on one of the lower levels. And once it has reached monotheism, there is little chance for a relapse to one of the earlier forms.[40]

While monotheism is the highest form of religious consciousness, it does not mean that for Schleiermacher all of the three great monotheistic religions (Judaism, Christianity, and Islam) are on equal footing in that regard. Schleiermacher quickly dismisses Judaism as being almost in the process of extinction, and in fact betraying a lingering affinity with fetishism.[41] He bases this on the numerous vacillations toward idol worship throughout Old Testament history.

Islam does not fare much better in Schleiermacher's hands. While Islam is certainly a strongly monotheistic religion for Schleiermacher, it also betrays an unrefined, sensuous character which has certain affinities with heathenism (polytheism).[42]

It is here that Schleiermacher then reveals the true religion which has the highest, most pure, and most vibrant religious consciousness. In his own words:

> Thus Christianity, because it remains free from both of these weaknesses, stands higher than either of those two other forms, and takes its place as the purest form of monotheism which has appeared in history. . . . Christianity is, in fact, the most perfect of the most highly developed forms of religion.[43]

THE AFFECTIONS AND ECUMENICAL THEOLOGY

In conclusion, I should like to draw out some of the implications of Schleiermacher's affective approach to theology for the ecumenical and interreligious strivings in our own time.

I think it can be said without hesitation that little can be salvaged from Schleiermacher's later thought on affections and world religions. His viewpoint seems to be reactionary and, I think, does not reflect the totality of what can be said from his perspective in this regard. The place to look for help in Schleiermacher is to his *Speeches*, for it is there that I think he is most true to his insights about the affective approach to God.

Schleiermacher's basic problem in the Speeches is similar to the problem faced by those wishing to develop ecumenical and interreligious theologies today. That problem is: how can one understand the relationship between the infinite and the finite in such a way that it is inclusive of all religious expressions, while not subsuming them one into another, or into an amorphous pseudo-religion. It is the latter, the amorphous pseudo-religion, which Schleiermacher attributes to the "cultured despisers." According to him, the cultured despisers had developed a form of religion which was without any but the most general qualities. In its attempt to become a religion for all people, it became a religion for none. It has no church, no distinct body of followers, thus it cannot be a true religion.[44]

By starting with feeling as the basis for religion, Schleiermacher provides us with a means of allowing all people to have the possibility of being religious. He thus begins with the unity of the religious quest for the infinite in the finite as a means of recognizing the diversity in unity that is a mark of the infinite. Schleiermacher uses the image of music as a means of expressing the necessity of maintaining the diversity within unity in religion. For Schleiermacher, relating with the infinite is comparable to the creation of a song. In the beginning, a few notes suggest the presence of a melody; later, the melody becomes clear and one is swept away into the fullest harmony of religious affections. Without religion, one's life remains a meager series of notes. With religion, it is raised from a simple song to a full-voiced harmony.[45] To extend this image a bit, for Schleiermacher each religion represents a single melody. All individual notes find their sense and meaning only in relationship to the whole. Discordant notes or other melodies cannot be tolerated within a single song. At the same time, however, different songs can have different melodies, each with its own validity and purpose. So too is it with specific religions. Each religion cannot tolerate discord within it, yet must allow for the possibility of other, possible relationships with the infinite which take on other forms. Various religions may have different sets of affections (melodies) but each is legitimate and rightful.[46]

For Schleiermacher, the infinite can only be infinite when it is inclusive of all religious experiences. When he states that no religion is universal he means that it is wrong to consider one religion as true and all others false.[47] All of human experience can take on religious significance, that is, all can be reflective of the infinite. In reflecting the infinite, inclusiveness, creativity, productivity, mutuality become the affections which best attest to its universal character. To exclude any set of affections as non-religious can only limit the infinite. In every religion there are traces of the quest for the unity of the finite and infinite. In Schleiermacher's words:

> If the proper religious view of all things is to seek even in things apparently common and base every trace of the divine. . . . You would find more than remote traces of the Divinity. . . . I invite you to study every faith professed by man, every religion that has a name and character. Though it may long ago have degenerated into a long series of empty customs, into a system of abstract ideas and theories, will you not, when you examine the original elements at the source, find that this dead dross was once the molten outpourings of the inner fire? Is there not in all religions more or less of the true nature of religion, as I have presented it to you? . . . Every positive religion, in its growth and bloom, when its peculiar vigor was most youthful, fresh and evident, did not concentrate and exclude, but expanded and pushed fresh shoots and acquired more religious matter to be wrought up in accordance with its own peculiar nature.[48]

This inclusiveness is not subsumption, however. As Schleiermacher points out, inclusion in the infinite does not ultimately destroy individuality but increases, strengthens and supports it. Recognition of the infinite in our own religion demands that we allow for the existence of the infinite in others because we must recognize that our own set of affections and experiences do not exhaust the reality of the infinite. To recognize the infinite in other religions means that we recognize that the infinite is capable of grasping all peoples and all communions, each according to its own nature. From the other side, it means the recognition that all religions are involved in a similar quest, the quest to search out, hold and reflect the infinite. By starting with the common experiences of the infinite in the finite, as did Schleiermacher, the unity of religions is the presupposition for the diversity of religions. No longer must we attempt to find what makes us distinct from other religions before we can attempt to find the unity between religions. Rather, the unity is presupposed and the diversity must somehow reflect that unity. Only in this way can we realize that the destiny of other religions is somehow contingent on our success at understanding and reflecting the diversity within the unity of the infinite, while our destiny is somehow contingent on their success at the same attempt.

NOTES

[1]Friedrich Schleiermacher, *On Religion: Speeches to Its Cultured Despisers*, tr. J. Oman (New York: Harper & Row, 1958); hereafter, *Speeches*.

[2]See Speech 3, particularly, pages 122-4.

[3]See Paul Misner, *Social Catholicism in Europe* (New York: Crossroad, 1991) for a discussion of the impact of industrialization on Europe during this period.

[4]S.H. Reimarus, *Fragments* (Philadelphia: Fortress, 1970) and G.E. Lessing, "On the Proof of the Spirit and of Power," in Henry Chadwick (ed.), *Lessing's Theological Writings* (Stanford: Stanford, 1956).

[5]*Speeches*, 27.

[6]Again Lessing comes to the forefront in this regard in his "On the Education of the Human Race," in Chadwick, *Lessing's Theological Writings*.

[7]*Speeches*, 27.

[8]I. Kant, *Critique of Practical Reason*, tr., L.W.Beck.
(New York: Bobbs-Merrill, 1956), pp. 128ff.

[9]*Speeches*, 35.

[10]*Speeches*, 36.

[11]See Hegel's critique of Schleiermacher in Hegel's forward to Hinrich's *Die Religion* (translated in F. Weiss (ed.), *Beyond Epistemology* (The Hague: Nijhoff, 1974).

[12]*Speeches*, 48.

[13]*Ibid.*

[14]*Ibid.*, 39, 56.

[15]*Ibid.*, 40.

[16]*Ibid.*, 47.

[17]*Ibid.*, 39, 44. This perspective is close to what Don Saliers contends is a primary characteristic of religious affections: "[a] basic attunement which lies at the heart of a person's being and acting. In quite specific ways religious affections qualify our perceptions, our fundamental attitudes and our behavior." Don Saliers, *The Soul in Paraphrase* (New York: Seabury, 1980), 7.

[18]Cf. R. Brandt, *The Philosophy of Schleiermacher*.
(New York: Greenwood, 1968), pp. 95ff.

[19]*Ibid.*, 42-44.

[20]*Ibid.*

[21]*Ibid.*, 4ff.

[22]*Ibid.*, 56.

[23]*Ibid.*, 49-50.

[24]*Ibid.*, 48-49.

[25]*Ibid.*, 36-37.

[26]*Ibid.*, 58.

[27]*Ibid.*, 150, 169-170.

[28]*Ibid.*, 43.

[29]Cf. R. Brandt, *The Philosophy of Schleiermacher.*

[30]*Ibid.*, 149.

[31]*Ibid.*

[32]*Ibid.*, 175-76, 180.

[33]*Ibid.*, 212.

[34]*Ibid.*, 211.

[35]*Ibid.*, 51-52.

[36]Schleiermacher is not totally against this possibility. See *Speeches*, 51, 224f.

[37]*Ibid.*, 219.

[38]F. Schleiermacher, *The Christian Faith*, H.R. Mackintosh & J.S. Stewart, eds. (Philadelphia: Fortress, 1976.), 34f.

[39]*The Christian Faith*, 34.

[40]*Ibid.*, 36.

[41]*Ibid.*, 37.

[42]*Ibid.*

[43]*Ibid.*, 37-38.

[44]*Ibid.*, 214f.

[45]*Ibid.*, 119, 87.

[46]*Ibid.*, 222-23.

[47]*Speeches*, 108.

[48]*Ibid.*, 216, 221.

Tropics of Autobiographical Discourse:
An Examination of Newman's *Apologia*

C. J. T. Talar

Since an autobiographical narrative practice seeks to order,
and reveal the truth about, 'real' past events, it is of a kind
with historical narrative *per se*, for the methodological
decisions that an autobiographer makes are historiographic
as well as literary, novelistic, and poetic ones.[1]

In order to emplot developments in theoretical and critical approaches
to autobiography, James Olney has decomposed the word into its constitu-
ent elements: *autos-bios-graphē*. Prior to the mid-1950s a focus on *bios*
rendered the self rather unproblematic: an autobiographical narrative
revealed a life in a manner "at least approaching an objective historical
account."[2] It is with the appearance of Georges Gusdorf's 1956 essay[3] that
a shift occurs: a turning from *bios* to *autos*, from the life to the self,
which signaled a turn in a philosophical, psychological, and literary
direction. From this perspective, in doing autobiography the self half
discovers, half creates itself: the narrated *bios* is not an objective reflection
of the self but its creative projection. More recently the third element,
graphē, increasingly has become the focal point.

In line with this last shift the autobiographer has been metaphorized
as "reader" of his or her past. As such, one does not "read" one's past
as a book in order to discern the "correct" meaning contained therein,
but in a manner analogous to the reader portrayed by reader-response criticism. The past is analogous to a textual structure which potentially admits
of multiple readings, although a given reading will produce a determinate
meaning in interaction with that text. In other words, the autobiographical
self comes into being in the act of writing, much as textual meaning comes
into being in the act of reading. The reader must constitute a perspective
that can be identified with a given character out of the various segments
of dialogue, events and narrator's commentary scattered throughout the
text, and then relate that perspective to those of other characters to

produce a continuous and ordered narrative. The autobiographer must constitute the chronologically discrete elements of experience supplied by memory, and organize those into a continuous and ordered life. "As a self-critic, then, who would *read* the meaning of his past, the traditional autobiographer can only succeed insofar as he projects onto his work (and his past) the meaning (coherence) he purports to be discovering."[4]

This characterization of autobiography as a narrative of events occurring in time invites comparison with historical narrative, as the epigraph indeed suggests. And an emphasis on *graphe*, on bringing the self into language invites retrieval of theoretical approaches to history concerned with the process of bringing the past into linguistic expression. The work of Hayden White falls into this category, being concerned with the figurative power of language and its implications for the narration of past events.[5] That work has proven to be of interest not only to historians, but to those interested in theoretical approaches to (auto)biography as well.[6]

White has stressed the role of the imagination in representing historical events. There is inevitably a fictive element in historical narrative—opening historiography to contributions from literary theory. Further, all historical accounts rely on a philosophy of history, whether articulated or implicit. White seeks to analyze the literary codes that shape the structure historical narrative. To do so he attends to the manifest dimensions of an historical work: the narrative's emplotment, the formal argument employed by the historian, and the historian's ideological stance. He further postulates a deep, precritical level of consciousness on which the historian adopts a tropological strategy of metaphor, metonymy, synecdoche, or irony. This deep structural level of the historical imagination linguistically constitutes the historical field on which the manifest functions of the historian are exercised.

Here White's analysis will be drawn upon to explore John Henry Newman's *Apologia Pro Vita Sua*, whose very subtitle, *A History of His Religious Opinions*, reinforces the connection between autobiographical and historical narrative.[7] The intent is to explore further the utility of this conceptual framework for illumining the *graphe* of the autobiographical genre. Since the framework can be rendered in terms of superstructural elements and a tropological infrastructure, the former will be taken up first, and parallels with autobiographical narrative suggested. The *Apologia* will serve to concretize the discussion. Following that the tropological infrastructure will be briefly presented, once again exploring the applicability to autobiography by examining Newman's text.

In Hayden White's *Metahistory* several levels dealing with historical narrative are distinguished:

1. Story: in contrast to chronicles with their chronological ordering of events, histories introduce cutting points into the historical continuum, delineating periods with their inaugural/transitional/and terminating motifs. Moreover, these motifs are given a direction, are emplotted as stories of a given type which serve to explain these events. A plot structure endows the story with a comprehensible process of development: a romance, comedy, tragedy, or satire.[8]

2. Argumentation: historical explanations are themselves products of metahistorical presuppositions about the nature of the historical field: what will count as an historical problem, the form that an historical explanation must take, and the kinds of evidence that will be permitted to count as data. Put another way, formal argumentation specifies the significance of historical emplotments: different for a Marxist than for an Idealist. Consonant with the fourfold typology of modes of emplotment, modes of argument are also quadriform: formist, organicist, mechanistic and contextualist.[9]

3. Ideological implication: the existence of alternative modes of representing the historical field poses a choice for the historian. White sees that decision informed by opinions about the nature of humanity and society, opinions which are ideological in nature. Every historical account of any scope would therefore presuppose a specific set of ideological commitments which would inform its very notion of "objectivity," "explanation." The work of Karl Mannheim is adapted to preserve symmetry with previous typologies, yielding anarchism, conservatism, radicalism, and liberalism.[10]

For White, then, a given historiographical style represents a particular combination of modes of emplotment, argument, and ideological implication. Further, although in principle any combination of these modes is theoretically possible, in practice there exist "elective affinities" among them, reflecting their varying degrees of compatibility. These affinities may be rendered schematically:[11]

Mode of Emplotment	Mode of Argumentation	Mode of Ideological Implication
Romantic	Formist	Anarchist
Tragic	Mechanistic	Radical
Comic	Organicist	Conservative
Satirical	Contextualist	Liberal

Having privileged these combinations over other possibilities, White immediately adds a qualification: affinities are not to be taken as *necessary* combinations. Indeed it is from combinations of variables not consonant with one another that there arises the "dialectical tension" present in the work of "master historians."[12]

The emphasis on formal elements of historical narrative, which ultimately undermines any neat distinction between form and content, finds its analogues in theoretical approaches to autobiography such as Jean Starobinski's.[13] His work challenges a notion of autobiography which views the author's past as existing as a unified, logically articulated whole prior to its representation in language. Rather, the autobiographical act is constructive, performative: "It is a way of doing things with words, not a passive description of something already there."[14]

On one level, one of the things autobiography does with words is tell the story of a life. It gives shape to this life, representing it as a triumphal or tragic story, a story that begins at birth, accords a number of events a transitional significance, and finds some concluding point of resolution. That is to say that, just as do classic novels, autobiographies employ plots in their shaping and structuring of the lives they treat. In doing so they impose a narrative pattern on the discrete events of a lifetime in order to explain those events, to render that life meaningful. White's observation made with reference to historical narrative would apply equally to autobiographical narrative:

> Since no given set or sequence of real events is intrinsically tragic, comic, farcial, and so on, but can be constructed as such only by the imposition of the structure of a given story type on the events, it is the choice of the story type and its imposition upon the events that endow them with meaning.[15]

Less than surprisingly, then, Northrop Frye's four archetypal story forms resurface among autobiographical theorists.[16]

Moving from autobiographical theory to autobiographical practice in Newman's *Apologia*, one encounters an embarrassment of riches where candidates for emplotment are concerned. Victorian biography in general depicted its subject as hero: as "the good man with a purpose overcoming the obstacles of the outside world."[17] Portions at least of Newman's book appear to reflect this approach. Characterizations of Newman as having created in the *Apologia* "a self-image that can be described as a conquering hero"[18] suggest a "romantic" mode—archetypally stressing conflict of hero and adversary, in which good triumphs and the hero transcends a fallen world. Taking as her point of reference Newman's Anglican career, however, Mary Lenz emplots Chapters I through IV as a tragedy: the first two chapters depict the rising action, with growing strength in the Anglican position, with the next two telling the story of the decline, "the final catastrophe of Newman's Anglican career being his conversion to Catholicism in Chapter IV."[19] A tragic note is also sounded by Martin Svaglic in his assessment of the book's structure, though with the suggestion that the tragedy is only apparent and that something deeper is at work. Noting the prominence of military metaphors throughout the book, he judges it "the drama of a soldier who, through defeat and submission, at last finds peace: a loving defeat ostensibly by his enemies but in reality by the 'sweet and mysterious influence which called him on'."[20]

At the end of his article Svaglic surfaces another image, expressed in a different set of metaphors: "faith as a journey in response to a vision, a voyage on the sea."[21] Calling it the "minor motif of the imagery" he quotes a number of texts reflective of it, the most telling of which for our purposes occurs at the outset of the final chapter. At this point Newman's own story is really concluded; Chapter V provides a direct answer to some of the charges Charles Kingsley and others have leveled against Catholicism. Accordingly Newman begins that chapter:

> From the time that I became a Catholic, of course I have no further history of my religious opinions to narrate. In saying this, I do not mean to say that my mind has been idle, or that I have given up thinking on theological subjects; but that I have no variations to record, and have had no anxiety of heart whatever. I have been in perfect peace and contentment. . . . I was not conscious to myself, on my conversion, of any change, intellectual or moral, wrought in my mind. . . . but it was like coming into port after a rough sea; and my happiness on that score remains to this day without interruption.[22]

These various emplotments surfaced, or suggested, by critical readings of the *Apologia* need not be mutually exclusive. Just as the same set of historical events can be rendered from more than one point of view, and endings linked to beginnings in a variety of ways; and just as a novel can incorporate simultaneously several points of view, distributed among its several characters; so with autobiography. While from one point of view Newman's conversion to Roman Catholicism could be (and indeed was) regarded as the tragic end of a promising career in both Anglicanism and the academy, a tragic fall into popery, from another—long a standard of Christian biography antedating even Augustine's *Confessions*—it could be represented as coming into safe harbor after the struggle with storms at sea. Indeed, the journey metaphorical network, relegated to the status of "minor motif" by Svaglic, is regarded as central to the *Apologia* by Sidney Mendel.[23] As such it becomes a story of Newman's leaving one home—the Anglican communion—in order to find his true home in Roman Catholicism.

Thus the overall framework which emplots the story of Newman's life can be considered a "comedy" the dynamic of which tends toward integration. In comedy the goal is reconciliation of the forces at play in personal and interpersonal worlds, a reconciliation achieved at a personal level at the beginning of Chapter V and still hoped for on a collective level in its concluding paragraph.

On another level, one of the things one does with language is construct a mode of argumentation. The controversial circumstances out of which the *Apologia* emerged have left their stamp on its form.[24] Even though Newman compressed much of the original material bearing on the controversy raised by Charles Kingsley into a relatively brief preface in the second edition (1865), thus enhancing the work's autobiographical status, it still reflects its origins.

Newman perceived that Kingsley's original charge, essentially one impugning his integrity, could not be met effectively by a point-by-point logical refutation. To establish his personal integrity he would have to reveal the integral nature of his life. Further, it must be noted that Kingsley served more as occasion than as primary audience for the *Apologia*, which also had in view Newman's former friends and associates at Oxford, his fellow Catholics—particularly those of the ultramontane party, and the broader English public.[25] Both out of conviction that the truth is presented more effectively when presented concretely, and out of aims larger than the immediate controversy with Kingsley, Newman set out to answer the latter's challenge, *What, Then, Does Dr. Newman Mean?* While certain logical argumentation is not absent from the *Apologia* that work relies more fundamentally on an ethical mode of persuasion, grounded on the personal character of the speaker.[26] Despite the book's subtitle, "meaning" will refer less to propositions which Newman holds than with the direction his life has assumed.

In White's schema comedy bears an elective affinity for an organicist mode of argumentation. Therefore we shall begin by looking for evidence of that. Commentators on the *Apologia* frequently relate it to both *An Essay in Aid of a Grammar of Assent* and to *An Essay on the Development of Christian Doctrine*: to the *Grammar* in that Newman's autobiographical approach permits truth to emerge from life rather than simply logical process[27]; to the *Essay on Development* in that ecclesiastical history provides an analogue for Newman's personal development. It is the latter treatise's focus on development which provides the point of contact with an organicist mode of argumentation. Indeed, in establishing contact between the evolution of church doctrine and Newman's personal evolution Olney himself employs an organic metaphorical network:

> In this matter of evolution, there is a clear analogy to be drawn between scriptural revelation, which is the objective, historical, and public seed of all church doctrine, and Newman's conversion at fifteen, the subjective, momentary, and private seed of personality, thereafter to be exfoliated in years of experience.[28]

This theme of development and growth is not merely the product of reader perception but is raised in the preface of the *Apologia*:

> I must, I said, give the true key to my whole life; I must show what I am, that it may be seen what I am not. . . . I will draw out, as far as may be, the history of my mind; I will state the point at which I began, in what external suggestion or accident each opinion had its rise, how far and how they developed from within, how they grew, were modified, were combined, were in collision with each other, and were changed. . . .[29]

Keeping in mind, however, the analogue between the *Essay on Development* and the *Apologia* one must be careful regarding how evolutionary development is to be understood in Newman. As Nicholas Lash has pointed out in his analysis of the *Essay* the organicist analogy coexists with others in the text, and indeed is not the prime analogate nor the leading idea.[30] Moreover in materialist hands the argument of progressive growth was used against Catholicism and religion generally—indeed with greater frequency than it was employed in their favor.

In the *Essay on Development* Newman is less concerned with tracing the progressive steps in a developmental process than with demonstrating consistency between the Roman Catholic Church of the nineteenth century and the Church of the first centuries. In that sense the point to be demonstrated is couched in negative terms, i.e., the Church has not substantially changed in the intervening centuries, despite apparent differences between its origins and contemporary expression. This is the point of contact between the *Essay* and the *Apologia*: that the fundamental change in

Newman's life occurred close to its origins, the conversion at age fifteen which Olney has alluded to above; and that subsequent transitions in Newman's life, his involvement in the Tractarian movement in 1833 and his conversion to Roman Catholicism in 1845 are continuous with that originary event. Newman's own account of it occurs close to the origins of his story of his personal history:

> When I was fifteen (in the autumn of 1816,) a great change of thought took place in me. I fell under the influences of a definite Creed, and received into my intellect impressions of dogma, which, through God's mercy, have never been effaced or obscured.[31]

Newman's aim in the book was to demonstrate that he had not substantially changed in that interval between initial conversion and commitment to Roman Catholicism; this in an effort to show his life as a unity. His form of argumentation, then, would be integrative rather than dispersive, would draw upon organicism or mechanism rather than formism or contextualism. While the search for cause-effect relationships characteristic of mechanism is not absent from Newman's autobiography, the terms in which that life is understood are more reflective of White's depiction of organicism.[32] The discrete events that occur in the course of a life are discerned as components of a synthetic process, as aggregating into a whole greater than the sum of its parts. Organicists "tend to structure their narratives in such a way as to depict the consolidation or crystallization, out of a set of apparently dispersed events, of some integrated entity whose importance is greater than that of any of the individual entities analyzed or described in the course of the narrative."[33] While close attention must be given to the ways in which this organicist strategy is enacted in metaphorical networks, it is the strategy which can be said to dominate the autobiographical narrative in the *Apologia*.

A combination of factors evokes the expectation of a conservative ideological orientation underlying the organicist mode of argumentation and predominantly comic mode of emplotment.

Victorian sensibilities were shaped by changes produced by the French Revolution and social transformations wrought by technological and economic innovation. Inheritors of a commitment to the aristocratic tradition of hierarchy as foundational to order, they observed the breakdown of authority and hierarchy around them. In Newman's age this supported a conviction that the hierarchy needed to be revivified, especially in view of challenges issuing from liberalism with their corrosive effects on dogma and established authority, ultimately on social and spiritual order.[34]

These sensibilities translated into a view of change as a necessary concomitant of stability. In the midst of change there is a quest for the permanent. Certainly an appreciation of change is not lacking in Newman: "In a higher world it is otherwise, but here below to live is to change, and to be perfect is to have changed often."[35] Much less often quoted is the sentence which immediately precedes, and which underscores a valuation of change only as a means to what is unchanging: an idea "changes . . . in order to remain the same." Development of doctrine is not innovation, but rather a clearer statement for a fallen humanity of what is originally given in Revelation, of what is permanent and unchangeable. Organic metaphors in the *Essay on Development* are counterweighted by logical ones, which push a reading of the former in the direction of emphasizing the substantial *identity* of initial point and maturity, of child and adult, rather than on the evolutionary *process* of growth itself. This is evidenced in the function of the seven "notes" set forth in the *Essay*: "[T]hese are seven tokens that [the idea] may rightly be accounted one and the same all along."[36]

The operation of one of these notes, continuity of principles, may serve as a bridge to Newman's understanding of his own past in the *Apologia*. Distinguishing between principles and the doctrines which embody them, Newman argues that a change in doctrinal expression of a principle is not a corruption if the principle is preserved intact. If the principle undergoes alteration, however, corruption ensues. And what is true in the life of Christianity is apparently held to be true in the lives of individuals.

Newman judges this continuity to have been operative in his own life:

I have changed in many things: in this I have not. From the age of fifteen, dogma has been the fundamental principle of my religion: . . .
I cannot enter into the idea of any other sort of religion; religion, as
a mere sentiment, is to me a dream and a mockery. . . . What I held
in 1816, I held in 1833, and I hold in 1864. Please God, I shall hold
it to the end.[37]

Based on this foundation of dogma Newman believed in "the truth of a certain definite religious teaching" which centered on a visible Church and a sacramental life. Once more continuity throughout his life is stressed: "Here again, I have not changed in opinion; I am as certain now on this point as I was in 1833, and have never ceased to be certain."[38] The changes which have occurred in converting to Roman Catholicism, and prior to that, within his Anglican position itself are described as strengthening those beliefs, not fundamentally altering them. "I have added Articles to my Creed; but the old ones, which I then held with a divine faith, remain."[39]

What Newman has renounced is the third point of his original beliefs: his former view of the Church of Rome. But he is able to interpret this as necessarily being true to the former two points of belief. Returning to these "three original points of belief": the principle of dogma, the sacraments, and anti-Romanism, he notes: "Of these three the first two were better secured in Rome than in the Anglican Church."[40] His process of conversion to Roman Catholicism thus involved bringing that opinion to the firmness of intellectual conviction.

Rooted in a Victorian sensibility, expressed theoretically in a theory of doctrinal development, a conservative orientation pervades Newman's self-understanding in the *Apologia*. Further, it will be noticed that a conservative mode of ideological implication bears an elective affinity with comedy and organicism. One would expect such consonance in a work aimed at seeking to convince its audience(s) of its point of view.

Judging from published criticism of White's work, his analysis of historical narrative in terms of emplotment, argumentation, and ideological implication has been the less controversial aspect. Indeed, singling out the four forms of emplotment, Maurice Mandelbaum has stated that "White has made an important and suggestive contribution to the theory of historiography in having called attention to them."[41] However, reaction to the tropological portion of White's conceptualization has been more reserved. It is therefore necessary to consider this aspect of the framework before going on to note its application to autobiographical theory, and to the *Apologia* in particular.

An historical narrative places events in relationships—relationships which are not immanent in the events themselves but which are the product of the mind of the historian reflecting on those events. Prior to constituting those relationships the historian must describe the events themselves, bring them to linguistic expression. For White both the kinds of objects which are permitted to appear in the historical field as data and the possible relationships that are conceived to be possible among them are products of a deeper interpretive ground, linguistic in nature, which constitutes the field itself as an act of mental perception. This prefigurative act is precognitive and precritical within consciousness, assuming the form of a preconceptual linguistic protocol. To classify this there is yet another fourfold structure: the distinction among tropes as metaphor, metonymy, synecdoche, and irony. The tropes, then, are invested with the power of determining the process of thought as it works itself out discursively. In White's terms,

> even the simplest prose discourse, and even in one in which the object of representation is intended to be nothing but fact, the use of language itself projects a level of secondary meaning below and behind the phenomena being 'described.' This secondary meaning exists quite apart from both the 'facts' themselves and any explicit argument that might be offered in the extradescriptive, more purely analytical or interpretive, level of the text. This figurative level is produced by a constructive process, poetic in nature, which prepares the reader of the text more or less subconsciously to receive *both* the description of the facts and their explication as plausible, on the one side, and as adequate to one another, on the other.[42]

Underlying the "surface" of the discourse, the facts and their formal explanation, is the figurative language used to characterize the facts and to privilege some sets of possible relationships over others—the "deep-structural" level of meaning. Underlying emplotment, formal argumentation, and ideological implication, in other words, are the tropes of metaphor, metonymy, synecdoche, and irony which give shape to the narrative discourse.

To acknowledge the constitutive role of figurative language in historical narrative is to admit an inescapably literary or fictive element in every historical account. Similarly, the shift in autobiographical theory to *graphe* has highlighted the literary—hence fictive—elements in the autobiographical act. Meaning is not simply construed from the sequence of events that make up a life, but is constructed in the act of bestowing coherence on those events, in patterning them as a story of a particular type. The autobiographical self is thus an emergent structure, product of an intricate process of self-discovery and self-creation, revealing as much or more of its author's present point of view as of past events. While the autobiographer is not free to invent just any self—there are after all the events which have occurred in the course of a lifetime—those events are subject to being constituted and interpreted in a variety of ways. Hence "the self that is the center of all autobiographical narrative is necessarily a fictive structure."[43]

Susanna Egan's extended analysis of Newman's accounts of his 1833 illness in Sicily provides a good illustration of this fictive element. She compares the various accounts of that event in contemporary letters to friends, in a private journal account begun in 1834 and revised on a number of occasions thereafter, and in the *Apologia* at the end of chapter I. While earlier accounts interpret that illness in terms of God's punishment for his sins and God's mercy and election for divine work, or as an obstacle placed by Satan, and include numerous details of symptoms and surroundings, in the *Apologia* "Newman extracts only those that make sense in this particular narrative and adhere to the pattern that we call 'conversion'."[44]

A focus on the literary form of autobiography has necessarily entailed focus on the literary act of composition and the dependence of the autobiographer on language to express a life-story. From there it is but a short step to connecting autobiographical narrative to White's tropological analysis of historical narrative. In making that connection with respect to biography Ira Nadel emphasized the roles of metaphor and metonymy as guiding tropes of a subject's life, imparting coherence to that life and organizing reader perceptions of it. However, with respect to Newman's representation of his life in the *Apologia* I shall argue that synecdoche plays the predominant role, while irony is also present and cannot be neglected.

As a skilled controversialist Newman was certainly practiced in the art of logical argumentation. Indeed his skill in turning an opponent's strongest arguments to his own advantage has received comment.[45] And while Newman gave an autobiographical answer to Kingsley's charge rather than a point-by-point refutation, logical argument does have a prominent role in the *Apologia*. The presence of such argument signals the presence of metonymy, which figures objects/events as parts of larger wholes, those parts being related in terms of cause and effect, agent and act. In Chapter I, for instance, Newman gives an account of the formation of his beliefs and intellectual habits, emphasizing their Anglican and Protestant sources and his lack of contact with Roman Catholic influences. Prominent as these metonymical representations are, however, they will not bear the burden of adequately representing the integral nature of Newman's life: "[I]t was not logic that carried me on; as well might one say that the quicksilver in the barometer changes the weather. It is the concrete being that reasons; . . . the whole man moves; paper logic is but the record of it."[46] While Newman sets out in the *Apologia* the record of his development, proceeding step by metonymical step, ultimately he has to take the next, synecdochic step in order to draw all the parts into an integral whole.

White categorizes metonymy and synecdoche, along with metaphor, as constructive tropes. Irony, on the other hand, is deconstructive—in a sense metatropological, since it brings into awareness the problematical nature of language in its attempts to depict reality. Irony harbors an "apprehension of the capacity of language to obscure more than it clarifies in any act of verbal figuration." In irony the potential of figurative language for distorting perception is questioned, the "very effort to capture adequately the truth of things in language" subjected to criticism.[47]

The very act of bringing the events of one's life into discursive coherence cannot but produce a sense of the omissions and inadequacies of that account.[48] In his preface Newman reflected on the inherent difficulties of his enterprise, noting problems of speaking adequately "in a reasonable compass," the lack of adequate documentation to compensate the fragility of memory, the necessarily "incomplete" nature of such a "sketch."[49] This sense of inherent inadequacy is raised again at the beginning of Chapter III:

> For who can know himself, and the multitude of subtle influences which act upon him? And who can recollect, at the distance of twenty-five years, all that he once knew about his thoughts and his deeds, and that, during a portion of his life, when, even at the time his observation, whether of himself or of the external world, was less than before or after, by very reason of the perplexity and dismay which weighed upon him. . . .[50]

Michael Ryan in his grammatological analysis of the *Apologia* pushes the problematic character of autobiography to the level of the very adequacy of language itself to represent the person. He notes that in the final chapter where casuistry is discussed Newman must argue that a writer can condone lying while not lying himself. Thus is a distinction possible between the representation and the person: "A man in his own person is guided by his own conscience; but in drawing out a system of rules he is obliged to go by logic, and follow the exact deduction of conclusion from conclusion, and must be sure that the whole system is coherent and one."[51] The writing may not be the representation of the person.

While the self-reflexive character of Newman's autobiographical act raises an ironic mode of consciousness in White's sense, ultimately the book is figured in the trope of synecdoche. Or in Ryan's terms, Newman's "seeming ambivalence" toward writing "might rest on the distinction he seems to make between the writing in which the writer 'is guided by his own conscience' and that in which 'he is obliged to go by logic'."[52]

Deriving as it does from Newman's inner voice, laying bare his conscience, the *Apologia* may indeed serve to represent Newman's integrity, even given the obstacles and limits he raises.

To do so the account must come to grips with an issue that is central: continuity and change. How can Newman claim to be consistent when his faith, his allegiance has changed? He is confronted by the need to convince his readers that he *has* changed—that he was not a crypto-"Romanist" "in Protestant livery and service."[53] Yet this need to show that he was truly Anglican and became truly Roman Catholic is complicated by his desire to suggest that he has not truly changed after all.[54] The continuity in the midst of difference that is suggested by an organic development from seed to mature plant may preserve both aspects. Commentators have remarked on the frequency of the images of growth in the *Apologia*. And unsurprisingly an organicist mode of argumentation is held to have an elective affinity for the trope of synecdoche in White's framework. For synecdoche stresses part-whole relationships in an integrative way, which makes it suitable for autobiography and Newman's purposes in particular:

> [T]he relation of surface to depth in autobiographical narrative can best be understood as a synecdochal relation. Like metaphor, the trope of synecdoche stands for a part-whole relation. Unlike metaphor, however, which connotes an image in space, synecdoche suggests a quality in time. Only inside of time and displayed in the world can the self participate in depth.[55]

I have argued that White's analysis of historical narrative can fruitfully illumine aspects of autobiographical narrative, resolving that into its levels of emplotment, argumentation, ideological implication, and tropological deep structure. On this basis the *Apologia* can be represented as comic, organicist, and conservative, undergirded by a synecdochic mode of consciousness. The synecdochic consciousness of a divine providence ordering the developments of sacred history finds its resonances in his own religious development that reflects a greater integrity.

Autobiography, then, has an essentially "poetic" character. As Ernest Renan remarked at the outset of his own autobiographical reflections, "What one says of oneself is always poetry. . . . One writes of such things in order to convey to others the world view that one carries in oneself."[56]

NOTES

[1]Paul Jay, *Being in the Text* (Ithaca, Cornell University, 1984), pp. 108-109.

[2]James Olney, "Autobiography and the Cultural Moment: A Thematic, Historical, and Bibliographical Introduction" in James Olney, ed., *Autobiography: Essays Theoretical and Critical* (Princeton, Princeton University, 1980), p. 20.

[3]"Conditions et limites de l'autobiographie." Eng. tr. "Conditions and Limits of Autobiography" in Olney, ed., pp. 28-48.

[4]Candace Lang, "Autobiography in the Aftermath of Romanticism" *Diacritics* 12 (1982), p. 14. In this review article which discusses Olney's earlier work, *Metaphors of Self* (1972) as well as his edited volume *Autobiography*, Lang criticizes Olney for not taking sufficient account of the more radical implications of the shift to *graphe*, as in deconstructionism. On the autobiographer as "reader" of the self see Janet P. Gunn, *Autobiography: Towards a Poetics of Experience* (Philadelphia, University of Pennsylvania, 1982).

[5]White's analytical scheme is set out and applied to various nineteenth-century historians and philosophers of history in *Metahistory* (Baltimore, Johns Hopkins University, 1973). See also his *Tropics of Discourse* (idem, 1978) and *The Content of the Form* (idem, 1987). This work is situated in relation to the traditional historiography by Lloyd S. Kramer, "Literature, Criticism, and Historical Imagination: The Literary Challenge of Hayden White and Dominick LaCapra," Lynn Hunt, ed., *The New Cultural History* (Berkeley: Unniversity of California, 1989), 97-128.

[6]*History and Theory* devoted one of its supplements to critical response to White's work: *Beiheift* 19 (1980), while Ira B. Nadel draws on it in *Biography: Fiction, Fact & Form* (New York, St. Martin's, 1984). James Mellard has provided a number of applications of White's approach to literature, including the genre of autobiography in *Doing Tropology* (Chicago, University of Illinois, 1987). Ch. 3 is devoted to *The Education of Henry Adams*.

[7]Newman's *Apologia* as combination of both autobiography and memoir renders it an especially good text with which to explore this connection. See A.O.J. Cockshut, *The Art of Autobiography* (New Haven, Yale University, 1984), p. 2. The circumstances surrounding the *Apologia*'s initial appearance are summarized in Martin Svaglic, "Why Newman Wrote the *Apologia*," and a history of its various editions with their contents in Francis Connolly, "The *Apologia*: History, Rhetoric, and Literature," both in Vincent Blehl, S.J. and Francis Connolly, eds., *Newman's "Apologia": A Classic Reconsidered* (New York, Harcourt, Brace & World, 1964), pp. 1-25 and 105-24 respectively.

[8]Here White is adapting to the historian's enterprise the typology developed by Northrop Frye in his theory of fictions. See Northrop Frye, *Anatomy of Criticism* (Princeton, Princeton University, 1973). For White's adaptation see *Metahistory*, pp. 7-11.

[9]White is incorporating the work of Stephen Pepper, *World Hypotheses* (Berkeley: University of California, 1970). In work subsequent to *Metahistory* White has substituted the term "idiography" for Pepper's formism, as better reflective of historical concerns.

[10]These ideologies are derived from Karl Mannheim's *Ideology and Utopia* (New York, Harcourt, Brace & World, 1964) and discussed in *Metahistory*, pp. 22-29.

[11]*Metahistory*, p. 29.

[12]Critics of *Metahistory* find White less than clear on the source of these elective affinities. Manifestly they are accorded the role of a synthetic principle, one which seeks to pattern potential diversity among the twelve variables. But the process by which a given historiographical style is generated and regenerated is "mysterious." By extension much the same can be said of the "dialectical tension" among variables in a given style. See Philip Pomper, "Typologies and Cycles in Intellectual History," *History and Theory*. *Beiheift* 19, pp. 32-33. Hans Kellner, writing in the same supplement, makes much the same point: "A Bedrock of Order: Hayden White's Linguistic Humanism," p. 27.

[13]See Jean Starobinski, "The Style of Autobiography" in Olney, ed., *Autobiography*, pp. 73-83.

[14]J. Hillis Miller, "Prosopopoeia and *Praeterita*" in Laurence Lockridge *et al.*, ed., *Nineteenth-Century Lives* (Cambridge, Cambridge University, 1989), p. 129.

[15]White, *The Content of the Form*, p. 44.

[16]See Susanna Egan, *Patterns of Experience in Autobiography*. (Chapel Hill: University of North Carolina, 1984), pp. 23, 41ff.

[17]Robert Blake, "The Art of Biography," in Eric Homberger and John Charmley, ed., *The Troubled Face of Biography* (New York, St. Martin's, 1988), p. 86.

[18]Edward Kelly, "Newman's Reputation and the Biographical Tradition" in *Essays in Honor of the Centenary of John Henry Cardinal Newman (1801-1890)* (Christendom Press, 1989), p. 154. Cf. Egan, pp. 57-58.

[19]Sister Mary Lenz, "A Rhetorical Analysis of Newman's *Apologia Pro Vita Sua*," (Ph.D. dissertation, University of Notre Dame, 1962), p. 146.

[20]Martin Svaglic, "The Structure of Newman's *Apologia*" in A. Wright, *Victorian Literature* (New York: Oxford University, 1961), p. 231.

[21]Ibid., p. 235.

[22]John Henry Newman, *Apologia Pro Vita Sua* (London: Longmans, 1934), p. 238.

[23]Sidney Mendel, "Metaphor and Rhetoric in Newman's *Apologia*," *Essays in Criticism* 23 (1973): 357-71.

[24]In the course of a book review published in *Macmillan's Magazine* for January, 1864, the reviewer stated, "Truth, for its own sake, had never been a virtue with the Roman clergy. Father Newman informs us that it need not, and on the whole ought not to be; that cunning is the weapon which Heaven has given to the Saints wherewith to withstand the brute male force of the wicked world . . . ." Upon learning the reviewer's identity as Charles Kingsley, Newman entered into a correspondence seeking redress for the unjustified slander. He failed to obtain satisfaction and the correspondence escalated into an exchange of pamphlets. The *Apologia* emerged from this controversy as Newman's mode of reply to Kingsley. It initially took the form of seven pamphlets issued weekly between April 21 and June 2, 1864, together with an appendix published on June 16. Its full title, *Apologia Vita Sua: Being a Reply to a Pamphlet Entitled "What, Then, Does Dr. Newman Mean?"* indicates its controversial origins. Svaglic, "Why Newman Wrote the Apologia."

[25]See Svaglic, "Why Newman Wrote the *Apologia*," pp. 9ff. and Edward Kelly, "The *Apologia* and the Ultramontanes" also in Blehl and Connolly, pp. 26-46.

[26]See Lenz's analysis of the rhetorical argumentation in the *Apologia* with its assessment of the roles accorded logical and ethical modes of persuasion.

[27]His autobiography has been described as "the practice for which the *Grammar* would be the theoretical expression." Michael Ryan, "A Grammatology of Assent: Cardinal Newman's *Apologia pro vita sua*" in George Landow, ed., *Approaches to Victorian Autobiography* (Athens, OH: University of Ohio, 1979), p. 129. Cf. Jonathan Robinson, "The *Apologia* and the *Grammar of Assent*" in Blehl and Connolly, pp. 145-64.

[28]James Olney, *Metaphors of Self* (Princeton: Princeton University, 1972), p. 225.

[29]*Apologia*, pp. xxiv-xxv. For the incidence of organic metaphors in the *Apologia* see the relevant sections of Lenz.

[30]See Nicholas Lash, *Newman on Development* (Shepherdstown, West Virginia: Patmos, 1975), ch. 4. Also Paul Misner, "The Liberal Legacy of John Henry Newman" in Mary Jo Weaver, ed., *Newman and the Modernists* (Lanham, University Press of America, 1985), p. 12.

[31]*Apologia*, p. 4.

[32]The organicism in Newman's work is reflective of its presence in the larger context of his times. For the Victorian sensibility "the purposiveness of the universe implies also an organic coherence, a world ordered, self-consistent, interdependent, and hierarchical. Clearly, the notion of a world interconnected at all points, like a kind of spider web, pervades Victorian thought." George Levine, *The Boundaries of Fiction: Carlyle, Macaulay, Newman* (Princeton, Princeton University, 1968), p. 182.

[33]*Metahistory*, p. 15.

[34]Levine, p. 185.

[35]John Henry Newman, *An Essay on the Development of Christian Doctrine* (London: Longmans, 1903), p. 40.

[36]Ibid., p. 206.

[37]*Apologia*, p. 49.

[38]Idem.

[39]Ibid., p. 52.

[40]Ibid., p. 120.

[41]Maurice Mandelbaum, "The Presuppositions of Metahistory" in *History and Theory. Beiheift* 19, p. 47.

[42]*Tropics of Discourse*, p. 110.

[43]Paul Eakin, *Fictions in Autobiography* (Princeton: Princeton University, 1985), p. 3.

[44]Egan, p. 56. She adds, "He does not need to discuss willfulness or even a struggle with Satan (he is, after all, underplaying his own leadership in the Oxford movement) so long as the sense of exalting mission emerges from delirium. Had Newman assumed a more significant role as leader in the Oxford movement, his fever might have played

a more significant part in this narrative as the source of inspiration from which his leadership derived," p. 57. Cf. the section, "Constructing a Conversion," in Jonathan Loesberg, *Fictions of Consciousness* (New Brunswick: Rutgers University, 1986), pp. 135-42.

[45]Levine, p. 197.

[46]*Apologia*, p. 169. This is but symptomatic of Newman's sense of the limitations of logic, both more generally and for him personally. Cf. p. 241 where he speaks of the force of arguments in proof of a God.

[47]*Metahistory*, p. 37.

[48]Louis Renza, "A Theory of Autobiography" in Olney, ed., p. 270.

[49]*Apologia*, pp. xxv-xxvi.

[50]Ibid., p. 92. Cf. pp. 147-148.

[51]Ibid., p. 276.

[52]Ryan, p. 140.

[53]*Apologia*, p. xix.

[54]See Heather Henderson, *The Victorian Self* (Ithaca: Cornell University, 1989), pp. 52-53.

[55]Gunn, p. 10.

[56]Ernest Renan, *Souvenirs d'enfance et de jeunesse* (Boston: D.C. Heath, 1902), p. 6.

Love Safeguarding Faith:

The Ethical Commitment to

Ecumenical Dialogue

in Newman's Theory of Religious Assent

Gerard Magill

INTRODUCTION

John Henry Newman (1801-90) was hardly complacent about doctrinal truth. In his spiritual autobiography, written in 1864, he professed his confidence in religious doctrine, proclaiming that "the principle of dogma" was "the fundamental principle of my religion."[1] Yet, he was no sedentary ideologist. That conviction led him from Anglicanism to Catholicism in 1845, and inspired him to publish in 1870 an account of the religious epistemology that undergirded his shifting assent to divergent doctrine. It is his highly original justification of that movement (both philosophical and theological) from one set of beliefs to another that can illumine dialogue between religions and churches today.

There are several ways to investigate Newman's contribution to ecumenism. One approach might be to consider his theological writings that can be construed as ecumenical. For example, in his Anglican theory of the *via media*, published in 1837,[2] he sought a *via media* between the sixteenth-century reformers and Romanism by portraying the Anglican Church as the reformed Catholic Church that remained more faithful to the doctrines of the early Church. In another work, the *Lectures on Justification* (1838), Newman applied his Anglican method of the *via media*[3] to resolve the Reformation debate between Protestant and Catholic theologies.[4] However, that approach for ascertaining Newman's ecumenical contribution is destined to frustration, partly because he rejected his argument of the *via media* by 1839, but more importantly because these works do not address the philosophical questions of assent and belief that provide the best vantage point for appreciating his contribution to ecumenical dialogue.

A second approach might be to consider Newman's personality as conducive (or not) for inspiring interreligious dialogue by examining his significance both for the Anglican Church and the Catholic Church.[5] That approach is more promising because of his conversion experience and also because of the leadership that he provided to both communions in the nineteenth century, as unofficial leader of the Oxford Movement in the 1830s and as the inspiring focus of liberal Catholics in the two decades preceding the declaration of infallibility in 1870. Such a study would explore, for example, his controversial spirit, his unashamed bigotry against Catholicism as an Anglican, and his apparently unflinching confidence in Catholicism after his conversion as exemplified in his view of the disjunction between Catholicism and atheism.[6] However, because Newman's explicit involvement in ecumenical dialogue was minimal, this more historical approach could offer only a rhetorical, personalistic stimulus for interreligious inquiry today.

A third approach, and the most promising of all, is to extract from Newman's religious epistemology some guidance for the process of interreligious dialogue. The advantage of such an approach is that it deals with Newman's major works in philosophy and theology to gain insights that transcend his personality quirks and cultural biases. Adopting this approach, I argue that his religious epistemology can illumine the process of ecumenical dialogue among the Christian denominations and interreligious dialogue among the world churches. I combine the terms ecumenical dialogue and interreligious dialogue to emphasize that Newman's religious epistemology illumines the *process* of interpretation and understanding that underlies each of them.

Newman's theory of religious assent remained substantially the same throughout his theological and philosophical writings. He established the basis of his theory in the theological thought of the *Oxford University Sermons* (1826-43),[7] preached as a young Anglican vicar, and he presented its final crafting in the philosophical thought of the *Grammar of Assent* (1870),[8] written as a Catholic priest in advanced years. His famous conversion in 1845 represented how his theory could be implemented concretely. My argument is that there is an ethical commitment to ecumenical dialogue in Newman's theory of religious assent. There are three stages in my essay. With regard to Newman's epistemology (part 1) I explain the significance of *Love safeguarding Faith* as a religious metaphor for his theory of assent. Then, I argue that the point of his metaphor is to highlight the role of *ethical commitment in assent* (part 2), clearly exemplified in his own conversion. With regard to Newman's theology I show that his ethical commitment in assent illumines the meaning of *ecumenical dialogue* today (part 3) by integrating his theories of education and doctrinal development with his religious epistemology. By examining the metaphor of love safeguarding faith from the perspective of ethical commitment I suggest that Newman's theory of religious assent illumines the process of dialogue today, thereby contributing to our Convention's theme, "Descendants of Abraham: Judaism, Christianity, Islam."

LOVE SAFEGUARDING FAITH

Newman had two major conversion experiences. As a youth of fifteen, his first conversion was deeply emotional. Impressed by Calvinistic and the Evangelical writings, his lack of religious convictions yielded to an affective awareness of divine presence. This conversion led him to Anglican Orders in 1822, and he never lost this emotional sense of divine presence in his life. But his second conversion, to Catholicism nearly thirty years later in 1845, was much more rational. That was clearly evident in the argument of *An Essay on the Development of Christian Doctrine*,[9] never completed owing to his conversion. These two conversion experiences displayed an entwining of emotion and reason that personalized the interaction between subjectivity and objectivity in his thought, ultimately presented as ethical commitment in assent in his *Grammar of Assent* (1870).

Newman addressed the complexity of this interaction by using a metaphor, "love safeguarding faith," in a sermon preached at St. Mary's, Oxford in 1839, "Love the Safeguard of Faith against Superstition" (*Sermons*, pp. 222-50). This metaphor is replete with meaning specifically to avoid the nineteenth century exaggerations of romanticism and rationalism in religious belief.[10] Romanticism, Newman argues, tends to encourage "a religion . . . of sacred scenes and pious sentiment" (*Grammar*, p. 56) while in rationalism "love was cold" (*Sermons*, p. 197). In contrast, Newman argues that love is the "illuminating principle of true faith" (*Sermons*, p. 234). Faith requires an act of the intellect, but it cannot be reduced to objective reasoning alone: faith "is itself an intellectual act, and it takes its character from the moral state of the agent" (*Sermons*, pp. 249-250). In other words, faith engages objectivity and subjectivity, intellectual reasoning and moral disposition: "Right Faith is an intellectual act, done in a certain moral disposition" (*Sermons*, p. 239). In this integration of objectivity and subjectivity Newman provides a valuable contribution to the process of ecumenical dialogue.[11]

For Newman, this moral disposition of love as an "illuminating principle" includes divine grace, "the Light of heaven which animates and guides [faith]" (*Sermons*, p. 249). Because the light of love illumines faith, he poetically describes faith as "a moving forward in the twilight" (*Sermons*, p. 249). Previously, in 1833 while sailing in the Mediterranean on his return from Italy, he expressed even more eloquently the same insight of love illuminating faith in the renowned metaphor: "Lead, Kindly Light, amid the encircling gloom."[12]

Here Newman is arguing that love (as moral disposition) is the safeguard of faith (as intellectual reasoning). However, to interpret "love" as moral disposition alone opens his account of faith to the charge of relativism. The Canadian philosopher Jay Newman makes this association between love and moral disposition (or virtue) in Newman's thought to argue that the thesis, love (rather than reason) being the safeguard of faith, is false. Jay Newman contends that the thesis reveals an anti-intellectualism in Newman's attempted response to rationalism.[13] Unfortunately, Jay Newman fails to notice that Newman's language of love safeguarding faith is metaphorical, a characteristic literary device in his writings. My subsequent analysis of Newman's use of the word "love" suggests that his view is neither relativist nor anti-intellectual. That is, Newman did not reduce the meaning of "love" to moral disposition alone (relativism), nor did he use it to undermine the role of reason (anti-intellectualism).

Several years prior to this sermon on love and faith Newman openly eschewed relativism. In one of the *Parochial and Plain Sermons* in 1835 at St. Mary's he recognized the danger of "making the test of our being religious, to consist in our having what is called a spiritual state of heart, to the comparative neglect of the Object from which it must arise" (*PS*, II, p. 154).[14] Similarly, his sermon on love and faith in 1839 was intended not to reduce religious belief to moral disposition alone (relativism) but to promote the interaction between subjectivity and objectivity. This interaction between love (which he also called devotion) and faith appears explicitly in his letter to the Reverend E. B. Pusey in 1865: "That distinction between faith and devotion on which I am insisting . . . is like the distinction between objective and subjective truth."[15] Newman understood love as safeguarding faith metaphorically in order to establish a sound interaction between subjectivity and objectivity in religious belief.

In the *Grammar* it is clear that the interaction is neither relativist not anti-intellectual: this is apparent in his explanation of ethical commitment in assent.

ETHICAL COMMITMENT IN ASSENT

In the 1871 edition of the Oxford sermons Newman clarifies the meaning of love safeguarding faith ("we *believe* because we *love*") in a footnote: "This means, not love precisely, but the virtue of religiousness, under which may be said to fall the *pia affectio*, or *voluntas credendi*" (*Sermons*, p. 236, n.4). This terminology appeared earlier in a theological paper written by Newman in 1853: "A pia affectio, or voluntas credendi" means "determining and commanding the intellect to believe" (*Papers*, p. 37).[16] Newman never explains the meaning of these terms but his argument on conscience and assent in the *Grammar* is instructive to understand them, and thereby to appreciate the "depth of meaning" (*Grammar*, p. 316) in using the metaphor of love safeguarding faith. This metaphor portrays the epistemological significance of ethical commitment in assent.

First, Newman's explanation of conscience illumines the meaning of "love" as the "virtue of religiousness." He explains that "conscience . . . is a moral sense, and a sense of duty" (*Grammar*, p. 105). He describes the "sense of duty" as "the creative principle of religion" being "a connecting principle between the creature and his Creator" (*Grammar*, pp. 110, 117). This means that there is a *subjective obligation* with religious significance (the sense of duty as the creative principle of religion) to embrace what reason discerns as ethically right (the moral sense). Similarly, love as the "virtue of religiousness" can be construed as the *subjective obligation* with religious significance to embrace what reason discerns as sufficient for belief.

Second, Newman's explanation of assent explains the meaning of this *subjective obligation* and therefore illumines the meaning of "love" as "commanding the intellect to believe." Some Newman commentators refer to this "commanding" as indicative of a volitionist account of belief.[17] However, a stronger case has been made for interpreting this "commanding" as the obligation of the agent to embrace what reason discerns as sufficient for assent.[18] Hence Newman describes the assent of religious certitude as "the perception of a truth" (*Grammar*, p. 197). Therefore, the meaning of "commanding the intellect to believe" (as the *pia affectio*, or *voluntas credendi*) can be interpreted as the ethical responsibility upon the agent to recognize what reason presents as sufficient for assent—that is, ethical commitment in assent. Further evidence for the legitimacy of this interpretation appears in the same theological paper of 1853 when Newman explains that the "pia affectio" must not act (command) "without a sufficient ratio volendi" (*Papers*, p. 38). Clearly, the emphasis here is upon what reason presents as sufficient for assent (belief).

Therefore, "commanding the intellect to believe" does not entail an act of will primarily. Rather, the command indicates the *subjective obligation* to accept what reason presents as sufficient for belief, just as the sense of duty in conscience indicates the *subjective obligation* to embrace what reason discerns as ethically right. In each case Newman was concerned to highlight the interaction of subjectivity and objectivity: the subjectivity of the agent's responsibility to follow reason, the objectivity of using reason to interpret the data. In each case Newman eschews relativism (by avoiding a resort to will alone) and anti-intellectualism (by defending the role of reason). His metaphor of love safeguarding faith, then, has epistemological significance the nuance of which took a lifetime to unveil.

One of the most recognized statements of this interaction between subjectivity and objectivity in assent appears in his final work on religious epistemology in 1870: "We judge for ourselves, by our own lights, and on our own principles; and our criterion of truth is not so much the manipulation of propositions, as the intellectual and moral character of the person maintaining them" (*Grammar*, p. 302). His point is not to argue that character is the criterion of truth (that is the relativist trap of Romanticism that he wanted to circumvent) but that the intellectual perception of assent requires ethical commitment (that is his response to "the manipulation of propositions" that characterized rationalism). The moral and intellectual dimensions of religious perception are thus inseparable: "We rightly lean upon ourselves, directing ourselves by our own moral or intellectual judgment, not by our skill in argumentation" (*Grammar*, p. 342).

Assent, therefore, is an intellectual perception of truth that requires ethical commitment. Therefore, the "depth of meaning" in his metaphor of love safeguarding faith is to convey the radical importance of ethical commitment in assent. And that ethical comment constitutes an obligation (a sense of duty) to embrace what reason presents as sufficient for belief. The legitimacy of this interpretation is most apparent in Newman's description of the assent of certitude: "Certitude is not a passive impression made upon the mind from without, by argumentative compulsion, but . . . an active recognition of propositions as true, such as it is the duty of each individual himself to exercise at the bidding of reason, and, when reason forbids, to withhold" (*Grammar*, pp. 344-5).

Ethical commitment in assent, therefore, entails "an active recognition" that arises from the obligation to accept what reason presents as sufficient. He describes that recognition in his Dublin university discourses (1852) as the capacity "to reach out towards truth, and to grasp it" (*Idea*, p. 126).[19] This combination of rational inquiry with ethical obligation is precisely the same as that used by Newman to explain conscience as a moral sense and a sense of duty. The epistemology of assent is the same as that of conscience.[20] Hence, Newman's metaphor of love safeguarding faith impacts as much upon the judgment of assent as upon the judgment of conscience, emphasizing the role of ethical commitment in each.

It was the ethical commitment to assent that inspired Newman's conversion to Catholicism. Arguably, then, that ethical commitment in assent, with its intellectual, moral, and religious dimensions, anticipated Bernard Lonergan's theory of intellectual, moral, and religious conversion to show that "objectivity is reached through the self-transcendence of the concrete existing subject."[21] Newman felt deeply the *subjective obligation* (as bearing profound religious significance in the sense of a vocation) to embrace what his reason discerned as sufficient for turning to the objective truth-claims of Catholicism. His metaphor of love safeguarding faith inspired him in 1845 to a new ethical commitment in assent: his conversion. His metaphor anticipated the integration of subjectivity and objectivity in his conversion experience. That integration he expressed imaginatively in an earlier sermon with another metaphor, the heart: "When men change their religious opinions really and truly, it is not merely their opinions that they change, but their hearts" (*PS*, VIII, p. 225). Playing on this metaphor of the heart, the Louvain theologian Terrence Merrigan imaginatively depicts "the interaction of intellection and duty" in Newman's religious epistemology in the title of his book, *Clear Heads and Holy Hearts*.[22] It was this ethical commitment in assent (Merrigan's interaction of intellection and duty) that inspired Newman's conversion. Therefore, it is mistaken to interpret his conversion as indebted to a particular doctrine. That, for example, is the central claim in a recent biography of Newman's spiritual pilgrimage from Evangelicalism to Anglicanism and then to Catholicism (until 1852). There, Michael Ffinch, an English poet and broadcaster, claims that a growing devotion to the real presence in the Eucharist led to Newman's conversion.[23] That view

is mistaken. Rather, it is the profound understanding of ethical commitment in assent, pervading all of Newman's doctrinal inquiries, that offers
the most coherent account of his conversion.

Being sensitive to Newman's highly imaginative use of metaphor
provides insight into the drama of his conversion and the intricacy of his
religious epistemology. In this case, the metaphor of the heart became for
Newman the *leitmotif* of his intellectual, moral, and spiritual life. Just as
he anticipated the metaphor of love safeguarding faith with that of "Lead,
Kindly Light" as an Anglican, in old age as a Catholic he expanded that
metaphor in his cardinalate coat of arms: "heart speaks to heart"—*cor ad
cor loquitur*. The metaphor of love safeguarding faith illumined the
meaning of ethical commitment in assent as integrating subjectivity and
objectivity. And that integration, depicted in the metaphor of the heart,
provides a moral and intellectual challenge for interreligious dialogue
today—*cor ad cor loquitur*.

ECUMENICAL DIALOGUE

Newman's metaphor of love safeguarding faith, as illustrative of
ethical commitment in assent, illumines the ethical commitment to ecumenical dialogue that is implied in his religious epistemology. To the extent
that ecumenism seeks greater recognition of shared belief among the
churches involved, Newman's theory of assent clarifies the role of ethical
commitment in interreligious dialogue.[24] Ethical commitment in assent
(involving the integration of subjectivity and objectivity) implies that the
fundamental process of ecumenical and interreligious dialogue requires
ongoing interpretation and understanding. Hence, ecumenism today involves a process of graduality that encourages the contributing churches
to increase their mutual commitment through interim stages of assent and
ensuing praxis.[25] That is, the process of ecumenical dialogue necessitates
a subjective commitment to perceptive learning as the *sine qua non* for
objective assent about shared belief. Newman addressed these concerns
in his theories of liberal education (the process of perceptive learning) and
doctrinal development (the process of ascertaining new assents about
shared belief), each crafted by his understanding of ethical commitment
in assent.

Ecumenical progress requires a form of education among the contributing churches that transcends the polite acknowledgement of differing
beliefs. Education, Newman argued, implies "a digestion of what we

receive" (*Idea*, p. 134). This involves a "process of enlightenment or enlargement of mind" (*Idea*, p. 130) that means "making the objects of our knowledge subjectively our own" (*Idea*, p. 134).[26] Here, in Newman's discourses (1852) for the new Catholic university at Dublin, the integration of subjectivity and objectivity illustrated his understanding of ethical commitment in assent. A decade earlier, in a sermon preached in 1841, Newman emphasized the role of ethical commitment that should characterize this process of education by employing another metaphor, that of living knowledge: "It is not the mere addition to our knowledge which is the enlargement, but . . . the movement onwards, of that moral centre, . . . It is . . . *living knowledge*" (*Sermons*, p. 287, emphasis added). Therefore, the role of education in ecumenical progress requires a moral involvement on the part of the contributors with the beliefs of the different churches, an ethical commitment in assent that engages the whole person in "living knowledge"—*cor ad cor loquitur*.

Four years later, in 1845, Newman adapted this metaphor of living knowledge to articulate his theory of doctrinal development. He explains how ideas develop in this way: "And the more claim an idea has to be considered *living*, the more various will be its aspects; . . . mutually connected and growing out of one another" (*Development*, p. 56, emphasis added). Ecumenism cannot advance without understanding how religious doctrine develops. To illumine that development Newman argues that doctrine is *living* because it is not merely a statement of propositional truth. Rather, doctrine, like liberal knowledge, integrates subjectivity and objectivity, engaging our "moral centre" as ethical commitment in assent. Just as love safeguarding faith is under the influence of grace, so this highly personal component of doctrinal development is under the guidance of God's grace in divine providence.[27] Interreligious dialogue, then, will flourish when doctrines are open to new interpretation and meaning whose growth is nourished by incorporating fresh insights, not stultified by ecclesial isolation. Newman observes astutely that the development of doctrine leads to "new meaning and direction, . . . It grows when it incorporates, and its identity is found, not in isolation, but in continuity" (*Development*, p. 39). He recognized that even heresy, which he placed outside authentic Christian discourse, can provoke real development. In a recent study of Newman on heresy, the English theologian Stephen Thomas insightfully shows that in allowing a dialogue between heresy and orthodoxy Newman recognized that the latter can enhance ecclesial understanding, doctrinal orthodoxy, and theological language.[28]

In this process of discerning doctrinal development Newman strongly emphasized the communal role of the ecclesial community. In his theological essay "On Consulting the Faithful" (1859) he alluded to the ethical commitment in assent that characterizes the entire community when referring to the "Consent of the faithful" as the *"conscience de l'Eglise"*—the conscience of the Church.[29] And, as if to strengthen the communal character of this ethical commitment in assent that generates doctrinal development, in 1871 he again resorted to his metaphor of *living knowledge*: "The voice . . . of the whole Church diffusive," including "the living tradition of the faithful," will generate "a momentous addition to the faith."[30] This appeal to communal discernment represents a theological development of his educational ideal that in the "acquisition of truth . . . the process is one of not only many stages, but of many minds" (*Idea*, 474). For Newman, this *process* of acquiring truth implies the corollary of maintaining a healthy openness to theological and doctrinal pluralism.[31] Of course, different understandings of communal discernment will yield varying degrees of pluralism in ecumenical dialogue. In this regard, the theologian George A. Lindbeck distinguishes between a sense of community that is constructed from below, building to higher organizational levels, and a sense of community that proceeds from top to bottom, being more hierarchical and juridical.[32] In either case, however, a plurality of doctrinal belief that celebrates a legitimate diversity in whatever unity can be achieved will prevail as characteristic of ecumenical dialogue.[33]

Conclusion

Newman's life-growing view of ethical commitment in assent crafted his theories of liberal education and doctrinal development, which, taken together, contribute to ecumenism today by illumining the integration of subjectivity and objectivity in interreligious dialogue. That integration involves a subjective commitment to perceptive learning as the *sine qua non* for objective assent about shared belief. His theory of assent presented a grammar for a legitimate discourse to justify belief. And I contend that his theory implicitly contains a grammar for interreligious discourse to advance ecumenism. In his religious epistemology he understood that human language is incapable of adequately expressing divine mystery: "Almighty God has condescended to speak to us so far as human thought and language will admit, by approximations" (*Sermons*, p. 269). He specifically employed the metaphor of love safeguarding faith to address this complexity of language whose human constructs in doctrine unavoidably compound the difficulty of grasping the mystery of divine revelation. His metaphor depicted the importance of ethical commitment in assent to engage each individual and ecclesial community as subjectively as possible in the historical quest of an increasingly objective language for doctrinal agreement. In this process of interreligious dialogue the integration of subjectivity and objectivity constituted his creative originality, challenging us today to develop doctrine for ecumenical assent. Newman's genius was to recognize that our confusion of language necessarily engages us in "a sort of night battle" where we try to "understand each other's meaning" (*Sermons*, p. 201).

NOTES

[1]John Henry Newman, *Apologia Pro Vita Sua*, 1864, edited, introduction and notes by M. J. Svaglic (Oxford: Clarendon Press, 1967), noted as *Apologia*; p. 54.

[2]John Henry Newman, *Lectures on the Prophetical Office of the Church* (Oxford: Rivingtons, 1837), later published as the first of two volumes with a Catholic preface in 1877, *The Via Media of the Anglican Church*, 2 vols. (London: Longman and Green, 1891).

[3]John Henry Newman, *Lectures on the Doctrine of Justification* (London: Rivingtons, 1874). Ian Ker, Newman's recent Catholic biographer, describes this a "a pioneering classic of 'ecumenical' theology" (*John Henry Newman: A Biography* [Oxford: Clarendon Press, 1988], p. 157). Sheridan Gilley, Newman's recent Anglican biographer, contends that the *Lectures on Justification* were Newman's greatest attempt at deploying the *via media* to a particular theological subject, (*Newman and His Age* [London: Darton, Longman, and Todd, 1990], p. 165).

[4]Justification remains a crucial stumbling block for Catholicism today, either as a doctrine (Joseph Ratzinger, "Luther und die Enheit der Kirchen. Fragen an Joseph Kardinal Ratzinger," *Internationale Katholische Zeitschrift* 12 [1983]: pp. 568-82), or as a hermeneutical principle for christian faith (Walter Kasper, "Basic Consensus and Church Fellowship," in, *In Search of Christian Unity*, ed. Joseph A. Burgess [Minneapolis: Fortress Press, 1991], p. 29). For a detailed study see, *The Condemnation of the Reformation Era. Do They still Divide?*, ed. Karl Lehmann and Wolfhart Pannenberg (Minneapolis: Fortress Press, 1989).

[5]Fine examples of this sort of study are, Henry Chadwick, "Newman's Significance for the Anglican Church," in, *Newman: A Man for Our Time*, ed. David Brown (Harrisburg, PA: Morehouse Publishing, 1990), pp. 52-74, and Eric D'Arcy, "Newman's Significance for the Roman Catholic Church," ibid., pp. 75-97.

[6]In 1860 he wrote to his brother Francis, "In truth, I think that *logically* there is *no* middle point *between* Catholicism and Atheism" (John Henry Newman, *Letters and Diaries*, ed. Charles Stephen Dessain, vol. XIX [London: Nelson, 1969], p. 286). For a fascinating study of the intellectual and psychological features in Newman that contribute to this attitude, see Edward E. Kelly, "Atheism or Catholicism: Stark Disjunction from Complex Newman," in *Newman the Theologian*, ed. Michael E. Allsopp and Ronald R. Burke (Hamden, CT: Garland Publishing, 1992), forthcoming.

[7]*Newman's University Sermons. Fifteen Sermons Preached before the University of Oxford 1826-43* (3rd. edition, 1871), introductions by D. M. MacKinnon and J. D. Holmes (London: S.P.C.K., 1970), noted as *Sermons*.

[8]John Henry Newman, *An Essay in Aid of a Grammar of Assent*, edited with notes and introduction by I. T. Ker (Oxford: Clarendon Press, 1985), noted as *Grammar*.

[9]John Henry Newman, *An Essay on the Development of Christian Doctrine*, foreword by Ian Ker (Notre Dame, IN: University of Notre Dame Press, 1989), p. x, noted as *Development*.

[10]Ian Ker also understands this sermon as standing in opposition to romanticism and rationalism (*John Henry Newman: A Biography*, p. 262).

[11]On the importance of the integration of objectivity and subjectivity for ecumenical dialogue, see Walter Kasper, "Basic Consensus and Church Fellowship," p. 26.

[12]John Henry Newman, "The Pillar of the Cloud," *Verses on Various Occasions* (London: Burns and Oates, 1883), p. 152.

[13]Jay Newman, "Newman on Love as the Safeguard of Faith," *Scottish Journal of Theology* 32 (1979): pp. 139, 144-45.

[14]John Henry Newman, *Parochial and Plain Sermons*, from 1834 (London: Longmans, Green, and Co., 1891), eight volumes, noted as *PS*.

[15]John Henry Newman, "A Letter Addressed to the Rev. E. B. Pusey, D.D., on Occasion of his Eirenicon" (1865), in *Certain Difficulties Felt by Anglicans in Catholic Teaching*, vol. II (London: Longmans, Green, and Co., 1898), pp. 27-28.

[16]*The Theological Papers of John Henry Newman on Faith and Certainty*, ed. Hugo M. de Achaval and J. Derek Holmes (Oxford: Clarendon Press, 1976), noted as *Papers*. Despite this technical language here, Newman's religious epistemology was quite unscholastic in its language and method. In a recent work Robert Pattison mistakenly claims that Newman's approach was mainly that of scholasticism (*The Great Dissent: John Henry Newman and the Liberal Heresy* [Oxford: Clarendon Press, 1991], pp. 129, 158).

[17]David Pailin, *The Way to Faith* (London: Epworth Press, 1969), pp. 103, 168, 170, 177; W. R. Fey, *Faith and Doubt* (Shepherdstown, W.VA: Patmos Press, 1976), pp. 105, 114, 120; and Louis Pojman, *Religious Belief and the Will* (New York: Routledge and Kegan Paul, 1986), p. 86.

[18]J.-H. Walgrave, *Newman. The Theologian* (London: Chapman, 1960), p. 235; M. Jamie Ferreira, *Doubt and Religious Commitment. The Role of the Will in Newman's Thought* (Oxford: Clarendon Press, 1980), p. 23; Ian Ker, *John Henry Newman: A Biography*, p. 648; and Gerard Magill, "Imaginative Moral Discernment: Newman on the Tension between Reason and Religion," *The Heythrop Journal* XXXII (1991): pp. 499-504.

[19]John Henry Newman, *The Idea of a University, Defined and Illustrated* (1873), edited with introduction and notes by I. T. Ker (Oxford: Clarendon Press, 1976), noted as *Idea*.

[20]Gerard Magill, "The Living Mind: Newman on Assent and Dissent," in *Discourse and Context: An Interdisciplinary Study of John Henry Newman*, ed. Gerard Magill (Carbondale, IL: Southern Illinois University Press, 1993), pp. 253-259.

[21]Bernard Lonergan, *Method in Theology* (London: Darton, Longman, and Todd, 1973), pp. 217, 338.

[22]Terrence Merrigan, *Clear Heads and Holy Hearts: The Religious and Theological Ideal of John Henry Newman* (Louvain: Peeters Press, 1991), also see p. 247. This title "clear heads and holy hearts" is a citation from John Henry Newman, *The VIA MEDIA of the Anglican Church*, ed. H. D. Weidner (Oxford: Clarendon Press, 1990), p. lxxv.

[23]Michael Ffinch, *Newman: Towards the Second Spring* (San Francisco: Ignatius Press, 1991), pp. x, 113, 135-36.

[24]George A. Lindbeck reiterates the importance of both commitment and assent (recognizing agreements in faith, in the proclamation of the word and celebration of the sacraments) for ecumenical dialogue as "covenantal engagement" ("Episcopacy and the Unification of the Churches: Two Approaches," in *Promoting Unity*, ed. H. George Anderson and James R. Crumley [Minneapolis: Augsburg Press, 1989], p. 56).

[25]Michael Kinnamon, *Truth and Community. Diversity and its Limits in the Ecumenical Movement* (Grand Rapids, Michigan: Eerdmans Publishing, 1988), p. 86, and William G. Rusch, *Ecumenism-A Movement Toward Church Unity* (Philadelphia: Fortress Press, 1985), pp. 72, 117, 128.

[26]This anticipates his explanation of real assent in 1870, see *Grammar*, pp. 75-88.

[27]For an excellent account of Newman's two views of providence in the two realms of nature and the Church, especially with regard to doctrinal development under the guidance of the Holy Spirit, see L. O. Frappell, "John Henry Newman: History and the Two Systems of Providence," *The Journal of Religious History* 15 (1989): pp. 470-87, at 477-79.

[28]Stephen Thomas, *Newman and Heresy: The Anglican Years* (New York: Cambridge University Press, 1991), pp. 228-36.

[29]John Henry Newman, *On Consulting the Faithful in Matters of Doctrine*, edited with an introduction by John Coulson (London: Chapman, 1961), p. 73.

[30]*The Letters and Diaries of John Henry Newman*, vol. XXV, ed. Charles Stephen Dessain and Thomas Gornall (Oxford: Clarendon Press, 1973), p. 284.

[31]I have studied the theological significance of Newman's openness to pluralism in "Newman on Liberal Education and Moral Pluralism," *Scottish Journal of Theology* 45 (1992): pp. 45-64, at pp. 55-64. Also, see the essays in Gerard Magill, ed., *Discourse and Context: An Interdisciplinary Study of John Henry Newman* (Carbondale, IL: Southern Illinois University Press, 1993).

[32]George A. Lindbeck, "Episcopacy and the Unification of the Churches: Two Approaches," p. 58.

[33]Walter Kasper, "Basic Consensus and Church Fellowship," pp. 24, 28, 37. Here Kasper is developing the thought of Yves Congar, *Diversity and Communion* (Mystic, CT: Twenty-third Publications, 1985) and Oscar Cullmann, *Unity Through Diversity* (Philadelphia: Fortress Press, 1988).

WEIGHING THE ALTERNATIVES:
POSSIBLE FUTURES FOR THE CHURCH

Joseph G. Ramisch

For some time now, it has seemed that careful and critical dialogue about the church of the West and the kind of future it may have is an urgent task facing contemporary theology. For such dialogue, some of the directions theology has recently taken are more promising than others, and the recently emerging tendencies in critical theology seem of particular value here. Theological discussions about the church can benefit greatly from the perspectives of critical social theory, in addition to the insights generally of the social sciences. What emerges from such a consideration is not so much a set of blueprints for the church of the future as a clarification of the frameworks theologians use to make sense of the issues.

As one contribution to that discussion, this paper examines the positions of two theologians whose work is much influenced by critical theory, and the implications of their positions for the future of the church. The theological positions developed by Charles Davis and Gregory Baum share a wide-ranging appropriation of many modern thinkers and schools of thought, but in particular reflect the influence of the critical theory of the Frankfurt School—and in Davis's case, its later exponents such as Jürgen Habermas.[1] Their positions, while quite similar in some respects, differ markedly with respect to the future of the church. Both agree on the necessity for a critical theology which would (among other things) use the liberating potential of the tradition to critique the dehumanizing tendencies within both the church and society. Such a critique depends upon theology's being in dialogue with both the contemporary situation and also with other religious traditions. Each theologian, however, presents a different vision of how such a critical dialogue might reshape the church.

INITIAL DIALOGUE ON THE CHURCH

The work of Davis and Baum taken together constitutes some of the most important contributions in English applying critical social theory to theological discourse. The dialogue between the two is now more than a quarter of a century old, going back as it does to the publication of Davis's *A Question of Conscience*,[2] to which Baum so thoroughly and ably responded in his *The Credibility of the Church Today*.[3] In that response, Baum himself stated that while he and Davis agree in many of their criticisms of the church, he comes to a "totally different interpretation" of what to do about it.[4]

That statement of Baum's indicates clearly how their positions differ, even today after so much development in their respective thoughts. They agree on the nature of the problems attending the church, but differ as to the solutions. Furthermore, while it is obvious that in the late 1960s both were speaking directly about the Roman Catholic Church, it becomes apparent in their subsequent writings that most of their reflection on the church deals with the Christian churches in a much wider sense. Their prescriptions and proscriptions can therefore be extended much more broadly to many if not most organized communities of Christian believers.

By 1967, Davis had basically concluded that the church was not able to change sufficiently or radically, and he announced his decision to abandon it. The church was so fundamentally static and hierarchical, he thought, that institutional churches would necessarily disintegrate over time, eventually to be replaced by other social forms expressive of new understandings of life and new patterns of communicative action.

For Baum, there was ample evidence—and still is—that the church does have the power to change and reform itself. He continues to describe himself as "hopeful" and "cheerful" about the church's prospects.[5] Their different perspectives no doubt reflect their different experiences throughout their careers. It is worth noting that as they have lived through the past quarter of a century in continuing dialogue with each other and with the changing churches and world around them, their positions now are less sharply opposed. Still, the differences remain and continue to be significant, as the concluding part of this paper will argue.

Toward the end of his *The Credibility of the Church Today*, Baum gives his concrete vision of the church of the future: it will become more like a movement that is outer-oriented, open to all the world, in solidarity with all who suffer, serving by reconciling.[6] People will belong to this movement "in different ways and in different degrees,"[7] and hierarchical authority will eventually be replaced by the authority of consensus.[8]

A more recent expression of that vision occurs at the end of *Faith That Transforms*, in his response to the other essays in that Festschrift.

There Baum speaks of

> networks of Christian groups and individual Christians for whom Jesus
> Christ is the transformer of culture and society. . . . It is from these
> Christians, a radical minority, that a new movement in the church has
> gone forth, a movement that has come to influence the ecclesiastical
> leadership.[9]

Baum feels part of that movement and does his theology within its context,
reflecting its beliefs and values as his own.[10]

GREGORY BAUM

A closer examination of the frameworks of each theologian's work,
and the significance of critical social theory within it, should clarify the
nature of their differences. Baum has been writing theology about and in
the service of the church and the ecumenical movement for more than
thirty years. He has dealt with sociology and critical theory as part of his
work for the past twenty years. The most notable shift in his work
occurred after two years at the New School for Social Research in New
York spent reading sociology. Following that, Baum began a campaign
to bring the tradition of critical sociology into theology. One of the first
major fruits of that effort was his book *Religion and Alienation: A
Theological Reading of Sociology*,[11] in which he states that religion
always has political implications; "it is never socially neutral." He argues
that "religious symbols are inevitably a hidden political language."[12] A
twenty-page bibliography of his books, articles, and reviews from the
1970s and 1980s shows that most of them deal with the application of
critical theological reflection to current social and ethical issues.[13]

As for the impact of critical theory on his work, he speaks of that
in an essay entitled "Humanistic Sociology: Scientific and Critical," where
he states:

> The claim of value-neutrality made by social science has removed
> ethics from the public debate of social policies. A humanistic, critical
> social science would give ethical reflection a recognized standing in
> social and political policy discussions. This value-oriented understand-
> ing of social science was my point of entry into the study of the
> Frankfurt School. I was greatly impressed by critical theory's critique
> of domination, by its analysis of the political relevance of culture, and
> by its insistence on an emancipatory commitment in the social sciences.
> I was also impressed by the dialectical critique of the Enlighten-

ment.[14]

Still, Baum's use of critical theory is not in itself uncritical. In that same essay on "humanistic sociology," he says:

> While I have great sympathy for critical theory, I feel that its retrieval of the ethical dimension is too unhistorical, too rational, too indifferent to the religious sources of the human quest for value and meaning. I am persuaded therefore that a humanistic sociology that is both scientific and emancipatory remains incomplete as long as the ethical dimension and the understanding of liberation are not rooted in a religious tradition.[15]

These statements of Baum's point to an aspect of his work that seems important for an overall assessment of his contribution. In the last sentence of the quotation above, he talks about the need to be "rooted in a religious tradition." Does it matter which religious tradition? What would one's criterion of selection be? Baum's tremendous contributions to ecumenical dialogue over his lifetime leave little doubt about the value he attaches to pluralism and dialogue. Still, he is a Christian theologian, and therefore it is invariably the Christian religious tradition to which he turns for his fundamental values, specifically the Roman Catholic tradition; even more specifically, the papal social teachings of the past one hundred years. It seems an odd position for a radical (not a liberal), critical theologian to be in, the position of being a presenter and defender of papal teaching. Baum's task has not always been an easy one, or one widely appreciated, but he has been largely successful at it, and his own theological values emerge clearly in the way he presents and interprets papal teaching.

For Baum, what is most authentic in the church, where it is most truly church, is in its struggle for justice. But that is because the struggle for justice is where God is most vitally present in the world, empowering all who work in solidarity with the suffering.[16] Liberation theology and the church's "preferential option for the poor" are further supported by the social and economic critiques of papal encyclicals and the pastoral letters of Canadian and United States bishops, who are in the tradition of the biblical prophets. As the prophets met resistance, so too does the "explosion of solidarity" in the church divide "people of good will," and evoke "strong resistance in the churches."[17] Clearly the church is not yet all it could be and should be for Baum. In fact, he does not hesitate to call some of its hierarchical decisions "mean-spirited and devious."[18]

His theological hermeneutics deserves some comment at this point. Baum argued forcefully in *Religion and Alienation* (following Karl

Mannheim's usage) that religion can be both *ideological* (supportive of the status quo) and *utopian* (that is, critical, prophetic, subversive or transformative).[19] As Baum says, religion is capable of generating its own critique,[20] and it is precisely the task of critical theology to do so. Hence Baum uses the Hebrew prophetic tradition, and elements drawn from papal social teaching, to reinterpret Christianity, to reinterpret Christian symbols and myths, and to reorient and redirect Christian praxis. In effect, Baum makes a theological value judgment; he has a canon within the canon, and uses some elements from the tradition to criticize other aspects of the tradition. What then are the criteria for and limits to this process? How far can the process go? What is the relationship between critical praxis and the symbols of the Christian tradition? Are there two kinds (or many kinds) of critical, humanizing praxis: Christian and non-Christian?

Baum himself has said that early in his work he became convinced "that there was not much difference between Christians and non-Christians," but he puzzled over what that meant for the church's unique mediating role.[21] It was from Karl Rahner that he learned how to reconcile "the universality of divine grace and the uniqueness of Christ and the Christian church." The divine power available to all throughout the world "has become visibly, fully, and definitively manifest in the person of Jesus Christ."[22] Baum would seem to be saying here that Christian symbols—and praxis?—are directly connected to, or expressive of, the mysterious depths of God's presence in our lives, our beings.

If critical praxis in the form of commitment to liberation is truly *prior* to theory or theology, should not the possibility of going beyond Christian symbols or myths altogether be considered? In what sense are *Christian* notions of liberation prior to others, or more basic than they? Is it simply a matter of faith or tradition that Christian models of liberation are considered more adequate than others? Critical praxis can be inspired or directed by the prophetic, liberating elements in the Christian tradition, but should it be bound by them? These questions seem related to ones about how flexible a religious symbol system can be: how does a religious tradition grow, develop, or change, and what are the limits—if any—to that growth? When does it become something else?

The issue at stake here may be elucidated by a comparison between theology and sociology, that is, between Baum's critical theology and his discussion of the need for a critical sociology. With respect to critical sociology, he talks about the importance of an ethical commitment on the part of the social science researcher:

> That social science and ethical commitment must go in tandem is a thesis that is controversial in most sociology departments. For what this thesis means is that sociological research carried on without an emancipatory commitment will arrive at conclusions that in one way or another strengthen the power of the dominative forces. And if sociology is practiced without respect for the spiritual and its historical sources, its conclusions will contribute to the spiritual empoverishment of the present age. Here engagement precedes science, here engagement is the pre-condition of scientific truth. And here the cultural and political impact of sociological research is one of the norms by which its truth is validated.[23]

Furthermore, ". . . Sociology is grounded in values and in turn promotes values. Science and commitment go hand in hand."[24] Although he does not say so, the question to be raised here is a simple one: do the same critical standards apply to theology as to sociology? What happens when the notion of "critical theology" is substituted here for "sociology" in Baum's texts? Can it not be reasonably argued that theology—and for that matter papal encyclicals as well—need to have their truth validated by their "cultural and political impact?" It is easy for the theologian to criticize the social scientist for insensitivity to "the spiritual and its historical sources." But cannot Baum's language be turned around onto *critical theology* itself, and onto the central symbols of the Christian tradition? Would it not be valid to substitute for "sociological research" in the above text parallel notions more familiar to the theologian? Read, for instance: "The cultural and political impact of theology is one of the norms by which its truth is validated." Or, "The cultural and political impact of the church and its work is one of the norms by which its truth is validated."

CHARLES DAVIS

Davis addresses similar issues at some length, so it is appropriate now to consider his work. In his *Theology and Political Society*, he speaks of the dilemma of critical faith left us by the Enlightenment: "To use external criteria to criticize faith is to subordinate faith to secular reason and thus to destroy it as faith. On the other hand, to refuse reason an independent critique of faith is irrational dogmatism."[25]

The emergence of a modern critical theology following the Enlightenment is one response to this dilemma. Davis also sees the dilemma of modern faith shaped by basic social changes such as the emergence of the bourgeois public sphere. His historical, sociological, and theological analysis of these eighteenth and nineteenth century developments helps us understand the fundamental shifts taking place in theology and the notion of the church at that time. He suggests that "the changing concept of the Church may give the clue to what was happening in theology. The basic criterion for distinguishing critical from pre-critical theology would then be the varying concept of the church."[26] During that period, the conception of the church shifted from its earlier social and legal terms, perhaps where it was seen as an ethical institution, to being seen in mystical terms, as a community embodying a common spiritual life and tradition.[27] Furthermore,

> the change in the church may be related to . . . the emergence of the
> bourgeois public sphere . . . and to . . . the rise of criticism [as] the
> intellectual expression of the rise of the bourgeois class. . . . [W]hat
> happened in the eighteenth and nineteenth centuries was the attempt
> to refashion the church, so that it no longer stood on the side of the
> State as an institution of power, but belonged as a social system to the
> bourgeois public sphere, which was grounded upon the principle of
> freedom and mutual exchange.[28]

But, although "the eighteenth century reconceived the Church, [it] did not succeed in creating a new sociological form in the concrete. The problem still remains with us."[29]

Further twentieth century developments led to the break between orthodoxy and what Davis calls political theology. Davis criticizes pre-political theology—or pre-critical theology—as "orthodoxy," where ortho-*doxy* is contrasted to ortho*praxis*. Orthodoxy, as the term implies, makes doctrine a norm, and implies therefore the priority of theory over practice. Political theology (Baum's "critical theology") reverses that priority in the light of the fundamental shift implied in Marx's critique with its stress on the priority of praxis over theory.

Davis, perhaps more fully and carefully than Baum, discusses the implications of Marxist theory, the critical theory of the Frankfurt School, and habermas's permutations and combinations, at some length in his *Theology and Political Society*,[30] and more recently in his *What is Living, What is Dead in Christianity Today?*[31] In the latter work, political theology takes the form of a pragmatic Christianity, Christianity as a way of life contributing to common action. There Davis begins where he left off in *Theology and Political Society* with a call for theology to take pluralism seriously and open Christianity up to the insights of other traditions.[32] In 1980, he had closed *Theology and Political Society* with a discussion of the "breakdown of the old Christian identity and the emergence of a new identity."[33] What is that new identity, and how new and different can it be?

Davis's answer to that question was that many Christians no longer found membership in a particular Christian church meaningful, but rather saw themselves "as participants with others in a continuous collective process of learning to be Christians."[34] Formal church membership is being replaced by "a network of relationships with others that ignore the boundaries of particular churches."[35] He argues that "basic religious identity . . . is not given by belonging to a particular religious tradition, but by active participation in the present shaping of a universality to be realized in the future."[36]

The position that emerges in Davis's work seems to point in a different direction from what one sees in Baum's theology. As Davis states in *What Is Living, What Is Dead in Christianity Today?*, six years after the previous work,

> What I was pointing to in my remarks on pluralism and new religious identity in *Theology and Political Society* was that the living out of the present situation was breaking apart Christian exclusiveness and transforming the Christian tradition so as to open it to the complementary insights and affirmations of the other major religious traditions. The present social, cultural, and political demands cannot be met from within an exclusively Christian horizon or from the resources of the Christian tradition alone.[37]

> I am not so sure . . . that the corporate, global self-consciousness now struggling to be born will find adequate expression through adapting the existing religious traditions. . . . No doubt there will be continuity as well as discontinuity, but how far present identities and distinctions will be preserved is difficult to determine.[38]

Furthermore,

> one cannot continue to suppose that the Christian religion in its inherited form has some exclusive and final answer to the problems of humankind. It is one element in a complex whole, subject to a dialectical development in a movement towards a world order of a yet unforeseen composition.[39]

Elsewhere, in his *Soft Bodies in a Hard World*, Davis has said:

> Religion itself . . . is relative, changing, dispensable, and not to be
> made an absolute, which would make it an idolatry. This opens the
> way to a religionless Christianity, not in the sense of a Christianity
> without customs, ritual, institutions, or traditions, but a Christianity
> able to change or surrender any of these elements when the ongoing
> presence of the transcendent in history calls for that.[40]

Our response to that call can and should take the form of communicative action—Davis's term borrowed from Habermas—which aims at
"mutual understanding and agreement." Such action-in-relationship where
all participate creates something new, "a genuinely new order," a "genuine community."[41]

> If there is one witness that is needed from Christians today, it is
> the witness of genuine community, which includes genuine individuali-
> ty and freedom. The world is seeking a way out of its politics of
> power, which are leading to annihilation. Unfortunately, the churches
> seem more concerned to preserve the tattered remnants of a past social
> order than to show how to create a new one. They should be preaching
> the kingdom of God, which in literal terms means community, individ-
> uality and freedom, based upon the love of a transcendent God.[42]

This is Davis's vision of the future of Christianity, then, as it
becomes transformed into something quite other than its traditional forms.
Some would doubtless find such a vision disturbing. It is worth noting,
however, that the transformation at work is not random or totally arbitrary
but that the Christian tradition itself has resources with humanizing and
liberating potential; furthermore, that there is a divine Spirit at work in
that wider, worldly, common action of which Christianity is only a part.

CONCLUSION

The groundwork has already been laid in the above discussions of
Baum and Davis for a final comparison of their theological positions.
Clearly they share a commitment to the development of a critical theology
in which orthopraxis—as humanizing, liberating praxis—takes priority over
orthodoxy. Their analyses of the liberating potential of the Christian
symbol systems are also similar; so too is their recognition of the necessity
for a common communicative praxis, a movement, a network of individuals working together. Both offer attractive models for the future of

theology and to some extent the future of the church. Those are, however, two different models, and ultimately mutually exclusive ones.

One can argue, further, that they not only offer alternative models for the future shape of theology, but that these likely represent the only two *possible* models. They have both abandoned the deadends of traditional, orthodox, male-centered, purely theoretical theology, in favor of a critical theology where priority is given to praxis over theory. They are fundamentally at one in that regard.

Where they diverge is in their respective assessments of the dynamic, symbolic elements in Christianity, the degree to which the Christian tradition can grow and change, the extent to which the church can or should be transformed. The differences between them in this area were already signalled twenty-five years ago when Davis made his dramatic announcement in his *A Question of Conscience* of his decision to leave the priesthood and the Catholic Church, and when Baum made his reply to the arguments Davis offered for doing so by stressing that Church's credibility. While their theological positions have obviously matured over the past quarter of a century, there are clear continuities as well. Davis has consistently done theology in a way that is open to the truths and values of other religious and non-religious traditions, and has developed that approach at some length over the years. Just as consistently, Baum has continued to work within the Catholic Church—or the churches—and to argue that the Christian tradition, rooted in the prophetic-liberating tradition of the bible, has sufficient resources for the necessary reconstruction of the social order. Baum would probably not deny that other (non-Christian) transformative models are possible, but he is not committed to developing them. He is in effect content to remain within the symbolic categories of the Christian tradition, even when it might appear to go against the logic of his own theological premises to do so.

A critique of Baum's position might validly be drawn from a slightly different context in Davis's work, where he is in fact criticizing Johann-Baptist Metz, who "will not allow that the truth of Christianity, eschatological in nature as it is, is socially and politically mediated in its entirety."[43] Such a comment might well be applied to Baum's position as well. The reference to the eschatological dimension of Christianity also leads into a warning Davis issues at the end of *What Is Living, What Is Dead in Christianity Today?*, a warning directed at those who would suppose

> that there is some radical, clearly delineated, once-for-all solution to the ills of human society. . . . to criticize what is wrong with society

is not the same as having a ready-made correct solution to its problems. . . . [One cannot] justify the translation of the absoluteness of Christian love into a political radicalism holding that the present evils of the human condition can be definitively overcome by social and political change and a radically new social order of justice, freedom, and equality created.[44]

One could question whether in the light of this statement Baum might want to nuance or redefine his own Christian and political radicalism.

In conclusion, then, it appears that the options for theology and the future of the church consist of variations of some kind on the themes so clearly and cogently presented by Baum and Davis. The basic choices to be made turn around the extent to which one is willing to go beyond the traditional categories and confines of Christianity in openness to other traditions and possibilities. The option taken by Charles Davis is aptly described by Matthew Lamb as the "central thrust of critical theory: a refusal to cut off further relevant questions even when they lead us into the darkness of negativity."[45]

NOTES

[1] If recognized at the outset, the potential ambiguity surrounding the term "critical theory" or "critical social theory" can be eliminated or at least reduced. The term is used here in the context of the Frankfurt School which began in the Germany of the 1920s and 1930s, then flourished in the United States for a time before returning to Frankfurt in the late 1940s. In the classical expression of Max Horkheimer—following Karl Marx^_^_explaining his notion of critical theory as opposed to traditional theory, the point of most theory is to understand the world; the point of critical theory is to change it. Mark Poster has written: "Critical theory . . . attempts to promote the project of emancipation by furthering what it understands as the theoretical effort of the critique of domination begun by the Enlightenment and continued by Karl Marx." Critical Theory and Poststructuralism: In Search of a Context (Ithaca: Cornell University, 1989), p. 1.

[2] London: Hodder and Stoughton, 1967.

[3] The Credibility of the Church Today: A Reply to Charles Davis (New York: Herder and Herder, 1968).

[4] Credibility of the Church, p. 11.

[5] In Faith That Transforms: Essays in Honor of Gregory Baum, Mary Jo Leddy and Mary Ann Hinsdale, eds. (New York: Paulist, 1987), pp. 150-51.

[6] Credibility of the Church, pp. 196ff.

[7] Ibid., p. 200.

[8] Ibid., p. 206.

[9] Faith That Transforms, pp. 139-40.

[10] Ibid., p. 150.

[11] New York: Paulist, 1975.

[12] Religion and Alienation, p. 104.

[13] In Faith That Transforms, pp. 152-94.

[14] Theology and Society (New York: Paulist, 1987), p. 223.

[15] Ibid., pp. 227-28.

[16] Compassion and Solidarity: The Church for Others, The CBC Massey Lectures (Toronto: CBC Enterprises, 1987), p. 19.

[17] Ibid., pp. 30-31.

[18] Theology and Society, p. 234.

[19] Religion and Alienation, p. 104.

[20] Ibid., p. 110.

[21] Journeys: The Impact of Personal Experience on Religious Thought (New York: Paulist, 1975), p. 21.

[22] Ibid., p. 22.

[23] Theology and Society, pp. 225-26.

[24]Ibid., p. 227.

[25]*Theology and Political Society* (Cambridge: Cambridge University, 1980), p. 121.

[26]*Community and Critique in Nineteenth Century Theology*, ICES Research Report 3 (Montreal: Interuniversity Centre for European Studies, 1980), p. 9.

[27]Ibid., p. 10.

[28]Ibid., p. 13.

[29]Ibid., p. 20.

[30]*Passim*, but especially in chapters four and five, pp. 75-132.

[31]San Francisco: Harper & Row, 1986.

[32]Ibid., pp. 3-4.

[33]*Theology and Political Society*, p. 166.

[34]Ibid.

[35]Ibid., p. 167.

[36]Ibid., p. 173.

[37]*What Is Living, What Is Dead in Christianity Today?*, p. 3.

[38]Ibid., p. 2.

[39]Ibid., p. 3.

[40]*Soft Bodies in a Hard World: Spirituality for the Vulnerable* (Toronto: Anglican Book Centre, 1987), p. 14.

[41]Ibid., pp. 41-42.

[42]Ibid., p. 42.

[43]*Theology and Political Society*, p. 7.

[44]*What Is Living, What Is Dead in Christianity Today?*, p. 121.

[45]Matthew L. Lamb, *Solidarity with Victims: Toward a Theology of Social Transformation* (New York: Crossroad, 1982), p. 31.

CONTRIBUTORS

MAHMOUD AYOUB, Professor of Religion, Temple University, Philadelphia, Pennsylvania.

RICHARD J. BEAUCHESNE, Professor of Religious Studies, Emmanuel College, Boston, Massachusetts.

WILLIAM CENKNER, O.P., Professor of Religion and Religious Education, The Catholic University of America, Washington, D.C.

ANNE M. CLIFFORD, C.S.J., Associate Professor of Theology, Duquesne University, Pittsburgh, Pennsylvania.

RALPH DEL COLLE, Assistant Professor of Theology, Marquette University, Milwaukee, Wisconsin.

ROBERT T. CORNELISON, Assistant Professor of Theology, Fordham University, Bronx, New York.

JOSEPH DEVLIN, Associate Professor of Religion, LaSalle University, Philadelphia, Pennsylvania.

SUSANNAH HESCHEL, Associate Professor of Religion, Case Western Reserve University, Cleveland, Ohio.

PETER HUFF, Assistant Professor of Theology, St. Anselm's College, Manchester, New Hampshire.

FREDERICK KECK, Mercyhurst College, Erie, Pennsylvania.

ALICE L. LAFFEY, Associate Professor of Religious Studies, College of the Holy Cross, Worcester, Massachusetts.

GERARD MAGILL, Associate Professor of Theological Studies, St. Louis University, St. Louis, Missouri.

MARIE ANNE MAYESKI, Professor of Theological Studies, Loyola Marymount University, Los Angeles, California.

FREDERICK G. MCLEOD, S.J., Associate Professor of Theological Studies, St. Louis University, St. Louis, Missouri.

ELIZABETH NEWMAN, Assistant Professor of Religious Studies, St. Mary's College, Notre Dame, Indiana.

TERENCE L. NICHOLS, Assistant Professor of Theology, University of St. Thomas, St. Paul, Minnesota.

PETER C. PHAN, Professor of Theology, The Catholic University of America, Washington, D.C.

BERNARD P. PRUSAK, Associate Professor of Religious Studies, Villanova University, Villanova, Pennsylvania.

JOSEPH G. RAMISCH, Associate Professor of Religion, Carleton University, Ottawa, Ontario.

GERARD S. SLOYAN, Professor Emeritus of Religion, Temple University, Philadelphia, Pennsylvania.

C. J. T. TALAR, Associate Professor of Theology, Alvernia College, Reading, Pennsylvania.

PATRICIA TALONE, R.S.M., Associate Professor of Humanities, Gwynedd-Mercy College, Gwynedd Valley, Pennsylvania.

STEPHEN A. WERNER, Assistant Professor of Theological Studies, St. Louis University, St. Louis, Missouri.